From
☑ W9-CFF-867

Grand Canyon National Park

4th Edition

by Shane Christensen

Here's what critics say about Frommer's:

"Amazingly easy to use. Very portable, very complete."

—*Booklist*

"Detailed, accurate, and easy-to-read information for all price ranges."

—*Glamour Magazine*

WILEY
Wiley Publishing, Inc.

Published by:

WILEY PUBLISHING, INC.

111 River St.
Hoboken, NJ 07030-5774

ISBN 0-7645-4284-2

Editor: Richard Goodman
Production Editor: Bethany André
Photo Editor: Richard Fox
Cartographer: Elizabeth Puhl
Production by Wiley Indianapolis Composition Services

For information on our other products and services or to obtain technical
support, please contact our Customer Care Department within the U.S. at
800/762-2974, outside the U.S. at 317/572-3993 or fax 317/572-4002.

Wiley also publishes its books in a variety of electronic formats. Some content that appears in print may not be available in electronic formats.

Manufactured in the United States of America

5   4   3   2

Contents

List of Maps

ABOUT THE AUTHOR

Shane Christensen, a California native, has written extensively about the United States, South America, and Western Europe for Berkeley Guides, Fodor's, and the *Wall Street Journal*. He is also a co-author of *Frommer's South America* and *Frommer's Argentina & Chile*.

AN INVITATION TO THE READER

In researching this book, we discovered many wonderful places—hotels, restaurants, shops, and more. We're sure you'll find others. Please tell us about them, so we can share the information with your fellow travelers in upcoming editions. If you were disappointed with a recommendation, we'd love to know that, too. Please write to:

> *Frommer's Grand Canyon National Park,* 4th Edition
> Wiley Publishing, Inc. • 111 River St. • Hoboken, NJ 07030-5774

AN ADDITIONAL NOTE

Please be advised that travel information is subject to change at any time—and this is especially true of prices. We therefore suggest that you write or call ahead for confirmation when making your travel plans. The authors, editors, and publisher cannot be held responsible for the experiences of readers while traveling. Your safety is important to us, however, so we encourage you to stay alert and be aware of your surroundings. Keep a close eye on cameras, purses, and wallets, all favorite targets of thieves and pickpockets.

Frommer's Star Ratings, Icons & Abbreviations

Every hotel, restaurant, and attraction listing in this guide has been ranked for quality, value, service, amenities, and special features using a **star-rating system.** In country, state, and regional guides, we also rate towns and regions to help you narrow down your choices and budget your time accordingly. Hotels and restaurants are rated on a scale of zero (recommended) to three stars (exceptional). Attractions, shopping, nightlife, towns, and regions are rated according to the following scale: zero stars (recommended), one star (highly recommended), two stars (very highly recommended), and three stars (must-see).

In addition to the star-rating system, we also use **seven feature icons** that point you to the great deals, in-the-know advice, and unique experiences that separate travelers from tourists. Throughout the book, look for:

Finds	Special finds—those places only insiders know about
Fun Fact	Fun facts—details that make travelers more informed and their trips more fun
Kids	Best bets for kids—advice for the whole family
Moments	Special moments—those experiences that memories are made of
Overrated	Places or experiences not worth your time or money
Tips	Insider tips—some great ways to save time and money
Value	Great values—where to get the best deals

The following **abbreviations** are used for credit cards:

AE	American Express	DISC	Discover	V	Visa
DC	Diners Club	MC	MasterCard		

Frommers.com

Now that you have the guidebook to a great trip, visit our website at **www.frommers.com** for travel information on more than 3,000 destinations. With features updated regularly, we give you instant access to the most current trip-planning information available. At Frommers.com, you'll also find the best prices on airfares, accommodations, and car rentals—and you can even book travel online through our travel booking partners. At Frommers.com, you'll also find the following:

- Online updates to our most popular guidebooks
- Vacation sweepstakes and contest giveaways
- Newsletter highlighting the hottest travel trends
- Online travel message boards with featured travel discussions

Welcome to the Grand Canyon

Years ago, upon completing a hike in the Grand Canyon, I stood at the rim, gazing one last time at the colors below, and vowed right then to inform everyone how lucky they were to be alive. My good intentions lasted for only a day, but it was an unforgettable one, and when it was over I realized that the canyon had moved me the way religion moves fervent believers. At the time I wasn't sure why. Only after I began work on this book did I begin to understand all those things that, for me, make the canyon not just a beautiful place, but a sacred one as well.

When I returned to the canyon, I was awed by the terraced buttes and mesas, rising thousands of feet from the canyon floor and dividing the many side canyons. Early cartographers and geologists noticed similarities between these pinnacles and some of the greatest works of human hands. Clarence Edward Dutton, who scouted the canyon for the U.S. Geological Survey in 1880–81, referred to them as temples and named them after eastern deities such as Brahma, Vishnu, and Shiva. François Matthes, who drew up a topographical map of the canyon in 1902, continued the tradition by naming Wotans Throne and Krishna Temple, among other landmarks.

The temples not only inspire reverence but tell the grandest of stories. Half the earth's history is represented in the canyon's rocks. The oldest and deepest rock layer, the Vishnu Formation, began forming 2 billion years ago, before aerobic life-forms even existed. The different layers of sedimentary rock that piled up atop the Vishnu tell of landscapes that changed like dreams. They speak of mountains that really did move, eroding away into nothingness; of oceans that poured forth across the land before receding; of deserts, swamps, and rivers the size of the Mississippi—all where the canyon now lies. The fossils in these layers illustrate the very evolution of life.

Many of the latest products of evolution—over 1,500 plant and 400 animal species—still survive at the canyon today. If you include

Grand Canyon Overview

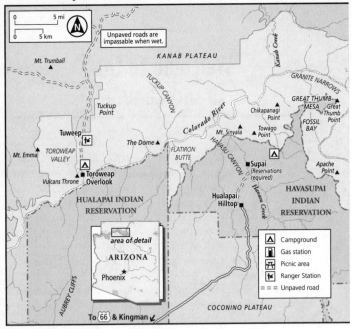

the upper reaches of the Kaibab Plateau (on the canyon's North Rim), this small area of northern Arizona includes zones of biological life comparable to ones found as far south as Mexico and as far north as Alaska. The species come in every shape, size, and temperament, ranging from tiny ant lions dwelling on the canyon floor to 1,000-pound elk roaming the rims. And for every species, there is a story within the story. Take the Douglas fir, for example. Once part of a forest that covered both rims and much of the canyon, this tree has endured since the last Ice Age on shady, north-facing slopes beneath the South Rim—long after the sun-baked rim itself became too hot and inhospitable.

As much as I like the stories, I also enjoy the mysteries that can't be explained. The web of ecological cause-and-effect among the canyon's species is too complicated for any mortal to untangle. It leaves endless questions to ponder, such as why the agave blooms only once every 20-odd years. Similarly, the canyon's rocks withhold as much as they tell. More than a billion years passed between the time the Vishnu Schist formed and the Tapeats Sandstone was

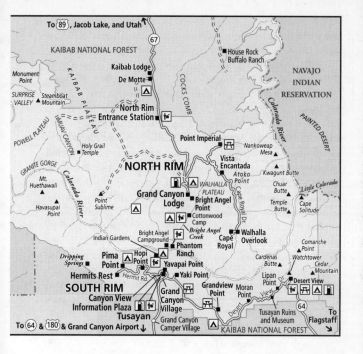

deposited atop it—a gap in the geological record commonly referred to as The Great Unconformity. Other gaps—or unconformities—exist between other layers. And river gravels that would have explained how the canyon was cut have long since washed away.

The more time I spend inside the canyon, the better I hope to understand the first people who dwelt here. A number of different tribes have lived in or around the canyon, and the Navajo, Havasupai, Kaibab Paiute, Hopi, Zuni, and Hualapai tribes still live in the area. Before the white man arrived, they awakened to the colors of the canyon, made their clothes from its plants and animals, smelled it, touched it, tasted it, and felt it underfoot. The Hopi still regard the canyon as their place of emergence and the place to which their dead return. Native Americans have left behind more than 3,000 archaeological sites and artifacts that may be as old as 10,000 years. All this runs through my mind when I walk the canyon floor.

I also contemplate some of the first white people who came to this mystical place. The canyon moved them to do extraordinary, if not always productive, things. I think about the prospectors who clambered through the canyon in search of precious minerals, and then wonder about the ones who stayed here even after their mines proved unprofitable. I wish I could have met icons like Georgie White, who began her illustrious river-running career by *swimming* 60 miles down the Colorado River in the western canyon; and Mary E. Jane Colter, the brilliant architect who obsessed over creating buildings that blended with the landscape, even going so far as to grow plants out of the stone roof at the Lookout Studio. I'd still like to meet David Brower, who, as executive director of the Sierra Club, helped nix a proposal to dam the Colorado River inside the Grand Canyon. He did so by running full-page ads in the *New York Times* that compared damming the canyon to flooding the Sistine Chapel. I admire these people, who felt blessed and inspired by the canyon.

Theodore Roosevelt would also belong in this group. During his 1903 visit, the canyon moved him to say: "Leave it as it is. You cannot improve on it. The ages have been at work on it, and man can only mar it. What you can do is to keep it for your children, your children's children . . . as the one great sight which every American . . . should see." That wasn't just talk. He backed up his words, using the Antiquities Act to declare the Grand Canyon a National Monument in 1908. Congress established Grand Canyon National Park in 1919.

Although Congress called it a "park," the canyon still has a daunting, even ominous side. Everyone, no matter how many times they enter it, must negotiate with it for survival. One look at the clenched jaw of a river guide as he or she rows into Lava Rapids will remind you that the canyon exacts a heavy price for mistakes. And the most common error is to underestimate it. Try to escape, and it becomes a prison 10 miles wide (on average), 277 (river) miles long, and with walls 4,000 feet high. The canyon's menace, for me, is part of its allure—a reminder that we're still living creatures who haven't completely conquered nature.

Clearly, you can suffer here, but reward is everywhere. It's in the spectrum of colors: The Colorado River, filled with runoff from the Painted Desert, runs blood red beneath slopes of orange Hakatai Shale; cactus flowers explode in pink, yellow, and red; and lichens paint rocks orange, green, and gray, creating art more striking than the works in any gallery. It's in the shapes, too—the spires, amphitheaters, temples, ramps, and cliffs—and in the shadows that bend across them before lifting like mist. It's in the myriad organisms and their individual struggles for survival. Perhaps most of all, it's in the

---

The Grand Canyon Has a New Concessionaire

Xanterra Parks & Resorts has been authorized to provide visitor services to Grand Canyon National Park through 2012. As the park's concessionaire (and the largest park and resort management company in the United States), it operates all lodging and dining on both the South and North Rim, as well as motor coach tours and mule rides on the South Rim. Previously named Amfac, Xanterra offers online reservation services for visitors to the Grand Canyon at www.xanterra.com, where you can also learn more about the company.

---

constancy of the river, which, even as it cuts closer to a beginning, reminds us that all things break down, wash away, and return to the earth in time.

1 The Park Today

The new millennium finds Grand Canyon National Park considering an ambitious plan for altering the park. This plan, known as the **General Management Plan,** dates to the mid-'90s, the tail-end of a 2-decade period during which park visitation more than doubled to 4.6 million. By the mid-'90s, the park's resources were badly strained. On a typical summer day, some 6,500 vehicles drove to the South Rim, only to find 2,400 parking places. Faced with gridlock, noise, and pollution from emissions during high season, the park planned major changes, designed to accommodate the 6.8 million annual visitors that the park, at that time, expected to receive in 2010. However, a 10% decline in the number of tourists to the park since the September 11, 2001, terrorist attacks has left implementation of the General Management Plan uncertain.

Under the plan, private vehicles would eventually be barred from most areas along the South Rim, including the historic district in Grand Canyon Village, Hermits Rest Route, and all but one overlook (Desert View) on the Desert View Drive. Instead of driving, visitors would travel by light rail from a new transportation staging area in Tusayan (just south of the park's south entrance) to a larger orientation center—the Canyon View Information Plaza—inside the park near Mather Point. A second light rail line would link the Canyon View Information Plaza with the Village Transit Center in Grand Canyon Village. At both the Canyon View Plaza and the

Village Transit Center, visitors would be able to board shuttles that would transport them to other developed areas on the South Rim.

Private cars would not be banned altogether from this part of the park. Visitors camping or staying in lodges and campgrounds away from the rim would be allowed to drive directly to those areas. Those staying nearer the rim would be driven by van from parking areas farther out. Visitors would also be able to drive through the park on Highway 64, a through-road connecting the towns of Williams and Cameron, Arizona. However, they would not be allowed to park at the overlooks west of Desert View.

The plan also calls for an extensive "greenway" trail for cyclists (rental bicycles will eventually be available), walkers, and equestrians. Paved in places, it would cover 38 miles on the South Rim between Hermits Rest and Desert View. Another 8-mile branch of the greenway would link Tusayan with the Canyon View Information Plaza. An additional 28 miles may eventually be constructed on the North Rim.

In time, the new transit and trails system should help the National Park Service achieve its goal of restoring the rim areas to a quieter, less polluted state. Other parts of the General Management Plan move commercial activity and housing away from the rim and, in some cases, out of the park. For starters, the rim-side Kachina and Thunderbird lodges would be razed; the area they occupy would become open space. Their guest rooms may be replaced by new ones away from the rim at Maswik Lodge and in historic buildings that now serve as employee dormitories. Visitors hoping to learn in depth about the park would be able to do so in a cluster of historic buildings in Grand Canyon Village known as the **Heritage Education Campus.**

Implementing the General Management Plan has proved even more challenging than expected. The park has been able to pay for some of the changes itself, using a percentage of the fees charged for admission and other park usage. But the most ambitious elements, including light rail service, require appropriations from Congress. The light rail plan alone would cost nearly as much as the entire construction budget for the Park Service.

Congress may have lost an impetus for funding major improvements when visitation to Grand Canyon leveled off in the late 1990s and declined after September 11, 2001. In Fall 2001, the National Park Service gave Congress a report on bus alternatives that might serve as a less-expensive substitute for light rail, but two years later no decision to move forward had been made.

In the meantime, the park has slowly moved forward with other elements of the General Management Plan. One major piece, the visually stunning Canyon View Information Plaza, opened in October 2000. A 2.1-mile stretch of greenway between Yavapai and Mather points has been completed.

At present, visitors can ride the park's existing shuttle bus system around Grand Canyon Village, to all overlooks on Hermits Rest Route, and to Mather, Yaki, and Yavapai overlooks. Yet automobiles still strongly affect the visitor experience in most of the park's developed areas, at least in peak season. As long as most people still drive into the park, the Canyon View Information Plaza, which was designed as a mass transit center and lacks automobile parking, will look strangely out of place.

2 The Best of the Grand Canyon

Choosing the best things at Grand Canyon is like naming the best thing about your true love. Especially when your true love—all 277 miles of it—is divine. But, since every vacation consists of smaller parts, I've done my best to isolate a few of the best places and ways to appreciate the larger beauty of Grand Canyon.

- **The Most Dramatic Rim View: Lipan Point** (on the Desert View Drive, South Rim). Located above a sweeping curve in the river and with views far downstream to the west, Lipan Point is the nicest, most easily accessible place to view the canyon and a great place to watch the sunset. The **Unkar Delta,** one of the most archaeologically rich areas in the park, is visible directly below the overlook. See "Desert View Drive" in chapter 3. That said, all of the points overlooking the Colorado River along the rim offer dramatic views. These include Pima, Mohave, Hopi, Moran, Lipan, and Desert View.

- **The Best Scenic Drive: Desert View Drive** (South Rim). You'll see more of the canyon on this route than on the canyon's other two main drives (The Cape Royal Rd. and Hermits Rest Route). The westernmost overlooks open onto the monuments of the central canyon; the eastern ones have far-ranging views of the Marble Platform and the northeast end of the canyon. Along the way, you can stop at the 825-year-old Tusayan Pueblo, which was once occupied by the Ancestral Puebloans. The Watchtower, a historic building artfully fashioned after towers built by the Ancestral Puebloans, is a perfect place to finish the drive. See "Desert View Drive" in chapter 3.

- **The Best Historic Building: Hermits Rest** (at the western terminus of Hermits Rest Route). On the outside, this 1913 building resembles a crude rock shelter like one built by a hermit. Inside, it has an enormous, cavelike fireplace, original furniture, and candelabra on the walls. Built as a rest stop for travelers en route to a camp inside the canyon, Hermits Rest is still a great place to collect oneself before returning to Grand Canyon Village. See "Historic & Man-Made Attractions" in chapter 3.

- **Best Place to Picnic: Vista Encantadora** (on the North Rim's Cape Royal Rd.). The picnic tables here afford canyon views and provide a convenient stopping point when you're visiting the overlooks on the Cape Royal Road. On the South Rim, there are few tables along the rim, so you'll need to be more creative. If the weather is calm, pack a light lunch and walk along one of the rim trails until you find a smooth rim-rock or bench on which to picnic. See "North Rim: Cape Royal Drive" in chapter 3.

- **The Best Bike Ride: Hermits Rest Route in summer** (South Rim). During high season, when this road is closed to most private vehicles, motorized traffic consists mostly of the occasional shuttle bus. Between shuttles, you'll often have the gently rolling road and some of the overlooks to yourself. See "Other Sports & Activities" in chapter 4.

- **The Best Rim Walk: Greenway between Yavapai and Mather Points.** This stretch of the park's ambitious greenway project travels right along the rim, affording views straight down into the canyon. Paved and smooth, it lets walkers enjoy the scenery without worrying too much about their footing. Its 10-foot width allows groups of friends to stroll side by side. And, given its location between two of the park's busiest overlooks, it can be surprisingly quiet. On the North Rim, try the Widforss Trail. See "Trails on the South Rim" in chapter 4.

- **The Best Day Hike Below the Rim: Plateau Point Trail** (accessible via the Bright Angel Trail). With views 1,300 feet down to the Colorado River, Plateau Point is a prime destination for fit, well-prepared day hikers. The hardest part of this 6.1-mile (each way) trip is on the Bright Angel Trail, which descends 4.6 miles and 3,060 vertical feet from Grand Canyon Village to Indian Garden. The trailhead for the Plateau Point Trail is a half-mile west of Indian Garden on the Tonto Trail.

From there, it's a smooth and relatively level stroll to the overlook. See "South Rim Corridor Trails" in chapter 4.

- **The Best Corridor Trail: North Kaibab** (North Rim). For people backpacking into the canyon for the first time, this is a scenic, less-crowded alternative to the South Rim corridor trails. During its 14-mile-long, 5,850-vertical-foot descent from rim to river, the trail passes through vegetation ranging from spruce–fir forest to Sonoran desert. It ends near Phantom Ranch, the only lodging inside the canyon within the park boundaries. See "North Rim Corridor Trail" in chapter 4.

- **The Best Active Vacation: Oar-powered raft trips through Grand Canyon.** Expensive and worth it, these trips negotiate thrilling rapids on the Colorado River. Between the rapids, they move slowly and quietly enough to reveal the subtle magic of the canyon. During stops hikers have access to some of the prettiest spots anywhere. See "Other Sports & Activities" in chapter 4.

- **The Best RV Park: Kaibab Camper Village** (Jacob Lake, © 928/643-7804). For once, an RV park that doesn't look like the lot at a drive-in movie. Old growth ponderosa pines and views of Jacob Lake (the tiny pond) make this RV park, located about 45 miles from the North Rim entrance, the best by far in the Grand Canyon area. Campers can pick up a few supplies at nearby Jacob Lake (the motel, store, gas station, and restaurant). Now it even has showers. See p. 109.

- **The Best Car Campground in the Park: North Rim Campground** (© 800/365-2267 or 928/638-9389). The campsites along the rim of Transept Canyon have pleasing views and are well worth the extra $5. Ponderosa pines shade all the sites, which are far enough apart to afford privacy. For hikers, the Transept Trail begins just a few yards away. If you're on the South Rim, try **Desert View Campground** (p. 101). See p. 104.

- **The Best Historic Hotel: El Tovar Hotel** (Grand Canyon Village, © 928/638-2631). Made of Oregon pine, this grand 1905 hotel rises darkly above Grand Canyon Village on the canyon's South Rim. Inside, moose and elk heads, copper chandeliers, and rooms with classic American furnishings add to its almost-spooky character. By far the most luxurious in the park, this hotel is the only one with room service. See p. 112.

- **The Best Bar in the Park: Bright Angel Lounge** (inside Bright Angel Lodge in Grand Canyon Village, ✆ **928/638-2631**). Every night, tourists from around the world perch atop the stools at this long bar, their backs to a mural by a renowned Hopi artist Fred Kabotie, their elbows resting atop a coated bar top displaying historic postcards, old horseshoes, and other canyon relics. During high season, you'll hear more languages here than at the United Nations. See "The Grand Canyon After Dark" in chapter 6.

- **Best Place to Watch the Sunset: Westernmost Deck of Grand Canyon Lodge.** While the sun disappears behind the pines along the rim, you can soak up the colors on the horizon while sitting in a comfortable chair and sipping a beverage from the nearby saloon. After the sun sets, warm up by the immense outdoor fireplace on the lodge's eastern deck. For unobstructed views, go to Lipan Point on the South Rim or Cape Royal on the North Rim. See p. 118.

- **The Best Accessible Backcountry Destination: Waterfalls of Havasu Creek.** Surrounded by the red-rock walls of Havasu Canyon, these turquoise-colored falls seem to pour forth from the heavens into the cauldron of Grand Canyon. Travertine dams the creek in places, forming many seductive swimming holes. The 10-mile hike or mule ride from Hualapai Hilltop helps ease you into this area, home to the Havasupai Indians. See "Havasu Canyon & Supai" in chapter 7.

- **The Best B&B: The Inn At 410 Bed & Breakfast** (Flagstaff, ✆ **800/774-2008** or 928/774-0088). Your journey doesn't end at the door of this inn. Inside, each of the elegantly decorated rooms recalls a different setting. One room celebrates the cowboy way of life, another recalls a 19th-century French garden, and a third is fashioned after a turn-of-the-20th-century Mexican courtyard. The intriguing decor, together with the kindness of innkeepers Sally and Howard Krueger, helps you travel the world—while catching up on your rest. See p. 131.

- **The Best Expensive Hotel: Best Western Grand Canyon Squire Inn** (Tusayan, ✆ **800/622-6966** or 928/638-2681). Located just a mile outside the park, this hotel offers many of the amenities generally associated with resorts in big cities. Here, you'll find the town's best dining (in the elegant Coronado Room), its liveliest watering hole (downstairs, in the bar that locals call "The Squire"), and its only tennis courts for guests—not to mention luxuries such as a beauty shop and concierge. Located in the main building, the deluxe rooms equal the area's best. See p. 138.

- **The Best Expensive Restaurant: Cottage Place** (Flagstaff, ℂ **928/774-8431**). The quiet serenity of Flagstaff's most elegant restaurant is ideal for special occasions, a wonderful spot to peacefully celebrate your vacation to the Southwest. Original artwork decorates three rose-colored rooms, where soft conversations are heard from the candlelit tables. Chateaubriand (for two) is Executive Chef/Owner Frank Branham's signature dish. See p. 133.

- **The Best Moderately Priced Restaurant: Pine Country Restaurant** (Williams, ℂ **928/635-9718**). The pie here is so good, many locals order dessert first. Others can't wait to dine on straightforward dinner entrees like baked chicken, pork chops, and fried shrimp, most of which go for under $8. Alas, certain misguided customers enjoy their dinners so much, they spoil their appetites for dessert. See p. 149.

- **The Best Inexpensive Restaurant: The Black Bean Burrito Bar and Salsa Company** (Flagstaff, ℂ **928/779-9905**). Get a burrito as heavy as a hand weight, at a price that makes it feel like a handout. Wrapped in aluminum foil and served in plastic drive-in baskets, this may be the best food value in the whole Grand Canyon area. The food is ready within seconds after you order, making this a great place to get a quick fix after a long day. See p. 135.

- **The Best Steakhouse: Rod's Steak House** (Williams, ℂ **928/635-2671**). Beef lovers won't want to miss this Route 66 landmark, identifiable by the cow-shaped sign out front. After 50 years, the tiny menus here are as laconic as cowboys—seems the restaurant would rather serve its giant steaks than write about them. Don't miss the mud pie, the perfect finish to a simple, yet delicious, meal. See p. 149.

- **The Best Area Museum: Museum of Northern Arizona** (Flagstaff, ℂ **928/774-5213**). One of the most extensive collections of Native American art makes this museum unique. Both functional and striking, the artifacts are compellingly displayed, in exhibits that illuminate the close relationship between the indigenous people and the land of the Colorado Plateau. There's no better place to begin learning about the area. See p. 128.

- **Best Place to Escape the Crowds: Anywhere More Than a Half-Mile From the Nearest Parking Lot or Shuttle Bus Stop.** The vast majority of park visitors seldom venture farther than a half-mile from a parking area. If you're willing to walk a half-mile or more, whether it's on a corridor, rim, or wilderness trail, you'll begin to experience some quiet and solitude. This may be the single best way to enjoy the canyon.

2

Planning Your Trip to Grand Canyon National Park

According to Park Service studies, the average visit to Grand Canyon National Park lasts about 3 hours—and many people spend even less time than that. At the other end of the spectrum lies a handful of people who spend lifetimes exploring the canyon, logging hundreds of miles on its hiking trails or weeks at a time on its river. How much time you allow depends on how well you'd like to know the canyon.

I recommend spending at least 1 full day and night inside the park, if possible. This will give you a chance to watch a sunset or (better still) a sunrise. It will also give you enough time to find a quiet place on the rim for writing postcards or listening to the canyon. If you spend 2 full days, you can hike 1 day and take a scenic drive the next. Another day is better still. A lifetime is best.

1 Getting Started: Information & Reservations

Grand Canyon National Park distributes a free trip planner that should answer most of your questions about the park. To get a copy of the planner, you can call © **928/638-7888** or visit the park's website at **www.nps.gov/grca/grandcanyon**.

MULE RIDES

Mule trips to Phantom Ranch can fill up months ahead of time, so it's wise to make your reservations as early as possible, especially if you hope to visit during September or October. For detailed information about mule rides and how to make reservations, see "Other Sports & Activities," in chapter 4.

MAPS

The best driving map of the Four Corners area—the point at which Arizona, Utah, Colorado, and New Mexico intersect—is **AAA's Guide to Indian Country** ($3.95), which shows many of the more remote roads. **Trails Illustrated** publishes an excellent large-scale

Planning Tip

For every season but winter, reservations for campsites, raft trips, backcountry permits, motel rooms, and train and (South Rim) mule rides should be made well in advance. Mule trips and raft trips should be booked as early as possible, since they're the most likely to fill up. However, don't assume that the canyon's lodges and activities are always booked solid. Travel has slowed somewhat since September 11, 2001, leaving the park with mid-season vacancies. There are also some periods that are surprisingly slow every year, like the weeks before and after Labor Day.

(1:73,500) topographical map of the Grand Canyon ($9.95). Waterproof and tear-proof, it shows both rims and all the canyon trails from Lee's Ferry to west of Havasu Canyon, with the eastern canyon displayed on one side and the western canyon on the other. These maps, as well as more than 200 titles about the canyon, are available through the **Grand Canyon Association,** P.O. Box 399, Grand Canyon, AZ 86023 (© **800/858-2808; www.grandcanyon.org**).

Detailed topographical maps of the canyon are helpful for those hiking the canyon's wilderness trails. You can order **U.S. Geological Survey (USGS) 7.5-minute maps** of the canyon, which roughly cover a 7-mile by 7-mile square area, by calling the USGS directly (© **888/ASK-USGS**) or by visiting the USGS website (**www.usgs. gov**). Cost for direct orders is $6 per map plus a $5 handling fee (you can also download the maps for free). Once ordered, products are delivered within 3 weeks. The backcountry office can tell you which USGS maps show particular areas of the canyon. The 7.5-minute maps are also usually available at **The Canyon Village Marketplace** (© **928/638-2262**) on the South Rim, open daily 7am to 8:30pm. The nearest North Rim outlet is at **Willow Creek Books** in Kanab, Utah (© **435/644-8884**). However, these stores, unlike the USGS, won't always have the map you need.

If you're planning to travel through the Kaibab National Forest to a remote campsite or trailhead, a map can be a lifesaver. The Kaibab National Forest Tusayan, Williams, and Chalender Ranger Districts map ($6) covers the Forest Service land along the South Rim. To buy one, stop by the **Kaibab National Forest Tusayan Ranger District Office** (© **928/638-2443**), outside the park's south entrance. The Kaibab National Forest North Kaibab Ranger District map shows the Forest Service land along the North Rim, much of which extends to the rim itself. The **Kaibab Plateau Visitor Center** (*©* **928/643-7298**) at Jacob Lake sells these $7 maps.

USEFUL BOOKS & PUBLICATIONS

Among the hundreds of books written on the canyon, several stand out. For a general overview, leaf through *Grand Canyon: A Natural History Guide* (Houghton Mifflin Co., 1993) by Jeremy Schmidt. Schmidt reveals the larger beauty of the canyon by exploring the smaller relationships between its dwellers—human and otherwise.

If you're the type who doesn't know schist (but would like to), pick up *An Introduction to Grand Canyon Geology* (Grand Canyon Association, 1999) by L. Greer Price. The author explains the geology of Grand Canyon in terms anyone can understand.

For a popular but morbid look into the Canyon's history, check out *Over the Edge: Death in the Grand Canyon* (Puma Press, 2001) by Michael P. Ghiglieri and Thomas M. Myers. The book records all known fatal mishaps (some 550) in the Grand Canyon dating back to Powell's river exploration in 1869.

The Man Who Walked Through Time (Vintage Books, 1967), by Colin Fletcher, provides a more personal look at the canyon. As he chronicles his own solitary 300-mile walk through the canyon, the author explores how the land moves him. If people interest you most, look for *Living at the Edge* (Grand Canyon Association, 1998) by Michael F. Anderson. This carefully researched book traces the canyon's human history from the prehistoric desert cultures through the present. All of the above titles can be ordered through the **Grand Canyon Association** (*©* **800/858-2808**).

Packing Tips

A wide-brimmed hat, sunglasses, and sunscreen are standard equipment at the canyon in all seasons. If you're planning to hike in cool weather, you'll be most comfortable in a water-resistant, breathable shell and several layers of insulating clothing, preferably polypropylene, polar fleece, or other fabrics that remain warm when wet. The shell-and-layers technique works especially well in spring and fall, when extreme swings in temperature occur regularly. Even in summer, you'll still want a shell and at least one insulating layer (more on the North Rim) for cold nights or storms.

---

2 When to Go

The **South Rim** is open year-round. But don't plan on driving on Hermits Rest Route (also known as West Rim Drive) from March 1 to November 30—during that period, if you don't want to walk or ride a bicycle, you'll have to rely on the park's free shuttles to move you from lookout to lookout.

Weather permitting, the **North Rim** is open from mid-May to mid-October. After this date, the park remains open (without most guest services, including gas) until the first major snowstorm. The road from Jacob Lake into the park closes during the first storm and remains closed until spring.

AVOIDING THE CROWDS

When planning your trip, remember that high season runs from April through October. If you come during high season, plan on entering the park before 10am or after 2pm, so you can avoid the lines at the entrance gates and the parking challenges inside the park.

Although mass transit won't help you avoid the crowds, it might make those crowds more bearable. A wonderful historic train travels to Grand Canyon Village year-round from Williams. There are also buses to the Grand Canyon originating in Flagstaff and Williams, as well as taxi service offered from Tusayan.

If you are driving to the South Rim, it is easiest to park your car at a designated parking spot and then take one of the Grand Canyon's free shuttles. There are a number of lots available in Grand Canyon Village, and you can refer to the park's free newspaper, *The Guide*, for a map of specific parking lot locations. Three shuttle routes together serve all of **Grand Canyon Village, Canyon View Information Plaza, Mather Point, Yavapai Point, Yaki Point,** and **Hermit Road.** The shuttles run year-round in Grand Canyon Village and March through November on Hermit Road. When the

---

Tips Buying Park Entrance Permits Outside the Park

Vending machines located outside the Flagstaff Visitors Center, the Williams–Grand Canyon Chamber of Commerce, and the IMAX Theater in Tusayan sell entrance permits to the park. By using these machines, you can avoid waiting in line at the park entrance during peak hours.

shuttles run, Hermit Road and Yaki Point (including the South Kaibab Trailhead) are closed to private vehicles.

FLOOD WARNING

In mid-July, the monsoons usually begin. As hot air rises from the canyon floor, moist air is swept up along with it. As this moist air rises, it condenses, forming towering thunderheads that unloose short-lived but intense afternoon thunderstorms. These localized storms frequently drench the park during August, the wettest month of the year, when nearly 2.25 inches of rain falls on the South Rim.

When rain threatens, hikers should avoid slot canyons, whose steep walls make climbing to safety nearly impossible. Even in wide, dry washes, hikers should be aware of the possibility of sudden, unexpected floods and be prepared to move to higher ground. One especially dangerous, commonly visited area prone to flash floods is Havasu Canyon.

INSECTS

Mosquitoes and biting flies sometimes breed near standing water (which is, itself, a rarity) on the North and South rims; and near springs in the inner canyon. However, most canyon areas are free of mosquitos and biting flies the vast majority of the time.

CLIMATE

Month	South Rim		Inner Gorge		North Rim	
	High °F (°C)	Low °F (°C)	High °F (°C)	Low °F (°C)	High °F (°C)	Low °F (°C)
Jan	41 (5)	18 (–8)	56 (13)	36 (2)	37 (3)	16 (–9)
Feb	45 (7)	21 (–6)	62 (17)	42 (6)	39 (4)	18 (–8)
Mar	53 (12)	36 (2)	72 (22)	59 (15)	57 (14)	32 (0)
Apr	60 (16)	32 (0)	82 (28)	56 (13)	53 (12)	29 (–2)
May	70 (21)	39 (4)	92 (33)	63 (17)	62 (17)	34 (1)
June	81 (27)	47 (8)	101 (38)	72 (22)	73 (23)	40 (4)
July	84 (29)	54 (12)	106 (41)	78 (26)	77 (25)	46 (8)
Aug	82 (28)	53 (12)	103 (39)	75 (24)	75 (24)	45 (7)
Sept	76 (24)	47 (8)	97 (36)	69 (21)	69 (21)	39 (4)
Oct	65 (18)	36 (2)	84 (29)	58 (14)	59 (15)	31 (–1)
Nov	52 (11)	27 (–3)	68 (20)	46 (8)	46 (8)	24 (–4)
Dec	43 (6)	20 (–7)	57 (14)	37 (3)	40 (4)	20 (–7)

The climate at the Grand Canyon varies greatly not only from season to season but from point to point. At 8,000 feet and higher, the North Rim is by far the coldest, dampest part of the park. Its temperatures run about 30°F cooler than Phantom Ranch at the bottom of the canyon, more than 5,000 vertical feet below. The North Rim averages 25 inches of precipitation per year, compared with just 8 inches at Phantom Ranch and 16 inches on the South Rim. Phantom Ranch is more than 4,000 feet lower and up to 25°F warmer than the South Rim.

IF YOU'RE GOING IN SPRING   The North Rim doesn't open until mid-May, so in early spring your only choice is the South Rim, which is cool and breezy at this time of year. The South Rim's daily highs average 60°F (16°C) and 70°F (21°C) in April and May, respectively. Nights can be very cold, with lows in April around freezing. Travelers should be prepared for late-winter storms, which occasionally bring snow to the rim. Storms aside, this is an ideal time to hike the inner canyon, with highs in April averaging 82°F (28°C). It's also the most popular, so make reservations early. Many of the canyon's cacti bloom in spring, dotting the already colorful walls with lavenders, yellows, and reds and making this perhaps the prettiest time of year to visit.

IF YOU'RE GOING IN SUMMER   The South Rim seldom becomes unbearably hot, and the North Rim never does. During July, the average highs on the South and North rims are 84°F (29°C) and 77°F (25°C) , respectively. Although the temperatures on the rim are pleasant, the crowds there can feel stifling. Escaping into the canyon may not be an alternative—at this time of year; the canyon bottom can be torrid, with highs averaging 106°F (41°C), and considerably hotter along the dark-colored rocks near the river. However, on the North Rim especially, summer nights can still be nippy. Even during July, low temperatures there average a chilly 46°F (8°C).

IF YOU'RE GOING IN FALL   After the monsoons taper off in mid-September, fall is a great time to be anywhere in the park. The crowds fall off before the red, orange, and yellow leaves on the rim-top trees follow suit. The North Rim, with its many aspens, is brightest of all. Highs on the South Rim average 76°F (24°C) in September, 65°F (18°C) in October, and 52°F (11°C) in November. The North Rim has highs of 69°F (21°C) in September and 59°F (15°C) in October. (It closes in mid-Oct.) Highs average 97°F (36°C) in the Inner Gorge in September. In October, however, the days cool off by 13°F, and backpackers can sometimes enjoy perfect weather. The first winter storms can hit the North Rim as early as mid-October.

What Things Cost at the Grand Canyon	U.S. $	U.K. £
Local fare on Fred Harvey/Xanterra Taxi Service (from Grand Canyon to Tusayan, 1 person)	20	12
(Each additional adult)	2	1
7-lb. bag of ice at Canyon Village Marketplace	2	1
"I Hiked Grand Canyon National Park" T-shirt at Yavapai Lodge gift shop	19–23	11–14
Open Roads Tours bus from Flagstaff to Grand Canyon Village (round-trip fare for adults)	69	41
(kids 11 and under)	35	21
Small cup of coffee at Yavapai Cafeteria (inexpensive)	1	.70
Room with bed and sink only at Bright Angel Lodge (inexpensive)	55	33
Double-occupancy high-end "view suite" at El Tovar Hotel (expensive)	295	177
Double-occupancy canyon-side room at Kachina Lodge (moderate)	122–132	73–79
Double-occupancy room at Holiday Inn Express in Tusayan (moderate)	97	58
(in low season)	69	41
Double-occupancy room at Super 8 Motel in Flagstaff (inexpensive)	70	42
(in low season)	50	30
Site at Mather Campground	15	9
Water/electric hookup site at Grand Canyon Trailer Village	25	15
Mule day trip to Plateau Point	129	77
Gallon of gas in Tusayan (in Aug 2003) (.30/.17 more than in Flagstaff)	2	1
7-day Park admission (per car)	20	12
One-Time Backcountry permit (plus 5.00/2.90 per person per night)	10	6
Big Mac burger at Tusayan McDonald's	3	2
Slice of pie at Pine Country Restaurant	3.25	1.95

Also in the fall, for 3 weeks every September, the **Grand Canyon Music Festival** brings together world-renowned classical musicians. The offerings, consisting primarily of chamber-music concerts, are held in the intimate, acoustically superb **Shrine of the Ages Auditorium** on the canyon's South Rim. Tickets for the 7:30pm concerts cost $18 for adults and $8 for children (park admission not included) and are available at the door or in advance through Grand Canyon Music Festival (© **800/997-8285** or 928/638-9215; www. grandcanyonmusicfest.org), P.O. Box 1332, Grand Canyon, AZ 86023. Check the website for the concert schedule, and to ensure that you receive the tickets you want, order by early July.

IF YOU'RE GOING IN WINTER   If you don't mind the cold, you'll love the canyon in winter. Winter is by far the quietest and most peaceful time to visit. Backcountry permits are easy to come by, the overlooks are virtually empty, and storms sprinkle snow across the red rocks. These storms, unlike summer monsoons, are not localized disturbances. Rather, they're the same large Pacific fronts that drop snow throughout the West. Closed in winter, the North Rim sometimes receives more than 200 inches of snow in a season. Although the South Rim gets considerably less, drivers should still be prepared for icy roads and occasional closures. Though trails remain open, hikers must often walk on snow and ice, especially near the tops of trails on north-facing slopes. (Small crampons can be useful for winter hiking.) When the snow isn't falling, the South Rim warms up nicely. High temperatures average 41°F (5°C) in January and 45°F (7°C) in February. The inner canyon can be pleasant during the coldest months. Even in January, its highs average a balmy 56°F (13°C), although snow does occasionally reach the floor.

3 Getting There

Las Vegas and Phoenix are the major cities closest to the North and South Rims, respectively. You can save money by flying into these cities, but they're too far from the canyon to stay in during your visit. Flagstaff, AZ, Williams, AZ, Tusayan, AZ, and Kanab, UT, are better choices for lodging near the Grand Canyon.

BY PLANE

Many travelers opt to fly into either the **Phoenix Sky Harbor International Airport** (© **602/273-3300**), 220 miles from the South Rim, or **McCarran International Airport** (© **702/261-5743**), in Las Vegas, 263 miles from the North Rim. Both airports are served by most major airlines.

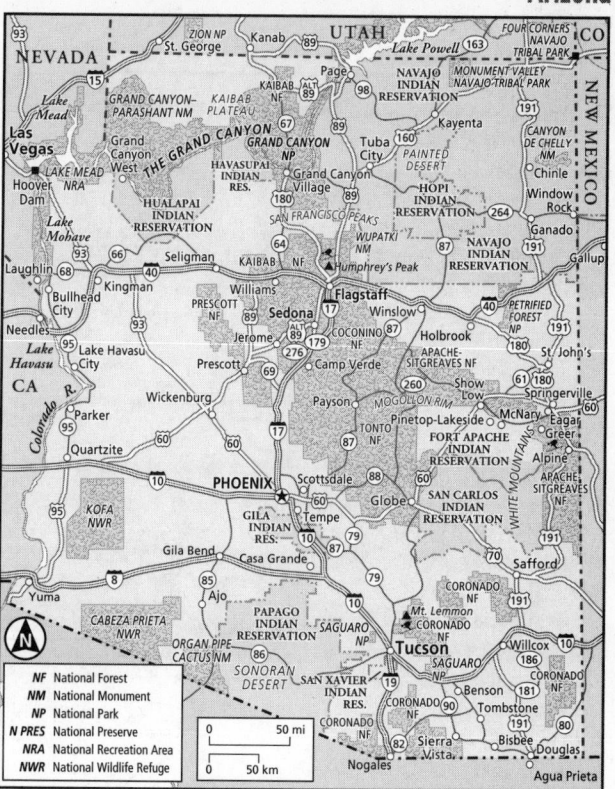

NF National Forest
NM National Monument
NP National Park
N PRES National Preserve
NRA National Recreation Area
NWR National Wildlife Refuge

0   50 mi

0   50 km

For those who would like to fly closer to the canyon, **America West Express** (✆ 800/235-9292) has daily jet service (round-trip cost $200 and up) connecting Phoenix Sky Harbor International Airport and **Flagstaff Pulliam Airport,** roughly 80 miles from the park.

Closer still is **Grand Canyon National Park Airport** (✆ 928/638-2446) in Tusayan, 1.5 miles south of the park's south entrance. **Air Vegas** (✆ 800/255-7474 or 702/736-3599) and **Scenic Airlines** (✆ 800/634-6801 or 702/638-3300) both offer daily service between Las Vegas and Grand Canyon National Park Airport in Tusayan. Air Vegas, whose round-trip fare is $200, departs from **North Las Vegas Airport** (✆ 702/261-3806); Scenic, which charges $227 round-trip, also leaves from North Las Vegas Airport.

Driving Distances

Mileage from the South Rim (entrance) of Grand Canyon National Park to:

Albuquerque, NM	407
Bryce Canyon National Park, UT	310
Cameron, AZ	57
Canyon de Chelly National Monument, AZ	243
Denver, CO	649
Flagstaff, AZ	78
Gallup, NM	273
Grand Canyon National Park Airport	9
Kanab, UT	222
Kingman, AZ	188
Las Vegas, NV	290
Los Angeles, CA	556
North Rim Grand Canyon National Park	215
Petrified Forest National Park	189
Phoenix, AZ	220
Williams, AZ	59
Zion National Park, UT	272

Mileage from the North Rim (entrance) of Grand Canyon National Park to:

Flagstaff, AZ	193
Fredonia, AZ	71
Jacob Lake, AZ	30
Kanab, UT	78
Las Vegas, NV	277
Phoenix, AZ	335
Salt Lake City, UT	438
Williams, AZ	225
Zion National Park, UT	119

BY CAR
RENTING A CAR

Major rental-car companies with offices in Arizona and Las Vegas include **Avis** (② 800/230-4898), **Budget** (② 800/527-0700), **Dollar** (② 800/800-4000), **Hertz** (② 800/654-3131), **National** (② 800/227-7366), and **Thrifty** (② 800/367-2277).

Grand Canyon Driving Times & Distances

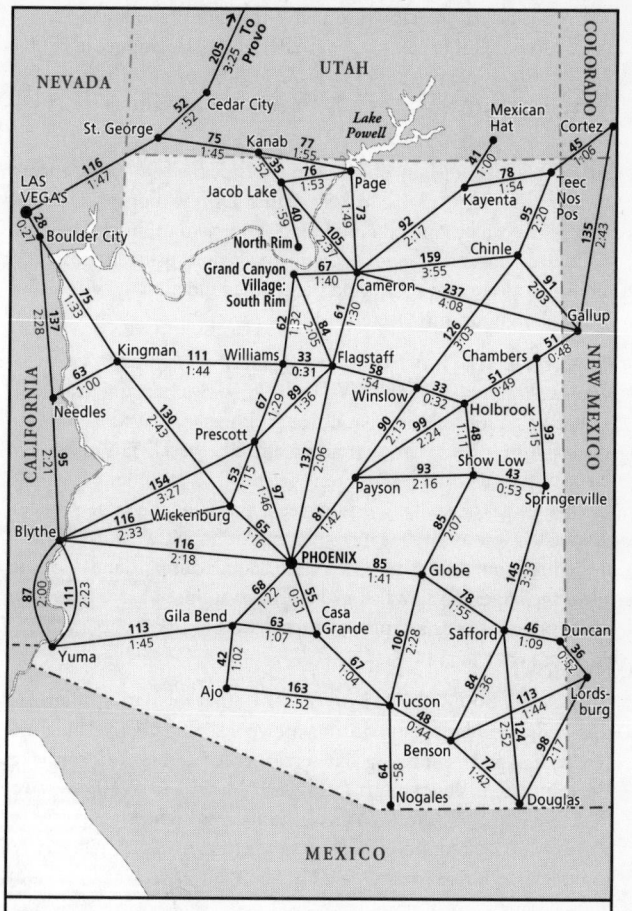

Lightface numbers *indicate driving times*
Bold numbers *indicate distances in miles*

In this schematic we assume 100 miles will take an
average of 1 hour, 49 minutes (excluding stops)
at an average speed of 55 miles per hour

In Flagstaff, car rentals are available through the following companies: **Avis** (℘ 800/230-4898 or 928/774-8421), **Budget** (℘ 800/527-0700), **Enterprise** (℘ 800/325-8007 or 928/526-1377), **Hertz** (℘ 800/654-3131 or 928/774-4452), and **National** (℘ 800/227-7368 or 928/779-1975).

DRIVING TIP   Many of the Forest Service roads to remote areas on the rims are impassable in wet weather. During monsoon season, these roads can become too muddy or slippery to negotiate. In winter, there's no snow removal on them. People using these roads should be aware that they could be stranded indefinitely by a heavy snowfall, rain, or other factors.

RENTING AN RV FOR YOUR TRIP

Cruise America (℘ **800/RV-DEPOT;** www.cruiseamerica.com) rents RVs nationwide and has offices in Phoenix, Flagstaff, and Las Vegas. During 2003, Cruise America offered a weekly rate of $1,165 for a 25-foot, C-class motor home getting 8 to 10 miles per gallon (with a 40-gal tank). Low-season weekly rates for the same vehicles dropped as low as $910. Thirty-foot motor homes went for $1,295 in high season, $1,005 in low season. Some campgrounds do not allow the largest RVs. When making reservations at a campground, make sure that your RV meets its regulations.

BY TRAIN

Amtrak (℘ **800/872-7245** or 928/774-8679 for station information only) regularly stops in downtown Flagstaff, where lodging, rental cars, and connecting bus service are available. You can take the train from Albuquerque to Flagstaff for $59 to $110 one-way. The one-way fare from Los Angeles to Flagstaff ranges from $50 to $119. Amtrak also serves Williams, where connecting rail service (on the historic and lively Grand Canyon Railway) is available. Fares are the same as for Flagstaff.

BY BUS

Open Road Tours (℘ **800/766-7117**) has bus service linking Flagstaff with Grand Canyon National Park.

Daily shuttle service between the North and South rims is available from mid-May through mid-October on the **Trans-Canyon Shuttle** (℘ **928/638-2820**). The fare is $65 one-way, $110 round-trip, for adults. For kids 12 and under, the fare is $55 one-way, $90 round-trip. You must make a reservation to take the shuttle.

4 Learning Vacations & Special Programs

The Grand Canyon Field Institute, a nonprofit organization cosponsored by the Grand Canyon Association and Grand Canyon National Park, lets you experience the canyon with those who understand it best. Every year it schedules dozens of backpacking trips and outings lasting from 2 to 9 days. Some explore broad subjects such as ecology, paleontology, and archaeology; others hone narrow skills such as orienteering or drawing. People intimately familiar with the canyon, who are experts on the topics covered, guide all of the excursions. Because the courses vary greatly, the Field Institute assigns a difficulty level to each and attempts to ensure that participants find ones suited to their skill levels and interests. If you love the canyon, there's no better way to pass a few days. To contact the Field Institute you can call ✆ **928/638-2485;** write to P.O. Box 399, Grand Canyon, AZ 86023; or check out its website at **www.grandcanyon.org/fieldinstitute/**.

5 Tips for Travelers with Disabilities

The steep, rocky trails below the rim pose problems for travelers with disabilities. People with limited vision or mobility may be able to walk the Bright Angel or North Kaibab trails, which are the least rocky in the canyon. If you need to take a service dog on trails below the South Rim, check in with the ranger office at the corner of Center Road and Village Loop Road. On the North Rim, check in at the Backcountry Office.

On the rims themselves, many attractions are accessible to everyone. On the **South Rim,** the Desert View Drive is an excellent activity. Four of its overlooks—Yaki, Grandview, Moran, and Desert View—are wheelchair accessible, as are Tusayan Museum and Pueblo. (Ask for assistance at the information desk.) At Desert View, the bookstore and grocery store are accessible, but no designated seating is available in the snack bar. Along this drive, restrooms for the mobility impaired can be found at Yavapai Point, Tusayan Museum, Desert View (just east of Desert View General Store), and Desert View Campground. (The campground has no designated sites.)

Hermits Rest Route (the West Rim Drive) poses more problems. For starters, most of the shuttles serving it are not wheelchair accessible. Advance reservations are required for accessible shuttle service (✆ **928/638-0591**). It's easier for people in wheelchairs to drive themselves. Although the drive is closed to most private cars when the shuttles are running, people with disabilities can obtain permits for their vehicles at **Canyon View Center.** On the drive itself, Hopi Point, Pima Point, and Powell Memorial are all wheelchair accessible. The road also affords a number of nice "windshield views" from pull-outs where one need not leave the car to see the canyon. To reach the gift shop at Hermits Rest, you'll have to negotiate two 5-inch steps and a route that slopes gently sideways. Near Hermits's Rest is a wheelchair-accessible chemical toilet. Despite having many historic buildings, most of **Grand Canyon Village** is wheelchair accessible. The notable exceptions are Kolb Studio and Lookout Studio. Hopi House is accessible only through a 29-inch-wide door on the canyon side of the building. Also, some hallways in Yavapai Lodge are too narrow for wheelchairs. Wheelchair-accessible restrooms are found at the Canyon View Information Plaza, Canyon Village Marketplace, Yavapai Observation Station, the El Tovar Hotel, Bright Angel Lodge, Mather Campground, and Maswik Lodge. Mather Campground has six sites for people with disabilities.

The South Rim's new visitor center, the Canyon View Center, has been tailored to people with disabilities. Walkways and doorways are gradual and open. People with disabilities can drive to nearby Mather Point, which is wheelchair accessible, and reach the plaza via a paved walkway. (***Note:*** If, as planned, the National Park Service closes Mather Point to private vehicles, people with disabilities will need to obtain permits to park at Mather Point. These permits will be available at the park entrances.)

Those who have difficulty walking can usually negotiate the 1.5-mile-long rim trail between Bright Angel Lodge and Yavapai Point (except when icy). If they desire, they can continue an additional 0.5 miles to Mather Point on a stretch of the Park's new greenway. Wide and smooth, the greenway has moderate grades and offers stunning canyon views.

On the North Rim, the gas station and grocery pose problems for people in wheelchairs, but most other buildings are wheelchair accessible. The two most popular North Rim overlooks—Point Imperial and Cape Royal—are each accessible, although neither has a designated parking space. Grand Canyon Lodge is accessible via both a lift and a ramp, and the North Rim Campground has two accessible sites. Wheelchair-accessible restrooms are located at the Backcountry Office (assistance required), Grand Canyon Lodge (assistance may be required), the North Rim Campground, and behind the visitor center.

The canyon's mule-trip concessionaires accommodate people with certain disabilities, as do many river companies. Also, **Fred Harvey** (✆ **928/638-2822**) can sometimes arrange for buses with lifts for its bus tours if it's informed in advance. For details about the accessibility of park buildings and facilities, pick up the park's free *Accessibility Guide* at the park's information centers.

As for raft companies, **Western River Expeditions** (✆ 800/453-7450), **Arizona Raft Adventures** (✆ 800/786-RAFT), **Grand Canyon Expeditions** (✆ 800/544-2691), and **Canyon Explorations, Inc.** (✆ 800/654-0723) are all good choices for people with certain disabilities.

6 Tips for Travelers with Pets

Hot weather and crowds make the canyon a bad place for pets. If you do bring your dog to the South Rim, you can take it on a leash on rim trails inside the park's developed areas, but not in the backcountry, below the rim, on buses, or inside public buildings. Rather than leave your dog in the car, use the **Grand Canyon Kennel** (✆ **928/638-0534**), near Maswik Lodge in Grand Canyon Village. Open daily 7:30am to 5pm, it will care for your pet during the day and overnight. Cost for day care is $9 for dogs, $6 for cats. Overnights cost $13.50 for dogs over 50 pounds, $10 for dogs under 50 pounds, and $7.50 for cats. Payment is by cash only. Be sure to call ahead for reservations, as this kennel frequently sells out. Upon arriving, you'll be asked to show proof that your pet's shots are up to date. There's no kennel on the North Rim, and the Park Service discourages people from bringing pets there. On the North Rim, the only trail open to pets is the bridle path linking the lodge with the trailhead for the North Kaibab Trail.

7 Tips for Travelers with Children

The park's **Junior Ranger** program can help engage your kids during your stay. Register for the program at the Grand Canyon Visitor Center (also called the Canyon View Information Plaza) on the South Rim or the Grand Canyon Lodge on the North Rim. You can also pick up a guide outlining steps to complete the Junior Ranger program at the Visitor Center, Yavapai Observation Station, or the Tusayan Museum information desk. These steps include attending a walk or talk by a ranger, completing educational games and puzzles, and picking up litter or recyclables inside the park (or simply listing reasons for protecting the area). The activities are tailored to three age groups, together spanning ages 4 to 14. After completing the steps, your youngster will receive a certificate and be eligible to purchase (for $1.50) a Junior Ranger patch. The park also has a Junior Ranger program in which participants use a field guide and binoculars to identify species, and another with a special focus on geology.

During summer, the park offers additional programs aimed at children, including daily nature walks. Parents must accompany their children on these activities. For a complete listing of kids' activities, consult the park's free newspaper, *The Guide*.

The canyon may not be as huggable as Barney (far from it) or as mesmerizing as a GameBoy, but its size, beauty, and danger (especially danger) still impress many kids. In addition to the Junior Ranger program described above, kids may also enjoy the following activities:

- **Look for deer.** At sunset, take a quiet walk in the grass along the train tracks by Grand Canyon Village, or watch a meadow along the entrance road on the North Rim. See how many deer you can count. But please don't feed or approach them.

- **Hike a rim trail.** If your kids are too small to make the steep descent into the canyon, take them walking on the canyon rim. This gets them away from the car and into less crowded areas. On the South Rim, the greenway from Grand Canyon Village to Mather Point is a nice option. On the North Rim, the Transept or Cliff Springs trails are both fun for kids.

- **Go birding.** During the daytime, sit on the rim and watch raptors and ravens ride the thermals. See if you can identify eagles, hawks, or vultures—and perhaps even California condors. Watch swifts and swallows dart around the rim. Use chapter 8, "A Nature Guide to Grand Canyon National Park," to help identify many of the different animals and plants.

- **Watch the wranglers prepare the mules for the trip into the canyon.** At 8am daily (9am in winter), the wranglers bring the mules to the corral on the South Rim just west of Bright Angel Lodge. While the mules entertain the kids, the wranglers will entertain the adults with their humorous lecture on mule-ride protocol. One word of caution: Certain tourist-weary mules have copped an attitude and will bite when petted.

- **See the canyon on the big, big screen.** When the canyon fails to entertain your young ones in person, show it to them on the 82-foot-high screen at the IMAX Theater outside the park in Tusayan.

8 Protecting Your Health & Safety

In 2001, two Arizona writers published a disconcertingly thick book detailing every known fatal accident within the canyon. *Over the Edge: Death in Grand Canyon* (Puma Press, Flagstaff, 2001) not only tells captivating stories but serves as a handy reminder of what *not* to do in the park. (For starters, don't remove your hiking boots and run barefoot toward the river.) Below is a list of guidelines that will keep you from becoming a subject of *Over the Edge: Volume II.*

- **Choose reasonable destinations for day hikes.** Although most park visitors quickly recognize the danger of falling into the canyon, they don't always perceive the danger of walking into it. Every year, the canyon's backcountry rangers respond to hundreds of emergency calls, most of them on the corridor trails (Bright Angel, North Kaibab, and South Kaibab). Day hikers are lured deep into the canyon by the ease of the descent, the sight of other hikers continuing downward, and (sometimes) the goal of reaching the river. As they drop into the canyon's hotter climes in late morning, temperatures climb doubly fast. By the time they turn around, it's already too late. They are hot, fatigued, and literally in "too deep." When hiking in the canyon, particularly during the summer months, pick a reasonable destination, and don't hesitate to turn back early.

- **Don't hike at midday during hot weather.** When hiking at temperatures over 100°F (38°C), you'll sweat fluids faster than your body can absorb them, no matter how much you drink. For this reason, hiking in extreme heat is inherently dangerous.

- **Drink and eat regularly.** During a full day of hiking, plan to drink more than a gallon of fluids—on the hottest days, make it more than two. Consume both water and electrolyte-replacement drinks such as Gatorade. Also, remember that eating carbohydrate-rich, salty foods is as important as drinking. If you consume large amounts of water without food, you can quickly develop an electrolyte imbalance, which can result in unconsciousness or even death.

- **Wear sunscreen and protective clothing.** Even during winter, the Arizona sun can singe unsuspecting tourists. To protect your skin and cool your body, wear long-sleeved white shirts, wide-brimmed hats, sunglasses, and high-SPF sunscreen.

- **Move away from rim overlooks during thunderstorms.** On the rim, you may be the highest point—and best lightning rod—for miles around.

- **Exercise caution on the rims.** Every year a handful of people fall to their death in the canyon. To minimize risk, don't blaze trails along the rim, where loose rock makes footing precarious. Use caution when taking photographs and when looking through the viewfinder of your camcorder (unless, by chance, you want your final footage to wind up on the FOX Network). Be prepared for gusts of wind, and keep an eye on your children.
- **Yield to mules when hiking.** If you encounter mules, step off the trail on the uphill side and wait for instructions from the wranglers. This protects both you and the riders.

3

Exploring the Grand Canyon

At the edge of the Grand Canyon, even the breezes seem to take a deep breath. Sometimes the best thing to do at the canyon is to take one yourself. Find a quiet place on the rim or off a trail and sit for an hour or so. Feel the warm air rise, watch the shadows and light play across the monuments, and listen to the timeless hush. No matter how fast you drive, and no matter how many angles you see the canyon from, you'll never completely "do" the canyon. So relax.

1 Essentials

ACCESS/ENTRY POINTS

The park has three gated entrances—two on the **South Rim** and one on the **North Rim.** The one that's most convenient to travelers from Flagstaff, Williams, and Phoenix is the park's **South Entrance Gate,** 1 mile north of Tusayan on Highway 64. Traffic occasionally backs up here during peak hours in high season. Many travelers from Flagstaff, as well as those from points east, prefer entering the South Rim area through its **East Entrance Gate,** near Desert View, 28.5 miles west of Cameron, Arizona, on Highway 64. From Flagstaff, the drive to the East Entrance Gate is about 8 miles longer than to the South Entrance.

The gate to the **North Rim** (separated from the South Rim by 210 highway miles) isn't convenient to anywhere, except perhaps the small store, motel, and gas station at Jacob Lake, Arizona, 30 miles north on Highway 67. (The North Rim itself is 14 miles south of the gate.) The closest real town is **Fredonia, AZ,** 71 miles to the north on Highway 89A. Parts of the park can also be accessed via Forest Service dirt roads.

INFORMATION CENTERS

CANYON VIEW INFORMATION PLAZA   Completed in Fall 2000 near Mather Point, the Canyon View Information Plaza was designed to orient visitors arriving at the park via a new light-rail system. Though the rail system has not yet been built, the Information Plaza has the streamlined appearance of a modern mass transit

Tips   Exploring the Park Without a Car

The best time to be car-less inside the park is from March 1 to November 30, when all of the park's free shuttle routes are operating. Departing regularly from 1 hour before dawn until 1 hour after sunset, the shuttle buses serve all of **Grand Canyon Village, Canyon View Information Plaza, Mather Point, Yavapai Point, Yaki Point,** and **Hermit Road.** Because the buses run every 15 to 30 minutes (depending on the time of day and the route), you seldom have to wait too long at a stop. The shuttles operate seasonally on Hermits Rest Route, and year-round in Grand Canyon Village. Consult the park's free publication, *The Guide,* for detailed information on shuttle stops and schedules.

When the shuttles aren't running, you may need to take advantage of the park's **Fred Harvey's 24-hour taxi service** (© 928/638-2822). These taxis do not have meters. Their fares vary according to distance and the number of passengers. For example, a trip between Bright Angel Lodge and Market Plaza costs $5 for the first person, $2 for each additional adult. The trip from Grand Canyon Village to Tusayan costs $10 for one or two adult passengers, plus $5 for each additional adult. Alternatively, you can catch a taxi from Tusayan into the park with **Grand Canyon Coaches** (© 928/638-0821), also for $10 one-way. **Open Road Tours** (© 800/766-7117) has bus service linking Flagstaff with Grand Canyon National Park for $26 one-way; $40 round-trip. It also offers 3½ hour tours of the Grand Canyon for $69, departing Flagstaff at 9:30am and returning at 5:30pm.

hub, with ample room for crowds and no automobile parking lots. Outdoors in the landscaped plaza, kiosks provide basic information on tours, trails, canyon overlooks, cycling, and other topics. The main South Rim visitor center is located inside the long, glass-fronted building known as the **Canyon View Center.** Here, you'll find additional displays on the canyon and the Colorado Plateau, an area for Ranger presentations, a bookstore, an information desk, and restrooms. To get here, you'll need to take a free shuttle, walk, or park at nearby Mather Point. The Information Plaza is open daily 8am to 6pm.

YAVAPAI OBSERVATION STATION   Located a ½ mile west of Canyon View Center on Yavapai Point, this historic station has an observation room where you can identify many of the monuments in the central canyon. Rangers frequently lead interpretive programs here. (For more information, see the section on the Desert View Drive, later in this chapter.)

DESERT VIEW CONTACT STATION   Staffed by volunteers, this small station 26 miles east of Grand Canyon Village sells books and has information on the canyon. This station is just inside the park's East Entrance, 29 miles west of Cameron on Highway 64.

TUSAYAN MUSEUM   Located 3 miles west of Desert View, Tusayan Museum has an information desk staffed by rangers in addition to displays on the area's indigenous peoples.

KOLB STUDIO   Located on the rim at the west end of Grand Canyon Village, Kolb Studio houses a small bookstore and an art gallery with free exhibits.

NORTH RIM VISITOR CENTER   This visitor center near Grand Canyon Lodge has a small bookstore and information desk.

ENTRANCE FEES

Admission to Grand Canyon National Park costs $20 per private vehicle (includes all occupants) and $10 for adults (ages 17 and over) on foot, bicycle, or motorcycle. The receipt is good for a week and includes both rims. Adults who enter the park in organized groups or on commercial tours usually pay about $8 each, though the rates vary some.

SPECIAL DISCOUNTS & PASSES

A number of special passes are available at the park's entrance stations. **Golden Eagle Passports** entitle holders to unlimited use of all National Park Service sites, including Grand Canyon, for 1 year from the date they make this $65 purchase. A **Grand Canyon National Park Pass** ($40) entitles the holder to free admission to Grand Canyon for one calendar year. For $10, U.S. residents aged 62 and older can purchase a **Golden Age Passport,** which admits the holder, free of charge, for life at all National Park Service sites. Another card, the **Golden Access Passport,** entitles U.S. residents with permanent mental or physical disabilities to the same privileges afforded by the Golden Age Passport. This card is free, but the applicant must apply in person at Canyon View Center.

CAMPING FEES

Camping at **Mather Campground,** the largest on the South Rim, costs $15 per site during high season. **Desert View Campground,** open from mid-May to mid-October, costs $10 per site. And the **North Rim Campground,** also open from mid-May to mid-October, costs $15 per site. At all three campgrounds, no more than two vehicles and six people can share a site. **Trailer Village,** an RV park on the South Rim, charges $25 per hookup for two people, plus $2 for each additional adult. For more information, see chapter 5.

PARK RULES & REGULATIONS

The following list includes a set of rules established to protect both the park and its visitors:

- Bicycles must stay on roads. That means no mountain biking on the trails or on the park's new stretch of greenway.
- It's illegal to remove any resources from the park. This can be anything from flowers to potsherds. Even seemingly useless articles such as bits of metal from the canyon's old mining operations have historical value to the park's users and are protected by law.
- Dogs must be leashed at all times. They're allowed on certain rim trails in developed areas of the park, but are banned from trails below the rim, buses, or in park lodging. The only exceptions are certified service dogs.
- Fires are strictly prohibited except in the fire pits at North Rim, Desert View, and Mather campgrounds. In the backcountry, you can use a small campstove for cooking.
- Weapons including guns, bows and arrows, crossbows, slingshots, and air pistols are all prohibited, as are all fireworks. If, by chance, you have a hang glider and are considering jumping into the canyon, forget it. It's illegal, and you'll be fined.

FAST FACTS: The Grand Canyon

ATM The lone ATM in the park is on the South Rim at Bank One, located in Market Plaza next to the Canyon Village Marketplace. Due to the limited availability of ATMs, it is best to bring sufficient cash for your trip to the Grand Canyon.

Fuel There is only one gas station inside the park on the South Rim. **Desert View Chevron,** on Highway 64, 25 miles east of Grand Canyon Village, is open daily from late April through September. Hours vary seasonally. If you're entering the park from the south and are running low on fuel, make sure to gas up in **Tusayan,** 1 mile south of the park's south entrance. On the North Rim, the **Chevron Service Station** is open daily 8am to 5pm (7am to 7pm in summer), also seasonally. You can also get gas at the general store across from Kaibab Lodge, 18 miles north of the North Rim on Highway 67.

Garages A public garage with 24-hour emergency towing service ($\textcircled{C}$ **928/638-2631**) currently operates inside the park on the South Rim. The garage itself is open from 8am to noon and 1pm to 5pm daily. The nearest automotive service to the North Rim is at **Judd Auto** ($\textcircled{C}$ **928/643-7107**) in Fredonia. Judd Auto has 24-hour towing and a reputation for being honest.

Health Services If you have a medical emergency on either rim, dial $\textcircled{C}$ **911** (or 9911 from motel rooms) to obtain assistance from Park Rangers. On the South Rim, a **health clinic** ($\textcircled{C}$ **928/638-2551**) is located on Clinic Road, off Center Road between Grand Canyon Village and the South Rim entrance road. The clinic is open on weekdays from 9am to 6pm, Saturday 10am to 2pm. The nearest pharmacies are in Williams, AZ. Health services have been nonexistent on the **North Rim** ever since the small clinic there closed in 2000. In non-emergency situations, you'll need to drive all the way to the hospital in Kanab, UT. North Rim emergency medical services are provided by rangers on duty.

Laundry Laundromats can be found inside the park on both rims. Open 7am to 9pm daily (8am to 6pm in winter), the **South Rim's Laundromat** is in the Camper Services building near Mather Campground. Open 7am to 9pm daily, the **North Rim's Laundromat** is near the North Rim Campground.

Lost & Found For items lost in or near the park's South Rim lodges, call $\textcircled{C}$ **928/638-2631.** For those lost elsewhere on the South Rim, call $\textcircled{C}$ **928/638-7798** Tuesday to Friday 8am to 5pm. Found items can be returned to the Canyon View Information Plaza. On the North Rim, report lost and found items in person at the visitor center or at the Grand Canyon Lodge front desk ($\textcircled{C}$ **928/638-2611**).

Outfitters On the South Rim, **Canyon Village Marketplace** ($\textcircled{C}$ **928/638-2262,** open daily 8am to 8pm in summer, 8am to

7pm in winter) in Grand Canyon Village rents and sells camping and backpacking equipment. There is no equipment for rent on the North Rim, but the **North Rim General Store** (ℂ 928/ 638-2611, ext. 270), usually open from 7am to 9pm, sells a very limited supply of camping equipment.

Police For emergencies dial ℂ **911** (9911 from motel rooms).

Post Offices On the **South Rim,** the post office (ℂ **928/638-2512**) in Market Plaza has window hours from 9am to 4:30pm on weekdays and from 11am to 3pm Saturdays. On the **North Rim,** a tiny post office at Grand Canyon Lodge is open Monday to Friday 8am to 4pm and Saturday 8am to 1pm.

Supplies There are three grocery stores inside the park. The largest, **The Canyon Village Marketplace** (ℂ 928/638-2262), is in Market Plaza in Grand Canyon Village. Its hours are usually 8am to 8pm in summer, 8am to 7pm the rest of the year. **Desert View General Store** (ℂ **928/638-2393**), at Desert View (25 miles east of Grand Canyon Village on Hwy. 64), is open daily 8am to 7pm in summer, 9am to 5pm the rest of the year. On the North Rim, the only provisions are at the **North Rim General Store** (ℂ **928/638-2611,** ext. 270), adjacent to North Rim Campground. It's usually open daily 7am to 9pm.

Weather Updates Recorded weather information, updated every morning, is available by calling ℂ **928/638-7888.** Forecasts are also posted at the main visitor centers.

2 How to See the Park in Several Days

The itineraries below list some captivating activities for your visit. These same activities are described in detail later in the book. And remember, the rims are 210 highway miles apart.

IF YOU HAVE 1 OR 2 DAYS

ON THE SOUTH RIM   After stopping at the visitor center, hike a short distance down the **Bright Angel Trail** in the morning. (If the weather is hot or if your condition is not top-notch, walk a portion of the **greenway** between Grand Canyon Village and Mather Point.) During midday, attend a Ranger presentation, for which times and locations are posted at the visitor centers. Later in the day, take the shuttle along **Hermits Rest Route.** From any of the stops on the drive, you can walk a short distance along the **West Rim**

Trail to quiet spots where you can savor the canyon. If possible, watch the sunset from **Hopi Point.**

The next morning, get an early start and watch the sunrise from **Desert View** on the South Rim. (Be sure to go up into The Watchtower.) On your way back to Grand Canyon Village, stop at the viewpoints along **Desert View Drive.** Most of these viewpoints are open to cars year-round and have expansive views of the central and northeastern canyon. Upon returning to Grand Canyon Village, take a walking tour of the historic buildings. Relax over an iced tea on the veranda of the lounge at the El Tovar Hotel.

ON THE NORTH RIM   In the morning after checking in at the visitor center, hike down the top of the **North Kaibab trail.** A less-strenuous option is the short walk from Grand Canyon Lodge to Bright Angel Point. In the afternoon, drive down the **Cape Royal Road.** After returning to Grand Canyon Lodge, buy a cold beverage at the saloon, then sip it while sitting on the lodge's enormous, canyon-facing deck. After sunset on calm evenings, warm yourself by the fireplace on the deck of Grand Canyon Lodge.

If you're an early riser, head to **Point Imperial** before dawn the next day to watch the sun rise. Then take a walk on one of the rim

---

How Grand Is the Grand Canyon?

Size: 1,904 square miles (more than 1½ times the size of Rhode Island)
Length of River in Canyon: 277 miles
Vertical Drop of River in Canyon: 2,215 feet
Average Width of Canyon: 10 miles
Widest Point: 18 miles
Narrowest Point: 600 feet (in Marble Canyon)
Average Depth: 1 mile
Lowest Point: 1,200 feet (at Lake Mead)
Highest Point on South Rim: 7,400 feet
Highest Point on North Rim: 8,801 feet

COLORADO RIVER FACTS (as it flows through the canyon)
Length: 277 miles
Average Width: 300 feet
Average Depth: 40 feet
Average Gradient: 8 feet per mile

trails—**the Transept Trail, the Uncle Jim Trail** (to Uncle Jim Point), or, my favorite, **the Widforss Trail** (to Widforss Point).

IF YOU HAVE 3 OR 4 DAYS
With 3 or 4 days at the canyon, 3-day hikes may be in order.

ON THE SOUTH RIM   Choose from the Bright Angel, South Kaibab, Grandview, Hermit, and West Rim trails.

ON THE NORTH RIM   Try the North Kaibab Trail and two rim trails. There are fewer diversions on the North Rim, so be prepared for deep relaxation on the third and fourth days.

ON BOTH RIMS   Consider riding a mule into the canyon, accompanying a Ranger on a guided walk, or sitting and reading on the porch of one of the canyon's lodges.

3 Driving Tours

The South Rim is easily accessible by car off Highway 64, which connects Williams and Cameron. Inside the park's southern gate, the South Entrance Road diverges from Highway 64 and leads to **Grand Canyon Village.** A National Historic District, the village feels like a small town, with hotels, restaurants, shops, and a train depot. The loop road can be confusing, so take your time, watch carefully for signs, and use the village map included in the park newspaper, *The Guide.*

Scenic drives hug the canyon rim on either side of the village. **Hermits Rest Route** (also known as West Rim Drive, closed to private vehicles during high season) heads west along Hermit Road for 8 miles to its terminus at Hermits Rest. **Desert View Drive** covers 25 miles between Grand Canyon Village and the Desert View overlook on the southeastern edge of the park. The two scenic drives have numerous pull-offs that open onto the canyon, some with views of the river.

Some 210 highway miles and 4 hours of driving separate the North Rim from the South Rim. On the way, Highway 89A crosses the Colorado River near the canyon's northeastern tip, where the river begins cutting down into the rocks of the Marble Platform and the Grand Canyon begins. As you drive west from Lees Ferry, you'll see where rocks make a single fold along a fault line and rise more than 4,000 vertical feet from the Marble Platform to the level of the Kaibab Plateau—the canyon's North Rim.

Hermits Rest Route & South Rim Trails

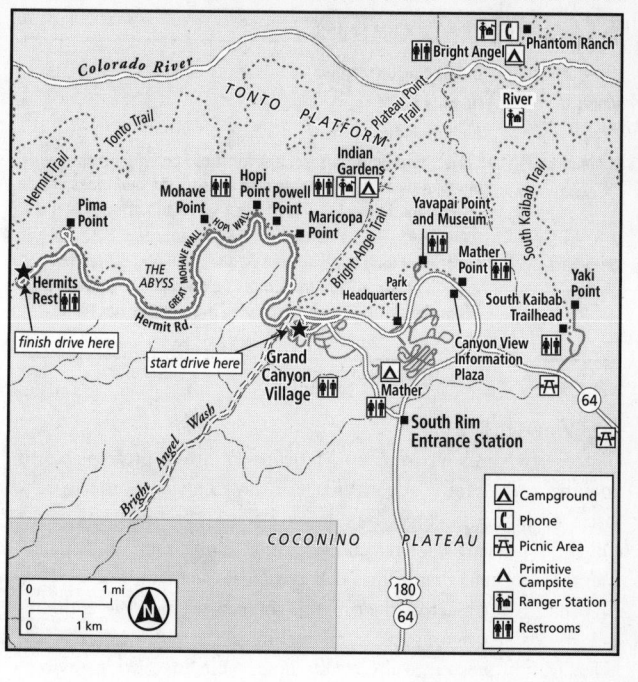

The **North Rim** stretches more than 1,000 feet above the busier South Rim. Highway 67 travels south 44 miles from Highway 89A at Jacob Lake to where it dead-ends at Bright Angel Point, site of the Grand Canyon Lodge. A 23-mile-long paved scenic drive travels from Highway 67 southeast to the tip of the Walhalla Plateau, a peninsula east of Bright Angel Point. This drive, which ends at Cape Royal, has overlooks of the eastern Grand Canyon. On this curvy road, signs appear quickly. Pay attention, as there are few places to turn around. The 3-mile-long spur road to Point Imperial, the highest point on the North Rim, forks to the northeast off this road.

The rims at the **western end of the canyon** are lower, rockier, and more remote than those in the central canyon. Only a few roads cross these lands. The canyon ends abruptly at the Grand Wash cliffs, where the Colorado River flows out of Grand Canyon and into Lake Mead. To drive from rim to rim around the western end of the canyon, you'd have to cross the Colorado River at the Hoover Dam, near Las Vegas.

HERMITS REST ROUTE

Start:	Grand Canyon Village.
Finish:	Hermits Rest.
Time:	About 3 hours.
Highlights:	Closed to private cars (except for those carrying people with physical disabilities) during high season, the overlooks are quieter than those on Desert View Drive and afford excellent river views.
Drawbacks:	Occasional long waits for buses. The 8-mile-long road from Grand Canyon Village to Hermits Rest is open to private cars when the shuttles aren't running. (The shuttles run Mar 1–Nov 30.)

Stop 1
Trailviews 1 & 2

These viewpoints en route to Maricopa Point are great places to look back at Grand Canyon Village. Below the village, the switch-backs of the Bright Angel Trail descend along a natural break in the cliffs. This break was created by erosion along the Bright Angel Fault, one of many fault lines that crisscross the main canyon.

Looking north across the canyon, you can see how the fault created two side canyons in a straight line, on opposite sides of the river. Runoff seeps into the cracks along fault lines, beginning the process of forming side canyons such as these. Below, Indian Garden, where Havasupai Indians farmed for generations, is identifiable by the lush vegetation that grows around the spring there. Past Indian Garden a trail travels straight out to the edge of the Tonto platform, where it dead-ends. This is not the Bright Angel Trail, which descends another side canyon to reach the Inner Gorge, but a spur known as the Plateau Point Trail.

Stop 2
Maricopa Point

The Orphan Mine southwest of this point produced some of the richest uranium ore in the Southwest during the 1950s and 1960s. Below and to the west, you can see some of the metal framework of the tramway that moved ore to the rim from 1956 to 1959. Later, a 1,500-foot-high elevator replaced the tramway. A metal headframe from that elevator remains visible on the rim, directly above the old shaft. Mining continued here, sometimes at night, through 1966.

Stop 3
Powell Memorial

Here you'll find a large memorial to John Wesley Powell, the one-armed Civil War veteran who is widely believed to have been the first person to float through the canyon. Funded in part by the Smithsonian Institute, Powell first drifted into the canyon on August 5, 1869. He and his crew of eight portaged around rapids when the walls were gradual enough to allow it. In parts of the canyon's Inner Gorge, however, the walls became too steep to climb, and the men were forced to float blindly, in wooden boats, through some of the world's most dangerous waters.

Parts of the Inner Gorge are visible below this point, but only a tiny stretch of the river can be seen. Where Powell saw the Inner Gorge's dark, steep rocks lining the water, he thought not of their beauty but of the peril they represented. He called the gorge "our granite prison" and described his men "ever watching, ever peering ahead, for the narrow canyon is winding and the river is closed in . . . and what there may be below, we know not."

When the men stopped above what appeared to be another set of dangerous rapids after 3 weeks in the canyon, three of them left the expedition by walking out into what is now known as Separation Canyon, but were never seen again. The irony here was that the expedition had already passed most of the worst rapids. The remaining crew negotiated the last white water and soon arrived at a small Mormon outpost bearing the first records of the inner canyon's rocks, geography, and life-forms. Powell later fleshed out these records and notes in a lengthy diary, "The Exploration of the Colorado River and its Canyons." The names of the three crew members who left at Separation Canyon do not appear on the monument.

Stop 4
Hopi Point 🔊

Because it projects far into the canyon, the tip of Hopi Point is the best place along Hermits Rest Route to watch the sunset. As the sun drops, its light will play across four of the canyon's loveliest temples. The flat mesa almost due north of the point is Shiva Temple. The temple southwest of it is Osiris; the one southeast of it is Isis. East of Isis is Buddha Temple.

Named for a destructive yet popular Hindu god, Shiva Temple was the site of a much-ballyhooed 1937 mission by a team of scientists from the American Museum of Natural History. Believing that the

canyon isolated the forest atop Shiva Temple the same way oceans isolated the Galapagos Islands, the team set out to find species that had
evolved differently from those on the rim. The East Coast press
drummed up sensationalistic stories about the trip, even going so far
as to hail it as a search for living dinosaurs. Alas, the search didn't turn
up any new species, let alone dinosaurs. Rather, the team learned that
cliffs and desert didn't bar the movements of most Grand Canyon
species. (The Colorado River poses a more significant barrier.) The
most noteworthy discovery: an empty Kodak film box and soup cans
deliberately left behind by canyon local Emery Kolb, who was upset
when the expedition declined his offer to help. Kolb easily made the
ascent himself, proving that the cliffs were hardly a barrier.

Stop 5
Mohave Point ⟨𝒦⟩

This is a great place to observe some of the Colorado River's most
furious rapids. Farthest downstream (to your left) is Hermit Rapids.
Above it, you can make out the top of the dangerous Granite
Rapids, one of the steepest navigable rapids in the world. Just above
Granite Rapids, the bottom of Salt Creek Rapids is visible. As you
look at Hermit Creek Canyon and the rapids below it, you can easily visualize how flash floods washed rocks from the side canyon into
the Colorado River, forming the natural dam that creates the rapids.

Stop 6
The Abyss

The walls in this side canyon steeply fall 2,600 feet to the base of the
Redwall Limestone. The best way to experience the steepness is to
follow the rim trail a few hundred yards west of the overlook, where
the cliffs are most sheer.

Stop 7
Pima Point ⟨𝒦⟩

Three thousand feet below Pima Point—which offers a stunning
view of the Colorado River—you can see some of the foundations
and walls from the old Hermit Camp, a tourist destination built in
1912 by the Santa Fe Railroad. Situated alongside Hermit Creek,
the camp featured heavy-duty tents, each with stoves, Native American rugs, and windows. An aerial tramway connected this point
with the camp below. Used to lower supplies, it made the 3,000-foot
descent in roughly a half hour.

To get to Hermit Camp, tourists traveled 51 miles by train from
Williams to Grand Canyon Village, 9 miles by stagecoach from the
village to the top of the Hermit Trail trailhead, and 8 miles by mule

to the camp. After the Park Service wrested control of the Bright Angel Trail from Ralph Cameron in the 1920s, Phantom Ranch became a more popular tourist destination, and Hermit Camp closed its doors in 1930.

The Hermit Trail, however, remains popular. North of the overlook, below the fin of rock known as Cope Butte, you can see it zigzagging down the blue-green Bright Angel Shale.

Stop 8
Hermits Rest ⚔

Before descending to Hermit Camp, tourists rested at this Mary Colter–designed building, built in 1914. Here, Colter celebrated the "hermit" theme, making the building look as if an isolated mountain man had constructed it. It resembles a crude rock shelter, with stones heaped highest around the chimney. A large fireplace dominates the interior. Colter covered the ceiling above it with soot, so that the room had the look of a cave warmed by fire—much like the nearby Dripping Springs overhang where "The Hermit of Hermit Canyon," Louis Boucher, once passed time. Colter had a knack for finding the perfect details. Note the anthropomorphic rock above the fireplace, the candelabra, and the hanging lanterns. Some of the original hand-carved furniture is still here.

A snack bar sells candy, ice cream, chips, soda, and ham or turkey sandwiches. Two heavily used restrooms are behind the main building. Before leaving, take one last look at the canyon. The three-pronged temple across the canyon to the north is the Tower of Ra, named for the always-victorious Egyptian sun god. Seen from above, each prong points to a different set of rapids: the near arm to Hermit Creek, the middle to Boucher, and the far one to Crystal—waters that have triumphed over more than a few river guides.

DESERT VIEW DRIVE

Start:	Yavapai Point, about a mile east of Grand Canyon Village.
Finish:	Desert View overlook, near the park's east entrance.
Time:	About 4 hours.
Highlights:	Spectacular views of both the central and northeastern canyon.
Drawbacks:	Packed parking lots in summer.

Desert View Drive travels 2 miles on the South Entrance Road, which links Tusayan and Grand Canyon Village. The remaining 23 miles are on the stretch of Highway 64 linking the South Entrance

Road and the Desert View overlook. The Yavapai and Mather overlooks are on the South Entrance Road; the remaining seven stops, including six canyon overlooks, are accessible from Highway 64.

Stop 1

Yavapai Observation Station

Yavapai Point features some of the most expansive views both up and down the canyon. A historic observation station here has huge plate glass windows overlooking the central canyon, along with interpretive panels identifying virtually all the major landmarks.

From here you can spot at least five hiking trails. To the west, the Bright Angel Trail can be seen descending to the lush Indian Garden area. The straight white line leaving from this general area and eventually dead-ending, is the Plateau Point Trail. Directly below the overlook and to the north, the Tonto Trail wends its way across the blue-green Tonto Platform. Across the Colorado River, find the verdant area at the mouth of Bright Angel Canyon. The North Kaibab Trail passes through this area yards before ending at the river, just below Phantom Ranch. Turning to face east, find the saddle just south of O'Neill Butte. The South Kaibab Trail crosses this saddle.

Stop 2

Mather Point ⊛

Visitors who see the canyon only once often do it from here. People entering the park from the south generally catch their first glimpse of the canyon in this area, which offers an expansive, 180 degree view. Many of them immediately steer off the highway, sometimes onto the dirt alongside the road, and rush to the overlook. It can be a clamorous place in high season, epitomizing the "industrial tourism" that the late author Edward Abbey so dreaded.

Grand Canyon National Park, perhaps sensing that this was a natural stopping point, built a large, new visitor center a short walk from this overlook. The only automobile parking near the visitor center is at Mather Point, so visitors now park at Mather Point and walk about 5 minutes to the new plaza (free shuttles are available for travelers with disabilities).

Stop 3

Yaki Point ⊛

Accessible by car when the shuttles aren't running, this overlook is one of the best places to see some of the canyon's most notable monuments, including Vishnu Temple, Zoroaster Temple, and Wotans Throne. As erosion and runoff cut side drainages into the land

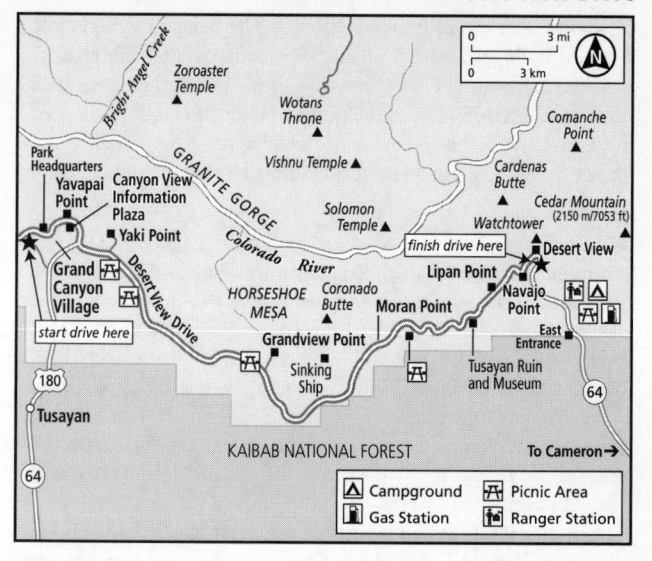

around the larger canyon, pinnacles such as these are sometimes isolated between the drainages. In time, these monuments will erode
away altogether, as will more of the rims. The South Kaibab trailhead is located nearby.

Stop 4

Grandview Point 🔎🔎

At 7,406 feet, this is one of the highest spots on the South Rim. In
the 1890s, it was also one of its busiest. In 1890, one of the canyon's
early prospectors, Pete Berry, filed a mining claim on a rich vein of
copper on Horseshoe Mesa, visible to the north of the overlook. To
remove ore from the mine, Berry built—and in some cases hung—
a trail to it from Grandview Point. He erected cabins and a dining
hall on the mesa, then, as visitors began coming, added a hotel a
short distance away from Grandview Point. Built of ponderosa pine
logs, the Grand View Hotel flourished in the prerailroad days. To
reach the hotel, which for a brief period was considered the best
lodging at the canyon, tourists took a grueling all-day stagecoach
ride from Flagstaff.

In 1901, however, the Santa Fe Railroad linked Grand Canyon
Village and Williams, putting an end, almost immediately, to the
Flagstaff-to-Grandview stagecoach run. Once at Grand Canyon Vil-
lage, few tourists wandered 11 miles east to Grandview Point, and

the hotel went out of business in 1908. The mine fared no better. Plagued by high overhead, it shut down shortly after the price of copper crashed in 1907. Only a trace of the foundation remains of the Grand View Hotel, but the historic Grandview Trail is still used by thousands of hikers annually (see chapter 4 for details), and debris from the old mine camp still litters Horseshoe Mesa.

Stop 5

Moran Point ⚐

This point is named for landscape painter Thomas Moran, whose sketches and oil paintings introduced America to the beauty of the canyon in the years before landscape photography. After accompanying Maj. John Wesley Powell on a surveying expedition in 1873, Moran illustrated Powell's book, *The Exploration of the Colorado River and its Canyons.* Moran's painting, *The Grand Chasm of the Colorado,* later adorned one wall of the nation's capitol. These and other works helped lure some of the first tourists to the canyon in the 19th century.

Moran Point is the best place from which to view the tilting block of rock known as **The Sinking Ship.** Standing at the end of the point, look southwest at the rocks level with the rim. The Sinking Ship can be seen beyond the horizontal layers of Coronado Butte (in the foreground). It's part of the Grandview Monocline, a place where rocks have bent in a single fold around a fault line. Looking down the drainage below Coronado Butte, you'll see the red splotches of Hakatai Shale that give Red Canyon its name.

The first white people to see the canyon probably saw it from somewhere on the rim between here and Desert View. In 1540, Spanish explorer Francisco Vásquez de Coronado was scouring the Southwest for the mythical Seven Cities of Cíbola, with its equally mythical fortune in gold. After hearing of a great river and settlements north of the Hopi pueblo of Tusayan, he sent a small force led by Garcia Lopez de Cardenas to explore the area. Hopi guides led Cardenas and his men, who began the journey in armor, to the South Rim somewhere near here. Upon seeing the Colorado River, the Spaniards initially estimated it to be 6 feet wide. (It's closer to 200 in this area.) When Cardenas asked how to reach it, the Hopi, who had made pilgrimages to the bottom of the canyon for generations, professed not to know. For 3 days Cardenas's men tried unsuccessfully to descend to the river. In the process they learned what many canyon hikers would later discover: "What appeared to be easy from above was not so, but instead very hard and difficult." They gave up, and no white people returned to the canyon for 200 years.

Stop 6
Tusayan Pueblo 👁

By studying the tree rings in the wood at these dwellings, archaeologists determined that parts of this 14-room stone-walled structure were built in 1185 by the Ancestral Pueblo People. Among the pueblos that have been excavated near Grand Canyon, Tusayan Pueblo was the most recently occupied. By 1185 most of the Ancestral Puebloans had already left the canyon. For unknown reasons, however, the dwellers of this pueblo stayed on, despite a prolonged drought (also known from tree rings) and despite the nearest year-round water source being up to 7 miles away.

A self-guided tour takes you through this small collapsed pueblo, which includes the stone foundations of two kivas, living areas, and storage rooms, all connected in a U-shaped structure.

This dwelling, like many Ancestral Pueblo abodes in present-day northern Arizona, has a clear view of the San Francisco peaks, including Humphreys Peak, which at 12,633 feet is the highest point in Arizona. These peaks formed when volcanoes boiled up through weak spots in the earth's crust between 1.8 million and 400,000 years ago. The descendants of the Puebloans, the modern Hopi, believe these peaks are home to ancestral spirits known as Kachinas.

Built in 1932, **Tusayan Museum,** open daily 9am to 5pm, celebrates the traditions of the area's indigenous people. Displays in this dimly lit historic building include traditional jewelry, attire, and tools, as well as historic photos. It's worth coming here just to see the 3,000-4,000-year-old split-twig figurines, made by members of a hunter-gatherer clan known as the **Desert Culture.** These mysterious figurines of deer or sheep were found under cairns (piles of stones) in caves inside the canyon.

Note: There are bathrooms at Tusayan Pueblo.

Stop 7
Lipan Point 👁👁

With views far down the canyon to the west, Lipan Point is a supreme place to catch the sunset. It also overlooks the Colorado River where the river makes two sweeping curves. Between those curves, on the opposite bank, Unkar Creek has deposited a large alluvial fan. From A.D. 800 to 1150, the Ancestral Pueblo People grew beans and corn in this rich soil. Archaeologists have found many granaries and dwellings in the area—not to mention evidence of the use of astronomy. At least some of the Puebloans migrated to the rim during summer to hunt the abundant game and to farm there. Rangers offer free talks here daily at 3:30pm, with guided walks available year-round.

Stop 8
Navajo Point

Like Lipan Point, this one offers fine views of the Grand Canyon Supergroup, a formation of igneous and sedimentary Precambrian rocks that has eroded altogether in many other parts of the canyon. The long, thin streaks of maroon, gray, and black, which tilt at an angle of about 20 degrees, are layers of this formation. They're visible above the river, directly across the canyon. As you look at these rocks, note how the level, brown Tapeats Sandstone, which in other canyon locations sits directly atop the black Vishnu Formation, now rests atop the Supergroup—hundreds of feet above the schist. Where the Supergroup had not yet eroded away, the Tapeats Sandstone was often deposited atop it, protecting what remained. In still other locations, the Supergroup rocks formed islands in the ancient Tapeats Sea, and no sand—the raw material for Tapeats Sandstone—was deposited atop them.

Stop 9
Desert View 𝒜

Here you'll find the **Watchtower,** a 70-foot-high stone building designed by Mary Colter. Colter modeled it after towers found at ancient pueblos such as Mesa Verde and Hovenweep. To get an idea for the shape she wanted, she made a clay model of the building, atop an exact replica of the land at Desert View. Her model seems to have worked. Like Colter's other buildings, this one seems to emerge from the earth, the rough stones at its base blending seamlessly with the rim rock.

The Watchtower is connected to a circular observation room fashioned after a Hopi kiva—a ceremonial room that often adjoined the real pueblo towers. To climb the Watchtower (which is free), you'll first have to pass through this room, currently being used as a gift shop selling Navajo rugs and Native American artifacts. The shop is open daily 7:30am to 6pm; access to the observation deck until 5:30pm. The walls inside the watchtower are decorated with traditional Native American art. Some of the finest work is by Hopi artist Fred Kabotie, whose depiction of the Snake Legend, the story of the first person to have floated down the Colorado River, graces the Watchtower's Hopi Room. At the top is an enclosed observation deck, which at 7,522 feet is the highest point on the South Rim.

The rim at Desert View offers spectacular views of the northeast end of the canyon. To the northeast you'll see the cliffs known as the Palisades of the Desert, which form the southeastern wall of Grand Canyon proper. If you follow those cliffs north to a significant rock outcropping, you're looking at **Comanche Point.** Beyond Comanche Point, you can barely see the gorge carved by the Little Colorado River. In 1956, at the point where that gorge intersects the Grand Canyon, two planes collided and crashed, killing 128 people. Most of the debris was removed from the area around the confluence of the rivers, but a few parts, including a wheel from one of the planes, remain. (None are visible from the rim.)

The flat, mesalike hill to the east is **Cedar Mountain.** This is one of the few places where the story told by the rocks at Grand Canyon *doesn't* end with the Kaibab Limestone. Cedar Mountain and Red Butte (a hill just south of Tusayan along Hwy. 64) were both deposited during the Mesozoic Era (245–65 million years ago). They linger, isolated, atop the Kaibab Limestone, remnants of the more than 4,000 feet of Mesozoic deposits that once accumulated in this area. (Sedimentary rock like this is usually deposited when the land is near or below sea level, as the land in this area was for long periods in the past. It erodes when elevated, the way the Grand Canyon is now.) Though nearly all of these layers have eroded off Grand Canyon, they can be seen nearby in the Painted Desert, the Vermilion Cliffs, and at Zion National Park.

This is the last overlook on the Desert View Drive, where there is a general store and barbecue grill. Past Desert View, Highway 64 continues east, roughly paralleling the gorge cut by the Little Colorado River. It leaves the Grand Canyon, which follows a more northerly course upstream of Desert View. About 10 miles above the confluence, the canyon narrows and the walls begin to drop, eventually disappearing below river level at Lees Ferry (68 miles upstream of where the river passes Desert View), where the canyon begins.

NORTH RIM: CAPE ROYAL DRIVE

Start:	Grand Canyon Lodge.
Finish:	Point Imperial, at the northeastern end of the park.
Time:	About 4 hours—more if you do any hiking.
Highlights:	Sparse crowds and lovely views of the eastern canyon.

Drawbacks:	Has only one viewpoint (Cape Royal) from which to see the central canyon. The Colorado River is not visible from as many points on this drive as on the South Rim drives. From the Grand Canyon Lodge, I recommend driving 23 miles directly to Cape Royal, on the Walhalla Plateau. Make your stops on the way back to the Grand Canyon Lodge. That way, you can do the short hikes near Cape Royal while your legs are fresh, then stop at the picnic areas, closer to the lodge, on your way back.

Stop 1
Cape Royal 🐾🐾

Lined by cliff rose and piñon pine, a gentle, paved 0.3-mile (each way) trail opens onto some of the most stunning views in the park. It first approaches a natural bridge, Angel's Window, carved into a rock peninsula along the rim. Through the square opening under the bridge, a part of the lower canyon, including a slice of the Colorado River, can be seen from the trail. This opening in the Kaibab Limestone was formed when water seeped down through cracks and then across planes between rock beds, eventually eroding the rock from underneath.

The left fork of the trail travels about 150 yards, ending at the tip of the peninsula above **Angel's Window.** With sheer drops on three sides, Angel's Window is a thrilling place to stand.

The right fork of the trail goes to the tip of Cape Royal. From here, Wotans Throne, a broad mesa visible in the distance from many South Rim overlooks, looms only 1.5 miles to the south. Also to the south, and nearly as close, is Vishnu Temple. Closer still is Freya Castle, a pinnacle shaped like a breaking wave. Across the canyon, the tiny nub on the rim is the 70-foot-high Watchtower at Desert View.

> **OPTIONAL STOP**
> The **Cliff Springs Trail** (3 miles north of Cape Royal, in a small pullout). This
> $^1/_2$-mile walk ends at a small spring in a side canyon. (See "Trails on the
> North Rim," in chapter 4.)

Stop 2
Walhalla Overlook and Walhalla Glades 🐾

Ancestral Puebloans no doubt enjoyed the views from here. Follow the tan line of Unkar Creek as it snakes down toward Unkar Delta. Enriched by the river deposits of the creek, the soil and abundant water at the delta made for excellent farming. Many Ancestral

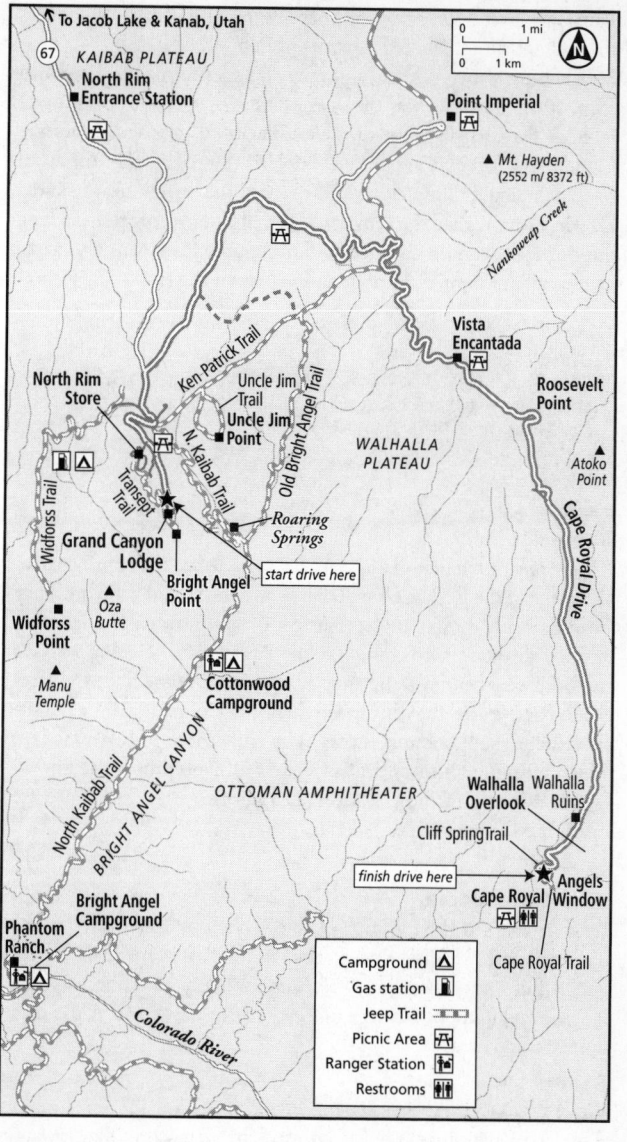

To Jacob Lake & Kanab, Utah
67
KAIBAB PLATEAU
North Rim Entrance Station

Point Imperial

▲ Mt. Hayden
(2552 m/8372 ft)

Nankoweap Creek

Vista Encantada

Roosevelt Point

WALHALLA PLATEAU

▲ Atoko Point

North Rim Store
Ken Patrick Trail
Uncle Jim Trail
Uncle Jim Point
N. Kaibab Trail
Old Bright Angel Trail

Transept Trail
Roaring Springs
start drive here

Grand Canyon Lodge
Bright Angel Point

Widforss Trail

Cape Royal Drive

Widforss Point

Oza Butte

▲ Manu Temple

Cottonwood Campground

North Kaibab Trail
BRIGHT ANGEL CANYON

OTTOMAN AMPHITHEATER

Walhalla Overlook   Walhalla Ruins

Cliff SpringTrail

finish drive here

Cape Royal   Angels Window

Cape Royal Trail

Bright Angel Campground

Phantom Ranch

Colorado River

	Campground	▲
	Gas station	🛢
	Jeep Trail	▪▪▪
	Picnic Area	⛺
	Ranger Station	🏠
	Restrooms	🚻

0   1 mi
0   1 km
N

Puebloans lived there, growing corn, beans, and squash on terraces that caught runoff and left deposits of rich soil.

When the canyon heated up, they also spent time on the North Rim, at dwellings such as the ones across the street from this overlook. A flat dirt path leads to Walhalla Ruin, which includes the foundations of two small pueblos. In this area, the Ancestral Puebloans could farm, taking advantage of the extra moisture and a growing season that was lengthened by the warm breezes blowing out of the canyon. In addition to farming, the Puebloans also gathered food and hunted the abundant game on the rim.

OPTIONAL STOP:
Cape Final Trail (4.9 miles south of Roosevelt Point). This gentle, 1.5-mile-long (one-way) hike follows an old Jeep trail to an overlook at Cape Final. (See "Trails on the North Rim," in chapter 4.)

Stop 3
Roosevelt Point
This is one of the best places in the canyon to see the confluence of the gorge of the Little Colorado River and the Grand Canyon. They meet at nearly a right angle, unusual in that most tributaries enter at close to the same direction as the larger rivers. Geologists have used this observation to buttress arguments that the ancestral Colorado River exited the canyon via the Little Colorado gorge, but little evidence supports this theory. The cliffs south of this junction, which form the southeast wall of Grand Canyon proper, are known as the Palisades of the Desert. Those north of the confluence are called the Desert Facade.

Stop 4
Vista Encantadora
By starting your driving tour of the Walhalla Plateau early in the day, you can reach Vista Encantadora in time for a late picnic lunch. You'll find several tables near the rim. While you picnic, you can look down an upper drainage of Nankoweap Creek and at the rock pinnacle known as Brady Peak.

Stop 5
Point Imperial 🔭🔭
A 3-mile spur road leads from the Cape Royal Road to Point Imperial, which at 8,803 feet is the highest point on the North Rim and the best place on either rim to view the northeastern end of the

---

Fun Fact **Wild Things**

If you watch carefully, you'll see wildlife everywhere during your stay. The best time to view larger animals is at dawn or dusk, when they become more active. To see large animals such as elk, drive into the **Kaibab National Forest** near Grand-view Point. On the North Rim, the meadows alongside the entrance road are frequented by **wild turkey, deer,** and (less often) **coyotes.** If you're serious about wildlife watching, bring binoculars. For more information, turn to the "The Fauna" section of chapter 8.

---

park. To the northeast, 3,000 feet below the overlook, you'll see the brownish-green plane known as the Marble Platform. The Colorado River cleaves this platform between Lees Ferry and where Grand Canyon proper yawns open just east of here. Because the Marble Platform has the same rock layers as Grand Canyon, **Marble Canyon** is considered by geologists to be the uppermost section of Grand Canyon.

Bordering the Marble Platform on the north are the **Vermilion Cliffs.** Located along the Utah-Arizona border, these cliffs are also the next steps up in the Grand Staircase, a geological formation in which progressively younger rock formations rise like steps from Marble Canyon to Bryce Canyon in southern Utah. The Vermilion Cliffs run southwest to northeast. Where this formation turns toward the south near Lees Ferry, the cliffs are known as the **Echo Cliffs.**

Looking southeast, you can see where the gorge of the Little Colorado River intersects the Grand Canyon. Past that confluence, the landforms of the Painted Desert stain the horizon a rich red. This desert, made up of badlands and other erosional features carved from the soft clays of the Chinle Formation, surrounds the Little Colorado River and one of its tributaries, the Puerte River. Like the Vermilion Cliffs, the Painted Desert is made up of "younger" rocks than are found in Grand Canyon.

4 Ranger Programs & Organized Tours

On both rims, the park offers a host of Ranger programs with schedules that change seasonally. A typical schedule includes guided hikes and walks, kids' programs, and discussions of geology, native plant and animal species, and natural and cultural history. Evening programs are offered nightly, all year-round. All the programs are free and open to everyone. You just need to show up at the meeting places, which are scattered around the park (overlooks, trailheads, archaeological sites, and so on). For an up-to-date schedule, consult the park newspaper, *The Guide*.

BUS TOURS

Of the many private companies that offer bus tours, **Fred Harvey** has the most extensive schedule. Among the choices are Desert View Drive (East Rim) and Hermits Rest Route (West Rim) tours ($28 and $16, respectively, for adults; under 16 free), sunset tours to Hopi or Mojave Point ($12.25), sunrise tours ($12.25) to one of several rim stops, and all-day outings ($34) that combine two of the shorter tours. Unlike the drivers on the free shuttles, Fred Harvey drivers narrate the tours. Don't believe everything they say. Though they mean well and offer some valuable information, they were not hired for their command of natural science and history. (Just be glad you don't have distracted professors driving the bus.) For advance reservations, call © **888/297-2757.** Once at the canyon, visit the transportation desks at Yavapai, Maswik, or Bright Angel lodges, or call © **928/638-2631,** ext. 6015.

Open Road Tours (© **800/766-7117**) offers 1-day guided canyon tours that depart from Flagstaff at 9:30am and return by 5:30pm. The cost is $69 for adults; $34.50 for 11 and under.

5 Historic & Man-Made Attractions

Please refer to the map "Grand Canyon Village" on p. 115 in chapter 6 to find the exact locations of the historic buildings in the South Rim.

SOUTH RIM

Most of the historic buildings on the South Rim are concentrated in Grand Canyon Village, a National Historic District. Outside of the village, **Hermits Rest** on the Hermits Rest Route and The **Watchtower** on the Desert View Drive are also of historical significance. For information on these two sites, refer to the West Rim (p. 40) and East Rim (p. 43) driving tours. Strange and beautiful, these historic buildings—like the canyon itself—take time to appreciate.

Mary Colter, a Minneapolis schoolteacher who in 1902 began decorating the shops that sold Native American art on the Santa Fe Railroad line, designed more than a half dozen of these historic buildings. As both a decorator and self-trained architect, Colter later designed these Grand Canyon landmarks: Hopi House (1905), the

Lookout (1914), Hermits Rest (1914), Phantom Ranch (1922), Watchtower (1932), and Bright Angel Lodge (1935). Colter's work drew heavily on the architectural styles of Native Americans and Spanish settlers in the Southwest, long before these styles became fashionable among Anglos. The most noteworthy historic buildings in Grand Canyon Village are detailed below.

THE BRIGHT ANGEL LODGE 🐾🐾   In the 1930s, the Santa Fe Railroad asked Mary Colter to design moderately priced accommodations for the many new tourists who had begun driving to the canyon. Colter laid out a number of cabins, as well as this rustic log-and-stone lodge, which would house a lounge, restaurant, and curio shop. Completed in 1935, the lodge, located near the west end of Grand Canyon Village, looks low from outside but has a spacious lobby with wood walls, flagstone floors, and a high ceiling with an exposed log framework. A remarkable hearth is found in what was once the lounge and is currently the site of the Bright Angel History Room. Known as "the geological fireplace," it features the rock layers found in the canyon, stacked in the same order in which they occur there. Rounded, smooth river stones lie at the bottom of this bell-shaped hearth and Kaibab Limestone, the rim rock, is on top.

The History Room tells the story of Harvey Girls—young women who came west during the years from 1883 through the 1950s to staff the Fred Harvey restaurants and hotels along the rail lines.

BUCKEY O'NEILL CABIN 🐾   This is the second-oldest surviving structure in Grand Canyon Village (the oldest being Red House Station, which was moved to the rim in 1890). It was the home of Buckey O'Neill, who in the 1890s worked at a number of jobs, including sheriff, judge, reporter, and prospector, in the area. After discovering what he believed to be a rich copper vein in Anita, 14 miles south of the canyon, he pushed for the construction of a railroad line connecting Williams with Grand Canyon—via Anita, naturally. A Chicago mining company bought out O'Neill, but the project collapsed when the mine turned out to be less than rich. In 1901, the Santa Fe Railroad, perhaps realizing that Canyon tourism would pay far greater dividends than copper, bought the line and laid the remaining track. When Mary Colter designed cabins for Bright Angel Lodge, she fought for the preservation of the O'Neill Cabin, eventually building her own ones around it. Today, this cabin, a few feet west of Bright Angel Lodge, is probably the most luxurious guest suite in the park.

THE EL TOVAR HOTEL ☆☆☆ A year after the Santa Fe Railroad linked the South Rim with Williams, Fred Harvey commissioned Charles Whittlesey, an architect who had worked alongside Mary Colter on the Alvarado Hotel in Albuquerque, to build a large luxury hotel on the rim. Whittlesey fashioned the El Tovar after the northern European lodges of that period. Built of Oregon pine, this 100-room hotel offered first-class luxury accommodations at the canyon, attracting luminaries such as George Bernard Shaw and Theodore Roosevelt. To find it, walk 200 yards east along the rim from Bright Angel Lodge. (For more on the El Tovar, see chapter 6.)

GRAND CANYON DEPOT Built in 1909, this is one of three remaining log train depots in the United States. It closed after the last train from Grand Canyon departed in 1968, then reopened in 1990, roughly a year after the railway resumed service. Located about 100 yards south of the El Tovar, this two-story depot is built of logs that are flat on three sides, making for smooth interior walls and a rounded, rustic exterior. Once home to the station agent and his family, the upstairs of the depot now houses Park Service offices.

HOPI HOUSE ☆☆ Aware that travelers were captivated by the idea of meeting Native Americans, Fred Harvey brought a group of Hopi artisans to Grand Canyon Village. At the same time that it was erecting the El Tovar Hotel on the rim, the company commissioned Mary Colter to design a structure 100 feet east of the hotel that could serve as both a dwelling for the Hopi and a place to market their wares.

Colter fashioned Hopi House after the pueblos in Oraibi, Arizona. Completed in 1905, this faux adobe structure rises in tiers, with each level connected by exterior wood ladders (and interior stairways). The roof of each level serves as the porch for the one above. Inside, low doorways and nooks in the walls recall the snug quarters found in real pueblos. The concrete floors are made to look like dirt, the plaster walls to look like adobe. Log beams support thatched ceilings.

Through 1968, the Hopi artisans lived on the top floor of this building while they created and sold their pottery, rugs, and jewelry on the lower floors. They chanted and danced nightly on a platform behind the building. Today, Hopi House still sells Native American art on the lower two floors (with higher quality art located on the second floor), and Native American dancers have recently begun performing again. Once used for religious purposes, the kiva on the second floor remains off-limits to non–Native Americans.

KOLB STUDIO ⚘ In 1902, two brothers, Emery and Ellsworth Kolb, began photographing tourists descending the Bright Angel Trail on mules. After snapping the photos, they ran to Indian Gardens, where they had water to develop their plates, then raced back to the rim in time to sell the photos. Flush with profits from the business, they built this home and studio alongside the trailhead of the Bright Angel Trail, along the rim at the westernmost edge of Grand Canyon Village, in 1904. Several years later the brothers launched a more ambitious project: a motion picture of a raft trip through Grand Canyon. Completed in 1912, the film earned them international fame and drew throngs of people to the studio's viewing room.

After clashing regularly throughout the years, the two brothers eventually flipped a coin to see which one would have the privilege of remaining at their beloved Grand Canyon. Emery won two out of three tosses. So while Ellsworth moved to Los Angeles, Emery continued to live and work at Kolb Studio, introducing the brothers' film to audiences each day until his death at age 95 in 1976, after which the Park Service took over the building. Today, Kolb Studio houses a bookstore and gallery (located in the former viewing room), which features exhibits year-round. Photos and clips from the Kolbs' films are shown in an interactive CD-ROM video (a must-see) inside the store.

LOOKOUT STUDIO ⚘ Seeing the crowds drawn to Kolb Studio, The Fred Harvey Company decided to launch a similar business, only closer to the railroad terminus. Mary Colter was hired to design the building, which she eventually named The Lookout. Unlike some of her buildings, which were fashioned after occupied pueblos or well-preserved ruins, this one, on the canyon rim about 100 yards east of Kolb Studio, resembled a collapsed ruin. Its original chimney and low-slung roof looked like a pile of rocks and seemed barely higher than the canyon rim. To add to the effect, Colter planted indigenous plants on the roof. After its completion in 1914, tourists came here to buy souvenirs or to photograph the canyon from the deck, where a high-power telescope was placed. Today, Lookout Studio still serves much the same purpose.

VERKAMP'S CURIOS A true visionary, John G. Verkamp may have been the first to sell curios at the Grand Canyon. In 1898, before the railroad even reached Grand Canyon Village, Verkamp was hawking souvenirs out of a tent on the grounds of the Bright Angel Lodge. Although his first attempt at the business failed,

Verkamp returned in 1905, after the trains began running, and opened a curio shop in a wood-shingled, Craftsman-style building 200 feet east of Hopi House. This time he succeeded. His descendants still run the store, making it one of the last privately held businesses in the park.

NORTH RIM

GRAND CANYON LODGE & CABINS ⍟   This lodge sits quietly on the North Rim, gracefully blending into its surroundings. Built in 1928 by the Pacific Railroad, the lodge burned down in 1932 and was rebuilt in 1937. Inside, an expansive 50-foot-high lobby opens onto an octagonal sunroom with three enormous windows offering picturesque views of the canyon. You can also enjoy the views in a chair on one of two long decks outside the sunroom. For a cool treat, descend the lodge's back steps and look directly below the sunroom. There, you'll find the much darker "Moon Room." For more information see chapter 6.

4

Hikes & Other Outdoor Pursuits in the Grand Canyon

There's no better way to enjoy the canyon than by walking right down into it and seeing all the rock layers and the plant and animal life up close. You can day-hike part of the way into the canyon on a number of trails.

Although hiking below the rims is the most stimulating way to experience the canyon, it can also be dangerous, especially at mid-day during summer. If it's hot out or you aren't up to climbing, consider walking on one of the rim trails or on the new greenway being constructed on the South Rim. The rim trails are especially nice in the forests on the North Rim.

On the South Rim, the wide, lush **Bright Angel Trail** is the least difficult canyon trail for day hikers. It is well maintained, has shade and drinking water, and is less steep than other canyon trails. A few well-prepared hikers will be comfortable traveling 6 miles one-way to the end of the **Plateau Point Trail** ⚑, which departs from the Tonto Trail just north of where the Tonto crosses the Bright Angel Trail. If you go any farther on a day hike, there's a good chance that you'll run out of energy and/or daylight while climbing back to the rim.

Other popular day hikes on the South Rim include the **South Kaibab Trail** to Cedar Ridge, the **Hermit Trail** to either Dripping Springs (via the Dripping Springs Trail) or Santa Maria Spring, and the **Grandview Trail** to Horseshoe Mesa. Because it is steeper and has no water and little shade, the South Kaibab Trail is considered more strenuous than the Bright Angel Trail, but it offers panoramic views. The Hermit and Grandview trails, which are unmaintained and very steep in places, are more rugged than the South Kaibab.

On the North Rim the **North Kaibab Trail,** which has seasonal water and abundant shade, is the best option for day hikers descending into the canyon. Day hikers, as a rule, shouldn't go farther than Roaring Springs, 4.7 miles and 3,000 vertical feet below the trailhead. Even strong hikers may have problems returning to the rim before sunset if they go past Roaring Springs on a day hike.

The trail descriptions later in this chapter cover many canyon paths, including turn-around points for day hikers. However, because of remote locations and/or rugged conditions, the **South Bass, North Bass, Nankoweap, Tanner, New Hance, Boucher, Thunder River, Bill Hall,** and **Deer Creek** trails are not covered in this book. You can ask questions about these trails and obtain free trail descriptions at the Backcountry Information Center (© **928/638-7875**), located in the Maswik Transportation Center. More detailed descriptions can be found in guidebooks and individual trail guides sold through the Grand Canyon Association (© **800/858-2808**).

Wherever you hike, carry plenty of water and know where the next water sources are. Eat and drink regularly. If you hike into the canyon, allow yourself twice as much time for the trip out as for the descent.

Recommended Hiking Distances

The following is a list of trails recommended for day hikers, and the farthest point that day hikers should try to go on them.

For Less-Experienced Hikers:

South Rim Trail	2.1 miles one-way
West Rim Trail	8 miles one-way
Bright Angel Point Trail	.3 miles one-way
Transept Trail	1.5 miles one-way
Widforss Trail	5 miles one-way
Bright Angel Trail to Mile-and-a-Half House	1.5 miles one-way
North Kaibab Trail to Supai Tunnel	2.7 miles one-way

For Fit, Well-Prepared Hikers:

South Kaibab Trail to Cedar Ridge	1.5 miles one-way
North Kaibab Trail to Roaring Springs	4.7 miles one-way
Bright Angel Trail to Indian Garden	4.6 miles one-way
or to Plateau Point	6.1 miles one-way
Grandview Trail to Horseshoe Mesa	3 miles one-way
Hermit Trail to Santa Maria Spring	2.5 miles one-way
Hermit and Dripping Springs Trails to Dripping Springs	3 miles one-way

BACKPACKING FOR BEGINNERS

By camping inside the canyon, you can give yourself time to explore the lower elevations of the park. However, the extreme changes in temperature and elevation can make the Grand Canyon a nightmare for inexperienced or unprepared backpackers. The jarring descent strains your knees; the climb out tests your heart. Extreme heat often precludes hiking during the middle of the day, and water is scarce. Because of these hazards, a first-time backpacker should consider hiking on gentler terrain before venturing into the canyon.

1 Preparing for Your Backcountry Trip

PACKING TIPS FOR BACKPACKERS

What you carry (or don't) in your pack is just as important as your choice of trails. Warm temperatures and dry weather make the canyon an ideal place for traveling light. Lighten your load by carrying dry food such as instant beans and ramen noodles. In summer, you can go lighter still by leaving the stove at home and preparing cold meals. Some foods that are usually heated, like ramen noodles or couscous, will soften in cold water—even inside a water bottle—over time. During early summer, carry a tent's rain fly or bivy sack instead of a tent. At this time of year, you're more likely to die of problems related to heat—and heavy packs—than from the cold. Just be sure you know how to rig your shelter, in case rain does fall.

Also, make sure you have enough water containers. I usually carry 6 to 8 quarts in summer and sometimes, for long, waterless walks, bring even more. Drink all the time—start before you get thirsty—and refill your bottles whenever you have the chance. Eating carbo-hydrate-rich, salty food is just as important. If you guzzle too much water without eating, you run the risk of developing an electrolyte imbalance that can result in unconsciousness or death. Loss of appetite is common during a hike. Try to eat every time you take a drink, even if you don't feel hungry. Also, carry powdered Gatorade or another electrolyte replacement drink. See "Equipment Checklist," below.

GETTING PERMITS

Permits are required for all overnight camping in the backcountry that falls within the park's boundaries. This includes all overnight stays below the rims (except in the cabins and dorms at Phantom

Equipment Checklist

- Tent or light shelter
- Ground cloth
- Sleeping bag (very lightweight in summer)
- Sleeping bag stuff sack (can be used to hang food)
- Sleeping pad
- Patch kit (if pad is inflatable)
- Backpack (external frame is better)
- Signal mirror
- Compass
- Headlamp with batteries
- Spare batteries and bulbs
- First-aid kit (adhesive tape, supportive elastic wrap, mole-skin, mole foam, iodine, gauze pads, bandages, aspirin, antihistamine, diarrhea medication, tweezers)
- Water-purifying tablets (pumps often clog)
- Two 1-quart unbreakable plastic water bottles plus one or two 4-liter nylon water bags
- Small plastic or collapsible metal shovel for burying human waste
- Waterproof matches
- Lightweight camp stove and fuel (optional)
- Stove repair kit and spare parts (if carrying stove)
- Topo maps
- Trail descriptions published by the Backcountry Information Center
- Swiss army knife
- Eating utensil
- Lightweight cooking pot
- Hiking boots
- Two long-sleeved T-shirts
- One pair shorts
- Thick socks

Ranch) and on park land outside of designated campgrounds. Good for up to 11 people, each permit costs $10 plus an additional $5 per person per night.

Regular hikers can purchase a **Frequent Hiker Membership,** which costs $25 but waives the $10 permit fee for a year from the date of purchase.

- Breathable water-resistant shell
- Polypropylene underwear (top and bottom)
- Polar fleece leggings and uppers (seasonal)
- Winter cap and gloves (seasonal)
- Wide-brimmed hat
- 100% UV protection sunglasses
- High SPF sunscreen and lip balm
- Extra plastic freezer bags
- Toilet paper
- Garbage bag
- Notebook and pen (optional)
- Lightweight camera and film (optional)
- ¼-inch nylon rope (if necessary for hike)
- Trail mix
- Ramen noodles
- Dehydrated beans
- Dried foods
- Granola bars
- Turkey or beef jerky
- Energy bars
- Dried milk
- Cold cereal
- Raisins
- Crackers
- Very hard cheese
- Salted peanut butter (in plastic jar)
- Bagels

Note: Dried or freeze-dried food is fine only if you have access to water. If not, take food that doesn't require water during preparation.

Permits for the month desired go on sale on the first of the month, more than 4 months earlier. For example, permits for all of May go on sale on January 1; permits for June go on sale February 1, and so on. If you're not purchasing a permit in person, you'll need to complete a **Backcountry Permit Request Form,** included in the free Backcountry Trip Planner mailed out by the park. The Backcountry

Backcountry Permit Waiting List

If you show up at the park without a permit and find the back-country booked, you may be able to obtain one by putting your name on the waiting list. If you want to hike the corridor trails during the spring, summer, and fall, you should expect to spend at least 1 day on the waiting list before obtaining a permit. To place your name on the waiting list, show up in person at the Backcountry Information Center. The ranger will give you a number at that time. To stay on the waiting list, you'll have to show up at the Backcountry Information Center at 8am every morning until you receive an opening. Usually permits are for the next night, but occasionally, permits for that night are issued. Even though cancellations don't always happen, the center sometimes sets aside a spot or two at the Bright Angel Campground or Cottonwood Campground for people on the list.

Trip Planners also suggest itineraries for first-time Grand Canyon hikers and offer advice on safe, low-impact hiking. To receive one, call the park's main extension at © **928/638-7888** and choose the "backcountry information" option. Or, write to Grand Canyon National Park, P.O. Box 129, Grand Canyon, AZ 86023, and request a **Backcountry Trip Planner** (not to be confused with one of the park's regular trip planners). You can also download a Permit Request Form and instructions by surfing to **www.nps.gov/grca**. To increase your odds of receiving a permit, be as flexible as possible when filling out the form. It helps to request three alternative hikes, in order of preference, and more than one starting date. Keeping your group small also helps.

Once you fill out your Permit Request Form, you can take it in person to the Backcountry Information Center on either rim; fax it to © **928/638-2125** no earlier than the date the permits become available, or mail it postmarked no earlier than that date. No requests are taken by phone. Allow 1 to 3 weeks for processing, after the Backcountry Information Center receives your form.

If you have questions about a trail or about the process itself, the Backcountry Information Center, at © **928/638-7875,** takes calls weekdays between 1 and 5pm Mountain Standard Time. You can visit the office in person from 8am to noon and 1 to 5pm daily.

Permits can sometimes be obtained in person outside the park's developed areas (and in some cases, outside the park) at the **Kaibab Plateau Visitor Center** (© **928/643-7298**) in Jacob Lake, AZ; at

Pipe Spring National Monument (© 928/643-7105) near Fredonia, Arizona; and at Ranger stations at **Tuweep, Meadview,** and **Lees Ferry.** The Kaibab Plateau location is particularly convenient for backpackers hoping to hike the Nankoweap, North Bass, Bill Hall, or Thunder River Trails, all of which are accessed via roads through the Kaibab National Forest. At the Pipe Spring, Tuweep, Meadview, and Lees Ferry locations, you may not always find personnel capable of processing your request.

2 Exploring the Backcountry

For the purposes of this book, I've divided the park trails into three categories: corridor, wilderness, and rim. In the Grand Canyon, most of the rim trails and all of the corridor and wilderness trails are considered part of the backcountry.

CORRIDOR TRAILS   When descending into the canyon for the first time, even experienced backpackers should consider one of the three **corridor trails,** North Kaibab, South Kaibab, or Bright Angel, discussed in detail below. Well maintained and easy to follow, these are regularly patrolled by park rangers. Each has at least one emergency phone and pit toilet. Drinking water is available at several sources along both the Bright Angel and the North Kaibab trails, but not on the South Kaibab. (Some of these sources are seasonal.) Check at the Backcountry Information Center for current water availability before starting your hike. While hiking the corridor trails, you can spend your nights at **Bright Angel, Cottonwood,** or **Indian Garden** campgrounds, each of which has a ranger station, running water (seasonal at Cottonwood), and toilets.

WILDERNESS TRAILS   By hiking on corridor trails, you can acclimate yourself to the conditions in the canyon without having to negotiate the boulder-strewn and sometimes confusing **wilderness**

(Tips) **Locations of Ranger Stations**

Backcountry ranger stations are found at **Indian Garden, Phantom Ranch,** and **Cottonwood Campground** (in summer only). Emergency phones, connected to the park's 24-hour dispatch, are at the rest houses along the Bright Angel Trail and near the intersection of the South Kaibab and Tonto trails. On the **North Kaibab Trail,** an emergency phone can be found near Roaring Springs.

A Note About Difficulty of Trails

Because of the huge elevation changes on the canyon trails, none should be called easy. (More people are rescued off the Bright Angel Trail, generally considered the easiest trail into the canyon, than off any other trail.) In general, please note that rating a trail easy, moderate, or difficult oversimplifies the situation. For example, the **Hermit Trail** is easy to follow and relatively gradual between the rim and just above Santa Maria Spring, but it's considerably more rugged after that; the **Tonto Trail** is easy to walk on in places, but has almost no water and very little shade. The following is a very subjective ranking of some of the most popular trails that go from the rim into the canyon from **least to most difficult.**

South Rim	North Rim
Bright Angel	North Kaibab
South Kaibab	Thunder River
Grandview	Bill Hall/Thunder River
Hermit	Nankoweap
Hermit/Dripping Spring/Boucher	North Bass

trails, which also go into the canyon. Rangers are seldom encountered on these trails, which are not maintained by the park. These trails have washed away in some places; in others, they descend steeply through cliffs. They can also be difficult to discern. On the less-traveled wilderness trails, help can be very far away if something goes wrong.

The corridor trails provide access to backcountry campgrounds, but most wilderness trails accommodate only **at-large camping,** meaning that it's up to each hiker to find his or her own campsite. Unlike the campgrounds, the campsites along wilderness trails do not have purified water or ranger stations nearby, and only a few have pit toilets. On the busiest wilderness trails, campers may be limited to **designated sites.**

RIM TRAILS   As the name implies, rim trails travel on the rim of the canyon and do not descend into the canyon's interior. Some rim trails stay inside the park's developed areas. These are usually paved, with relatively gradual inclines. These trails can be very busy, but they sometimes afford nice views. Other rim trails go farther away from developed areas and into the nearby piñon-juniper, ponderosa pine, and spruce-fir forests. These trails have a few rugged, steeply rolling stretches, but most are quite manageable. Often uncrowded, many of these trails lead to scenic canyon overlooks.

3 Trails on the South Rim

Visitors to the South Rim have two rim trails from which to choose: the **West Rim (Hermits Rest) Trail** and the **South Rim Trail.** Both start in Grand Canyon Village and travel in opposite directions along the rim, with the West Rim Trail traveling 8 miles west to Hermits Rest and the South Rim Trail extending 3.4 miles northeast past Mather Point to Pipe Creek Vista. Both can be very busy, especially near Grand Canyon Village. And both offer stunning canyon views while passing through rim-top scenery that is less than pristine. The South Rim Trail is paved, wide, and easy to walk on; the West Rim Trail is longer, more rugged, and has a few lonesome stretches. Unfortunately, much of it lies close to Hermit Road.

West Rim Trail   Highlights: Beats riding the bus to all the overlooks. **Drawbacks:** Seeing and hearing the buses, and the crowds at the overlooks. **Difficulty:** One steep climb; tricky footing in isolated locations.

Don't let the name of this trail confuse you. The West Rim Trail meanders along the *South Rim* of the canyon, from Grand Canyon Village all the way to Hermits Rest. (If you go looking for a west rim of the canyon, you may end up in Lake Mead.) In doing so, it parallels Hermit Road and passes through all the same scenic overlooks, described in the driving tour (see chapter 3). Walking instead of driving along this stretch of road is a great way to see the canyon while putting some elbow room between yourself and the crowds at the overlooks. The 1.3-mile stretch from the village to Maricopa Point is paved, with one 200-vertical-foot climb. Past Maricopa Point, the trail planes off somewhat and the pavement ends. For the rest of the way to Hermits Rest, the trail becomes a series of footpaths that meander through piñon-juniper woodland along the rim (when not crossing overlooks). Sagebrush roots and loose rocks make for tricky footing, but the scenery is lovely, and the crowds thin as you move farther west. The nicest stretch is between the Abyss and Pima Point. Here, the trail detours away from Hermits Rest Route, going towards the canyon and away from the road. This is one of the few places on the trail where you won't hear an occasional bus.

As 16 miles might be too much hiking for 1 day, I recommend hiking out on this trail from Grand Canyon Village and taking the shuttle back (mid-Mar through mid-Oct). By hiking out, you can avoid revisiting the same overlooks on the shuttle ride back—the shuttles stop at every turnout while en route to Hermits Rest, but only stop at Mohave Point and Hopi Point on their way back to Grand Canyon Village.

If you don't want to walk the whole 8 miles, here's a list of distances, which will help determine how far you've gone and whether you want to continue to the next lookout.

Trailhead to Trailview I:	.6 miles
Trailview I to Maricopa Point:	.7 miles
Maricopa Point to Powell Point:	.5 miles
Powell Point to Hopi Point:	.3 miles
Hopi Point to Mohave Point:	.8 miles
Mohave Point to the Abyss:	1.1 miles
The Abyss to Pima Point:	2.9 miles
Pima Point to Hermits Rest:	1.1 miles

8 miles to Hermits Rest. Access: Rim-side sidewalk at the west end of Grand Canyon Village. Water sources at Grand Canyon Village, Hermits Rest, Park Headquarters, and Yavapai Point. Maps: Trails Illustrated Topo Map or Village Area Map (included in *The Guide*).

South Rim Trail   **Highlights:** Paved, easy to walk on, and close to the edge. **Drawbacks:** More crowded than the West Rim Trail. **Difficulty:** A boulevard. The sidewalk is so wide, it's more like a road than a trail.

This smooth, paved trail connects Grand Canyon Village and Mather Point. Around the lodges, the path is a flat sidewalk teeming with people. The crowds dissipate somewhat between the east edge of the village and Yavapai Point. Near Yavapai Point, you'll find many smooth flat rocks along the rim—great places from which to contemplate the canyon. Located 1.5 miles northeast of the Historic

---

Note About Trail Descriptions

The trail descriptions in this chapter are not intended for use in route finding. It's up to each hiker to hike smart, be physically fit, and have the skills and equipment needed to stay on the trail. Also, more detailed trail descriptions are available. The Grand Canyon Association (✆ **800/858-2808**) publishes a number of guides to the most popular trails.

District in Grand Canyon Village, **Yavapai Point** has a historic (1928) observation station with large windows overlooking the canyon. From here, you can walk another .6 miles to Mather Point on a portion of the park's new greenway (and even farther in the near future). This 10-foot-wide, paved walkway usually travels within a few feet of the rim. It takes you away from the crowds and provides ever-changing canyon views. If you grow fatigued during your walk, you can catch shuttles at Mather or Yavapai Points.

2.1 miles to Mather Point. Access: Grand Canyon Village, along the rim behind the El Tovar Hotel. Water sources at Grand Canyon Village, Park Headquarters, and Yavapai Point. Maps: Trails Illustrated Topo Map or Village Area Map (included in *The Guide*).

4 Trails on the North Rim

The rim trails on the North Rim rank among the park's treasures. Start with either the **Transept Trail** or the **Bright Angel Point Trail,** which are different sections of the same pathway. At the bottom of the stairs behind Grand Canyon Lodge, the Bright Angel Point Trail goes to the left, while the Transept Trail goes right. The Bright Angel Point Trail is a short (¼-mile) paved path to a stunning overlook on a tiny peninsula between Transept and Bright Angel Canyons. It's nearly always crowded, but well worth seeing. The Transept Trail is longer, more thickly forested, and far less crowded, but it has less panoramic views.

Bright Angel Point Trail ⟨ **Highlights:** Stunning views of Transept and Bright Angel Canyons. **Drawbacks:** Crowds at Bright Angel Point Overlook. **Difficulty:** Safe and easy, unless there's lightning.

This paved trail travels a quarter mile along a narrow peninsula dividing Roaring Springs and Transept canyons. On the way, it passes a number of craggy outcroppings of Kaibab Limestone, around which the roots of wind-whipped juniper trees cling like arthritic hands. Although the trail stays at about the same level as the rim, junipers supplant ponderosa pines here because of the warm winds that blow out of the canyon. The trail ends at 8,148-foot-high Bright Angel Point. From this overlook you can follow Bright Angel Canyon (with your eyes) to its intersection with the larger gorge of the Colorado River. On a quiet day, you can hear Roaring Springs, a tributary of Bright Angel Creek and the water source for both the North and the South rims of the canyon.

.3 mile each way. Access: By descending the back steps off the patios at Grand Canyon Lodge. Water source at Grand Canyon Lodge. Map: *The Guide.*

The Transept Trail 🎦   **Highlights:** Ponderosa pine forest and views of Transept Canyon. **Drawbacks:** May be busy, especially near Grand Canyon Lodge. **Difficulty:** Generally easy. Its undulations provide interval training.

Traveling 1.5 miles northeast along the rim of Transept Canyon, this trail connects the lodge and the North Rim Campground. Passing through old-growth ponderosa pine and quaking aspen, it descends into, then climbs out of, three shallow side drainages, with ascents steep enough to take the breath away from people unaccustomed to the 8,000-foot altitude. A small Native American ruin sits alongside the dirt.

1.5 miles each way. Access: Behind North Rim General Store (near the campground), or by descending the back steps off the patios at Grand Canyon Lodge. Water source at North Rim Store. Map: *The Guide.*

Ken Patrick Trail 🎦   **Highlights:** A stretch skirts the rim; nice views of Nankoweap Creek drainages. **Drawbacks:** Mule-trampled near North Kaibab Trailhead parking lot, faint in other spots, and steeply rolling near Point Imperial. **Difficulty:** The longest, faintest, most scratchy—and all around toughest—rim trail, no water accessibility.

This long, steeply rolling trail travels through ponderosa pine and spruce-fir forest between the head of Roaring Springs Canyon and Point Imperial. Along the way, it poses a number of challenges. Starting at the North Kaibab end, the first mile of the trail has been pounded into a dustlike flour (where not watered down into something resembling cake batter) by mules. Where the mules turn around after a mile, the trail becomes faint. It becomes even less distinct about 4 miles in, after passing the trailhead for the old Bright Angel Trail.

After crossing the Cape Royal Road (the only road that you encounter, about two-thirds of the way to Point Imperial), the trail descends into, then climbs out of, a very steep drainage overgrown with thorn-covered New Mexican locust. While challenging, the 3-mile stretch between the road and Point Imperial is also the prettiest on the trail, skirting the rim of the canyon above upper drainages of Nankoweap Creek. In these areas you'll see plenty of scarlet bugler, identifiable by tubular red flowers with flared lower petals, as well as a number of Douglas firs interspersed among the ubiquitous ponderosa pines.

10 miles each way. Access: From the south side of the parking area for Point Imperial or from the parking area for the North Kaibab Trail (on the North Rim entrance rd., 2 miles north of Grand Canyon Lodge). No water sources. Maps: Trails Illustrated Topo Map.

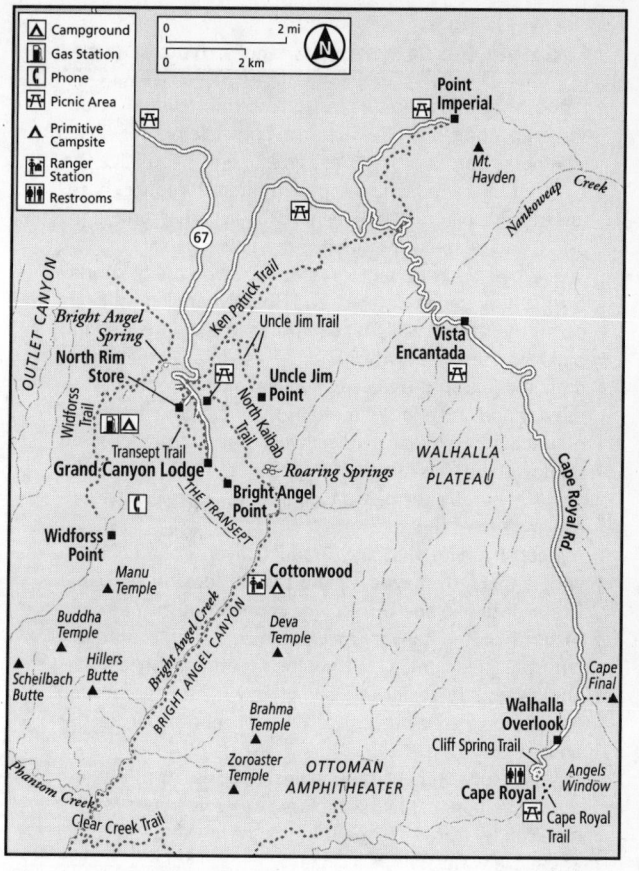

Trails on the North Rim

Legend:
- △ Campground
- 🅖 Gas Station
- 🅒 Phone
- 🖃 Picnic Area
- ▲ Primitive Campsite
- 🏠 Ranger Station
- 🚻 Restrooms

0 — 2 mi
0 — 2 km

Point Imperial
Mt. Hayden
Nankoweap Creek
Outlet Canyon
Bright Angel Spring
Ken Patrick Trail
Uncle Jim Trail
North Rim Store
Widforss Trail
Transept Trail
Grand Canyon Lodge
Uncle Jim Point
North Kaibab Trail
Vista Encantada
Roaring Springs
WALHALLA PLATEAU
Cape Royal Rd.
Widforss Point
Bright Angel Point
THE TRANSEPT
Manu Temple
Buddha Temple
Hillers Butte
Scheilbach Butte
Bright Angel Creek
BRIGHT ANGEL CANYON
Cottonwood
Deva Temple
Brahma Temple
Zoroaster Temple
OTTOMAN AMPHITHEATER
Phantom Creek
Clear Creek Trail
Cliff Spring Trail
Walhalla Overlook
Cape Final
Angels Window
Cape Royal
Cape Royal Trail
67

Uncle Jim Trail   Highlights: Views of Bright Angel and Roaring Springs canyons, and easy access make this a great place for a picnic. **Drawbacks:** Mule traffic. **Difficulty:** Has some hills, but is suitable for families.

A lasso-shaped loop accessible via the Ken Patrick Trail, the Uncle Jim Trail circles Uncle Jim Point, which divides Roaring Springs and Bright Angel canyons. By taking the right branch of the lasso, you'll soon reach an overlook near the tip of Uncle Jim Point, named for a former game warden, Jim Owens, who slaughtered hundreds of mountain lions on the North Rim in the early 1900s. (Owens's

Shooting the Canyon: Tips for Photographers

It's not easy to capture the canyon's spirit on film. Here are some tips to help you take the best possible photos:

A **polarizing filter** is a great investment if you have the kind of camera that will accept lens filters. It reduces haze, lessens the contrast between shadowy areas and light areas, and deepens the color of the sky.

The best times to photograph the canyon are at **sunrise** and **sunset,** when filtered and sharply angled sunlight paints the canyon walls in beautiful shades of lavender and pink. At these times the shadows are also at their most dramatic. To capture these ephemeral moments, it's best to use a tripod and a long exposure. The worst time to photograph the canyon is at noon when there are almost no shadows, and thus little texture or contrast. *The Guide,* the park's official visitor newspaper, includes a table with sunrise and sunset times.

Keep in mind that the Grand Canyon is immense. A wide-angle lens may leave the canyon looking on paper like a distant plane of dirt. Try zooming in on narrower sections of the canyon to emphasize a single dramatic landscape element. Or, if you're shooting with a wide-angle lens, try to include something in the foreground (people or a tree branch) to give the photo perspective and scale.

When shooting portraits against a sunrise or sunset, use a flash to illuminate your subjects; otherwise your camera meter may expose for the bright light in the background and leave your subjects in shadow.

—*by Karl Samson*

handiwork, part of a misguided predator-control program, may have contributed to an explosion in the deer population and an ensuing famine.) From here, you'll have views across Roaring Springs Canyon to Bright Angel Point and up Roaring Springs Canyon, to where the upper switchbacks of the North Kaibab Trail are visible. This overlook is a scenic, easily accessible spot for a picnic lunch. After passing it, the trail skirts the edge of Bright Angel Canyon before looping back.

5 miles round trip (including Ken Patrick Trail). Access: 1 mile down Ken Patrick Trail from North Kaibab trailhead parking area. No water sources. Maps: Trails Illustrated Topo Map.

Cape Final Trail **Highlights:** An uncrowded, flat, boulder-free walk to a canyon overlook. **Drawbacks:** Parking area is easy to miss. **Difficulty:** Nice and easy.

Because this trail is relatively flat and boulder free, it's a good choice for a first hike in the backcountry. It meanders through ponderosa pine forest on an old Jeep trail, ending at Cape Final, where you'll have views of the northern canyon and Juno Temple.

2 miles each way. Access: An unmarked dirt parking area off the Cape Royal Rd., 4.9 miles south of Roosevelt Point. No water sources. Map: Trails Illustrated Topo Map.

Cliff Springs Trail 🤾 **Highlights:** Passes springs and an Ancestral Pueblo granary. **Drawbacks:** A few rocky stretches. **Difficulty:** Craggy spots pose challenges for people lacking agility.

Both scenic and fairly short, this is a nice hike for most families. Although this dirt trail seems at first to head into forest *away* from the canyon, it quickly descends into a narrow, rocky canyon that drains into the larger one—a reminder that the Walhalla Plateau is a peninsula in Grand Canyon. Spruce and fir trees dominate the northern exposures in this side canyon, while ponderosa pines and even piñon and juniper trees grow in the sunnier spots. Roughly a quarter mile from the trailhead, the trail passes a small Ancestral Pueblo granary. After crossing a small drainage, it hugs the north wall of the side canyon, passing under limestone overhangs, in light colored green by the canopies of box elder trees (identifiable by their leaflets in groups of three and by their double-winged fruit). The springs drip from one of these overhangs, where mosses carpet the fissures in the rock. A waist-high boulder marks the end of the trail.

4 miles each way. Access: A small pullout .3 mile north of Cape Royal on the Cape Royal Rd. Water sources at Cliff Springs (purify before drinking). Map: Trails Illustrated Topo Map.

Widforss Trail 🤾🤾 **Highlights:** A nice escape into ponderosa pine forest, culminating with canyon views from Widforss Point. **Drawbacks:** Much of the trail is away from the rim, with the canyon out of sight, frequented by mules. **Difficulty:** Distance and rolling terrain combine to make this a challenge.

This trail, named for Gunnar Widforss, a landscape painter, may be the nicest rim hike in the park. It curves around the head of Transept Canyon before venturing south to Widforss Point. A brochure, sometimes available at the trailhead, explains points of interest in the first 2 miles, during which the trail undulates through ponderosa pine and spruce-fir forest.

At the head of Transept Canyon, about halfway to Widforss Point, you'll pass several nice overlooks that make for good resting spots. You'll also see a balancing rock, formed when water seeping across planes in the rock eroded beds of Kaibab Limestone from underneath the ones above.

Past the head of Transept Canyon, the trail heads south through old-growth ponderosa pine, and the canyon passes out of view. Under the red-orange-trunked trees, lupine blankets the forest floor with blue flowers. You'll also note a number of badly singed pines. In the late '90s the National Park Service conducted prescribed burns in this area, eliminating excess deadfall and undergrowth from the forest floor. Burns like these are designed to bring the forest closer to its natural state. Before humans began suppressing blazes, natural fires swept through the ponderosa pine forest an average of every 7 to 10 years. (For more on prescribed burns, see chapter 8.)

The trail, remaining hilly most of the way, reaches the rim again at Widforss Point. There, you'll have a nice view of five temples. The three to the southeast are Zoroaster (farthest south), Brahma (north of Zoroaster), and Deva (farthest north); to the southwest, Buddha Temple sits like a sphinx with two long legs. Out of one of those legs rises Manu Temple. Near the rim are a picnic table and several good campsites.

5 miles each way. Access: A dirt road .3 mile south of the Cape Royal Rd. Follow this road .7 mile to the parking area, which is well marked. No water sources. Map: Trails Illustrated Topo Map.

5 South Rim Corridor Trails

Bright Angel Trail 🐾🐾 **Highlights:** Long stretches near lush, cool creek beds. **Drawbacks:** During high season, you'll pass hundreds of hikers and a few mules. **Difficulty:** Water sources, ample shade, and a wide, well-maintained surface; the most accommodating trail into the canyon from the South Rim.

Both Native Americans and early settlers recognized this as a choice location for a trail into the canyon. First, there's an enormous fault line, along which so much erosion has taken place that even the usually sheer Redwall Limestone holds vegetation. Then there's the water—more of it than in any other place on the South Rim. The springs at Indian Garden supplied Grand Canyon Village as late as 1970.

Bright Angel & South Kaibab Trails (South Rim)

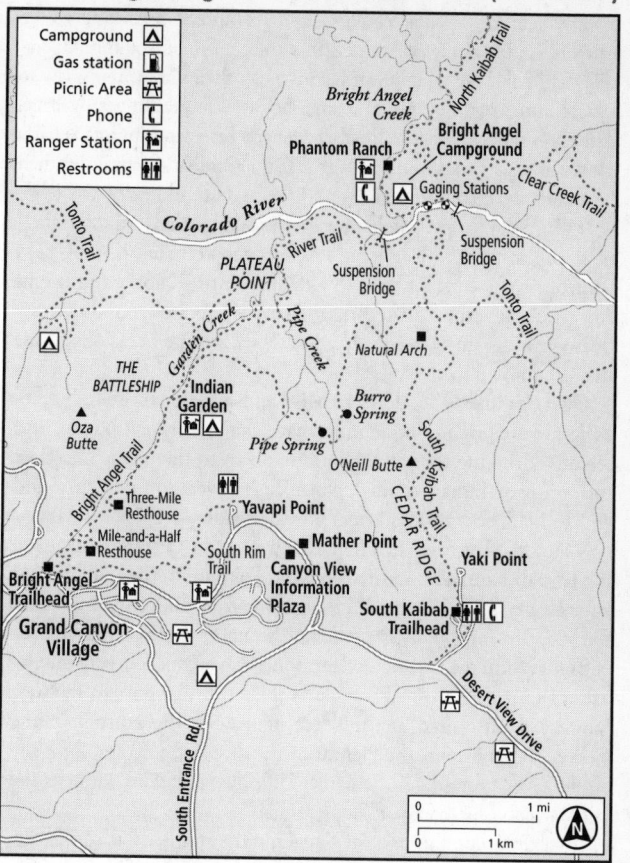

Campground	▲
Gas station	🛢
Picnic Area	🔥
Phone	📞
Ranger Station	🏠
Restrooms	🚻

Bright Angel Creek

Phantom Ranch

Bright Angel Campground

North Kaibab Trail

Clear Creek Trail

Gaging Stations

Colorado River

Tonto Trail

River Trail

PLATEAU POINT

Suspension Bridge

Suspension Bridge

Pipe Creek

Tonto Trail

Garden Creek

THE BATTLESHIP

▲ Oza Butte

Indian Garden

Pipe Spring

Natural Arch

● *Burro Spring*

▲ *O'Neill Butte*

SOUTH KAIBAB TRAIL

CEDAR RIDGE

Bright Angel Trail

■ Three-Mile Resthouse

Mile-and-a-Half Resthouse

Yavapi Point

South Rim Trail

■ **Mather Point**

■ **Yaki Point**

Bright Angel Trailhead

Canyon View Information Plaza

South Kaibab Trailhead

Grand Canyon Village

South Entrance Rd

Desert View Drive

0		1 mi
0		1 km

For centuries, the Havasupai used this trail to descend from the rim, where they hunted in winter, to Indian Garden, where they farmed year-round. This went on until the 1920s when the Park Service expelled the remaining tribe members. Although most of the Havasupai now live on a reservation in the central canyon, a few of their pictographs (rock paintings made with mineral dyes) remain along the trail. Some are high on the rocks just past the first tunnel; others can be seen on a sandstone overhang above Two-Mile Corner, the first switchback below Mile-and-a-Half Rest House.

When Pete Berry, Niles Cameron, and Ralph Cameron prospected for minerals here in the late 1800s, they improved the trail to the point where most people could hike it. As more visitors came to the canyon, Ralph Cameron realized that the trail might be more lucrative than gold. He bought out his partners, then used mining law to take control of the land near and below Grand Canyon Village. Although the Santa Fe Railroad challenged his authority in the early 1900s, it wasn't until the 1920s that Cameron lost the trail. By then he had charged countless hikers a $1 fee to descend it.

If Cameron earned a dollar for every hiker on this trail today, he'd be doing just fine. More than 500,000 people hike on the Grand Canyon's three corridor trails (South and North Kaibab, and Bright Angel) every year, and the Bright Angel is the most popular. It's a freeway: wide, dusty, relatively gradual, with some occasional mule manure thrown in.

On a day hike, walk down to **Mile-and-a-Half House** or **Three-Mile House,** each of which has shade, an emergency phone, and seasonal drinking water. Or continue down to the picnic area near the spring at Indian Garden, where lush vegetation will surround you and large cottonwood trees provide shade.

Watch the layers on this trail as you descend. As you move from the Kaibab Formation to the Toroweap Formation, the wall on your left will gradually turn from cream-colored to pinkish-white. After the second tunnel you'll start down through the steep buff-colored cliffs that form the Coconino Sandstone. As you do, compare the elevations of the cliffs on either side of the fault. The ones to the west have been offset and are 189 feet higher. At the bottom of the Coconino Sandstone, the Hermit Shale, deep red in color, is visibly eroding out from under the harder cliffs above it. This weakens the cliffs, which then break off along joints.

After dropping through the Supai Group and Redwall layers, the trail begins its long, direct descent to Indian Garden. As you near Indian Garden, you'll begin to see species found near water, including willow, mesquite, catclaw acacia, and even Arizona grape, a native species that grows tart but edible grapes. In spring, the purple blooms on the redbud are bright enough to be seen from the rim. Fit, well-prepared day hikers may wish to hike an additional 1.5 miles past Indian Garden on the Tonto and Plateau Point trails. The Plateau Point Trail eventually crosses the Tonto Platform to an overlook of the Colorado River, 1,300 feet below.

Below Indian Garden, the Bright Angel Trail follows Garden Creek down a narrow canyon in the Tapeats Sandstone. After leaving the Garden Creek drainage, the trail descends through much of the Vishnu Formation in a series of switchbacks known as the Devil's

Corkscrew. It then follows Pipe Creek to the Colorado River and the junction with the River Trail. There you'll find a small rest house with an emergency phone and pit toilet—but no pretreated drinking water. After skirting the river for 1.7 miles on the River Trail, you'll reach the Silver Suspension Bridge. When you cross it, you'll be near **Bright Angel Campground.** See "Backcountry Campgrounds," later in this chapter.

Round-trip length of the trail is 19 miles; 4.6 miles to Indian Garden; 7.8 miles to Colorado River; 9.3 miles to Bright Angel Campground. Access: Trailhead is just west of Kolb Studio, near Grand Canyon Village. Water sources at Mile-and-a-Half Rest House (seasonal), Three-Mile Rest House (seasonal), Indian Garden, Colorado River, Bright Angel Campground. Maps: Grand Canyon (7.5 min.), Phantom Ranch (7.5 min.). Parking can be found 1.2 miles of the trailhead in parking lots D and E.

South Kaibab Trail 𝄢𝄢𝄢 **Highlights:** Panoramic views for much of the distance from the rim to the river. **Drawbacks:** Mule traffic and its byproducts. **Difficulty:** You won't find water, abundant shade, or shelter; more dangerous than the Bright Angel—and steeper. This trail is very strenuous.

The South Kaibab Trail was the Park Service's way of bypassing Ralph Cameron, who controlled the Bright Angel Trail in the early 1900s. Cameron used mining law to lay claim to the land around the Bright Angel Trail and charged $1 to every person descending it. Later, as a senator, he pushed to deny funding for the Park Service. In 1924, exasperated by Cameron's maneuverings, the Park Service began to build the South Kaibab Trail, which, like the Bright Angel Trail, linked Grand Canyon Village with the Colorado River and Phantom Ranch. Unlike the Bright Angel Trail, which follows natural routes into the canyon, this one was built using dynamite and hard labor.

Tips Bright Angel or South Kaibab— Which to Choose?

The South Kaibab trail is steeper and shorter than the Bright Angel Trail. And while the Bright Angel offers ample shade and water, the South Kaibab has no water and little shade. Strong backpackers planning to do a loop hike to Phantom Ranch should descend the South Kaibab Trail and climb out on the easier Bright Angel Trail. To break up the hike, spend 1 night at Bright Angel Campground and 1 at Indian Garden. Do not attempt to do both in 1 day.

The South Kaibab Trail begins by making a series of switchbacks through the upper rock layers. As you descend the Kaibab Formation, note the Douglas firs, remnants of the last Ice Age. After that Ice Age ended 10,000 years ago, the firs retreated off the South Rim, clinging only to a few due-north slopes where they received almost no direct sunlight. As the trail descends the Coconino Sandstone, watch for evidence of cross-bedding—diagonal lines formed by windblown sand in an ancient desert.

Below the Coconino, the trail descends onto Cedar Ridge, a platform that has pit toilets and a hitching post for mules. This is an excellent place for day hikers to picnic and rest before hiking the 1.5 miles back out. Continuing northward down the ridge, it then reaches a saddle underneath O'Neill Butte, with views 1,000 feet down to the Tonto Platform on either side. The trail then rounds the east flank of the butte, eventually reaching another saddle. It descends in steep switchbacks through the Redwall, then slices downhill across the Tonto Platform toward the Inner Gorge. From the Tonto Platform, make sure to glance back at the natural rock bridge in the cliffs. At the tip-off, where the trail begins its drop into the Inner Gorge, an emergency telephone and toilet are available.

As you begin your descent of the Tapeats Sandstone, you'll see the Colorado River between the dark, sheer walls of the Inner Gorge. The pink in the otherwise black walls is Zoroaster Granite, formed 1.2 billion years ago when molten rock was squeezed into fissures in the Vishnu Schist. From here it's an hour's walk to the Kaibab Suspension Bridge and Bright Angel Campground.

Note: From March through November, you cannot drive to the South Kaibab trailhead. The park's free shuttle service begins ferrying hikers to the trailhead at least 1 hour before sunrise every morning.

6 miles to Colorado River; 7.3 miles to Bright Angel Campground. Hiking time 3–4 hr. down, and 6–8 hr. up. Do not attempt round trip in 1 day. Access: Trailhead at Yaki Point (Hwy. 64, E. Rim Dr., 5 miles east of Grand Canyon Village). Water sources at Colorado River and Bright Angel Campground. Maps: Phantom Ranch (7.5 min.) quadrangle.

6 North Rim Corridor Trail

North Kaibab Trail *★★*   **Highlights:** Less crowded than the Bright Angel Trail. Great for a first backpack trip into the canyon. **Drawbacks:** At 14.4 miles and with a vertical drop of 5,850 feet, it's much longer, and drops farther, than the South Rim corridor trails. **Difficulty:** Descends gradually from rim to river. Ample water and shade. Tests endurance more than agility.

North Kaibab Trail (North Rim)

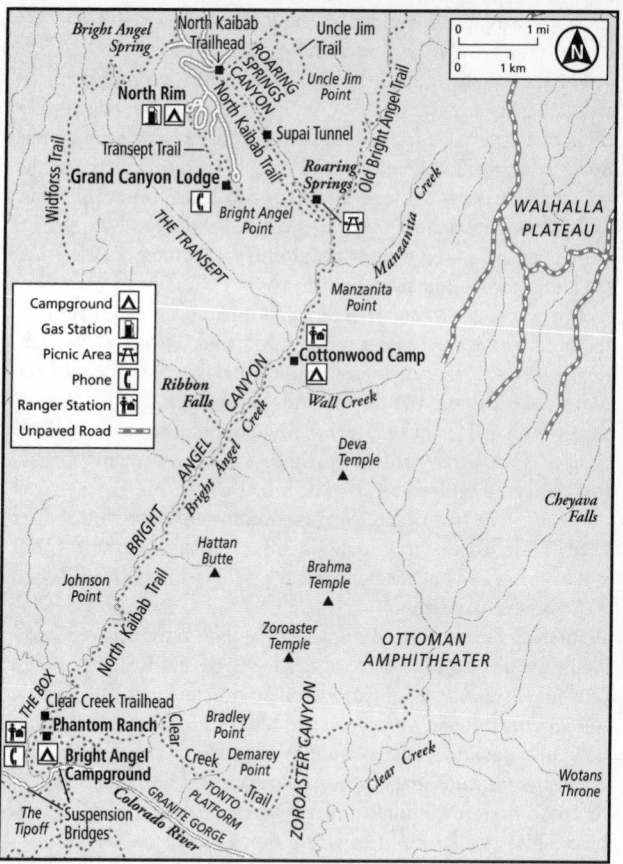

Forget the myth about corridor trails being easy. The North Kaibab Trail will test any hiker who attempts to go from rim to river (or vice versa) in a day. By comparison, the South Rim corridor trails, the Bright Angel and South Kaibab, travel 9.2 and 6.7 miles, respectively, and fall about 4,800 vertical feet from rim to river. Despite the length and the big vertical drop, the North Kaibab Trail may be the nicest place for backpackers to first experience the canyon. The scenery is lovely, the grades on the trail manageable. The North Kaibab has beautiful views down two side canyons—Roaring Springs and Bright Angel—but unlike the South Rim trails, you see less of the gorge cut by the Colorado River. It's also less crowded than the South Rim corridor trails.

The trail begins with a long series of switchbacks down the head of Roaring Springs Canyon. At over 8,000 feet, the first switchbacks are in thickly forested terrain that could just as easily be found in the Rocky Mountains. Aspen, Douglas fir, and Gambel oak shade the trail and hide many of the rocks in the Kaibab and Toroweap layers. The Coconino Sandstone, whose sheer cliffs hold too little soil for these trees, stands out against the greenery, its white rocks streaked tan and black by mineral deposits.

The next major landmark is **Supai Tunnel.** At 2.7 miles from the trailhead, and with seasonal water, shade, and restrooms available, this is an excellent turnaround point for day hikers. Beyond the tunnel, the canyon warms up, and heat-tolerant plants such as squaw-bush, pale hoptree, piñon pine, and juniper appear. The trail descends in relatively gradual switchbacks through the Supai Group, then crosses a bridge over a creek bed. Past the bridge, the creek plummets. The trail travels along the south wall of Roaring Springs Canyon, on ledges above Redwall cliffs. A spire of Redwall Limestone known as **The Needle** marks the point where the trail begins its descent of the Redwall.

Roaring Springs, the water source for both rims, becomes audible just above the confluence of Bright Angel and Roaring Springs canyons. A .2-mile-long spur trail descends to the springs, where water pours from an opening in the Muav Limestone and cascades downhill, pooling at the bottom of the creek bed. Around those pools grow Arizona grape, scouring rushes, and box elder and cottonwood trees. You'll find drinking water, shade, and picnic tables here. This is the farthest a day hiker should go.

Below the springs are a pump house, a heliport, and a residence for the pump house operator. In this area, the trail begins a long, gradual descent to the Colorado River, traveling on or near the floor of Bright Angel Canyon for most of the way. The rocks along this stretch can be difficult to sort out. In addition to the layers seen everywhere in the canyon, you'll find members of the Grand Canyon Supergroup, including the reddish-brown Dox Sandstone, purplish Shinumo Quartzite, orange-red Hakatai Shale, and numerous dikes and sills—places where lava filled cracks in the earth.

Two miles past Roaring Springs is Cottonwood Campground. By camping at Cottonwood Campground on the way to and from the river, backpackers can extend their trips while hiking reasonable distances.

About a mile past Cottonwood Campground, a spur trail leads to **Ribbon Falls,** the centerpiece of a large natural amphitheater. The waterfall is usually a short detour off the North Kaibab trail. But when the water level is high, you'll need to backtrack to the bridge after seeing the falls, instead of fording the river farther downstream. Even so, don't pass up a chance to hike to the base of these falls, which roll off a high sandstone ledge and arc gracefully to earth, skimming an apron of travertine on the way. This apron formed when calcium carbonate precipitated out of the water as rock. You may see small, brown birds known as dippers (the name alone describes them) fishing in the pools around these falls.

About 2.5 miles past the falls, the trail enters a long stretch of narrows known as **The Box** and remains there, winding alongside Bright Angel Creek, until just above Phantom Ranch. To keep hikers dry in these narrows, the Civilian Conservation Corps (CCC) in the 1930s built three bridges over the creek and blasted ledges in the cliffs of the Vishnu Formation. An immense flash flood swept away most of the originals—steel and all—in 1966. A flood in July 1999 damaged the trail so badly that it was closed for more than 2 months.

2.7 miles to Supai Tunnel; 4.7 miles to Roaring Springs; 6.8 miles to Cottonwood Campground; 14.4 miles to the Colorado River. Access: On North Rim entrance rd., 2 miles north of Grand Canyon Lodge. Water sources at Roaring Springs (seasonal), Bright Angel Creek, Cottonwood Campground (seasonal), Phantom Ranch, Bright Angel Campground. Maps: Bright Angel Point (7.5 min.) and Phantom Ranch (7.5 min.) quadrangles. Note that under no circumstances should you attempt to hike from the rim to the river and back in 1 day!

7 South Rim Wilderness Trails

Hermit Trail 🔍🔍   **Highlights:** Late-afternoon sun feels good on cold days. **Drawbacks:** Less panoramic than other trails from the South Rim to the river. **Difficulty:** Steep in places; washouts and rock fall complicate route finding. Cobblestone portions near the top are broken and rugged.

In 1912, the Santa Fe Railroad sought to establish a route into the canyon that Ralph Cameron, the "owner" of the Bright Angel Trail, couldn't control. So it built the Hermit Trail 8 miles west of Grand Canyon Village. Paved with sandstone slabs and with low walls on the outside, the Hermit Trail was generally regarded as the nicest in the canyon in the 1910s. The vine-covered shelter at Santa Maria Spring was built at about the same time, as was Mary Colter's new building known as Hermits Rest.

Today, the Hermit Trail remains wide at the top, with long, gradual switchbacks descending to the bottom of the Coconino Sandstone and onto the expanse of Waldron Basin. However, the old sandstone slabs have broken or slid in places, making the trail far more rugged than it was in the 1920s. Because the upper trail is on west-facing cliffs, it's cool in the morning and hot in the afternoon. Below the Coconino Sandstone, the trail, passing a few low-lying piñon and juniper trees, intersects both the Waldron and the Dripping Springs trails. Go right both times. Near the head of the brick-red Hermit Gorge, the trail makes a few switchbacks down into the Supai Group, eventually reaching a delicious water source, Santa Maria Spring. At 2.5 miles down, this spring is a nice turnaround point for day hikers. To be safe, treat the water before drinking.

Past the spring, the trail heads toward the tip of Pima Point, remaining fairly level—except when negotiating areas covered by rockfall or when making short descents, via switchbacks, lower into the Supai Group rocks. Finally, reaching a break in the Redwall, it careens downhill in tight switchbacks known as the Cathedral Stairs. Below the Redwall, the trail slices downhill, then makes a series of long switchbacks onto the Tonto Platform.

At the junction with the Tonto Trail, the Hermit Trail continues west (left) toward Hermit Creek. Later you'll reach another junction. The trail forking to the right from here descends to Hermit Creek between the Hermit Creek campsites and the Colorado River. Hikers camping at Hermit Rapids should take this shortcut. Others, including those using the Hermit Creek sites, should continue straight, passing this turnoff. In this area, you'll also find remnants of the old Hermit Camp. Guests here in the 1920s were shuttled around the camp in a Model T that had been transported to the camp in pieces and reassembled on-site—a luxury you may pine for by this point.

If you do walk the 1.5 miles down the creek to the beach at Hermit Rapids, you'll pass several nice pour-overs and small pools. Along the walls, watch for sacred datura, identifiable by its large, teardrop-shaped leaves and white, lilylike flowers. You may have company at the beach—river trips frequently stop here to scout the rapids below the confluence.

Note: Backpackers planning overnight trips on the Hermit Trail can receive special permits to drive on Hermit Road, at the Backcountry Information Center.

2.5 miles to Santa Maria Spring; 7.8 miles to Hermit Creek; 9.3 miles to Colorado River. Access: Parking area west of Hermits Rest. Water sources at Santa Maria Spring, Hermit Creek, and Colorado River. Maps: Grand Canyon (7.5 min.) quadrangle.

Hermit Trail/Dripping Springs/Boucher Trails (South Rim)

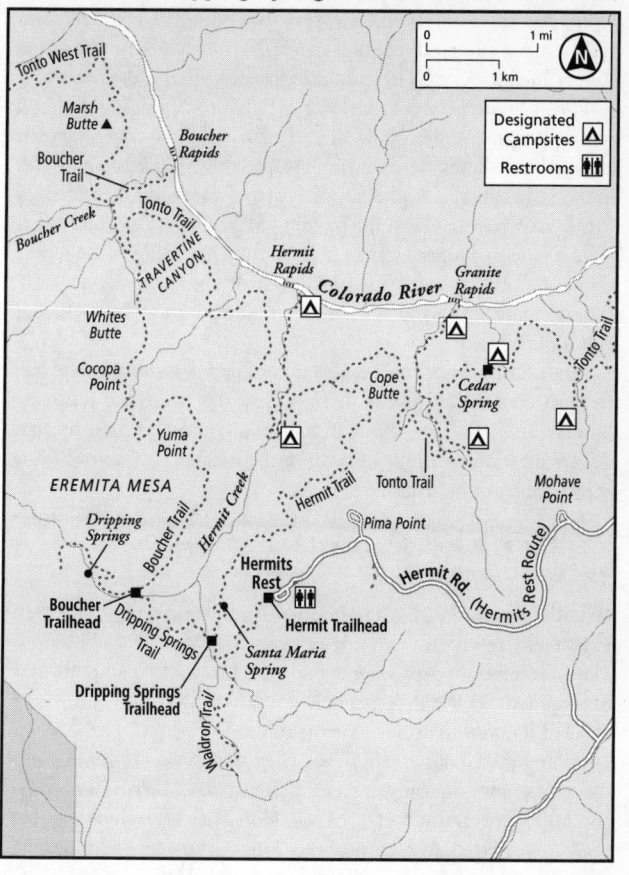

Dripping Springs Trail ⚐ **Highlights:** Uncrowded; ascends to springs in a deep alcove. **Drawbacks:** Does not afford expansive views. **Difficulty:** Relatively easy, but with a few steep inclines and some genuinely scary exposures.

Although this trail doesn't have expansive views of the inner canyon, it offers the peace and solitude needed to appreciate the desert's sounds, smells, and lighting. The most physically demanding part is the 1,340-vertical-foot descent from the Hermit Trail trailhead to the junction with the Dripping Springs Trail. On the Dripping Springs Trail, it's a gradual westward climb to the springs themselves. (There are, however, a few sections of trail near the head of Hermit

Gorge that roll steeply and are narrow and exposed.) The trail eventually curves into an upper drainage of Hermit Basin, rounding the base of Eremita Mesa. The springs are partway up this drainage.

The 30-foot-deep rock overhang at Dripping Springs looks like a great place for a hermit to live. Perhaps this is why everyone assumed that Louis Boucher, the prospector who lived in this area in the early 1900s, *was* a hermit. It even looks a bit like the oversized fireplace of Hermits Rest, the building Mary Colter designed as her own tribute to a loner's way of life. Not much remains of Boucher's camp. But the springs still trickle out of the overhanging rock, through moss and maidenhair fern, and drip into a pool below. If you fill up, purify the water.

Note: Dripping Springs is also accessible via a short, steep trail from the rim directly above it. To purists, this is the real Dripping Springs Trail. Because the road to the original Dripping Springs Trail is now closed a mile or so from the trailhead, the above route is preferable for most hikers.

3 miles from Hermit trailhead to Dripping Springs. Access: Located off of the Hermit Trail at the head of Hermit Gorge. Water sources at Dripping Springs (purify before drinking). Map: Grand Canyon (7.5 min.) quadrangle.

Grandview Trail 🐾🐾   **Highlights:** An historic trail, which provides views down into two side canyons. **Drawbacks:** Cobblestone ramps become slippery when wet or icy. In winter, crampons may be required. **Difficulty:** Suitable for most fit hikers; steep and exposed in a few locations near the top.

Hiking the Grandview Trail is a great way to take in human history along with the canyon scenery. Strong day hikers can descend the 2,600 vertical feet over 3 miles to Horseshoe Mesa, look over the remnants of Pete Barry's turn-of-the-20th-century copper mine, and still make it back to the rim for dinner. Backpackers can use it to begin or close out loop hikes. However, because the cobblestone ramps below Grandview Point become especially slick in wet weather, I'd avoid this trail during storms.

The trail itself is part of the history. All but the top 430 feet of it was built in the 1890s. (The current upper section was completed around 1910.) In some places, the trail builders used dynamite to blast away rock from sheer cliffs, forming ledges where none had been. In others they pinned a trail against the walls. To do this, they drilled holes into the rocks, pounded metal rods into the holes, then laid logs lengthwise above the rods. They then crammed rocks and dirt into openings and, as a finishing touch, paved the trail with a layer of cobblestones. Be sure to look at the trail from below to admire its structure.

For day hikers who are agile but not particularly strong, a smart place to turn around is at the saddle between upper Hance and Grapevine canyons. Known as the Coconino Saddle, it's about three-quarters of a mile from the rim. Here, you'll find shade, flat spots for resting, and views of both canyons. At the bottom of the Coconino Sandstone, the trail traverses east, then turns north, descending through the Hermit Shale and the Supai Group and onto Horseshoe Mesa. On the mesa, it intersects the Horseshoe Mesa Trail.

Whether you go right, left, or straight at this junction, you'll eventually intersect the Tonto Trail. By going right, you'll descend 700 feet through the Redwall Limestone on the southeast side of the mesa. Steep and rocky, this precarious route is the quickest path to water. Below the Redwall, a short spur trail leads to the perennial Miner's Spring. (Purify it for safety.) You'll also find several mines here, including the New Tunnel (new in 1906), with a boiler and a compressor outside. In addition to being unstable, the mines have high levels of radon, so it's best to stay out of them.

By going left, you'll descend the west side of the mesa to the ephemeral Cottonwood Creek, past where the first miners lived. By going straight, you'll travel out onto the northwest "arm" of the mesa, where you'll see the foundations of buildings from the mine camp, as well as old bottles, cans, and pieces of metal stoves. Also present, but less conspicuous, is evidence of past Native American activity: bits of chert (quartz rocks from which arrowheads were made) and old agave roasting pits. A pit toilet is available for campers in this area, who must camp in designated, posted sites.

3 miles from Grandview Trail trailhead to Horseshoe Mesa; 6.8 miles to Tonto Trail (via the East Horseshoe Mesa Trail). Access: From Grandview Point (on Hwy. 64, 12 miles east of Grand Canyon Village). No water sources on Horseshoe Mesa. Water source at Miner's Spring (off the east Horseshoe Mesa Trail, well below the rim of Horseshoe Mesa). Maps: Grandview Point (7.5 min.) and Cape Royal (7.5 min.) quadrangles.

Tonto Trail ★★ Highlights: Links many of the South Rim trails, creating some of the nicest loop hikes in the park. Drawbacks: Long, shadeless, dry stretches make knowledge of water sources imperative. Difficulty: Smooth and relatively level when not dipping into rocky, rugged drainages.

This 95-mile trail traverses much of the lower canyon atop the Tonto Platform. Rather than hike all of it, most people include parts in shorter loop hikes linking trails from the South Rim. Hiking here is often more strenuous than expected. Distances that look short on the map sometimes take long periods to cover, as the trail contours around numerous drainages that cut partway into the Tonto Platform. Because the platform has little to no shade, and because many of its water sources are seasonal, long hikes here during summer are ill advised. Especially dangerous are the stretches between the Grandview and South Kaibab trails and between Slate Canyon and the South Bass Trail, both of which lack reliable water.

95 miles from Red Canyon (east) to Garnet Canyon (west). Access: The Hance, Grandview, South Kaibab, Bright Angel, Hermit, Boucher, and South Bass trails all intersect the Tonto Trail. Water sources at Hance, Cottonwood (usually), Grapevine, Pipe, Monument, Hermit, and Boucher creeks, Indian Garden Spring, the Colorado River in several locations. Ask at the Backcountry Information Center about water sources before starting hike. Map: Topo map for section hiked.

8 North Rim Wilderness Trail

Clear Creek Trail ⋒   **Highlights:** A scenic, relatively flat spur off the North Kaibab Trail, with views of Zoroaster Temple, Clear Creek, and the Colorado River. **Drawbacks:** Dangerously hot and dry in summer. **Difficulty:** Like the Tonto, smooth and relatively level when not dipping into craggy drainages.

After leaving the North Kaibab Trail, the Clear Creek Trail climbs in steep switchbacks east of Bright Angel Creek, eventually reaching an overlook of the Colorado River, sandwiched between the dark walls of the Granite Gorge. The trail then travels east above the river, gradually ascending to the Tonto Platform.

Before it reaches that level, however, watch for the interface between the black, 2-billion-year-old Vishnu Formation and the flat brown facade of the Tapeats Sandstone. You can touch the point of contact between these layers. This is as close as you'll get to "touching" the Great Unconformity, the gap of 1.2 billion years in the geological record caused by past erosion.

After reaching the Tonto Platform, the trail continues to the east (and then southeast), veering around the tops of numerous drainages, all beneath the imposing presence of Zoroaster Temple to the north. This long, shadeless stretch, where blackbrush and agave are among the tallest plants, makes the Clear Creek Trail a risky place for summer hiking. Eventually the trail crests a small rise, revealing a view of the confluence of the Colorado River Gorge and the drainage cut by Clear Creek. Turning northeast, the trail crosses Zoroaster Canyon and then traverses above Clear Creek before finally descending to the creek bed itself.

There are a number of nice campsites in the area just west of Clear Creek, all within easy walking distance of a pit toilet. From these campsites you can strike out on a number of excellent day hikes. Follow the creek 4 miles north to Cheyava Falls, a seasonal waterfall that, at 800 feet, is tallest in the canyon. Or, walk (and down-climb) 6 miles south to the Colorado River. The narrows en route to the Colorado are subject to flash floods and should be avoided during wet weather and spring runoff.

8.7 miles from Phantom Ranch to Clear Creek Drainage. Access: .3 mile north of Phantom Ranch on the North Kaibab Trail. Water source at Clear Creek. Maps: Phantom Ranch (7.5 min.) quadrangle.

9 Backcountry Campgrounds

The park's three backcountry campgrounds—**Bright Angel, Cottonwood,** and **Indian Garden**—are located deep inside the canyon and are accessible only via hiking trails. To stay at these campgrounds, you must be willing to hike long distances into the canyon carrying the necessary clothes, shelter, food, and water, and then hike back out with all of the same belongings (including your trash). You will also need a permit from the park's Backcountry Information Center. If you lack either the necessary incentive or the necessary permit (or both), try camping at one of the car campgrounds in the park's developed areas. At these campgrounds, you can sleep under the stars, a few feet away from your loaded vehicle. For more information, see chapter 5, "Camping with a Car in the Grand Canyon Area."

Bright Angel Campground ✷✷✷   The **River Trail** (which begins at the foot of the Bright Angel Trail), the **South Kaibab Trail,** and the **North Kaibab Trail** all converge below Bright Angel Campground, which lies on the north shore of the Colorado River. The River Trail crosses the Colorado River on the Silver Suspension Bridge just west of the campground; the South Kaibab Trail crosses on the Kaibab Suspension Bridge just east of the campground. The

---

Tips **Camping Tip**

Permits to camp at **Bright Angel Campground, Cottonwood Campground,** and **Indian Garden Campground** are available through the park's Backcountry Information Center at P.O. Box 129, Grand Canyon, AZ 86023. All three campgrounds have pit toilets, drinking water, and picnic tables.

lowest section of the North Kaibab Trail parallels the campground on the opposite side of Bright Angel Creek. Bright Angel Campground is 14.4 miles from the North Kaibab trailhead; 9.3 miles from the Bright Angel trailhead; and 7.3 miles from the South Kaibab trailhead.

This long, narrow campground lies in a purgatory between the cool waters of Bright Angel Creek and black cliffs of the Vishnu Formation, which are hot as grills in the summer. At .5 mile away, the Colorado River rumbles past, eddying against a beach that is a popular stopping point for raft trips. A walkway divides the campground, which is open all year. Roughly half of the 31 campsites are on the cliff side; the other, nicer half are on the creek side. Most are shaded by cottonwood trees, a few of which were planted in the 1930s by CCC workers whose camp was here. (Most of the trees planted by the CCC washed away in a 1966 flash flood.) Phantom Ranch is a half mile to the north. Though all three of the campgrounds inside the canyon offer lovely surroundings, the proximity of Bright Angel Campground to the Colorado River makes it especially stunning.

Cottonwood Campground ⟨★★⟩ As you hike up the North Kaibab Trail from the Colorado River, the walls of Bright Angel Canyon part like the Red Sea below this campground. Between them rests a valley floor soft enough and damp enough to support a few cottonwood trees, most of which grow by the ranger station. Most of the 11 campsites are surrounded by shrub oak, whose low-slung branches barely shade the sites and picnic tables. Bright Angel Creek flows past the west side of the campground. On a hot summer day, it's the only cool place around.

Halfway between the North Rim and the Colorado, Cottonwood Campground is a great place to camp while en route to (or from) the river. For a nice 4-day hike from the North Rim, schedule 2 nights here around a night at Bright Angel Campground. But don't underestimate how hard it is to get here: The walk from the North Kaibab trailhead to Cottonwood Campground covers 6.8 miles and drops 3,170 feet—that's nearly a half mile longer than the entire length of the South Kaibab Trail, with nearly three-quarters of the vertical drop.

Cottonwood is the last camp in the canyon before you ascend to the North Rim. It remains open all year-round.

Indian Garden Campground ⟨★★⟩ You can use this campground, 4.6 miles from the Bright Angel trailhead and 3,100 vertical feet

Camping Etiquette & Special Regulations

First, the standard camping etiquette: Pack out all your garbage, including uneaten food and used toilet paper. You are *not* doing anyone a favor by leaving uneaten food in the ammo cans at the campgrounds. Stay on designated trails. Don't disturb plants, wildlife, or archaeological resources. Camp in obvious campsites—stay off the vegetation and cryptogamic soils. If pit toilets are not available, bury human waste in holes 4 to 6 inches deep, 6 inches across, and at least 200 feet from water and creek beds. When doing dishes, take water and dishes at least 200 feet from the water source, and scatter the waste water. When bathing, take water away from the water source. Use only biodegradable soap (or, better yet, none at all) for both dishes and bathing. Hang food and trash out of reach of wildlife.

There are also a few canyon-specific regulations. No campfires are allowed (only camp stoves). Also, be sure to camp inside the use areas specified on your permit. These are shown on the Trails Illustrated topographical map of the canyon. Finally, pay attention to trail-specific rules provided by the Backcountry Information Center. If you have any questions about the hike—especially water sources—ask a ranger. The Backcountry Information Center can't always determine whether a hike suits you. It's up to you to ask the necessary questions about trail conditions, water sources, and the location of campsites.

below the rim, to break up hikes from the South Rim to the Colorado River. The 14 sites are surrounded by lush riparian vegetation that taps into Indian Garden Spring, just a short walk down the canyon. For a nice 4-day hike from the South Rim, schedule 2 nights here around one at Bright Angel Campground.

10 Other Sports & Activities

CONDOR VIEWING

In recent years, many Grand Canyon visitors have spotted the largest land bird in North America. Members of the vulture family,

California condors will cruise up to 100 miles a day, at speeds approaching 50 mph. When mature, condors are grayish-black except on their heads, which are orange and featherless. Under each wing, a triangular white patch is sometimes visible.

In December 1996, six of these birds, whose wings can span nearly 10 feet, were released on the Vermilion Cliffs along Highway 89A near Lees Ferry. Twenty-two more have been set free in northern Arizona since then. Of the 55 California condors in the wild, 35 now live in the Grand Canyon area. The releases were part of a larger project aimed at reintroducing the birds to the wild after they nearly went extinct in the 1980s.

Because condors have poor olfactory senses, they sometimes follow turkey vultures and other raptors to carrion. Other than size, the easiest way to tell the two species apart is the way they soar: vultures hold their wings in a "V"; condors keep theirs in a plane. Unless the condors change their habits, they will probably reappear above the South Rim in the years to come.

In the summer of 2003 biologists confirmed that at least three pairs of California condors nesting in Arizona laid eggs. Two nests were unsuccessful, but one pair produced a young condor. It was the first time in hundreds of years that a condor hatched and survived in Arizona.

North of the canyon, you might spot a condor by driving 14 miles east of Jacob Lake on Highway 89A to House Rock Valley Road (the first road to your left after you leave the National Forest). Turn left (north) and go 2 miles to a small ramada. Scientists leave food for the youngest birds in the cliffs above the ramada. If the condors are in the area, you'll probably meet workers who are tracking them. They carry a spotting scope and binoculars and will help you sight the birds.

Wherever you spot them, please don't approach, feed, or otherwise disturb the condors. If you see one who appears to be hurt or endangered, notify the **Peregrine Fund Condor Project** (© **928/ 355-2270**). Be prepared to identify the time and location of the sighting and, if possible, the wing-tag number of the bird.

CROSS-COUNTRY SKIING

The crisp air, deep snow, and absolute silence make the **North Rim** a delightful place to ski. The closest skiing to the park starts south of Jacob Lake, at the gate that closes Highway 67; you can park your car here, and then ski south on the snow-covered highway. Snowmobiles are banned from the highway and the land east of the highway. If you'd like to ski into the park (44 miles and several days' travel from the gate) and spend a night on the North Rim, you'll need to obtain a backcountry permit from the **Backcountry Information Center** (© **928/638-7875**).

When snow sticks on the **South Rim,** you can cross-country ski at the Grandview Nordic Center in the Kaibab National Forest near Grandview Point. To get there, drive east toward Desert View on Highway 64. About 1.7 miles past the Grandview Point turnoff, turn right on the road to the Arizona Trail. Park where the snow begins, then ski or walk down the road roughly a quarter mile to a bulletin board with instructions for the trails. The Forest Service has marked three loops in this area, each meandering through meadows and ponderosa pine forest: the intermediate 7.5-mile-long Twin Lakes Loop; the easy 1.1-mile Grandview Lookout Loop; and the easy 3.7-mile Boundary Loop. There's no charge. For more information call the **Kaibab National Forest Tusayan Ranger District Office** at © **928/638-2443.**

CYCLING

Inside the park, cyclists are required to stay on roads, many of them narrow and crowded. Routes such as Highway 64 and the Cape Royal Road are inherently risky for cyclists. But at least two good rides exist. From March through November, Hermits Rest Route is closed to most private cars, making it a haven for cyclists. You'll still have to yield to tour buses, shuttles, and a handful of private vehicles, and watch out for people on foot, many of whom will be oblivious to your approach. On the North Rim, the entrance road is wide enough to accommodate experienced cyclists.

MOUNTAIN BIKING

To mountain bike near Grand Canyon, you'll need to cross out of Grand Canyon National Park into the Kaibab National Forest, which borders the park on both rims. On the North Rim, avid cyclists are flocking to the new **Rainbow Rim Trail**—an 18-mile stretch of expert-level single track (no motor vehicles allowed) that provides access to five remote canyon overlooks. Old logging roads, jeep trails, and footpaths crisscross other areas of the North Rim, providing a variety of cycling options. Visit the **Kaibab Plateau Visitor Center** in Jacob Lake (© **928/643-7298**) for directions, maps, road conditions, and trail descriptions.

On the South Rim, you'll find enjoyable mountain biking on a stretch of the **Arizona Trail** that starts at Grandview Lookout Tower. To reach the lookout, take Highway 64 east from Grand Canyon

Village. About 1.7 miles east of the Grandview Point turnoff, turn right (south) onto the road for the Arizona Trail. Leaving the park, follow this dirt road 1.3 miles to Grandview Lookout and the trail-head. Beginning here, you can ride more than 20 miles of intermediate-level single-track (with a few short, technically demanding stretches thrown in), much of it along the Coconino Rim.

Another trail system, with loops of 3.7, 10.2, and 11.2 miles, is located near Tusayan. These loops follow old Jeep trails through rolling hills in the ponderosa pine forest. The trails have a few steep, rocky areas, but most of the terrain is only moderately difficult. To reach them, find the marked parking area .3 miles north of Tusayan on the west side of Highway 64. A single trail heads north from there, eventually crossing under the highway through a concrete tunnel and providing access to the loops. (*Note:* This is also a great place to run when you're staying in Tusayan.) For information on these trails and maps of the Tusayan Ranger District (℗ **928/638-2443**), visit the **Forest Service Office** a half mile south of the park entrance on Highway 64. It's open weekdays 8am to 4:30pm.

BIKE RENTALS

SOUTH RIM   On the South Rim, higher-end bicycles can be rented in Flagstaff at **Absolute Bikes** (℗ **928/779-5969**), 18 N. San Francisco St. Prices vary from $25 to $45 for a full day, $20 to $30 for a half day.

NORTH RIM   On the North Rim **Kaibab Adventure Outfitters of Moab, UT** (℗ **800/451-1133** or 435/259-7423; www.kaibab tours.com) offers bike rental on a half/full-day basis at the cost of $40 and $33 respectively. For $175, bicycles may be hired for 7 days. Kaibab Adventure Outfitters offers van-supported 5-day mountain bike tours (cost: $895) of the North Rim.

FISHING

You're welcome to fish in the Colorado River, provided you have an Arizona Fishing Permit and trout stamp. One-day nonresident permits are available for $12.50 (or 5 days for $26) at the **Canyon Village Marketplace** (℗ **928/638-2262**) in Grand Canyon Village; at **Marble Canyon Lodge** (℗ **800/726-1789** or 928/355-2225), a quarter mile west of the Navajo Bridge on Highway 89A; and at **Lees Ferry Anglers Guides and Fly Shop** (℗ **800/962-9755** or 928/ 355-2261), at Cliff Dwellers Lodge, 9 miles west of Navajo Bridge on Highway 89A. **The Marble Canyon/Vermilion Cliffs** area is about 45 miles southwest of Page and 2½ hours north of Flagstaff.

Once you get your fishing permit, the next challenge is getting to the best fishing spots. To fish inside park boundaries, you either have to hike to the Colorado River or be on a river trip and fish during breaks from rafting (for information on river trips, see "River Rafting Trips," later in this chapter).

The best trout fishing inside the park is at the eastern end of the canyon—upstream of Phantom Ranch. The river is clear and cold (48°F/9°C) year-round directly below the dam, making this a great trout hatchery (and a chilling place for the native species, which evolved to live in muddy water and extreme variations in temperature). Downstream, the river gradually warms and gathers sediment from its tributaries, causing the trout population to dwindle and enabling the bottom-feeders to survive. The five most abundant fish species in the park are carp, speckled dace, flannel-mouth sucker, rainbow trout, and blue-head sucker.

Some of the best trout fishing in the Southwest is just upstream of the park's easternmost boundary, between Glen Canyon Dam and Lees Ferry. Most of the hot spots in this 16-mile-long stretch of river can be reached only by boat, but anyone can walk up a mile of shoreline from the parking area at Lees Ferry. If you don't have your rod and waders with you, you can rent them, and boats too, from **Lees Ferry Anglers Guides and Fly Shop** (© **800/962-9755** or 928/355-2261; **www.leesferry.com**). This shop, the best in the area, offers a complete guide service and carries a full line of fishing gear and tackle.

HORSEBACK RIDING
SOUTH RIM HORSEBACK RIDING

For horseback riding near the South Rim, go to **Apache Stables** (© **928/638-2891; www.apachestables.com**), which operates from April through October behind the now-closed Moqui Lodge, just outside the park's south entrance. Most of the horses at the stables are "dog-friendly," as our guide put it. They're retired ranch horses that average 15 years in age. Because they're gentle and know the trails around the stables, you need only kick your steed periodically to make sure it keeps going. The rest of the time, you can relax and enjoy your horse's swaying and the ponderosa pine forest.

The friendly horses make this a great, albeit expensive, family activity. Children as young as 8 (and 48 in. tall) are allowed on the 1-hour trail rides, which, like the 2-hour ones, loop through the Kaibab National Forest near the stables. Apache Stables also offers a 4-hour, 12-mile round-trip ride east through the forest to a view point at the East Rim. There, riders dismount and cross Highway 64 on foot to admire the canyon. You must be 10 or over to go on the 2-hour ride, 14 to go on the 4-hour ride. Weight limits are 235 pounds, 225 pounds, and 200 pounds for the 1-, 2-, and 4-hour rides, respectively.

Other options are an evening trail ride and a wagon ride, both going to a campfire where participants roast marshmallows and other food they bring. (No grill is available.) When the marshmallows have all been consumed (either by people or flames), everyone returns together on the wagon.

Prices are $95.50 (plus tax) for the 4-hour East Rim ride, $56 for the 2-hour ride, $31 for the 1-hour ride, $41 for the campfire trail ride, and $13 for the campfire wagon ride. Participants should wear long pants and closed-toed footwear, and bring plenty of water. Backpacks are not allowed, but fanny packs are okay.

NORTH RIM HORSEBACK RIDING

On the North Rim, **Allen's Guided Tours** (℡ **435/644-8150**) offers horseback rides from 8am to 6pm Monday to Saturday from May 15 through September 15. Departing from a corral a quarter mile south of Jacob Lake on Highway 67, the tours travel on gentle terrain in the Kaibab National Forest. 1- and 2-hour rides cost $20 and $35, respectively. Half-day rides, which follow a stretch of the Arizona Trail, cost $55. Full-day rides, which cost $85, travel to and from an overlook of the eastern canyon and include a bag lunch. The full-day ride must be booked a day in advance and requires a minimum group of four. Shorter rides don't require a reservation and leave every hour on the hour. There is no weight or age limit.

MULE TRIPS
SOUTH RIM MULE TRIPS

Wearing floppy hats and clutching rain slickers, the day's mule riders gather at 8am (9am in winter) every morning at a corral west of Bright Angel Lodge to prepare for their rides. You can almost hear the jangling nerves as they contemplate the prospect of descending narrow trails above steep cliffs on animals hardly famous for their intelligence. Although the mules walk close to the edges and have been known to *back* off the trails, accidents are rare, especially among riders who follow the wrangler's instructions. In fact, Fred Harvey has been guiding mule trips into the canyon for more than 90 years without a single fatality from a fall.

The rides, while usually safe, can nonetheless be grueling. Most people's legs aren't used to bending around a mule, and the saddles aren't soft. In addition to the pounding, the canyon can be scorching, and chances for breaks are few. Because the rides are strenuous for both riders and mules, the wranglers strictly adhere to the following requirements: You must weigh less than 200 pounds, be at least 4 feet 7 inches tall, and speak fluent English. If the wranglers think you weigh too much, they won't hesitate to put you on the scale. Acrophobes and pregnant women are also discouraged from taking the rides.

The least expensive ride—the 1-day trip to Plateau Point—may also be the most grueling, since it involves a whopping 6 hours in the saddle. It travels down the Bright Angel Trail to Indian Garden, then follows the Plateau Point Trail across the Tonto Platform to an overlook (Plateau Point) of the Colorado River. Having descended 3,200 vertical feet, the riders return on the same trails. This 12-mile round-trip ride, which breaks for lunch at Indian Garden, doesn't reach the rim until mid- to late afternoon. Cost: $129.

The other rides are part of 1- or 2-night packages that include lodging and meals at Phantom Ranch. Going down, they follow the Bright Angel Trail to the river, then travel east on the River Trail before finally crossing the river via the Kaibab Suspension Bridge. Coming back they use the South Kaibab Trail. The 10.5-mile descent takes 5½ hours; the 8-mile-long climb out is an hour shorter. The Phantom Ranch overnight costs $350 for one person, $623 for two, and $277 for each additional person. The Phantom Ranch 2-night trip, which is offered only from mid-November through March 31, costs $494 for one, $833 for two, and $320 for each additional person. A livery service is also available. One-way transportation of a 30-pound duffel (or less) costs $53.

NORTH RIM MULE TRIPS

Mule rides on the North Rim are through a small, family run outfit called **Canyon Trail Rides** (see "Reserving a Mule Trip," below). Four types of rides are offered. Open to ages 7 and up, the easiest ride goes 1 mile along the rim on the Ken Patrick Trail before turning back. This 1-hour ride costs $20 per person. Two half-day rides, each costing $45 per person, are offered. One stays on the rim, following the Ken Patrick and Uncle Jim trails to a canyon viewpoint; the other descends 2 miles into the canyon on the North Kaibab Trail, turning back at Supai Tunnel. The all-day ride, which includes lunch, travels 5 miles on the North Kaibab Trail to Roaring Springs before turning back. Cost for the all-day ride is $95. Riders must be at least 12 to go on the all-day ride. No one over 200 pounds is allowed on the canyon rides; for the rim rides, the limit is 220. All riders must speak English.

OVERFLIGHTS

Six companies at Grand Canyon National Park Airport in Tusayan currently offer scenic airplane or helicopter rides over the canyon. With more than 600,000 people taking air tours over the canyon every year, the flights, which generate a great deal of noise in parts of the park, have become a politically charged issue.

They also raise safety concerns. A total of 41 people, more than half of them sightseers, have died in seven plane and helicopter crashes in and around Grand Canyon since 1991. This includes six people who died in a helicopter crash in August, 2001, and another fatal crash in 2003.

For many vacationers, however, the question is not whether to fly, but whether to take an airplane or a helicopter. The airplane flights, by and large, last longer and cost less. Most airplane tours remain airborne (ideally) for 40 to 50 minutes, at costs ranging from $75 to $159 per person; most helicopter tours fly for 30 minutes, at costs

---

⌐ Tips Reserve a Mule Trip in Advance

Mule trips to Phantom Ranch can fill up months in advance, so make your reservations early. Reservations for the next 23 months can be made beginning on the first of the month. For example, all dates in December 2004 would have gone on sale January 1, 2002. For **advance reservations** call ℂ **888/297-2757.** The **Bright Angel Transportation Desk** at ℂ **928/638-2631,** ext. 6015, can tell you about openings the next day. If you arrive without reservations, you can put your name on a waiting list by going to the desk in person. Reservations for South Rim mule rides are easier to obtain in winter, a time when temperatures in the lower canyon are often very pleasant.

The mule rides on the North Rim tend to fill up much later than those on the South Rim—if at all. To sign up, visit the **Canyon Trail Rides** desk (open daily 7am–6pm) at Grand Canyon Lodge, or call ℂ **928/638-9875.** The off-season number is ℂ **435/679-8665,** and the Web address is **www.canyonrides.com.**

of $89 to $109. The planes also cover more ground, crossing the canyon near Hermits Rest and returning along the East Rim, near Desert View. The helicopter tours, meanwhile, usually fly out and back in the same corridor near Hermits Rest. (Some do go for the full loop.) The helicopters cruise lower—just above the rim. And while they're not immune to an occasional bump, they tend to be smoother. (*Tip:* Whether you take an airplane or helicopter, your flight will be smoother if you go early in the day.)

During my helicopter ride, cinematic scores played over headphones, setting an epic tone that didn't quite jibe with the canyon. The flight afforded stunning aerial views of the topography, but precluded smelling or touching it. It was also a bit stomach-churning. It didn't help that I was pinned in the helicopter's middle seat between two large, sweaty strangers. The IMAX movie often achieves similar effects—without disturbing the wilderness.

The following companies offer air tours originating from Tusayan: **Papillon Grand Canyon Helicopters** (© **800/528-2418** or 928/638-2419; **www.papillon.com**); **Air Grand Canyon/Sky Eye Air Tours** (© **800/247-4726** or 928/638-2686; **www.airgrandcanyon.com**); **AirStar Helicopters** (© **800/962-3869** or 928/638-2622; **www.airstar.com**); **Grand Canyon Airlines** (© **800/528-2413** or 928/638-2407; **www.grandcanyonairlines.com**); **Kenai Helicopters** (© **800/541-4537** or 928/638-2764; **www.flykenai.com**).

RIVER RAFTING

White-water raft trips inside the park generally last from 3 to 14 days and must be booked well ahead of time. However, several companies offer shorter trips on the Colorado River near or inside Grand Canyon.

Aramark-Wilderness River Adventures, 50 S. Lake Powell Blvd., Page, AZ (© **800/528-6154** or 928/645-3279), offers half-day and full-day smooth-water raft trips from the base of Glen Canyon Dam to Lees Ferry, where the companies floating into Grand Canyon *begin* their trips. You'll complete the motorized half-day trip, which travels below the sandstone walls of the Vermilion and Echo cliffs, in about 5 hours. On the full-day trip, the boat drifts, engines off, for more of the time, and a lunch is served on the beach. Cost for the half-day trip is $59 for adults, $39 for 11 and under. The full-day trip, which takes 7 hours, costs $79 for adults, $69 for 11 and under.

Grand Canyon Airlines offers the half-day trip, plus round-trip bus transportation (totaling 290 miles) from Grand Canyon

National Park Airport in Tusayan. Cost for this 12-hour tour is $101 ($61 for 11 and under). For reservations call ☎ **800/528-2413** or 928/638-2463.

One-day trips through the westernmost part of Grand Canyon are available through **Hualapai River Runners** (☎ **888/255-9550** or 928/769-2210), P.O. Box 246, Peach Springs, AZ 86434. These motorized trips, which cost $250 per person, begin with rapids in the lower Granite Gorge of Grand Canyon and end on Lake Mead. Trip participants meet at 7:30am at Hualapai Lodge, on the Hualapai Indian Reservation, and do not return until between 7 and 8pm that night. The reservation is more than 2 hours drive from Grand Canyon Village.

RIVER RAFTING TRIPS

MOTORIZED   Motorized trips are fastest, often covering the 277 miles from Lees Ferry (above the canyon) to Pierce Ferry (in Lake Mead) in 6 days, compared to as many as 19 for nonmotorized trips. The motorized trips use wide pontoon boats that almost never capsize, making them slightly safer. Also, it's easier to move about on these solid-framed boats than on oar or paddleboats, a plus for people who lack mobility. Because of the speed of the trips, however, there's less time for hiking or resting in camp. If motorized trips are for you, consider using the companies **Aramark-Wilderness Adventures** (☎ **800/992-8022** or 928/645-3296) or **Western River Expeditions** (☎ **800/453-7450** or 801/942-6669).

NONMOTORIZED   For mobile people who want to bask in the canyon's beauty, I strongly recommend nonmotorized trips, even if it means seeing half the canyon instead of all of it. A motorless raft glides at close to the water's pace, giving passengers time to observe subtle, enticing patterns—swirls of water in eddies; the play of shadows and light as the sun moves across rock layers; the opening, unfolding, and gradual closing of each side canyon. Without motors running, the sound of the river provides a dreamlike backdrop to the journey.

There are two types of nonmotorized boats: paddle boats and oar boats. **Oar boats** are wooden dories or rubber rafts, each of which holds six passengers and a guide who does most or all of the rowing. If the guides are highly skilled, the passengers on an oar-powered trip have an excellent chance of floating the entire river without taking a life-threatening swim in the rapids. (The latest statistics on river-related deaths show commercial river trips to be as dangerous as golf. Far more people get hurt in camp than on the river.)

In a **paddleboat,** six passengers paddle, assisted by a guide who instructs them and helps steer. This experience is ideal for fit people who want to be involved at all times. However, because of the inexperience of the participants, paddle boats are probably more likely to capsize than oar boats or motorized rigs. And paddling can become burdensome during the long, slow-water stretches, especially when a head wind blows. **Canyon Explorations/Expeditions** (© **800/654-0723** or 928/774-4559) and **Outdoors Unlimited** (© **800/637-7238** or 928/526-2852) both have excellent reputations for paddle trips.

If an oar-powered company appeals to you, I recommend the company known as **O.A.R.S.** ✦✦✦ (© **800/346-6277** or 209/736-2924, see listing below), which has some of the most experienced guides on the river. On my trip with O.A.R.S., the three guides had a combined 52 years on the Colorado. They were responsible, informative, and fun, sharing the joy they found in the canyon. During the busiest months, O.A.R.S. assures quality service by sending six crew members out with each group of 16 passengers—providing one of the best crew-to-client ratios on the river.

Another factor to consider before scheduling your trip is the season. In **April,** the cacti bloom in the lower canyon, splashing bright colors across the hillsides, and the river is relatively uncrowded. However, cold weather can occasionally make these trips a test of the spirit. In **May** the weather is usually splendid, but the river is at its most crowded. **June and July** can be oppressively hot. In **late July and August,** monsoons break the heat and generate waterfalls all along the river, but they also soak rafters. From **September 15 to the end of October,** no motorized rigs cruise the river, so the canyon is quiet, although cold weather can once again be a problem.

RIVER RAFTING COMPANIES

Aramark-Wilderness River Adventures   Aramark-Wilderness offers both motorized and oar-powered trips with trip lengths varying from 4 to 12 days; with 8-day motorized trips and 12-day oar trips. P.O. Box 717, Page, AZ 86040. © **800/992-8022** or 928/645-3296. **www.riveradventures.com**.

Canyon Explorations   Canyon Explorations offers oar-powered and paddle trips with lengths varying from 6 to 18 days, including one trip with a string quartet, and two trips that set aside extra time for hiking. P.O. Box 310, Flagstaff, AZ 86002. © **800/654-0723** or 928/774-4559. **www.canyonexplorations.com**.

O.A.R.S.　O.A.R.S. offers both oar-powered trips and paddle trips with trip lengths varying from 5 to 16 days. P.O. Box 67, Angels Camp, CA 95222. ✆ **800/346-6277** or 209/736-2924. **www. oars.com**.

Outdoors Unlimited　Outdoors Unlimited offers oar-powered and paddle trips with trip lengths ranging from 5 to 15 days. 6900 Townsend Winona Rd., Flagstaff, AZ 86004. ✆ **800/637-7238** or 928/526-2852. **www.outdoorsunlimited.com**.

Western River Expeditions　Western River Expeditions offers motorized trips mid-April to mid-September with trip lengths varying from 3 to 6 days. On the shorter trips, helicopters drop participants in the western Canyon, where they begin their trips to Lake Mead. 7258 Racquet Club Dr., Salt Lake City, UT 84121. ✆ **800/ 453-7450** or 801/942-6669. **www.westernriver.com**.

5

Camping with a Car in the Grand Canyon Area

This chapter focuses on camping with a car—that is, camping done in or near RVs and automobiles. Most car campgrounds have individual pullouts for parking, grassy spots for tents, picnic tables, fire rings or grills, toilets, and drinking water. A few so-called "primitive" campgrounds lack running water. Located in remote areas, these often consist of little more than open space and a pit toilet. In addition to car campgrounds, the Grand Canyon area is home to a handful of RV parks—places where recreational vehicles can tap into water and electricity during overnight stays.

Numerous car campgrounds and RV parks can be found in and near the developed areas of Grand Canyon National Park (as well as one primitive car campground near the western canyon). In addition to the campgrounds listed in this chapter, you'll find many other car campgrounds and RV parks farther from the canyon, in the gateway communities of Flagstaff, Williams, and Kanab.

For more information, see "Backcountry Campgrounds," in chapter 4.

1 Camping Inside the Park

NEAR THE SOUTH RIM

Desert View Campground ✦ At dusk, the yips of coyotes drift over this campground in piñon-juniper woodland at the eastern edge of the park. Elevated, cool, and breezy, the peaceful surroundings offer no clue that the bustling Desert View Overlook is within walking distance. The floor of the woodland makes for smooth tent sites, the most secluded being on the outside of the loop drive. The only drawback: The nearest showers are 28 miles away at Camper Services in Grand Canyon Village. During high season, this first-come, first-served campground usually fills up by noon. To secure a site, swing through in midmorning and see what's open. Backcountry permits are not required for this site.

28 miles east of Grand Canyon Village on Hwy. 64. No phone, no advance reservations. 50 sites. $10 per site. 7-day limit. No credit cards. Open mid-May to mid-Oct.

Mather Campground 🐾   Despite having 319 campsites in a relatively small area, this remains a pleasant place. Piñon and juniper trees shade the sites, which are spaced far enough apart to afford privacy to most campers. The Aspen and Maple loops are especially roomy. Also, it's good to be near, but not too near, the showers ($1 for 5 min.) located in the Camper Services building next to the campground. If you're too close, hundreds of campers tramp past.

Because Mather is the only campground in Grand Canyon Village, it tends to fill up before the others. You can make reservations up to 5 months in advance by calling the 800 number listed below. For same-day reservations, check at the campground entrance. Even when the campground is booked, sites sometimes become available when campers leave early or cancel. There's no waiting list, however, and no set time for the new spaces to be given away. By coming in the morning, however, you can avoid waiting in line at the campground entrance.

From December 1 to March 1, the campground is open on a first-come, first-served basis. No reservations are taken for these months, but sites are easy to obtain.

Near Grand Canyon Village on South Rim. 🕿 **800/365-2267** (301/722-1257 outside the U.S.) for advance reservations, or 928/638-7851 for campground-specific information. **http://reservations.nps.gov**. 319 campsites, 4 group sites. No hookups. $15 Apr 1–Nov 30; $10 Dec 1–Mar 31. $4 tent only (no car). DISC, MC, V. Open year-round.

Trailer Village   The neighbors are close, the showers far (about ½-mile away), and the vegetation sparse. In surroundings like this, you might want to draw the curtains and stay in your RV. The beauty of a hookup is that it lets you do that. If, however, you'd like to venture outside during your stay, scout the property before taking a site. A few sites at the north end of the numbered drives have grass, shade trees, room for a tent, and one neighbor-free side. If you'd like to leave your RV altogether, you can catch a shuttle bus at a stop near the campground.

Like the lodges inside Grand Canyon National Park, Trailer Village is overseen by Xanterra—and therefore subject to the same rules as the lodges (except pets are allowed here). That means reservations can be made in advance. If you don't have reservations, check at the campground entrance even if the sign says no openings exist. A few spots open up in the late mornings when campers depart early.

Grand Canyon Area Campgrounds

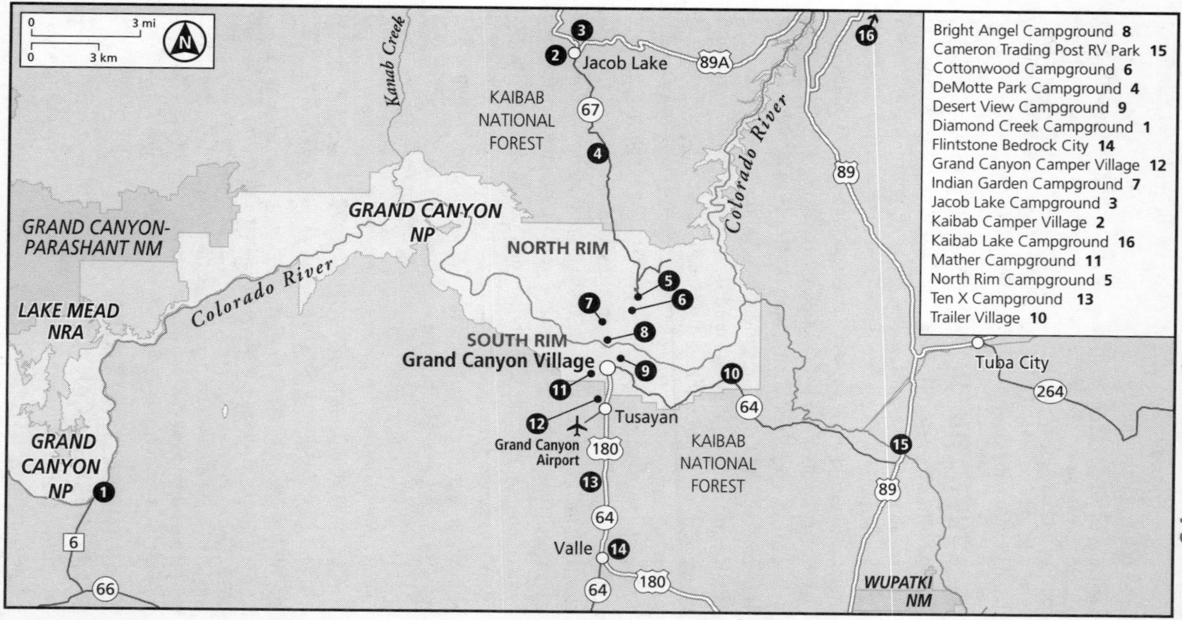

GRAND CANYON NP
GRAND CANYON-PARASHANT NM
LAKE MEAD NRA
Colorado River
Kanab Creek
GRAND CANYON NP
KAIBAB NATIONAL FOREST
NORTH RIM
SOUTH RIM
Grand Canyon Village
Grand Canyon Airport
Tusayan
Valle
KAIBAB NATIONAL FOREST
Colorado River
Jacob Lake
WUPATKI NM
Tuba City

Bright Angel Campground **8**
Cameron Trading Post RV Park **15**
Cottonwood Campground **6**
DeMotte Park Campground **4**
Desert View Campground **9**
Diamond Creek Campground **1**
Flintstone Bedrock City **14**
Grand Canyon Camper Village **12**
Indian Garden Campground **7**
Jacob Lake Campground **3**
Kaibab Camper Village **2**
Kaibab Lake Campground **16**
Mather Campground **11**
North Rim Campground **5**
Ten X Campground **13**
Trailer Village **10**

(Because reservations are guaranteed by credit card, few additional spots come open at night.)

Grand Canyon Village, P.O. Box 699, Grand Canyon, AZ 86023. ℂ 888/297-2757 advance reservations or 928/638-2631 same-day reservations, campground questions. Fax 928/638-9247. 84 sites with full hookups. $25 per site for 2 people, plus $2 for each additional adult (17 and over) after the first 2. AE, DISC, MC, V. Dump station located nearby (closed in the winter). Open year-round.

NEAR THE NORTH RIM

North Rim Campground 👧👧👧   Shaded by ponderosa pines and situated alongside Transept Canyon (part of Grand Canyon), this is a delightful place to pass a few days. The pines, which shade a soft, smooth, forest floor, are spaced just far enough apart to allow for a vigorous game of Wiffle ball, among other activities.

But there's more here than a field of dreams. The 1.5-mile-long Transept Trail links the campground to Grand Canyon Lodge. The North Rim General Store, a laundromat, and showers ($1.25 for 5 min.) are all within walking distance. The most spectacular sites are the rim sites, which open onto the canyon. These cost an extra $5 but are worth it, being some of the prettiest anywhere.

With only 87 sites, the North Rim Campground fills up for much of the summer. You can book a spot up to 5 months in advance. If you show up without a reservation only to find the "Sorry, campground full" sign on the entry booth, don't be afraid to ask what seems a stupid question. The gatekeepers often neglect to remove the sign after receiving cancellations, and you may just end up with a campsite. The best time to show up and ask about openings is at 8am. That's when sites made available by the previous night's cancellations go up for sale.

The campground sometimes stays open on a limited basis after October 15 until snow closes Highway 67, but few services are available in the park.

On Grand Canyon North Rim (44 miles south of Jacob Lake on Hwy. 67). ℂ 800/ 365-2267 advance reservations, or 928/638-9389 same-day reservations. **http://ressrvations.nps.gov**. 83 sites, 4 group sites. No hookups. $15–$20 per site and $40 per group site (group sites have a capacity to accommodate up to 25 persons per site); $4 for tent only (no car). DISC, MC, V. Open May 15–Oct 15.

NEAR THE EASTERN ENTRANCE & THE WESTERN CANYON

Diamond Creek Campground 👧   This primitive campground at the confluence of Diamond Creek and the Colorado River at the western end of the canyon is the only place where you can drive to the river inside the Grand Canyon. The gravel road, descending from 4,600 feet in Peach Springs to 1,350 feet at the campground, sometimes gets washed out, but high-clearance vehicles can negotiate it during dry weather. (Don't risk it during monsoon season.) Surrounded by cliffs of granite and schist, the campground is at a lovely spot. People who couldn't otherwise make it to the inner canyon will probably appreciate it most.

But there are some real drawbacks. You probably won't be alone; the beach serves as a popular pullout for raft trips, and the Hualapai River Runners begin their trips in the far western canyon here. If you don't commandeer one of the three metal ramadas, you could end up broiling in the midday sun. (Located just above the canyon's lowest point, this is one of its hottest places.) You'll need to bring your own drinking water and pack out your own garbage. Seldom pumped, the lone portable toilet tests the will.

Hualapai Indian Reservation (18.1 miles from Peach Springs, 19 miles from Hwy. 66 on the Diamond Creek Rd.). & 928/769-2210. Open tent camping. $10 per person for camping; $6.00 for sightseeing only. AE, DISC, MC, V. Open Mar–Sept. Pay and register before entering at the Hualapai River Trips Office, open daily 6am–6pm at Hualapai Lodge in Peach Springs. Closed in winter.

2 Camping Outside the Park

NEAR THE SOUTH RIM

Flintstone Bedrock City *Kids*   Cartoon lovers will be curious about this Flintstones-themed campground, restaurant, and store, whose multihued, faux-stone buildings cling like putty to the windswept land at the intersection of highways 64 and 180. In addition to peddling the ubiquitous Grand Canyon T-shirts and dead-scorpion paperweights, the gift shop sells all manner of Flintstones paraphernalia, including bibs, sweatshirts, T-shirts, key chains, and magnets. Fred's Diner serves up dishes such as the "Chickasaurus Sandwich" and the "Bronto Burger" for under $3.

One advantage to having a prehistoric theme is that no one can tell whether your campground is run-down. The buildings here seem about as old as caves. So nothing looks out of character. One problem, however, is obvious: the proximity of some tent sites to Highway 64. Services here include a small store, volleyball court, coin-op laundry, TV, and game room.

In Vallé (at junctions of Hwy. 180 and 64). HCR 34 Box A, Williams, AZ 86046. ☎ 928/635-2600. Unlimited tent sites, 27 hookups. $12 2-person tent; $14 electric hookup; $16 water/electric hookup; $2 each additional person after the first 2. AE, DISC, MC, V. Open year-round.

Campgrounds in the Grand Canyon Area

Campground	Rim	Total Sites	RV Hookups	Dump Station	Toilets	Drinking Water	Showers	Fire Pits/Grills	Laundry	Public Phones	Reserve	Fees	Open
Cameron Trading Post RV Park	South	48	48	yes	no	yes	no	no	no	yes	yes	$15	year-round
DeMotte Park Campground	North	23	no	no	yes	no	yes	yes	no	no	no	$12	mid-June to mid-Sept
Desert View Campground	South	50	no	no	yes	no	no	no	no	no	no	$10 per site	mid-May to mid-Oct
Diamond Creek Campground	South	open tent camping	no	no	yes	no	no	yes	no	no	no	$10 per person	except winter
Flintstone Bedrock City	South	unlimited tent sites	27	yes	yes	yes	yes	no	no	yes	yes	$12 two-person tent, $14 electric hookup, $16 water/electric, $2 each additional person	year-round
Grand Canyon Camper Village	South	300	250	yes	yes	yes	yes	yes	yes	yes	yes	$26 full hookup, $24 water/electric, $22 electric, $18 tent sites, $20 teepees	year-round

Campground													
Jacob Lake Campground	North	53	no	no	yes	yes	no	yes	no	no	no	$12	mid-May to mid-Oct
Kaibab Camper Village	North	130	70	yes	yes		yes	yes	yes	yes	no	$22 hookups, $12 dry sites, $12 tent sites, $12 cabin style rooms $65	May 15–Oct 15
Kaibab Lake Campground	South	72	no	no	yes	yes	no	yes	no	no	no	$12	May–Oct
Mather Campground	South	323	no	yes	yes	yes	yes	yes	yes	yes	Mar–Nov	$15 Apr–Nov, $10 rest of year	year-round
North Rim Campground	North	87	no	yes	yes	yes	nearby	yes	nearby	yes	yes	$15–$20 site, $4 tent only, no car	May 15–Oct 15
Ten X Campground	South	70	no	no	yes	yes	no	yes	no	no	no	$10	May–Sept
Trailer Village	South	84	84	nearby	yes	yes	nearby	yes	no	nearby	yes	$25 plus $1.75 each additional person	year-round

Grand Canyon Camper Village   This campground's advantage is its location: Just a mile south of the park entrance, it lies within easy walking distance of stores and restaurants on one side and of Kaibab National Forest on the other. Its disadvantages are its relatively narrow (average width: 27 ft.) campsites and the noise from the nearby Grand Canyon National Park Airport, whose constant daytime helicopter takeoffs, together with the throngs of people at the campground itself, may bring back memories of Woodstock. At least the restrooms are clean, and the showers (75¢ for 6 min.) hot. There's also a playground and a gravel basketball court.

In Tusayan (1 mile south of the park on Hwy. 64), P.O. Box 490, Grand Canyon, AZ 86023-0490. ✆ **928/638-2887**. 50 tent sites, 250 hookups. $18 tent sites; $20 teepees; $22 electric; $24 water/electric; $26 full hookups. AE, DISC, MC, V. Open year-round. Pets admitted under condition they are kept on a leash.

Kaibab Lake Campground 🌲🌲   The campsites at this Forest Service campground are on a forested hillside above the reddish waters of Williams Lake. There's no swimming in the lake, a reservoir for Williams, but the fishing for bottom-feeders isn't bad. Grand Canyon is only 60 miles away from the camping grounds. An Arizona fishing license is required for anyone over 14.

4 miles north of Williams on Hwy. 64. ✆ **928/699-1239**. 72 sites, 2 campsites accessible for people with disabilities; no hookups. $12 per site. No credit cards. Open May 15–Oct 31. Remains open winter in no-fee status, depending on road accessibility.

Ten X Campground 🌲🌲   Large, wooded campsites make this Forest Service campground the most peaceful open-air accommodations within 20 miles of the South Rim. With plenty of distance between you and your neighbors, this is a great place to linger over a fire. All sites have fire pits and grills, and the campground host sells wood. Later, you'll find the soft, needle-covered floor perfect for sleeping. Showers are located in the Grand Canyon Park Village. This first-come, first-served campground does sell out. If you're driving up from Flagstaff or Williams, consider snagging a site before going to the canyon for the day.

2 miles south of Tusayan on Hwy. 64. ✆ **928/638-2443**. 70 sites, no hookups. $10 per site. No credit cards. Open May–Sept.

NEAR THE NORTH RIM

DeMotte Park Campground 🌲🌲   Bundle up for the nights at this Forest Service campground. It's 8,760 feet high (10 ft. higher than Telluride, CO), in spruce-fir forest, so you're sure to be cool. It's so cool, in fact, that it closes in mid-October because the pipes freeze. The road through the campground curves sharply and some of the spaces are small, so this place may not work for large RVs. Because this campground is relatively small and located just outside the park entrance, it tends to fill up early. Try to get a site on your way *into* the park, instead of on your way out. Guided hikes and horseback rides are available at nearby concessions. Drinking water, toilets, cooking grills are available on the campground.

5 miles north of the park boundary on Hwy. 67. ℂ **928/643-7298.** 23 sites, no hookups. $12 per site. Open mid-May to mid-Oct.

Jacob Lake Campground 🏕🏕   Nestled into rolling hills covered with ponderosa pine forest, this is a beauty of a Forest Service campground. Towering pines shade sites only a short drive from the services at Jacob Lake Lodge. This first-come, first-served campground offers regular naturalist programs.

U.S. 89A, just north of Jacob Lake. No phone. 53 sites, no hookups. $12 per vehicle, second vehicle $6. Open mid-May to mid-Oct.

Kaibab Camper Village 🏕🏕   Compared to the South Rim RV parks, where sagebrush is often the largest plant in sight, this North Rim RV park is like a fairy tale. Everywhere inside the campground, ponderosa pines dust the sky like Jack's mythical beanstalk. Some campers even have a view past the trees to the puddle known as Jacob Lake. The setting makes this easily the prettiest RV park in the Grand Canyon area.

Tent campers will also be comfortable here, especially if they pay the extra $3 for one of the improved sites, which have sand rings and views of Jacob Lake. The use of generators is forbidden, so everyone can enjoy the quiet.

The owners recently added two public showers ($1.50 for 5 min.). Now the only thing missing is flush toilets. Several signs stress the fact that the current toilets are hooked up to a larger septic system. Still, they resemble portable toilets in every other conceivable way, including the fact that they're dark as caves at night.

½-mile west of Hwy. 67, just south of Jacob Lake. P.O. Box 3331, Flagstaff, AZ 86003. ℂ **928/643-7804** (when open); 800/525-0924 (Mon–Fri 8am–5pm) or 928/526-0924 (when closed). www.canyoneers.com. 50 tent sites, 80 RV sites (70 hookups, 10 dry sites). $22 for hookups (up to 4 people); $12 for dry sites (up to 4 people); $12 for tent sites (up to 2 people), plus $2 for each additional person. Cabin style rooms are available at $65 per room. MC, V. Open mid-May to mid-Oct (weather permitting).

NEAR THE EASTERN ENTRANCE

Cameron Trading Post RV Park   This is no-frills RV camping near the eastern entrance of the park: Hookups are in a field, with no showers available and only a few cottonwood trees for shade. A few sites at the north end of the campground overlook the Little Colorado River gorge—especially scenic when the river is flowing. Although there's nothing in the way of recreation at the campground, the Cameron Trading Post, with its restaurant and Native American art, is across the street.

U.S. 89 across from Cameron Trading Post (P.O. Box 339), Cameron, AZ 86020. © 800/338-7385 or 928/679-2231. No tent sites, 48 full hookups. $15 per site. AE, DISC, MC, V. Open year-round.

DISPERSED CAMPING IN KAIBAB NATIONAL FOREST

Park visitors can camp for free simply by driving out of the park and into the **Kaibab National Forest** 🐾🐾. The Forest Service's rules are simple: Camp at least a quarter mile from paved roads, campgrounds, and water, but never in meadows. (No camping is allowed near Hull Cabin or Red Butte.) Pack out your garbage, including used toilet paper, and remove any signs that you've been there. Bury human waste in holes 4 inches deep, 6 inches across, and at least 100 yards from water or creek beds. Completely douse campfires before leaving. If the forest seems dry, check with a local Forest Service office about burn restrictions.

The dispersed camping in the National Forest on the North Rim is among the best anywhere. Here, a number of Forest Service roads lead to canyon overlooks where you're free to spend the night. The most accessible of these used to be the East Rim Overlook, just 4.4 miles off of Highway 67 on FS Road 611. But the Forest Service, citing overuse, closed the rim area to motorized vehicles. Visitors can still park nearby and walk to the overlook, which opens onto views of the Marble Platform and the eastern Grand Canyon. Other overlooks, such as Crazy Jug Point and Parissawampitts Point, remain open to vehicles and have lovely views of the central Grand Canyon, but they require long, bumpy drives. For maps and information on dispersed camping on the North Rim, visit the **Kaibab Plateau Visitor Center** (© 928/643-7298) in Jacob Lake.

3 Picnic & Camping Supplies

If possible, stock up on your camping items at a large grocery store in a larger city such as Flagstaff. In general, prices are lowest in Flagstaff and rise steadily as you near the canyon, peaking at The Canyon Village Marketplace inside the park.

SOUTH RIM

The Canyon Village Marketplace &   Located in the business district of Grand Canyon Village, the general store on the South Rim is the largest and most complete retailer in the park, selling groceries, canyon souvenirs, liquor, electronic and automotive goods, provisions for camping, and hiking and backpacking gear. Some of the camping equipment can be rented for overnight use.

In Grand Canyon Village. ℂ **928/638-2262.** June–Sept 8am–8pm; Oct–May 8am–7pm.

Desert View Store   The Desert View Store has souvenirs, beer and wine, and a limited selection of groceries.

At Desert View (off Hwy. 64). ℂ **928/638-2393.** Summer 8am–7pm; rest of year 9am–5pm.

NORTH RIM

North Rim General Store   The North Rim General Store is small but well supplied with groceries, beer and wine, and a very limited supply of camping equipment. Unlike the General Store on the South Rim, the North Rim general store cannot outfit aspiring backpackers.

Adjacent to North Rim Campground. ℂ **928/638-2611,** ext. 270. 8am–8pm daily (may vary).

6

Where to Stay & Eat in Grand Canyon National Park

This chapter lists accommodations and dining available inside Grand Canyon National Park. Many other hotels and restaurants exist in the nearby communities of Tusayan, Williams, and Flagstaff, AZ, and in Kanab, UT. Rooms in Flagstaff, Williams, and Kanab—all three of which are more than 50 miles from the park—generally cost less than comparable ones inside the park. Tusayan, 1 mile from the park's south entrance, tends to be more expensive than the park. When planning a visit to Grand Canyon, I recommend reserving a place inside the park for at least 1 night. This lets you savor the twilight hours at the canyon without driving far in the dark.

If you're hoping to spend the night at or near the rim, be sure to call in advance of your stay. During busy years, the lodges inside the park and in Tusayan frequently fill up, forcing would-be lodgers to backtrack away from the park.

If you tire of relatively new rooms with Southwestern motifs, a few historic hotels and lodges do remain. In the park, stay at **Grand Canyon Lodge** (on the North Rim), the **Bright Angel Lodge,** or the **El Tovar Hotel.** Protected by law, these historic structures cannot be gutted during renovation, so their rooms and cabins remain entertainingly quirky—unlike the other park lodging, which tends to be uniform.

See chapter 7, "Gateway Towns," for more information on where to stay and eat, and what to do, outside of Grand Canyon National Park.

1 South Rim Lodging

EXPENSIVE

El Tovar Hotel 🌟🌟 *Moments*   With its European hunting-lodge style, the El Tovar offers a dark, cool counterpoint to the warm, pueblo-style buildings of Mary E. Jane Colter. Completed in 1905 to accommodate the influx of tourists on the Santa Fe Railroad, the

El Tovar, situated roughly 100 yards from the rim, casts a long shadow over Grand Canyon Village. A pointed cupola sits like a witch's cap above its three stories of Oregon pine and native stone, and spires rise above an upstairs deck. Nothing seems summery—from a distance, even its broad porches seem to recede into shadows.

The building's interior is as unforgettable as the outside. Moose and elk heads hang on varnished walls, dimly lit by copper chandeliers. Take away the modern-day tourists and the El Tovar probably looks much as it did at its inception, when it offered guests all manner of luxury, including a music room, art classes, and a roof garden.

While these amenities have gone the way of the Flagstaff-to-Grand Canyon stagecoach, the hotel is still the most luxurious at the canyon and the only one to offer room service and a nightly turndown. At its inception, the rooms were larger, with shared bathrooms at the end of each hall. When private bathrooms were installed, the rooms became smaller and more idiosyncratic. Today, many of the standard rooms are too small for a rollaway. The deluxe rooms are roomier than the standard rooms, but the most stunning accommodations by far are the four view-suites, each of which has a sitting room and a private deck overlooking the canyon. These suites, which cost $295, often fill up a year or more in advance.

© **928/638-2631** (main switchboard) or 888/297-2757 (reservations only). Fax 303/297-3175. 78 units. Standard rooms $120–$140; deluxe rooms $185; suites $210–$295. AE, DC, DISC, MC, V. **Amenities:** Restaurant (Continental) in a stunning dining room; lounge with veranda overlooking the rim; concierge; tour desk; room service. *In room:* A/C, TV.

MODERATE

Maswik Lodge 🌟 *Value*   Built in the 1960s, Maswik Lodge lies in a wooded area, a 5-minute walk from the rim. If you're not up to walking, you can catch a free shuttle directly in front of the lodge. The lodge has a cafeteria, sports bar, and gift shop.

The guest rooms are in 16 two-story wood-and-stone buildings known as Maswik North and South. Most Maswik North rooms have vaulted ceilings, private balconies, and forest views, making them among the most pleasant in the park. Rooms in Maswik South are 5 years older, a bit smaller, and have less pristine views. With only one window each, they can also be hot during summer. However, the Maswik South rooms were renovated in 2001, and their low cost—$45 less than Maswik North—makes them a good value despite their shortcomings. Maswik is especially good for families, and all rooms offer two queen-size beds. During summer, Maswik

Reserving a Room Inside the Park

Lodging inside the park is handled by **Xanterra Parks and Resorts**, 14001 E. Iliff, Aurora, CO 80014 (© **888/297-2757** or fax 303/297-3175; www.xanterra.com or www.grand canyonlodges.com). Book well ahead: the most desirable rooms, such as rim cabins at Bright Angel, go a year in advance. It is possible to reserve a room up to 2 years in advance (which you would need to do for Phantom Ranch). For example, on January 1, 2004, you could reserve rooms through the end of December 2006. If you're flexible with dates and choices or travel in the fall or winter, you can usually find rooms 1 or 2 months in advance. Because Xanterra allows cancellations without penalty up to 48 hours in advance, you can sometimes grab a room at the last minute, even at the busiest times, by directly calling the Xanterra switchboard (© **928/638-2631**). This is also the number to contact lodging guests. Xanterra accepts American Express, Discover, MasterCard, and Visa. Pets are not allowed in accommodations inside the park. Children under 16 stay free with their parents.

On the South Rim, the hotels themselves can be contacted through the same switchboard (© **928/638-2631** or fax 928/638-9247) and mailing address (P.O. Box 699, Grand Canyon, AZ 86023). The phone number for **Grand Canyon Lodge** on the North Rim is © **928/638-2611.** The hotels do not have specific street addresses. When you enter the park, you will receive a map locating all the hotels.

Most of the rooms in the park have relatively new furnishings, and all but a few have telephones and televisions. Only El Tovar and Yavapai East (at Yavapai Lodge) have air-conditioning (most of the others have swamp coolers). The only conspicuous difference in furnishings is at the El Tovar, where the furniture is more luxurious. Other than that, the buildings themselves are what differ most within the park.

also rents out 40 guest rooms in ten rustic, thin-walled cabins. If you're staying anywhere at Maswik, bring a flashlight, as the area is dark at night.

Grand Canyon Village

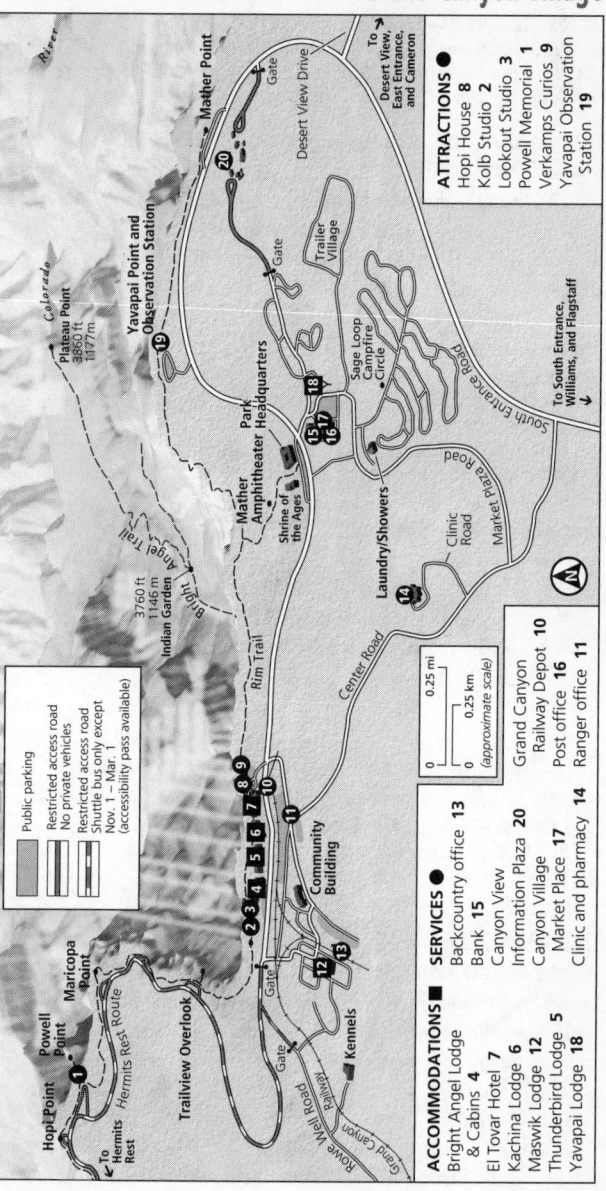

ATTRACTIONS ●
Hopi House **8**
Kolb Studio **2**
Lookout Studio **3**
Powell Memorial **1**
Verkamps Curios **9**
Yavapai Observation
Station **19**

ACCOMMODATIONS ■
Bright Angel Lodge
& Cabins **4**
El Tovar Hotel **7**
Kachina Lodge **6**
Maswik Lodge **12**
Thunderbird Lodge **5**
Yavapai Lodge **18**

SERVICES ●
Backcountry office **13**
Bank **15**
Canyon View
Information Plaza **20**
Canyon Village
Market Place **17**
Clinic and pharmacy **14**
Grand Canyon
Railway Depot **10**
Post office **16**
Ranger office **11**

0   0.25 mi
0   0.25 km
(approximate scale)

115

© **928/638-2631** (main switchboard) or 888/297-2757 (reservations only). Fax 303/297-3175. 278 units. Maswik South $80; Maswik North $125; cabin rooms $68. Winter rate for cabin rooms $66. AE, DISC, MC, V. **Amenities:** Cafeteria; sports lounge; tour desk. *In room:* TV, hair dryer (Maswik North only).

Thunderbird and Kachina Lodges 🔥 Fans of '60s-era dormitory architecture will admire the flat roofs, decorative concrete panels, and metal staircases on the buildings' exteriors, and the brick walls within. Inside, the rooms are surprisingly pleasant, with windows as wide as the rooms themselves. Most of the upstairs units on the more expensive "canyon side" have at least a partial view of the canyon. Check-in for the Thunderbird is at the Bright Angel Lodge; for the Kachina, it's at the El Tovar.

© **928/638-2631** (main switchboard) or 888/297-2757 (reservations only). Fax 303/297-3175. 55 units at Thunderbird, 49 at Kachina. Park side $122; canyon side $132. AE, DISC, MC, V. *In room:* TV.

Yavapai Lodge The largest lodge at the canyon, Yavapai is a mile from the historic district but close to Bank One, the post office, and the Canyon Village Marketplace. Built between 1970 and 1972, the A-frame lodge has a large cafeteria and gift shop. The 358 rooms, renovated in 2002, lie in ten single-story buildings known as Yavapai West and six two-story wood buildings known as Yavapai East. Most rooms in Yavapai West are compact with cinder-block walls, but they do afford guests the benefit of driving to the door. Yavapai East's units are larger, with king beds and air-conditioning, and many enjoy views of the forest. Most travelers would agree that they're worth the extra $13. The gravel paths connecting the buildings are very dark at night, so bring a flashlight.

© **928/638-2631** (main switchboard) or 888/297-2757 (reservations only). Fax 303/297-3175. 358 units. $95 Yavapai West; $108 Yavapai East. Winter $66. AE, DISC, MC, V. **Amenities:** Cafeteria; gift shop. *In room:* TV (A/C and hair dryer Yavapai East only).

INEXPENSIVE
Bright Angel Lodge & Cabins 🔥🔥 *Value* Guests of Bright Angel Lodge stay in tightly clustered buildings along the rim west of the main lodge. In the 1930s, the Fred Harvey Co. needed to develop new, affordable lodging for the many visitors who had begun driving to the canyon. At the company's request, Mary E. Jane Colter designed both the lodge and the cabins alongside it. The cabins were built around several historic buildings, including the park's old post office and the Bucky O'Neill Cabin, the oldest continually standing

structure on the rim. Since those days, Bright Angel Lodge has become the hub (and most crowded area) of the South Rim.

Low-end accommodations start with clean, spare rooms in two long buildings adjacent to Bright Angel Lodge. At $55 a night, the "hiker rooms" are the least expensive in the park. Each has a double bed and desk but no television or private bathroom. Other lodge rooms have double beds and toilets but no showers. Still others are appointed like standard motel rooms, only with showers instead of tubs.

Rooms in the historic cabins cost only about $10 more than the most expensive lodge rooms and are worth the extra money. These freestanding cabins, most of which house two guest rooms, recall a time when the canyon was a refuge from civilization. Most rooms have open-frame ceilings, brightly painted window frames, and windows to spare. The rooms nearer the rim are quieter than the ones along the Village Loop Road, where bus traffic can be heavy. At the high end of the price range are the twelve rim-side cabins, which have views of the canyon and cost from $107 to $130. The luxurious Bucky O'Neill Cabin, one of the oldest structures in the park, boasts a fireplace, wet bar, and canyon views. It goes for $245. The rim-side cabins tend to fill up far in advance.

© 928/638-2631 (main switchboard) or 888/297-2757 (reservations only). Fax 303/297-3175. 34 units, 14 with bathroom, 10 with sink only, 10 with sink and toilet; 55 cabin units. $55 double with sink only; $58 double with sink and toilet only; $70 double with bathroom; $85 historic cabin; $107–$130 historic rim-cabins; $245 rim-side Bucky O'Neill Suite with fireplace. AE, DISC, MC, V. **Amenities:** Arizona Room (American); snack bar; lounge (worth seeing); tour desk. *In room:* TV in most rooms.

2 Lodging Inside the Canyon

Phantom Ranch 🉐🉐   Accessible only by floating down the Colorado River or by hiking or riding a mule to the bottom of Grand Canyon, Phantom Ranch is the only park lodging below the canyon rims, and it often sells out on the first day of availability—more than 23 months in advance. To reserve a spot, call as early as possible. If you arrive at the canyon without a reservation, contact the **Bright Angel Transportation Desk** (© **928/638-2631,** ext. 6015) for information about openings the next day.

The reason for the booked slate? Clean sheets never felt better than at the bottom of the Grand Canyon, cold beer never tasted this good (not even close), and a hot shower never felt so, well, miraculous. Phantom Ranch is the only place below the rims inside the park that has these amenities.

The ranch's nine evaporatively cooled cabins are a simple pleasure. The famous Grand Canyon architect, Mary Colter, designed four of them—the ones with the most stone in the walls are hers—using rocks from the nearby Bright Angel Creek. Connected by dirt footpaths, they sit, natural and elegant, alongside picnic tables and under the shade of cottonwood trees. Inside each cabin, there's a desk, concrete floor, and four to ten bunk beds, as well as a toilet and sink. A shower house for guests is nearby.

While most of Phantom Ranch was completed in the 1920s and '30s, four 10-person dorms, each with its own bathing facilities, were added in the early 1980s. Used mostly by hikers, these are ideal for individuals and small groups looking for a place to bed down; larger groups are better served by reserving cabins, which provide both privacy and a lower per-person price than the dorms.

During the day, some guests hike to Ribbon Falls or along the River Trail, while others relax, read, or write postcards that, if sent from here, will bear the unique stamp, "Mailed by mule from the bottom of the Grand Canyon." In the late afternoon, many guests and hikers from the nearby Bright Angel Campground gravitate to the canteen, which sells snacks when not serving meals. (For more on dining at Phantom Ranch, see "Where to Eat Inside the Canyon," later in this chapter.)

Located at the bottom of the canyon, .5 mile north of the Colorado River on the North Kaibab Trail. ✆ **928/638-2631** (main switchboard) or 888/297-2757 (reservations only). Fax 303/297-3175. 7 4-person cabins, 2 cabins for up to 10 people, 4 dorms of 10 people each. $26 dorm bed; $70 cabin (for 2); $10.50 each additional person. Most cabins are reserved as part of mule-trip overnight packages (see "Mule Trips," in chapter 4, for details). AE, DISC, MC, V. **Amenities:** Canteen (American). *In room:* Evaporative coolers, no phone.

3 Lodging on the North Rim

Grand Canyon Lodge 🐾🐾   The lodge's architect, Gilbert Stanley Underwood, was best known for designing edifices such as train stations and post offices. Although Union Pacific Railroad built the lodge in 1928, the train never came closer than Cedar City, UT. A few tourists came there on "triangle" bus tours that also stopped at Bryce and Zion canyons, but most went to the South Rim. Most still do.

After burning in 1932, the lodge reopened in 1937 and now seems to have grown into the landscape. Its roof of green shingles goes with the needles on the nearby trees, its log posts match their trunks, and its walls of Kaibab limestone blend with the rim rock itself. In its expansive lobby, a 50-foot-high ceiling absorbs sound like the forest floor. Beyond it, the octagonal "Sun Room" has three enormous picture windows opening onto the canyon. Two long decks with imitation-wood chairs flank the sunroom, overlooking the canyon. The lodge also houses a saloon, a snack bar, a meeting room, and an excellent dining room.

Made of the same materials as the lodge, 140 cabins have sprouted like saplings around it. There are four types, all with private bathrooms. With wicker furniture, gas fireplaces, bathtubs, and small vanity rooms, the Western Cabins and Rim Cabins are the most luxurious. The Western Cabins cost $10 less than the four Rim Cabins, which have stunning views of Bright Angel Canyon. The Rim Cabins generally fill up on their first day of availability, nearly 2 years in advance.

The two other types—Pioneer and Frontier—are far more rustic inside. Tightly clustered along the rim of Transept Canyon, they have walls and ceilings of exposed logs, electric heaters, and showers instead of bathtubs. The Frontier Cabins each have one guest room with a double bed and a twin bed. The Pioneer Cabins, meanwhile, each have two guest rooms—one with a double bed and a twin bed, the other with two twins. For $94, a family of five can stay in comfort in one of the Pioneer Cabins.

Tip: If your reservations are for a Frontier or Pioneer cabin, ask for one that has a partial view of Transept Canyon. The lodge may be able to accommodate you, and there's no extra charge for the view.

A few motel rooms are also available. Although they're well maintained and were remodeled in 1999, their atmosphere doesn't compare to the cabins.

At North Rim, 214 miles north of South Rim on Hwy. 67. ℃ **928/638-2611** (main switchboard) or 888/297-2757 (reservations only). Fax 303/297-3175. 208 units. $92 Frontier Cabin; $91 motel unit; $101 Pioneer Cabin; $106 Western Cabin; $116 Rim-View Cabin. AE, DC, DISC, MC, V. **Amenities:** 2 restaurants (1 excellent dining room serving Continental fare, 1 snack bar); lounge.

4 Where to Eat on the South Rim

Arizona Room ◈◈ STEAKS   Lining up before this restaurant's 4:30pm opening isn't a bad idea. Instead of arriving after sunset to find an hour's wait, you can watch the changing colors through the long, canyon-facing windows. Or, when the days are longer, finish the meal in time to step outside for the evening's show. Either way, make sure you land a table, because the Arizona Room dishes up the most consistently tasty dinners on the South Rim. Entrees include broiled or blackened hand-cut steaks, mustard and rosemary crusted prime rib, marinated chicken breast, and pan-seared salmon with melon salsa. My favorite, the baby back ribs with prickly-pear or spicy *chipotle* barbecue sauce, taste delicious. To accompany your meal, you can choose from a variety of mid-priced California wines or flavored margaritas.

At Bright Angel Lodge. © **928/638-2631**. Reservations not accepted. Entrees $14.75–$20.75. AE, DC, DISC, MC, V. 4:30–10pm daily. Closed in winter.

Bright Angel Restaurant *(Kids* AMERICAN

Though this restaurant removed the words "coffee shop" from its name, it still serves average American coffee shop food. The breakfast fare, including omelets, French toast, and pancakes, is not bad. At lunch, the burgers, hot sandwiches, and large salads usually pass muster. At dinnertime, the restaurant supplements the lunch menu by adding palatable entrees such as grilled New York strip steak, chicken Alfredo, and stuffed shells.

This is a good place for families, who can dine here without worrying much about the children's behavior. The games on the **kid's menu** should distract the small fries until the french fries arrive.

Located in Bright Angel Lodge. © **928/638-2631**. Reservations not accepted. Breakfast $5.25–$7.40; lunch $7–$10; dinner $7–$16. AE, DC, DISC, MC, V. 6am–10pm daily.

Canyon Village Deli *(Value* DELI

Many Park Service employees duck into this delicatessen for lunch. Here you can sit in a corner booth, read the paper, and watch the tourists pass. The deli serves pre-made sandwiches, salads, pizza slices, calzones, and other hot dishes, including fried chicken, but the best offerings are often the daily specials.

In the South Rim's Canyon Village Marketplace (at Market Plaza). © **928/638-2262**. $3–$6. No credit cards. 8am–6pm daily.

Desert View Trading Post Cafeteria CAFETERIA

The pre-made sandwiches and burgers here will sustain you until you make it back to Grand Canyon Village. The breakfast offerings, including eggs and French toast, draw campers from nearby Desert View Campground.

At Desert View, 25 miles east of Grand Canyon Village on Hwy. 64. © **928/638-2360**. Reservations not accepted. $1.85–$4.40. No credit cards. Summer 8am–7pm; rest of year 9am–6pm.

El Tovar Restaurant *(★★* CONTINENTAL

One hundred years after opening its doors, this restaurant remains a unique dining experience. Best of all is the stunning room—walls of Oregon pine graced with murals depicting the ritual dances of four Native American tribes and banks of windows at the north and south ends.

At dinner, a Southwestern influence spices the Continental cuisine. One tasty appetizer is the black bean soup. For an entree, meat eaters will enjoy the flame-broiled peppercorn crusted filet mignon in roasted garlic sauce. Meanwhile, vegetarians can munch the *Cle-san-Du-Klish* (Native American vegan blue corn tamales).

The El Tovar accepts reservations for dinner only, but it's also open for breakfast and lunch. If you're traveling on a budget or prefer the dinner menu at the Arizona Room (as I do), try dining here during nondinner hours, when you can enjoy the lovely surroundings for just a dollar or two more than you'd spend at the other canyon restaurants. At breakfast, be sure to sample the coffee, the best inside the park, and order the eggs Benedict with smoked salmon. Expect large portions for all the restaurant's entrees.

In the El Tovar Hotel. **℃ 928/638-2631**, ext. 6432. Reservations accepted for dinner only. Breakfast $3.70–$10; lunch $6.95–$15.20; dinner entrees $17–$25.25. AE, DC, DISC, MC, V. 6:30–11am, 11:30am–2pm, and 5–10pm daily.

Maswik and Yavapai Cafeterias *Value* CAFETERIA For the price of a burger, fries, and a soft drink at the Tusayan McDonald's, you can eat a full meal at either Maswik or Yavapai cafeterias. Though the food costs about the same at either place, there are some key differences between the two. Maswik more closely resembles a food court, where meals come complete with side dishes. One Maswik station serves Mexican fare; another has hot sandwich plates; a third offers spaghetti and burgers; and a fourth serves barbecue chicken and steak.

At Yavapai, you can mix and match from a variety of stations, picking up a piece of fried chicken from one, a slice of pizza from another, a dish of mashed potatoes from another. (A case of indigestion, when you put it all together.) For $2.25, you can also assemble your own dinner salad at the salad bar. When dining here, try the turkey potpie.

Tips Ice Cream at the Fountain

Adjacent Bright Angel Lodge along the footpath overlooking the South Rim, the Fountain offers a great break from the midday sun. Order a hand-dipped cone with Dreyer's ice cream and relax on the patio in front. Open daily 11:30am to 5:30pm, the Fountain sells other reasonably-priced snacks.

Compared with Maswik's food, Yavapai's fare tastes less institutional. If you're hungry for a burger, however, go to Maswik, where the meat is grilled instead of fried.

Located at Maswik and Yavapai lodges, respectively. © 928/638-2631. Reservations not accepted. Breakfast $2–$5.25; lunch and dinner $2.25–$7. AE, DC, DISC, MC, V. Maswik 6am–9pm daily; Yavapai 6am–10pm daily (may fluctuate seasonally). Closed in low season.

5 Where to Eat Inside the Canyon

Phantom Ranch 🐝🐝 AMERICAN   At the bottom of the Grand Canyon, pretty much anything tastes good, so it's hard to say whether the food at Phantom Ranch would taste as great on the rim as alongside Bright Angel Creek. Whether you arrive by mule or on foot, the food almost always tastes fine.

If you want dinner served your way, however, bring a camp stove. Every evening, just three options are offered: a steak dinner at 5pm, a vegetarian dinner at 5pm, and a hearty beef stew at 6:30pm. The vegetarian plate consists of lentil loaf and the side dishes to the steak dinner: vegetables, cornbread, baked potato, and salad. With either dinner, the dessert is chocolate cake.

The family style, all-you-can-eat breakfasts are also excellent, with heaping platters of eggs, bacon, and pancakes laid out on the long tables in the canteen. The only disappointment is the box lunch, whose meager offerings (bagel, summer sausage, juice, apple, peanuts, raisins, pretzels, and cookies) don't seem worth the $9 price. Pack your own lunch and, if necessary, supplement it with snacks from the canteen.

Because the number of meals is fixed, hikers and mule riders must reserve them ahead of time through Xanterra (see earlier in this chapter) or at the Bright Angel Transportation Desk. As a last resort, inquire upon arrival at Phantom Ranch to see whether any meals remain. Up until 4pm this can be done in the canteen itself. After 4pm, ask at the side window behind the canteen. Between 8am (8:30am in winter) and 4pm and from 8 to 10pm, anyone is allowed in the canteen, which sells snacks, soda, beer, wine, basic first-aid items, souvenirs, and film.

Inside the canyon .5 mile north of the Colorado River on the North Kaibab Trail. To reserve meals more than 1 day in advance, call © 888/297-2757; to reserve meals for the next day, contact the Bright Angel Transportation Desk at 928/638-2631, ext. 6015. Steak dinner $28; vegetarian meal $19; stew $19; sack lunch $9; breakfast $16. AE, DC, DISC, MC, V (for advance reservations: AE, DISC, MC, V only).

6 Where to Eat on the North Rim

Café on The Rim AMERICAN   The cafe serves the best pizza on the North Rim, or so the joke goes. That speaks well for the pizza, which could just as easily—and no less truthfully—be called the worst. At $2.75 a slice, it's an economical alternative to firing up the camp stove; though not an ethereal experience. The snack bar also serves calzones, burgers, salads, made-to-order sandwiches, and breakfasts. If all you desire is good coffee and a muffin, stop by the saloon, where an espresso bar operates daily from 5:30 to 10am. Its prices are high—a tall double mocha runs $4—but the java is the strongest in the park. The saloon continues to serve espresso, minus the pastries, after the bar opens at 11am.

In the west wing of Grand Canyon Lodge. 𝄐 **928/638-2611.** Reservations not accepted. Breakfast $1.85–$4.80; lunch and dinner $2.75–$7; 14-in. Hawaiian-style pizza $16.80. AE, DISC, MC, V. 7am–9pm daily.

Grand Canyon Lodge Dining Room 𝄐𝄐 CONTINENTAL Long banks of west- and south-facing windows afford views of Transept Canyon and help warm this room, where the high, open-framed ceiling absorbs the clamor of diners. This is, without question, one of the most scenic dining rooms anywhere.

At dinner, pesto lovers will enjoy the Pasta Lydia—fresh asparagus and potatoes tossed in pesto sauce with bow-tie pasta. Other excellent choices are the pan-seared Atlantic salmon topped with blueberry chardonnay sauce, and the Four Corners lime chicken—a sautéed chicken breast with artichokes and capers in white wine sauce. The restaurant also offers steaks, prime rib, and salmon, as well as a varied wine list.

The lunch menu consists of mostly burgers, sandwiches, and salads. The best choice is probably the turkey Reuben, served with fries or pasta salad. At breakfast, a full buffet costs under $9, but the most delectable choice may be the artichoke and asiago cheese omelet.

Tip: Because of the volume of diners, the staff here does not accept reservations for window seats. However, they can often accommodate people who are willing to wait (though it could take up to an hour).

At Grand Canyon Lodge. 𝄐 **928/638-2611,** ext. 160. Reservations required for dinner, not accepted for breakfast and lunch. Breakfast $2.50–$9; lunch $4.75–$9.50; dinner $14.25–$25. AE, DC, DISC, MC, V. 6:30–10am, 11:30am–2:30pm, and 4:45–9:30pm daily.

7

Gateway Towns

The Grand Canyon isn't the only wonder in northern Arizona. The surrounding area on the Colorado Plateau is among the most stunning in the world, a sparsely populated landscape of 12,000-foot-high volcanoes and 3,000-foot-deep red-rock canyons—linked by the largest ponderosa pine forest on the planet. Lonely highways lace the countryside, inviting exploration. During your travels, you can track California condors, or watch elk wander the forests. You can walk the same paths and stand in rooms used for centuries by America's indigenous peoples, then learn about the cultures of their modern descendants. You can chat with cowboys in Williams or venture to Flagstaff's cultural attractions, including the Lowell Observatory and the Museum of Northern Arizona. The many diversions won't detract from your trip to the canyon; they'll simply enhance your appreciation of this area, with the canyon at its heart.

1 Flagstaff ★★

150 miles N of Phoenix; 32 miles E of Williams; 78 miles S of Grand Canyon Village

Home to Northern Arizona University, the Museum of Northern Arizona, and the Hansen Planetarium, as well as dozens of excellent restaurants and clubs, Flagstaff lets you nurture your intellect, dine on gourmet food, and dance to live music without losing sight of the more important things—the 12,000-foot-high San Francisco Peaks, which rise just north of town. Its historic downtown, with its many shops and galleries, attracts a mix of students, locals, and tourists. Freight trains regularly clatter past, shaking cappuccinos and drowning out street musicians before continuing to points less desirable. Flanked by motels with colorful names such as the Pony Soldier, Geronimo, and El Pueblo, Route 66 parallels the tracks.

ESSENTIALS

GETTING THERE   By Car   Flagstaff is on I-40, one of the main east-west interstates in the United States. I-17 also starts here and heads south to Phoenix. U.S. 89A connects Flagstaff to Sedona by way of Oak Creek Canyon. U.S. 180 links Flagstaff with Grand Canyon Village, and U.S. 89 goes from Flagstaff to Page.

By Plane   Flagstaff's Pulliam Airport, which is located 3 miles south of town off I-17, is served by **America West Express** (📞 **800/ 235-9292**) from Phoenix.

By Train   Flagstaff is also served by **Amtrak** (📞 **800/872-7245** for reservations, or 928/774-8679 for station information only) from Chicago and Los Angeles. The train station is at 1 E. Rte. 66.

VISITOR INFORMATION   The **Flagstaff Visitor Center,** at 1 E. Rte. 66 (📞 **800/842-7293** or 928/774-9541; **www.flagstaffarizona. org**), is open daily from 7am to 7pm during summer season, 7am to 6pm in winter.

GETTING AROUND   Car rentals are available from **Avis** (📞 **888/897-8448** or 928/774-8421), **Budget** (📞 **800/763-2999** or 928/779-5255), **Enterprise** (📞 **800/736-8222** or 928/526-1377), **Hertz** (📞 **800/654-3131** or 928/774-4452), and **National** (📞 **800/227-7368** or 928/779-1975).

If you need a taxi, call **Friendly Cab** (📞 **928/774-4444** or 928-214-9000), or **Sun Taxi & Tours** (📞 **800/483-4488** or 928/774-7400).

Mountain Line (📞 **928/779-6624**) provides public bus transit around the city every day except Sunday. The fare is $1 for adults.

ORIENTATION   Downtown Flagstaff is located just north of I-40. Milton Road, which at its southern end becomes I-17 to Phoenix, passes Northern Arizona University on its way downtown where it merges with Route 66. Part of Route 66, Santa Fe Avenue, parallels the railroad tracks, linking the city's historic downtown with its east side. Downtown's main street is San Francisco Street, while Humphreys Street leads north out of town toward the San Francisco Peaks and the south rim of the Grand Canyon.

SUPERMARKETS & GENERAL STORES   If you want to stock up on food before you hit the road, here are several places to stop: **Albertson's,** 1416 E. Rte. 66 (📞 **928/773-7955**), open daily 6am to midnight; **Basha's,** 2700 Woodlands Village Blvd. (📞 **928/774-3882**), open daily 5am to 1am; **Basha's,** 1000 N. Humphreys St. (📞 **928/774-2101**), open daily 6am to 10pm; and **Fry's,** 201 N. Switzer Canyon Dr. (📞 **928/774-2719**), open daily 6am to midnight.

WHAT TO SEE & DO

Lowell Observatory ⭐⭐ *Kids*   Percival Lowell, an amateur astronomer, realized that Flagstaff's dry, thin air made the town a choice location for observing the heavens. Hoping to find life on

Flagstaff

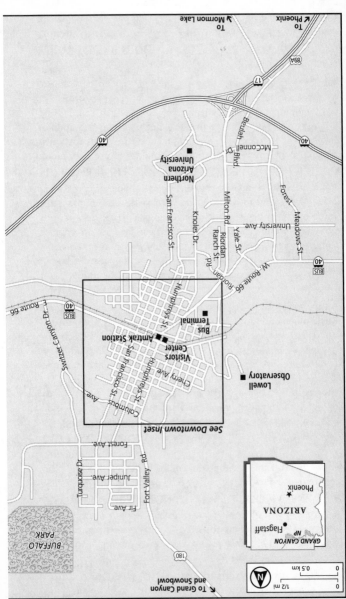

To Grand Canyon and Snowbowl ↖

To Phoenix ↗
To Mormon Lake ↖

BUFFALO PARK

Turquoise Dr.
Forest Ave.
Juniper Ave.
Fir Ave.
Fort Valley Rd.
180

Switzer Canyon Dr.
Columbus Ave.
San Francisco St.
Humphreys St.
Cherry Ave.
E. Route 66
BUS 40
BUS 40

See Downtown Inset

Visitors Center
Amtrak Station
Bus Terminal

Lowell Observatory

San Francisco St.
Knoles Dr.
Humphreys St.
Milton Rd.
Riordan Ranch St.
Riordan Rd.
Yale St.
W. Route 66
University Ave.
Forest Meadows St.
BUS 40

Northern Arizona University

McConnell Dr.
Beulah

40
40
40
17
89A

ARIZONA
Phoenix ★
Flagstaff ●
GRAND CANYON NP

N

0   1/2 mi
0   0.5 km

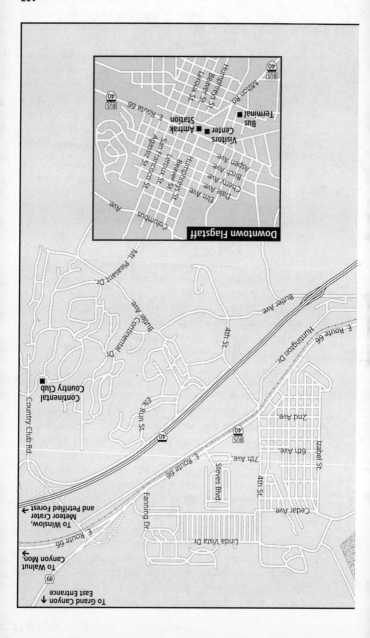

Downtown Flagstaff

Mars, the Boston aristocrat built an observatory atop a hill here in 1894, then used it to study the skies for the next 22 years. Though he never found life on Mars, the research done at his observatory has contributed greatly to our knowledge of the heavens. In the past century, Lowell Observatory discovered Pluto and helped map out the moon and provide evidence of an expanding universe.

Today, in addition to conducting research, the observatory's 22 PhD-level astronomers educate and entertain the public. It's most fun to come here on clear nights, when they'll help you peer through telescopes at stars far across the galaxy. (Call for a schedule of nighttime programs.) During daytime, tours of the observatory and historic rotunda library are offered. And, the Steele Visitor Center has exciting, state-of-the-art interactive displays, suitable for both adults and kids. They make a trip here worthwhile, any time.

1400 W. Mars Hill Rd., Flagstaff. ✆ 928/774-3358. www.lowell.edu. Admission $4 adults, $3.50 seniors and students, $2 ages 5–17, free for children 4 and under. AE, MC, V. Visitor center open 9am–5pm daily Apr–Oct; noon–5pm daily Nov–Mar. Nighttime hours vary (call for specific program information).

Museum of Northern Arizona 🌟🌟🌟 Founded in 1928 by a Flagstaff couple concerned about the widespread removal of artifacts from the area, this museum explores the history, science, and cultures of the Colorado Plateau. Its **Geology Room** has displays on the unique landforms in the area, and the **Special Exhibits Gallery** frequently shows art from the region. But the best attraction here—one of the best anywhere—is the display of Native American artifacts, culled from the museum's five-million-piece collection. Always beautiful and occasionally moving, they are arranged in a context that illuminates the history and spirit of the Native American people.

3101 N. Fort Valley Rd. (U.S. Hwy 180), Flagstaff. ✆ 928/774-5213. www.musnaz. org. Admission $5 adults, $4 seniors, $3 students with ID, $2 children ages 7–17, free for children 6 and under. AE, DISC, MC, V. Daily 9am–5pm.

Sunset Crater Volcano National Monument 🌟 Sunset Crater is one of the best preserved cinder cone volcanoes in the world. It was formed in 1064 atop a weak spot in the earth's crust. An underground gas chamber exploded, spewing tons of cinders around the newly created vent in the earth. Within a few months of the explosion, cinders had piled up to form a 1,000-foot-tall pyramid-shaped crater. Lava poured intermittently from openings near the bottom of the crater for the next 200 years, snaking across the land before ossifying in choppy mounds that to this day look viscous. In one final flourish of activity, small eruptions deposited red and yellow ash atop the otherwise black cone.

Bus Tours to the Canyon

Open Road Tours (© 800/766-7117, www.openroadtours.com) offers bus service linking Flagstaff with Grand Canyon National Park, including 1-day guided canyon tours that depart from Flagstaff at 9:30am and return by 5:30pm. The cost is $69 for adults; $35 for 11 and under. Other companies offering tours from Flagstaff to the Grand Canyon include **American Dream Tours** (© 888/203-1212,) and S.T.A.R. Tours (© 888/920-0237), both of which include the park entrance fee and lunch for $75.

The activity produced a landscape of eerie shapes and striking, subtle colors. During an expedition in the late 1800s, the explorer John Wesley Powell saw this colorful cone, perhaps in the low light in which it is most striking, and named it Sunset Crater. Today, the national monument has a picnic area, visitor center, and several walking trails. Try visiting here in early morning or late afternoon, when the colors are richest. The park stays open until dusk.

15 miles north of Flagstaff on Hwy. 89. © 928/526-0502. www.nps.gov/sucr. Admission $5 adults, free for children under 16. Fee also covers entrance to Wupatki National Monument. Cash or National Park passes only, at entrance gate. Summer 8am–6pm daily; spring and fall 8am–5pm daily; winter 9am–5pm daily.

Walnut Canyon National Monument ⭐⭐ The Sinagua (a subgroup of the Ancestral Puebloans) occupied this wooded canyon for roughly 125 years from 1125 to 1250. They built hundreds of dwellings under natural rock overhangs on sunny east- and south-facing cliffs, and tucked granaries into the smallest openings. Atop the canyon rims, they dug out terraces and check dams that would help keep their crops moist, and erected pit houses and pueblo-style dwellings.

Although most of the terraces and check dams have collapsed, 300 rooms remain. Twenty-five are on the **Island Trail,** a 1-mile-long loop that descends 185 feet (with over 100 steps) below the visitor center. Many others are visible from the trail, on the canyon walls. Another, relatively flat .7-mile trail travels along the rim of the canyon, affording views of the cliff dwellings in addition to skirting the rim-top ruins.

This is a lovely canyon and, with just 125,000 visitors annually, one of the quietest national monuments. By coming off-hours, you can sometimes find yourself alone here, and that's a great way to experience the world of the Ancestral Puebloans.

Tips **Planning Tip**

Using Flagstaff as a home base, one can easily visit Walnut Canyon, Sunset Crater, and Wupatki monuments in a full, rewarding day.

---

10 miles east of Flagstaff off I-40 (exit 204). © **928/526-3367**. www.nps.gov/waca/. Admission $5 adults, free for children under 17. Cash only at entrance gate. Summer 8am–6pm daily; spring and fall 8am–5pm daily; winter 8am–5pm daily.

Wupatki National Monument As their population grew in the 1100s, a large number of the Sinagua, Cohonna, and Kayonta Anasazi people moved onto the land north of Sunset Crater. Today, 800 ruins from this period are scattered across Wupatki National Monument. Some of the most remarkable are near the visitor center, including a mysterious ball court with walls 6 feet high, and pueblo ruins made from the same Moenkopi Sandstone atop which they're built. A blowhole, which releases air from underground caverns, may have had a special significance to the Native Americans who settled nearby. Other ruins are scattered along the road that loops through the monument, usually in elevated spots with expansive views of both the Painted Desert and San Francisco Peaks. Most of the Sinagua left in the 1200s and are believed to have become the modern-day Hopi (and perhaps Zuni).

35 miles north of Flagstaff on Hwy. 89. © **928/679-2365**. www.nps.gov/wupa/. Admission $5 adults, free for children under 16. Fee also good for Sunset Crater Volcano National Monument. Cash only at entrance gate. Visitor center June 1–Sept 30 8am–6pm daily; Oct 1–May 31 8am–5pm daily.

WHERE TO STAY
EXPENSIVE TO MODERATE

A recommended, expensive chain hotel in Flagstaff is **Radisson Woodlands Hotel Flagstaff** (© 928/773-8888), 1175 W. Rte. 66, which underwent a recent renovation. A recommended, mid-price chain hotel in Flagstaff is the **Holiday Inn Flagstaff** (© 928/714-1000), 2320 E. Lucky Lane (off I-40 Exit 198). In addition, a recommended B&B in Flagstaff is **Jeanette's Bed and Breakfast** (© 800/752-1912 or 928/527-1912), 3380 E. Lockett Rd.; double $115 to $145.

Comfi Cottages *Kids* In the 1970s Pat Wiebe, a nurse at the local hospital, began purchasing and renovating small homes in Flagstaff. Today, she rents out six of these quaint cottages, all but one of which were built in the 1920s and 1930s. Wiebe has modernized the cottages somewhat, adding thermostat-controlled fireplaces, televisions, VCRs, and washer/dryers. And, she goes out of her way to make them comfortable. In every unit you'll find fresh-cut flowers, antiques, cupboards stocked with breakfast foods, and rag dolls from her personal collection. Outside of each cottage is a picnic table and gas grill, and most have bicycles and sleds in the garage. These cottages, which sleep from two to six people, can make you feel as if you've acquired a new home, where kids are welcome. There's also a lovely new property at 710 W. Birch, with upstairs and downstairs units resembling contemporary town homes. Like most of the others, these are just a short walk from the historic business district.

1612 N. Aztec St., Flagstaff, AZ 86001. © **888/774-0731** or 928/774-0731. Fax 928/773-7286. www.comficottages.com. 8 cottages in different locations in Flagstaff. $120–$260 double. Extra $10 per person, per night, if more than 2 people. Rates include breakfast. DISC, MC, V. Inquire about pets. **Amenities:** Free use of bicycles. *In room:* A/C (in 4 cottages only), TV, kitchen, fridge stocked with breakfast foods, coffeemaker, iron, washer/dryer, gas barbeque, sleds.

The Inn At 410 Bed & Breakfast ★★★ *Finds*   Peering into each of the nine guest rooms at The Inn At 410 is like flipping the pages in an issue of *House and Garden.* Each expertly decorated room is daringly different, yet tasteful. Collectively, they make this 1894 home owned by Sally and Howard Krueger one of the most stunning B&Bs anywhere. One room, "Monet's Garden," is reminiscent of a French country garden. Sections of its walls have been painted to resemble broken plaster (far more appealing than the real thing, found in some Rte. 66 motels), while other areas have reproductions of Monet works brushed upon them. My favorite, "The Conservatory," celebrates classical music. It has an elegant sitting room with a fireplace and French sitting chairs; in the corner stands a violin and music stand. The walls are decorated with music sheet wallpaper and prints of the masters, and up a few stairs from the four-post bed lies a beautifully-appointed bathroom. All but one of the guest rooms here has a gas fireplace, and three of them have jetted tubs.

The gourmet Southwestern breakfast, served at your table, includes juice, fresh fruit, a homemade pastry, and a non-meat entree. Everything is baked from scratch, and the owner has even published a cookbook.

410 N. Leroux St., Flagstaff, AZ 86001. © **800/774-2008** or 928/774-0088. Fax 928/774-6354. www.inn410.com. 9 units. $145–$205 double. MC, V. *In room:* A/C, fridge, coffeemaker, hair dryer, no phone.

Little America Hotel ✦✦ *Value* Strangely enough, the best-regarded chain-hotel accommodations in Flagstaff adjoin a truck stop. Little America's rooms are enormous—they have sitting areas, dressing areas, dining tables, and oversized tubs. They're lavishly decorated in French Colonial style (think Versailles). And they're quiet—especially the ones farthest from I-40. On the downside, some of the rooms are aging and could stand for a bit of remodeling.

An even better surprise is the surroundings: 500 largely wooded acres, owned by the hotel, providing access to Flagstaff's urban trail system and, farther out, the Arizona Trail. From Thanksgiving through January, a million holiday lights sparkle on the forest trees. Closer to the rooms, there's a large outdoor pool, sand volleyball courts, horseshoe pits, and a 2-mile jogging trail. And if, by chance, you need 60 gallons of diesel, a mesh baseball cap with an enormous forehead, or coffee in an imposing Styrofoam cup, you won't have to go far. It's almost weird.

2515 E. Butler (off I-40 Exit 198), Flagstaff, AZ. ✆ **800/352-4386** or 928/779-7900. Fax 928/779-7983. www.flagstaff.littleamerica.com. 247 units, 8 specialty suites. Jan 1–Mar 8 $79–$89 double; Mar 9–Apr 30 and Nov 1–Dec 24 $89–$99 double; May 1–Oct 31 and Dec 25–31 $119–$129 double. AE, DC, DISC, MC, V. **Amenities:** 3 restaurants (deli, coffee shop, and fine dining); lounge; outdoor pool; exercise room; outdoor Jacuzzi; concierge; business center; gift shop; room service (6am–11pm); massage; coin-op washers/dryers; playground. *In room:* A/C, TV w/pay movies, dataport, fridge, coffeemaker, hair dryer, iron.

INEXPENSIVE

A recommended, inexpensive chain motel in Flagstaff is **Super 8 Motel** (✆ **888/324-9131** or 928/526-0818; fax 928/526-8786), 3725 N. Kasper Ave. (on Rte. 66, 1 mile west of I-40 Exit 201).

Hotel Weatherford *Value* Constructed in 1898, this hotel in downtown Flagstaff holds some fascinating common areas. An upstairs sitting room features quirky antiques such as a cider press and antique sewing machine, as well as panoramic photos of turn-of-the-20th-century Flagstaff. The Zane Grey Room, on the hotel's third floor, has a hand-carved Brunswick bar next to a fireplace and across from an original painting by the legendary 19th-century landscape artist Thomas Moran. Patrons of the Zane Grey Room can also enjoy the new wraparound balcony, overlooking the downtown streets.

The guest rooms, five of which have private bathrooms, are varied and eccentric. My favorite, no. 57, has hardwood floors, an Art Deco style bedroom set, and three 10-foot-high windows that date to its days as the hotel's sun parlor. A transom opens onto the hallway, helping create a draft. That said, the rooms are bare-bones: no TVs, no phones, and no amenities but a bedroom set and a heater. The main advantage to this hotel is its lively atmosphere. However, this can also become a drawback when loud partyers walk from the downstairs bar, where live music plays most nights, to the Zane Grey Room, which is situated just a few yards from some of the guest rooms. If you're planning to stay here, rest up plenty in advance and then join the party, starting with a meal at the hotel's restaurant, Charly's. For the least noise, get a room (like no. 57) at the end of the building farthest from the Zane Grey Room.

23 N. Leroux, Flagstaff, AZ 86001. (C) **928/779-1919.** Fax 928/773-8951. www. weatherfordhotel.com. 8 units, 3 with shared bathrooms. High-season $45–$70 double; low-season $35–$45 double. AE, DC, DISC, MC, V. Parking behind the hotel. **Amenities:** Restaurant (Southwestern/American); 3 delightful bars.

WHERE TO EAT
EXPENSIVE

Black Bart's Steak House, Saloon, and Musical Revue ✦ (Kids) AMERICAN   Initially I was less than enthralled by the prospect of dining at a steakhouse and musical revue named for a legendary robber. Past experience had convinced me that people who sing near steaks sing badly, and that people who cook near singers cook badly, and that people who run steakhouses offering bad singing and bad cooking were themselves legendary robbers. But this restaurant surprised me. First, the music is nicely performed by music students from Northern Arizona University. They capably croon country, blues, and cabaret songs, then hurry back to the tables they're serving. Even more surprising is the fact that the food—an assortment of hand-cut steaks and prime rib, salmon, grilled tuna, and ribs— can be pretty tasty (vegetarian dishes are available, too). The highlight is the all-you-can-eat sourdough biscuits with honey butter, served with every meal.

2760 E. Butler Ave., Flagstaff. (C) **928/779-3142.** Reservations accepted. Dinner $12–$26. AE, DC, DISC, MC, V. Daily 5–9pm.

Cottage Place ✦✦✦ (Moments) COUNTRY FRENCH   The quiet serenity of Flagstaff's most elegant restaurant is ideal for special occasions, a wonderful spot to peacefully celebrate your vacation to the Southwest. Original artwork decorates three rose-colored rooms, where soft conversations are heard from the candlelit tables. Chateaubriand (for two) is Executive Chef/Owner Frank Branham's signature dish, served with fresh vegetables, garlic Duchess potatoes, and tomato Provençal. Both the rack of lamb—seared on an open-flame broiler and accompanied by a port wine demi-glacé and

English mint sauce—and the *tornadoes gorgonzola*—choice medallions of beef tenderloin pan-seared, flavored with Gorgonzola and blue cheese—are equally recommended. All entrees are served with soup du jour, green salad, and fresh breads. The Caesar salad, which I also loved, is prepared table-side. A number of fish and seafood selections accompany the meat choices. For dessert, I recommend the delicious crêpes suzette. Service is refined, and the restaurant's impressive selection of wines has earned Wine Spectator's *Award of Excellence* most years over the past decade. A six-course tasting menu is offered Thursday through Saturday with or without matching wines.

126 W. Cottage Ave., Flagstaff. ℂ 928/774-8431. Reservations recommended. Dinner $20–$28; chateaubriand for 2 $60. AE, MC, V. Tues–Sun 5–9:30pm.

Josephine ⟨⟨ AMERICAN   This modern American bistro opened in 2002 in the historic Milton Clark house, previously home to Chez Marc restaurant. The bungalow-style building was the first constructed in Flagstaff (1911) using indigenous malpais rock. A large stone hearth forms the centerpiece of the main dining room and bar, with smaller rooms adjacent. The simple, creative menu offers dishes ranging from marinated lamb meat loaf to cilantro pesto halibut or grilled vegetables with couscous. At lunch, an uncommon but recommended choice is the Lebanese hummus and baba ghanouj platter, served with warm pita bread and a Mediterranean salad. Josephine's also serves a small selection of pizzas and calzones, washed down with a delicious glass of fresh lemonade. This is a great place to meet friends, and service is friendly and informal.

503 N. Humphreys, Flagstaff. ℂ **928/779-3400.** Reservations accepted. Lunch $7.25–$8.75; dinner entrees $14.50–$18.50. AE, DISC, MC, V. Mon–Sat 11am–2:30pm and 5:30–9pm. Closed Sun.

MODERATE

Brewer Street Brewery ⟨⟨ AMERICAN   This upscale whistle stop cafe became the first microbrewery in Flagstaff. Pot-belly stoves and railroad artwork decorate the high-spirited dining room, with an open-view kitchen and popular bar attached. For an appetizer, try one of the cheese fondues or pizza chips, sprinkled with Parmesan, Romano, mozzarella, and a dash of garlic. Pub-style platters include bratwurst sausages, crunchy Cajun catfish, a number of sandwiches, and wood-fired pizzas: The Enchanted Forest is smothered with portobello mushrooms, fresh spinach, roasted bell peppers, and French brie on an artichoke olive pesto base topped with walnuts, ground black pepper, Parmesan, and basil. It doesn't make a whole lot of sense to come here without trying one of the fresh brews, as well! Among the best are raspberry ale, Indian pale ale, and Railhead red ale (the most popular brew among locals).

11 S. Beaver St., Flagstaff. © **928/779-0079.** Lunch and dinner items $7.50–$9.25. AE, DISC, MC, V. Sun–Thurs 11:30am–11pm; Fri–Sat 11:30am–midnight.

Charly's 𝒦 SOUTHWESTERN/AMERICAN   Charly's is spacious and cool, both inside, where the 12-foot-high ceilings of the Hotel Weatherford (built in 1897) provide breathing room, and on the sidewalk, a favorite place for summertime dining. Besides steaks, fish, and burgers, the restaurant offers a number of vegetarian dishes that make for welcome light dining. Try the Durango Tacos—soft tacos with avocado, cilantro, and onions, filled with your choice of beef, chicken, fish, or grilled vegetables. After dinner, you can dance at the hotel bar, which features live entertainment nightly and has 20 beers on tap. Choose Charly's more for the entertainment than for the food, which is decent but not stellar.

In the historic Hotel Weatherford, 23 N. Leroux, Flagstaff. © **928/779-1919.** Reservations accepted. Lunch $5.75–$9.95; dinner entrees $7.95–$18.95. AE, DC, DISC, MC, V. Daily 11am–11pm (10pm in winter).

Monsoon on the Rim 𝒦𝒦 NEW ASIAN   Having moved to the center of town in 2002, Monsoon captured not just the city's dinner crowd, but much of the out-on-the-towners, as well. A sharp-looking waitstaff, dressed in black, dashes through the dining room faster than people in northern Arizona have heretofore been known to move. The food, which fuses Chinese, Japanese, Korean, and Pacific Island fare, has generated a buzz around town. Highlights include scallops on crispy spinach, and Thai spicy shrimp with green beans in brown sauce. Monsoon also serves as a sushi bar, martini bar, and Asian cafe. Come evening, this is wonderful place to start off with a drink (the martini bar stays open until 11pm weekdays, 1am weekends). A number of college bars are located along the same block.

6 E. Aspen, North corner of Leroux and Aspen, Flagstaff. © **928/226-8844.** Reservations accepted. Main courses $7.95–$12.95. AE, MC, V. Mon–Wed 11am–9pm; Thurs–Sat 11am–10pm.

INEXPENSIVE

The Black Bean Burrito Bar and Salsa Company 𝒦 *(Value* MEXICAN   The best burritos seem to turn up in the plainest environments. At the Black Bean, you'll eat out of plastic drive-in baskets while sitting at a counter that opens onto a pedestrian walkway. Sure enough, the burritos, which come with a choice of six different salsas, are delicious. A favorite among Northern Arizona University students, the Black Bean offers seven house specialty wraps (steamed or stir-fried food wrapped in tortillas), including exotic flavors such as Thai peanut tofu and roasted jalapeño chicken, as well as traditional bean, chicken, and steak burritos. Wrapped in aluminum foil, the burritos have the heft of hand weights. But with most under $5, they won't burden you financially.

12 E. Rte. 66, Gateway Plaza Suite 104, Flagstaff. *C* 928/779-9905. Reservations not accepted. $1.50–$5. MC, V. Summer Sun noon–8pm, Mon–Sat 11am–9pm; call for winter hours.

Cafe Espress *☆☆* NEW AMERICAN Like Macy's (see review in this section), Cafe Espress serves great vegetarian fare and displays paintings by local artists. But if the two restaurants were pastries, Macy's would be a nut bran muffin, while Cafe Espress would be a croissant. With hardwood floors and 12-foot ceilings, the interior of Cafe Espress seems brighter than Macy's, and its furniture, unlike the furnishings at Macy's, doesn't resemble something from a Rathskeller. Cafe Espress's food is slightly more refined, in terms of both preparation and ingredients. It may not be as healthful as the food at Macy's, but it sure tastes good (though service is sometimes slow). The breakfast fare includes delicious omelettes, huevos rancheros, and pancakes, with tofu available as a substitute for eggs. The lunch and dinner menu is a hodgepodge of soups, sandwiches, salads, and Southwestern fare. The most delectable items, however, are house specials like the ratatouille and veggie kabobs. Don't forget to order a slice of cheesecake or carrot cake, as the desserts here are among the best in town.

16 N. San Francisco St., Flagstaff. *C* 928/774-0541. Reservations accepted. Breakfast and lunch $2.75–$7.95; dinner entrees $7.95–$13.95. MC, V. Daily 7am–9pm.

Macy's European Coffee House Bakery & Vegetarian Restaurante *☆* *(Finds* VEGETARIAN/BAKED GOODS A refreshing breeze always seems to blow through this restaurant, skimming the dust off the elaborately drawn menus on the chalkboards and stirring aromas of patchouli, spices, and coffee. Macy's may not be able to save the world, but its fine vegetarian food, fresh pastries, and great coffee encourage people to slow down and smell the latte. It's a place where vegans are welcomed, where bikes lean against the building, and where the staff will (literally) carry your meal across a busy street for you. A cashier here earnestly told me that she loves everything on the menu. In addition to the standard menu items such as tempeh tuna and "tofurkey" (tofu made to taste like, but not too much like, turkey) sandwiches, Macy's serves daily specials, including a pasta of the day. Live music is featured nightly except Mondays, which is chess night.

14 S. Beaver St., Flagstaff. © **928/774-2243**. Fax 928/774-4242. Reservations not accepted. Main courses $3–$8. No credit cards. Sun–Thurs 6am–8pm; Fri–Sat 6am–10pm.

2 Tusayan ✦

1 mile S of Grand Canyon National Park; 60 miles N of Williams; 80 miles NE of Flagstaff; 340 miles N of Tucson

More a tourist outpost than a town, Tusayan has almost no houses. Most residents live in apartments or trailers behind the town's businesses. Employers pay a lot to house (or lure) workers, and to convince suppliers to lug their goods 60 miles off the interstate. So Tusayan isn't cheap. A cup of coffee costs about $1.50, and rooms generally go for about $20 more than in Williams or Flagstaff. Although most of the accommodations here are pleasant, the food is often bland, and the service can be unpredictable. Still, Tusayan's location makes it the next best thing to being inside the park.

ESSENTIALS

GETTING THERE   By Car   If you drive, make sure and fill your gas tank before setting out for Tusayan and the Grand Canyon; there's only one service station between Tusayan and Flagstaff, the nearest major city, which is almost 80 miles away. From Flagstaff, it's possible to take U.S. 180 and 64 directly to Tusayan.

By Plane   Grand Canyon National Park Airport in Tusayan is served by two airlines flying out of Las Vegas: **Air Vegas** (© **800/ 255-7474** or 702/736-3599), which charges $200 round-trip; and **Scenic Airlines** (© **800/634-6801** or 702/638-3300), which charges $227 round-trip.

Other than these options, you'll have to fly into Phoenix, Las Vegas, or Flagstaff and then arrange ground transportation to Tusayan and the national park.

GETTING AROUND   By Car   The nearest available rental cars are in Flagstaff. There's one **service station** in Tusayan and another at Desert View inside the park's east entrance (this station is seasonal). Be forewarned that gas at these stations costs about 25¢ more per gallon than in Flagstaff, downtown Williams (away from I-40) or Cameron, so make sure to top off in those places.

By Taxi **Xanterra/Fred Harvey** offers 24-hour **taxi service** to and from the airport, trailheads, and other destinations inside the park (✆ **928/638-2631**). **Grand Canyon Coaches** (✆ **928/638-0821**) offers year-round taxi service around Tusayan and into the park.

A SUPERMARKET **Tusayan General Store** is located 1 mile south of the park entrance on Highway 180/64 (✆ **928/638-2854**). It's open daily 7:30am to 9:30pm in summer, and 8am to 8pm during the slower times of the year. Or, try the larger **Canyon Village Marketplace** inside the park's business district.

WHAT TO SEE & DO

Grand Canyon IMAX Theater 🐾🐾 *(Kids)* If you quibble over facts, you'll detect flaws in the 34-minute IMAX presentation, *Grand Canyon—the Hidden Secrets,* which has been showing hourly in Tusayan since 1984. For example, it shows the ill-fated members of General Powell's crew leaving the expedition by going down a side drainage that is clearly *not* Separation Canyon. But if you concentrate on the big picture—and the picture here is very, very big—you'll love the IMAX. Every inch of the six-story-high, 82-foot-wide screen is taken up by stunning footage of the canyon. Among the highlights: whitewater rafting that makes you feel as if you might drown, insects blown up to the size of buildings, and aerial footage from inside some of the canyon's rock narrows.

Located on Hwy. 64 in Tusayan, 1.5 miles south of the park's south entrance. ✆ **928/638-2203**. www.grandcanyonimaxtheater.com. $10 adults, $7 ages 3–11, free for children under 3. Mar–Oct daily 8:30am–8:30pm; Nov–Feb daily 10:30am–6:30pm. Showings at half past the hour every hour.

WHERE TO STAY
EXPENSIVE

Best Western Grand Canyon Squire Inn 🐾🐾 There's a lot to do at this hotel, which prides itself on being the only full-service resort at Grand Canyon. You can play tennis, get a haircut, or pause to consider the three-story-high mural and waterfall in the lobby. The kids will love the family recreation center, which features a six-lane bowling alley and video games. Adults may gravitate to the Saguaro Food & Spirits Sports Bar, the most popular watering hole in Tusayan.

Costing $15 to $25 extra, the deluxe rooms are nearly spacious enough to justify their extra phones—found in the bathrooms, next to the oversized tubs. Thick-walled and quiet, they're among the most comfortable in town. The standard rooms, in two older buildings left from the Squire Motor Inn (1972), are no larger than the rooms at the other area motels, but they do offer amenities such as hair dryers and coffeemakers. And with so much activity at this inn, you probably won't spend as much time in them as you might elsewhere.

P.O. Box 130 (1.5 miles south of the park on Hwy. 64), Grand Canyon, AZ 86023. *(C)* 800/622-6966 or 928/638-2681. Fax 928/638-2782. . 250 units. Jan 1–Mar 31 $65–$135 double; Apr 1–Oct 31 $105–$185 double; Nov 1–Dec 22 $65–$135 double; Dec 23–Dec 31 $105–$185 double. AE, DC, DISC, MC, V. **Amenities:** 2 restaurants (coffee shop and dining room); 2 bars (lounge and sports bar); tennis courts; exercise room; Jacuzzi; bike rental; concierge/tour desk; coin-op washer/dryer; executive level rooms. *In room:* A/C, TV, dataport, fridge, coffeemaker, hair dryer, iron.

Grand Canyon Quality Inn and Suites 🌟🌟

In summer, guests here sun themselves around the large outdoor swimming pool and hot tub. In winter, they head for the hotel's atrium, where tropical plants and palm trees shade an 18-foot-long spa with a waterfall. As the area's hot tubs go, this one is the grandest, with jets to massage every aching joint. When the guests finally finish soaking, they find themselves occupying some of the most pleasant accommodations in town, including a number of rooms with private decks and refrigerators. A few rooms bordering the atrium have only tiny windows to the outside (and larger ones facing the atrium). Ask for a room with a large exterior window if dark rooms bother you.

Open from 7am to 9pm daily, the family style restaurant offers three buffets, which are popular with tour groups, as well as menu selections. The Wintergarten lounge, open only during high season, is situated in the pleasant confines of the hotel's atrium.

P.O. Box 520 (on Hwy. 64, 1 mile south of the park entrance, next to the IMAX Theater), Grand Canyon, AZ 86023. *(C)* 800/221-2222 (reservations only) or 928/638-2673. Fax 928/638-9537. www.grandcanyonqualityinn.com. 232 units, 56 suites. Apr 1–Oct 20 $118 double; Oct 21–Mar 31 $78 double. AE, DC, DISC, MC, V. **Amenities:** Restaurant; lounge (seasonal); outdoor pool; 2 Jacuzzis. *In room:* A/C, TV, minibar (60 rooms), fridge (suites only), coffeemaker, hair dryer, iron.

Grand Hotel 🌟🌟

This newest hotel in Tusayan is also its most stylish. Modeled after a lodge of the old West, the hotel's lobby features an enormous fireplace, hand-woven carpets, and hand-oiled, hand-painted goatskin lanterns. Imitation ponderosa pine logs rise from the stone-tile floors to the high ceiling. The rooms are also pleasant, though perhaps not large enough to justify the high price charged for them. The choicest ones are the third-story rooms that have balconies facing away from the highway.

The **Canyon Star Restaurant,** specializing in mesquite smoked barbecue and Southwestern cuisine, serves three meals daily and has nightly entertainment in summer. (See review in this chapter.)

Among Tusayan's upscale bars, the most appealing by far is the **Canyon Star Saloon.** Below its stamped copper ceiling, patrons belly up to the bar; one of the stools is an old saddle. Note that the hotel will pack box lunches ($9) for guests.

P.O. Box 331 (on Hwy. 64, 1.5 miles south of the park entrance), Grand Canyon, AZ 86023. *©* **888/634-7263** or 928/638-3333. Fax 928/638-3131. www.visitgrand canyon.com. 121 units. High-season $139 standard, $148 balcony; low-season $80 standard, $89 balcony. AE, DISC, MC, V. **Amenities:** Restaurant (Regional); bar; indoor pool; Jacuzzi. *In room:* A/C, TV, dataport, coffeemaker, hair dryer, iron.

MODERATE

A mid-priced chain hotel in Tusayan is **Grand Canyon Rodeway Inn Red Feather Lodge** (*©* **800/538-2345** or 928/638-2414), on Highway 64, 1 mile south of the park. Next door, you will find a **Holiday Inn Express** (*©* **888/473-2269** or 928/638-3000).

INEXPENSIVE

Grand Canyon Inn *(Value* Travelers can sometimes save $30 on a room simply by driving 23 miles south from Tusayan to this family run motel in Vallé, at the dusty crossroads of highways 180 and 64. Ironically, standard rooms cost the same as deluxe rooms, perhaps because the standard units are as large and pleasant as the slightly newer deluxe ones. Their entrances open onto the parking lot instead of a hallway. Located inside a '50s-era motel across Highway 64 from the main inn, the motel's budget rooms are cheaper still, but they're nowhere near as desirable and cannot be booked ahead. If you're looking for a variety of activities outside the motel, keep driving to Williams or Flagstaff.

P.O. Box 755 (in Vallé, at the junction of hwys. 180 and 64), Williams, AZ 86046. *©* **800/635-9203** or 928/635-9203. Fax 928/635-2345. Aug 1–Oct 31 $44–$89 double; Nov 1–Apr 30 $49–$69 double; May 1–Jul 31 $44–$79 double. AE, DISC, MC, V. **Amenities:** Restaurant; outdoor pool. *In room:* A/C, TV, dataport (deluxe rooms only).

7-Mile Lodge *(Value* Instead of taking reservations, the owners of this motel start selling spaces at around 9am and usually sell out by early afternoon. If you need a reasonably priced place to stay, think about stopping here on your way into the park. Don't be put off by the motel's cramped office—surprisingly, the rooms are quite pleasant and large enough to hold two queen beds. Built in 1984, they have 2-inch doors and walls thick enough to muffle the noise of planes from the nearby airport.

P.O. Box 56 (1.5 miles south of park entrance on Hwy. 64), Grand Canyon, AZ 86023. *©* **928/638-2291.** Reservations not accepted. 20 units. High-season $80 double; low-season $48 double. AE, DISC, MC, V. *In room:* A/C, TV, coffeemaker, no phone.

WHERE TO EAT

Cafe Tusayan AMERICAN/SOUTHWESTERN   Since opening Cafe Tusayan in spring 1999 in a space formerly occupied by
Denny's, the restaurant's owners have wisely kept the menu small.
They serve a few varieties of salads; appetizers such as jalapeño pop-
pers and sautéed mushrooms; and a half dozen entrees, including
salmon with herb butter, baked chicken, and stroganoff. Perhaps
because the chefs are able to focus on just a few dishes, the food is
some of the best in Tusayan. However, the servers tend to lose their
focus when busy, and the decor screams "chain restaurant."

Located next to the Rodeway Inn (1.5 miles south of the park on Hwy. 64), Tusayan.
© 928/638-2151. Reservations not accepted. Breakfast $3.75–$9.25; lunch
$5.95–$9.95; dinner $8.95–$17. MC, V. 7am–9pm daily during high-season; hours
vary during low-season.

Canyon Star Restaurant REGIONAL   The entertainment at
this sprawling restaurant seems designed to give foreign tourists
exactly what they hope to find in the American West. Most nights,
a lonesome cowboy balladeer and spiritual Native American dancers
take turns performing for the visitors. In case anyone gets bored
with the show, video clips of the canyon play constantly on moni-
tors above the dance floor. The distractions—especially the dances,
which can be captivating—are more than enough to make a person
forget the food, even the mesquite smoked barbecue.

In the Grand Hotel on Hwy. 64 (1.5 miles from the park's south entrance), Tusayan.
© 888/634-7263 or 928/638-3333. Reservations not accepted. Breakfast
$4.50–$8.95; lunch $3.95–$11; dinner entrees $12.95–$22.95. AE, DISC, MC, V.
Daily 7:30–10am, 11am–2pm, and 5–9pm.

Coronado Dining Room ⚜ CONTINENTAL   My last meal at
the Coronado Room felt like a guest appearance in the '70s TV
series "Fantasy Island." The nattily attired waiters, combined with
the high-backed wooden chairs and the dimly lighted metal chandeliers, made the room seem far more formal than other Tusayan
eateries. The busboy kept my water full all night, and used tongs to
plop a lemon wedge in my glass (but only after asking permission).
And the staff seemed to never stop watching. There were other nice
touches: tiny tabletop lamps; ample room between tables; and
moist, delicious dark bread.

This restaurant serves tasty steaks, chicken, and seafood, with a
few southwestern dishes thrown in. The most delicious entree may
be the elk tournedos served with sweet red wine demi-glacé. The
tasty food and attentive service together make this the best restaurant in Tusayan. The adjoining, family oriented Canyon Room

offers breakfast and lunch year-round and serves a dinner buffet for $15 during high season.

In the Best Western Grand Canyon Squire Inn (1.5 miles south of the park on Hwy. 64), Tusayan. ℰ **928/638-2681**, ext. 4419. Reservations accepted. Entrees $14–$25. AE, DC, DISC, MC, V. Daily 5–10pm.

We Cook Pizza and Pasta *Kids* ITALIAN   In this restaurant's lengthy name, the owners neglected to mention how much they charge. Prices here are high, even by Grand Canyon standards, especially for a place without table service. A large four-item pizza runs $22, and pasta dishes range in cost from $10 to $14. After paying dearly for your food, you'll have to sit at one of the long picnic tables and wait for your number to be called.

Since you can't reserve tables here, the only way to shorten your wait is by ordering your pizza by telephone ahead of time. At least the food, when it comes, is palatable. Pasta dishes such as the spicy shrimp linguine and the Cajun chicken fettuccini taste especially delicious to people who are salt-deprived, and the pizza pleases most diners, including locals. There are some lunch specials available from 11am to 4pm.

On Hwy. 64 (1 mile south of the park entrance), Tusayan. ℰ **928/638-2274.** Reservations not accepted. Pizza $7.95–$24. Pasta and calzones $9.25–$14. DISC, MC, V. Summer 11am–9:30pm; winter 11am–8pm.

3 Williams ★★

59 miles S of Grand Canyon; 32 miles W of Flagstaff; 220 miles E of Las Vegas

With timber above it, ranches below it, and railroads running through it, this town of 2,700 attracted one of the most raucous crowds in the West after being incorporated in 1892. Cowboys, loggers, prospectors, trappers, and railroad workers all frequented the brothels, gambling houses, bars, and opium dens on the town's infamous Saloon Row. Although quieter now, Williams has done an especially good job of packaging its lively past. Much of Saloon Row and many other 19th-century buildings have been restored. The town's renovated train depot now serves as the start and finish for the daily runs of the Historic Grand Canyon Railroad. To entertain the tourists, gun-slinging cowboys stage raucous (corny, but fun) shoot-outs in the streets every summer night. Don't look for much nighttime activity though: the only restaurant you'll find open after 10pm, for example, is Denny's. All told, this is a friendly, safe and very small town for families hoping to experience the old West without battling the traffic of the new West.

ESSENTIALS

GETTING THERE   By Car   Williams is on I-40 just west of the junction with Highway 64, which leads north to the South Rim of the Grand Canyon. Be careful of elk and deer crossing Highway 64 as you head north from Williams.

By Train   Amtrak (© **800/872-7245**) has a small station in Williams. A free shuttle bus brings departing passengers from the drop-off into town, to the station for the **Grand Canyon Railway.** The **Historic Grand Canyon Railway** (© **800/843-8724**) offers daily round-trip service linking Williams and Grand Canyon Village. For more on this historic railway, see "What to See & Do," below.

By Bus   Greyhound (© **800/231-2222**) has daily bus service from Williams to Flagstaff for $18 round-trip.

VISITOR INFORMATION   For more information on the Williams area, contact the **Williams–Grand Canyon Chamber of Commerce,** 200 W. Railroad Ave., Williams, AZ 86046-2556 (© **800/863-0546** or 928/635-1418; www.williamschamber.com). The visitor center here is open 8am to 5pm daily. A vending machine located outside the building sells entrance permits to the park.

GETTING AROUND   There are no car rental agencies in Williams. Taxi service is available through **Smitty's Taxi** (© **928/635-9825**), which operates on a flat rate basis.

SUPERMARKET   Safeway is located at 637 W. Rte. 66 (© **928/635-0500**); it's open daily from 5am to 10pm (hours may vary in winter).

WHAT TO SEE & DO

Grand Canyon Railway ★★★ *Kids*   In 1968, the automobile helped end the Santa Fe Railway's service between Williams and Grand Canyon. By 1989, when service resumed on the 65-mile-long line, automobiles were clogging the park's narrow roads. Thousands of visitors discovered that the historic train not only spared them the headache of driving, but was big-time fun. Today, the 100-year-old railroad carries more than 180,000 passengers annually, many of whom buy package tours that include transportation to Williams.

The trip starts at the historic Williams Depot and the original Fray Marcos Hotel. Built in 1908, this concrete building, on the National Register of Historic Places, survives today only because the railroad realized in the 1970s that to demolish it would cost more than to leave it standing. It now houses a gift shop, coffee shop, and a free museum tracing the history of the Grand Canyon Railway.

At 9:30 every morning, after local cowboys stage a Wild West gunfight outside the depot, conductors help passengers board the train. Coach passengers sit in restored 1923 Harriman coaches with Pullman windows, Art Deco–style lamps, and tiny ceiling fans. For $20 more, you can purchase an upgrade to the Club Car, with a fully stocked mahogany bar. For $55 more than coach fare, you can enjoy First Class treatment, including continental breakfast in the morning and champagne and appetizers on the trip home—all while sitting in comfortable recliner chairs. If you really want to savor the views of the high desert, however, I recommend purchasing a seat in the Deluxe Observation class, whose seats are in a glass dome atop the car. These seats cost $75 more than Coach Class (round-trip). I even prefer the Deluxe Observation class to the most expensive service, the Luxury Parlor Car, which boasts an open-air rear platform. In fact you can take one class of seating on the way to the Grand Canyon, and a different class back—this allows you to sample different cars inside the train, all of which are unique.

From Memorial Day through September 30, a rare steam engine pulls the train at speeds up to 30 miles per hour. (A vintage diesel locomotive often helps pull the train. In winter, only the diesel is used.) While the train chugs across the high desert, musicians wander through the compartments, playing folk and country standards. The trip *to* the canyon ends at the historic Grand Canyon Depot in Grand Canyon Village. From here, passengers can lunch at the historic El Tovar Hotel or take Fred Harvey bus tours of the rim. You can sign up for bus tours while reserving train tickets. I'd recommend sitting in a dome car on the way back to Williams, where you can watch a dazzling sunset with a glass of champagne accompanied by live guitar music. Wherever you sit, the train ride is a wonderful experience and a most memorable way to visit the Grand Canyon.

Williams Depot, 235 N. Grand Canyon Blvd. (take I-40 Exit 163, go .5 mile south), Williams. (C) **800/843-8724.** Fax 928/773-1610. www.thetrain.com. Round-trip coach tickets are $58 adult, $25 children 2–16 (plus tax and $8 National Park Service entry fees for ages 17–61), free for children under 2; upgrades cost $21–$89 per person, depending on class of service. AE, DC, DISC, MC, V. Train departs daily at 10am and arrives at Grand Canyon at 12:15pm. Leaves Grand Canyon at 3:30pm, arriving in Williams at 5:45pm.

Western-Style Gun Fights 𝒜 *Moments*   The same bad guys, sheriffs, and deputies who battle every morning near the Grand Canyon Railway Depot shoot at one another all over again at 7pm on summer nights in downtown Williams. The free show, which moves to a different block of Route 66 each night, entertains thousands of

visitors every year. If you're in town, don't miss it. These guys seem like real gunslingers, only they're funny. To find out where the show will be on a given night, consult one of the schedules available at the **Williams–Grand Canyon Chamber of Commerce** (© 800/863-0546 or 928/635-4061) or at businesses throughout town.

At various locations in Williams. © 800/863-0546. Free admission. Memorial Day–Labor Day 7pm nightly.

WHERE TO STAY
EXPENSIVE

Williams has one expensive chain hotel: **Best Western Inn of Williams** (© 928/635-4400), 2600 Rte. 66, Williams, AZ 86046.

Fray Marcos Hotel ⊛   Named for a Franciscan monk believed to have been the first white person in the region, this sprawling, luxurious hotel replaces the original Fray Marcos Hotel. (Located next door, the original hotel now houses a gift shop and the museum for the Grand Canyon Railway.) In the lobby of the new hotel, oil paintings of the Grand Canyon adorn the walls, and cushy chairs surround a flagstone fireplace. Bellhops carry luggage to the spacious but somewhat spartan Southwestern-style rooms.

The Grand Canyon Railway, which starts and ends its daily runs next to the hotel, has become hugely popular with tour groups, many of whom stay at the Fray Marcos. Its success has translated into rapid growth for the hotel, which now has 196 rooms. Although this is a quality hotel providing good service, it inevitably feels less intimate and more commercial than other area lodges. **Spenser's Lounge,** which features a beautiful 100-year-old bar imported from Scotland, offers simple dining and top-shelf liquor.

235 N. Grand Canyon Blvd., Williams, AZ 86046. © 928/635-4010. Fax 928/635-2180. www.thetrain.com/fares.cfm#fares_sub_fraymarcoshotel. 196 units. Mar 16–Oct 15 $121 double; Oct 16–Mar 15 $89 double. AE, DISC, MC, V. **Amenities:** Restaurant (American); lounge; indoor pool; exercise room; Jacuzzi. *In room:* A/C, TV.

Sheridan House Inn ⊛⊛   The home's interior bristles with bronze sculptures and shimmers with original paintings. Most guest rooms offer brass beds, glass-topped coffee tables, TVs, stereos, VCRs, and refrigerators stocked with cold drinks; the Aspen has a fireplace, impressionist paintings, and a large marble bathroom with separate shower and tub. Outside, under the ponderosa pines at the end of this quiet, dead-end street (a short walk from downtown Williams), the seasonal hot tub awaits. A fully-stocked bar is available to guests, as well. Making the setting all the more enjoyable are the friendly innkeepers, Steve and Evelyn Gardner, who serve a three-course dinner in addition to breakfast.

460 E. Sheridan Ave., Williams, AZ 86046. ℂ 888/635-9345 or 928/635-9441. Fax 928/635-1005. www.thegrandcanyon.com/sheridan/. 12 units. $135–$225 double. Rates include full breakfast and dinner. AE, DISC, MC, V. Ask about pets in advance. **Amenities:** Exercise room; Jacuzzi during summer season; washer/dryer; billiard table. *In room:* TV/VCR, stereo.

A Terry Ranch House Bed and Breakfast 🐾🐾 The most striking element of this 1994 Victorian Country home is the wood: walls of lodgepole pine; hardwood floors; and cherry and oak antiques. The wooden interior seems to inhale fresh air from the nearby mountains—each of the four guest units has large windows, a ceiling fan, a claw-foot tub (a Jacuzzi in the Charlotte Malinda room), and a private entrance with a screen door that opens onto the lodge's wraparound veranda. In addition, a separate bunk house with three two-room suites was under construction at press time. A full family-style breakfast is served come morning; note that this B&B does not serve alcohol. The owners will help guests arrange horseback riding, rafting, and guided tours.

701 Quarterhorse (near Rodeo Rd.), Williams, AZ 86046. ℂ 800/210-5908 or 928/ 635-4171. Fax 928/635-2488. www.terryranchbnb.com. 4 units. $139–$172 double for 1-night stay. AE, DISC, MC, V. Inquire about kids. *In room:* A/C, TV/VCR, hair dryer, radio/CD, thermostat-controlled gas fireplace. Phone with dataport and fridge are available in the common area.

MODERATE

Recommended mid-priced chain hotels in Williams include **Fairfield Inn by Marriott** (ℂ **928/635-9888**), 1029 N. Grand Canyon Blvd. (off I-40 Exit 163); **Quality Inn Mountain Ranch Resort** (ℂ **928/635-2693**), 6701 E. Mountain Ranch Rd. (8 miles east of Williams on I-40, exit 171); and **Holiday Inn Williams** (ℂ **928/ 635-4114**), 950 N. Grand Canyon Blvd. (off I-40 exit 163). Rates range $39–$79 for a double occupancy.

Canyon Motel *Value* In addition to having 18 rooms in historic flagstone cottages, this motel offers a total of five guest rooms in two railroad cabooses and one former Grand Canyon Railway coach car. From the outside, the cabooses resemble, well, cabooses, only with private decks. They even sit on segments of train track. Inside, however, my caboose seemed to morph into a single-wide trailer with a low ceiling, a compact bathroom and shower, and two narrow sleeping areas connected by a hallway. If you want to take the train, reserve one of the two largest guest rooms in the Grand Canyon

Railway car. Unlike the caboose rooms, these rooms have windows that open and enough space to accommodate a queen bed and futon. Still, the cottage rooms are the best deal at this motel and a wise choice for travelers on a budget.

1900 E. Rodeo Rd., Williams, AZ 86046-9527. ✆ **800/482-3955** or 928/635-9371. Fax 928/635-4138. www.canyonmotel.com 18 cottage units, 5 train-car units, 10 with shower only. Cottage unit $70–$85 double; train-car unit $75–$96 double. AE, DISC, MC, V. Pets accepted in smoking rooms only for $7 extra. **Amenities:** Indoor pool (may close seasonally). *In room:* A/C (11 units), TV, fridge (18 units), coffeemaker, microwave (18 units), no phone.

Mountain Country Lodge B&B *(Value)*   Art Deco paint, an out-of-order pay phone on the porch, and a location mere yards from Route 66 in historic Williams combine to make this 1909 house seem like an unlikely place for luxury. The surprise comes when you open the door to a guest room. Decorated in seemingly random themes such as "Alaska," "Route 66," and "Lavender," the nine refurbished guest units all have plush sofas or easy chairs, TVs with VCRs, refrigerators, and charming decor. My room, "The Cowboy Room," had metal cut-outs of cowboys, a replica of a sign from an old general store, and denim-colored linens. In addition to being luxurious, the room boasted its original trim and doors, exposed pine beams, and a brick hearth left over from the days when it served as the house's parlor. If you take advantage of the Internet booking discount, this lodge is a great value.

437 W. Route 66, Williams, AZ 86046. ✆ **800/973-6210** or 928/635-4341. Fax 928/635-1450. www.stayon66.com. 9 units, all with private bathroom and shower. $39–$109 double. 6 person family suite (for Internet bookings). Rates include continental breakfast. *In room:* A/C, TV/VCR, fridge.

The Red Garter Bed and Bakery *(★★ (Finds)*   In the early 1900s, this Victorian Romanesque building had a brothel upstairs, a saloon downstairs, and an opium den in the back. The innkeeper, John Holst, has worked hard to preserve both the building, built in 1897, and its colorful history. A general contractor specializing in restoration work, he fully refurbished the structure, which served as tire storage in the early 1970s. Using early family and city records, he also fleshed out the building's history, which he gladly shares with visitors.

Each of the four guest rooms has custom-made (by Holst himself) moldings, a 12-foot-high ceiling, a ceiling fan, and antique furnishings. My favorite guest room, **The Best Gals' Room,** overlooks Route 66 and is the largest and most luxurious of the four. Its two adjoining rooms were once reserved for the brothel's "best gals," who would lean out of the double hung windows to flag down customers. This unusual B&B boasts "more than 100 years of personal service."

137 W. Railroad Ave. (P.O. Box 95), Williams, AZ 86046. ℂ **800/328-1484** or 928/635-1484. www.redgarter.com. 4 units, all with private bathroom, 3 with shower only. $85–$125. Rates include continental breakfast. AE, DISC, MC, V. Closed Dec–Jan. *In room:* TV.

INEXPENSIVE

Inexpensive chain hotels in Williams include **Travelodge** (ℂ **928/635-2651**), 430 E. Rte. 66; **Motel 6 East** (ℂ **928/635-4464**), 720 W. Rte. 66; **Motel 6 Premier** (ℂ **928/635-9000**), 831 W. Rte. 66.

El Rancho Motel ℝ *(Value)*   It's sure not much from the outside, but this two-story 1966 Motor Court between the eastbound and westbound lanes of Route 66 is one of the best lodging values in Williams. Guests can swim in the outdoor pool, cook out on barbecue grills, or recline in the spotless rooms, which come with a host of amenities. The only drawback is the proximity of certain rooms to the westbound traffic. As for the decor, one owner aptly describes it as "blue."

617 E. Route 66, Williams, AZ 86046. ℂ **928/635-2552**. Fax 928/635-4173. www. thegrandcanyon.com/elrancho/. 27 units. Winter $35–$50 double; summer $57–$63 double. AE, DISC, MC, V. One small pet allowed per room for $5 extra. **Amenities:** Outdoor pool; barbecue grills. *In room:* A/C, TV/VCR (videos available for $2 each), fridge, coffeemaker, microwave.

WHERE TO EAT

Cruisers Cafe 66 ℝ *(Kids* AMERICAN   Built in an old Route 66 gas station, this restaurant is jammed with gas-station memorabilia, including stamped glass, filling-station signs, "Sky Chief" gas pumps, and photos of classic service stations. Served up with plenty of napkins as well as drinks in unbreakable plastic mugs, the roadhouse-style food will fuel you for days to come. Start with the sampler of appetizers—wings, chicken strips, mozzarella sticks, and fried mushrooms—served on a real automobile hubcap. The burgers are tasty, but the best choice, if you really want to fill up, is the pork back ribs. Alternatively, try the chicken-fried chicken—a tastier, and healthier, choice than the chicken-fried steak. Even the help calls to mind the road trips of years past—on a busy day, the waitresses can be as slow with your change as those old gas station attendants used to be.

233 W. Rte. 66, Williams. ℂ **928/635-2445**. Reservations not accepted. Lunch and dinner $7.95–$18. AE, DISC, MC, V. Daily 4–9.30pm (may vary seasonally).

Pine Country Restaurant ⭐ *(Value)* AMERICAN   Many locals who dine at this no-frills restaurant in downtown Williams eat their pie first, and then order dinner. One taste of any of this restaurant's 25 plus (over 60 in summer) varieties of fresh-baked pie—including unusual flavors such as banana peanut butter and strawberry cream cheese—will convince you that the pie-eaters have their priorities straight. But pie (at just $3.25 a piece) is just a slice of the offerings. Dinner entrees like roast beef, pork chops, and fried shrimp all cost under $10 and taste like meals your mother should have made. The lunch menu mostly consists of burgers and hot sandwiches. One winner: the turkey melt with bacon, green chiles, and Swiss cheese on grilled sourdough.

107 N. Grand Canyon Blvd., Williams. © 928/635-9718. Reservations accepted. Breakfast $2.95–$6.25; lunch $4.50–$6.25; dinner $6.95–$12. AE, DISC, MC, V. Daily 5:30am–9pm.

Rod's Steak House ⭐⭐ STEAKS   If you're a steak lover, brake for the cow-shaped sign on Route 66 as you would for real livestock. This landmark restaurant, sprawling across a city block between the highway's east- and westbound lanes, has hardly changed since Rodney Graves, an early member of the U.S. Geological Survey, opened it in 1946. Printed on a paper cutout of a cow, the menu is still only about 6 inches across—more than enough space for its laconic descriptions of the restaurant's offerings. You can choose non-steak items such as "beef liver grilled onions and bacon" and "jumbo fantail shrimp tempura battered"; or prime rib in three sizes, from the 9-ounce "ladies lite cut" to the 16-ounce "cattleman's hefty cut." But the best choices are probably the corn-fed mesquite-broiled steaks, which have kept this place humming for a half-century. For dessert, try the mud pie. This service is, well, let's say "service with an attitude."

301 E. Rte. 66, Williams. © 928/635-2671. Reservations accepted. $9–$29. AE, DISC, MC, V. Daily 11:30am–9:30pm. Closed first 2 weeks of Jan and Sun Oct–Feb.

Rosa's Cantina ⭐ *(Finds)* MEXICAN   Unless you thrill to the sight of inflatable beer bottles hanging from the roof of a former bowling alley, don't come to this restaurant for its ambience. But come anyway, in order to dine on traditional Mexican cuisine that, given the surroundings, deserves a score of 300. Never mind that a local might just tell you which lane you're sitting in. Concentrate on the delightful tastes of the fajitas, enchiladas, and (best of all) chile rellenos; soothe your nerves, if not your eyes, by drinking a neon-colored margarita; and marvel at the immensity of the portions.

411 N. Grand Canyon Blvd., Williams. ℂ **928/635-0708.** Reservations not accepted. $3.25–$12. AE, DISC, MC, V. Tue–Thurs 11am–9pm; Fri–Sat 11am–10pm; Sun 11am–8pm; closed Mon.

4 Cameron

51 miles N of Flagstaff on U.S. 89, and 30 minutes from Desert View and the eastern entrance to the park

Cameron is a convenient place to stay if you plan on exploring the eastern end of the park or visiting destinations inside the Navajo Nation.

SUPERMARKET Simpson's Market (ℂ **928/679-2340**) is located at the junction of highways 89 and 64, next to the Chevron. It's open daily from 6am to 9:30pm (7am to 8:30pm in winter).

WHAT TO SEE & DO

The **Cameron Trading Post** (ℂ **800/338-7385** or 928/679-2231), 1 mile north of the crossroads town of Cameron (where Hwy. 64 to Grand Canyon Village branches off U.S. 89 on the Navajo Reservation), merits a stop. When here, be sure to visit the original stone trading post. Built in the 1910s, this historic building now houses a gallery of museum-quality Native American artifacts, clothing, and jewelry. Even if you don't have $10,000 or $15,000 to drop on an old rug or basket, you can still look around. The main trading post is a more modern building and is the largest trading post in northern Arizona. If you shop here, you will probably pay a little more than you should. You can usually negotiate up to a 20% discount, but the prices remain high. Even so, I prefer taking my chances at the open-air stands scattered along highways 64 and 89, where you can sometimes chat with the artists or their families.

WHERE TO STAY

Cameron Trading Post Motel ☆ Renovated in the early 1990s, the rooms in this motel are among the most stylish in the Grand Canyon area. Each features its own unique Southwestern-style furnishings, many of them handmade by the motel's staff. The motel's Hopi building borders a terraced garden with stone picnic tables, a fountain, and a large grill. The campground opposite the motel offers full hookups for $15 per night.

P.O. Box 339 (54 miles north of Flagstaff on Hwy. 89), Cameron, AZ 86020. ℂ **800/ 338-7385** or 928/679-2231. Fax 928/679-2350. 66 units. Jun 1–Oct 15 $89–$119 double; Oct 16–Jan 31 $59–$79 double; Feb 1–Mar 1 $49–$69 double; Mar 2–May 31 $69–$99 double. AE, DC, DISC, MC, V. Pets accepted. **Amenities:** Restaurant (Regional); trading post/gift shop/gallery. *In room:* A/C, TV, coffeemaker.

WHERE TO EAT

Cameron Trading Post Dining Room REGIONAL   The menu at this eclectic restaurant draws upon a variety of cultures. The tin ceiling dining room features a grand fireplace, Native American wall rugs, mahogany wood, and antique Tiffany glass. As you might guess from the location, the Navajo dishes are the tastiest—particularly the hot beef sandwich, available only at lunch. A taste of the seafood, meanwhile, might remind you the ocean is a long way away.

On U.S. 89, Cameron. ℭ **800/338-7385** or 928/679-2231. Reservations not accepted. Breakfast $4–$9; lunch $4–$9; dinner $7–$18. AE, DC, MC, V. Summer 6am–10pm daily; winter 7am–9pm daily.

5 Towns & Outposts Near the North Rim

The area surrounding Grand Canyon north of the Colorado River is some of the most sparsely populated—and scenic—in the continental United States. Highway 89A crosses the Colorado River at the northeastern tip of Grand Canyon—just 5 miles downstream of **Lees Ferry,** where most river trips in the canyon begin. Continuing west from the bridge on Highway 89A, you'll pass three lonely lodges—**Marble Canyon Lodge, Lees Ferry Lodge,** and **Cliff Dwellers Lodge**—each a few miles apart, at the base of the aptly named Vermilion Cliffs. This eerie desert landscape, which features balancing rocks and other striking landforms, gives way to forest when you begin the 4,800-vertical-foot climb from the Marble Platform to the Kaibab Plateau. Because the area surrounding the park's North Rim is largely National Forest, you may have to travel a ways if you fail to find a room inside the park. The closest lodging to the park's northern entrance is at **Kaibab Lodge,** 18 miles north of the North Rim on Highway 67, and at **Jacob Lake,** 44 miles north of the North Rim. If those two lodges are full, you may have to drive as far north as Fredonia, Arizona, or Kanab, Utah, to find a room.

WHERE TO STAY & EAT
NEAR THE PARK

Jacob Lake Inn 𝒜   In 1922, Harold and Nina Bowman bought a barrel of gas and opened a gas "stand" near the present-day site of the Jacob Lake Inn. Seven years later they built this inn at the junction of highways 67 and 89A. Today, Jacob Lake Inn is the main hub of activity between the North Rim and Kanab, UT. To serve the growing summer crowds, the Bowmans' descendants and their friends travel south from their homes in Utah. Together, they run the Inn's various businesses: the bakery, churning out excellent

> **Tips   A View from the Bridge**
>
> The old Navajo Bridge, completed in 1928, now serves as a footbridge over Marble Canyon. When traveling on Highway 89A near Lees Ferry, park your car in one of the lots on either side of the gorge, then walk across the old bridge. More than 800 feet across, it affords stomach-churning views straight down 467 feet to the Colorado River, and several miles to the south down Marble Canyon (the northeastern tip of Grand Canyon).

fresh-baked cookies; the soda fountain, which serves milkshakes made from hard ice cream; the gift shop, which features museum-quality pieces by Native American artists; not to mention the restaurant, the motel, and the full-service gas station. *Note:* The ATM at the inn is the nearest one to the North Rim.

Lodgers can choose between motel units and cabins. Though pleasant inside, the motel rooms in the front building are not nearly as peaceful as the rooms and cabins behind the lodge. Built in 1958, the motel rooms in back are solid and clean. The bathrooms have showers but no tubs, and many of them drain onto the same tile floor as the bathroom itself—a curious design. Most people prefer the rustic cabins, which cost less than the motel rooms. The cabin floors creak, the guest rooms (from one to four per cabin) are cramped, and most smell like soggy pine needles. In other words, they're exactly how cabins should be. (Unfortunately, two have been lovingly restored and therefore ruined.) Another advantage to the cabins is that each has its own private porch, either attached to the building or standing alone in the ponderosa pine forest.

The Jacob Lake restaurant ☞, with both a U-shaped counter and a dining room, serves burgers, sandwiches, and steaks, but the most appetizing entree may be the grilled trout. A delicious lunch item is the cranberry cream cheese chicken sandwich. Even if you don't need a meal, it's worth stopping at Jacob Lake Inn to buy a few home-baked cookies or a real milkshake.

Junction of Hwy. 67 and 89A, Jacob Lake, AZ 86022. © 928/643-7232. Fax 928/643-7235. www.jacoblake.com. 12 motel units; 27 cabins, all with shower only. May 14–Nov 30 $72–$90 double; Dec 1–May 13 $52 double. Pets accepted for $10 extra. **Amenities:** Restaurant; playground. *In room:* No phone.

Kaibab Lodge   The main lodge here feels as warm and comfortable as a beloved summer camp. It has an open-framed ceiling and enormous pine beams that date from its construction in the 1920s. Perhaps because the guest rooms lack phones and all but two lack televisions, guests tend to congregate in the Adirondack-style chairs in front of the 5-foot-wide fireplace, in the small television room, or at the tables across from the counter that doubles as front desk and beer bar.

Each cabin-like building houses two to four of the 24 guest rooms, which sleep from two to five people. The rooms are spare but clean, with paneling of rough-hewn pine. Most have showers but not tubs. One luxury room has a queen bed, microwave, refrigerator, and coffeemaker. Because the walls of the older units are very thin, it's best to share a cabin with friends. Located roughly a quarter mile from the highway, the rooms open onto the broad expanse of DeMotte Park, one of the large, naturally occurring meadows on the Kaibab Plateau.

Like most summer camps, this lodge isn't perfect. Parts of its exterior are biodegrading; the front desk occasionally finds itself overwhelmed, and the food lacks consistency. But the surrounding meadows soothe the mind.

HC 64, Box 30 (26 miles south of Jacob Lake on Hwy. 67), Fredonia, AZ 86022. ℂ **928/638-2389** May 15–Nov. 1; 800/525-0924 or 928/526-0924 rest of year. Fax 928/638-9864. www.kaibab.org. 29 units. $85–$99 double. DISC, MC, V. **Amenities:** Restaurant; bar. *In room:* No phone.

NEAR LEES FERRY

Cliff Dwellers Lodge 🐾 *(Finds)*   Cliff Dwellers Lodge sits in the most spectacular setting in the Marble Canyon area. It's just a few hundred yards from an eye-catching area of balancing rocks (formed when boulders, having toppled off the nearby Vermilion Cliffs, "capped" the softer soil directly underneath them, thereby slowing its erosion). Against the side of one of these boulders, two former New Yorkers built a house in the 1920s and began serving dinner and drinks to the occasional passerby. Known simply as "Old Cliff Dwellers," the house still stands—barely.

The "new" Cliff Dwellers, which dates from the '50s, is set back 50 yards or so from the highway, so the rooms are very quiet. Unless you strongly prefer a bathtub to a shower, ask for a room in one of the older buildings, some of which have carports and recessed patios. Located in the oldest building, my favorite rooms have wood paneling even on the ceilings and in the bathrooms, which look a bit like saunas. The pace at the lodge is very relaxing, making it my favorite place to sleep in this area.

The best known fishing guide service in the area, Lees Ferry Anglers Fly Shop and Guide Service, relocated here from Lees Ferry Lodge. There's also a restaurant and package liquor store on the premises. Cliff Dwellers also rents a nearby, three-bedroom house for $175 per night.

HC 67-30 (9 miles west of Navajo Bridge on North Hwy. 89A), Marble Canyon, AZ 86036. © **800/433-2543** or 928/355-2228. Fax 928/355-2271. www.leesferry. com. 20 units. $60–$70 double. AE, DISC, MC, V. **Amenities:** Restaurant; fly shop; package liquor store. *In room:* A/C (or evaporative cooler), TV, no phone.

Lees Ferry Lodge ⊛   Some of the world's best porch-sitting can be enjoyed on the patios outside the low sandstone buildings of this 1929 lodge, a popular stopping place for trout fishers trying their luck above Lees Ferry. The patios, like those at nearby Cliff Dwellers, afford stunning views south across the highway toward greenish-pink Marble Platform or north to the Vermilion Cliffs. Although the motel sits close to the road, traffic is slow at night.

The older rooms, which are small and rustic, have been redecorated in themes ranging from cowboy to—yes—fish. Double rooms in newer, prefab style buildings are available for groups. When you tire of porch-sitting, shamble a few feet to the adjacent bar and grill, which serves the best food near Lees Ferry.

The only thing not restful are the showers, which erupt like Old Faithful, only less faithfully.

After rigging boats for trips down the Colorado, many river guides come to the restaurant here, the **Vermilion Cliffs Bar & Grill** ⊛⊛, and not just because it stocks nearly 130 types of bottled beer. They also come for nicely prepared steaks, chicken, and fish, and for imaginative sandwiches such as the "Turkey in a Straw"— sliced turkey breast, sauerkraut, and Swiss cheese grilled on sourdough bread and served with Thousand Island dressing. The staff provides low-key, friendly service, in a dining room whose wood walls, tables, chairs, and bar seem to all have been sawed from the same tree. The restaurant can be very crowded at dinnertime during peak fishing periods (generally fall and spring).

HC 67-Box 1 (4 miles west of Navajo Bridge on North Hwy. 89A), Marble Canyon, AZ 86036 (located in the tiny "Arizona designated place" of Vermilion Cliffs). © **928/355-2230** or 800/451-2231. www.leesferrylodge.com. 10 units. $56–$95 double. MC, V. Pets accepted. **Amenities:** Excellent restaurant; bar; flyshop; artist's guild with on-site silversmith. *In room:* A/C, coffeemaker, no phone.

Marble Canyon Lodge   The closest to Lees Ferry, this lodge frequently fills up with rafters eagerly awaiting the journey into the canyon or fishermen stocking up for their next excursion. The traffic gives the place a busier, less personal feel than at the nearby Cliff Dwellers and Lees Ferry lodges. The rooms here vary, but the ones in the 300 building are brightest and most pleasant. Although a restaurant and lounge are on the premises, I usually come here to browse the selection of unusual books on the region. Marble Canyon Lodge also rents eight two-bedroom apartments at prices ranging from $125 to $142.

P.O. Box 6001 (¼ mile west of Navajo Bridge on Hwy. 89A), Marble Canyon, AZ 86036. © 800/726-1789 or 928/355-2225. Fax 928/355-2227. 55 units. $64–$70 double. AE (lodge only), DISC, MC, V. **Amenities:** Restaurant; lounge; coin-op washer/dryer. *In room:* A/C, TV, no phone.

6 Kanab, Utah ★

78 miles NW of Grand Canyon National Park; 80 miles S of Bryce Canyon National Park; 42 miles E of Zion National Park; 303 miles S of Salt Lake City

The Navajo ran off the first Mormon settlers in this area. The second group, who arrived in the 1870s, managed to hold on. Brigham Young himself surveyed the land in Kanab and helped lay out the downtown, which remains largely unchanged today. For years Kanab survived on ranching. Later, in the 1960s, uranium mining boosted the economy. So did film crews who shot Westerns in the spectacular red-rock canyons that surround the town. Today, tourism drives the economy as travelers stay here while visiting Grand Canyon (though not in winter, when access to the north rim is closed), Bryce, and Zion parks, and the comparatively new Grand Staircase–Escalante National Monument. The town doesn't even have a bar that serves liquor, but the people are friendly, the food wholesome, and the nights serene. Seven miles south of Kanab is the smaller town of Fredonia, Arizona. Fredonia has all the sagging trailers, junk cars, dusty lots, and rusting bulldozers that one expects to find in rural Arizona. That's the downside. The upshot is that it also feels like a place where people measure time in sunrises and sunsets instead of seconds.

ESSENTIALS

GETTING THERE   By Car   Kanab is located on U.S. 89 at the junction of U.S. 89A, which crosses into Arizona just 7 miles south of town. To reach Fredonia from the North Rim, take Highway 67, 44 miles north to Jacob Lake, then take Highway 89A, 29 miles northwest to Fredonia.

Highway 12 between Boulder, UT, and Tropic, UT, crosses the north end of the monument, and Highway 89 between Kanab, UT, and Page, AZ, clips the monument's southernmost tip. Linking these highways are a number of gravel roads, which travel through the heart of the monument. If your aim is simply to cross the monument's boundary, drive 12 miles east of Kanab on Highway 89. To really experience it, however, do one of the following: Eight miles east of Kanab on Highway 89, turn north on the Johnson Canyon road. After 16 miles, turn right onto the gravel Skutumpah Road. The Skutumpah Road leads to some of the best areas for hiking in the area—not to mention some incredible scenery. Or, visit "The Toadstools"—an area of hoodoos and balancing rocks near the Paria Contact Station, 43 miles east of Kanab on Highway 89. Or, picnic near the Paria Movie Set, where rainbow-like cliffs of clay rise above a replica movie set. To reach the movie set, drive 37 miles east of Kanab on Highway 89A, then 5 miles on the bumpy dirt road. (*Note:* Do not attempt this road during rainy weather or in an RV.) Be sure to obtain additional information from locals about the roads and trails before going into the heart of the monument (see below).

VISITOR INFORMATION   The **Kane County Travel Council and Film Commission** is located at 78 S. 100 E., Kanab, UT 84741 (✆ **800/SEE-KANE** or 435/644-5033; www.kaneutah.com).

The **Kane County Office of Tourism** (✆ **800/733-5263** or 435/644-5033), 78 S. 100 E., Kanab, UT 84741, has more information on the many movie sets around Kanab.

GETTING AROUND   The only way to reach Kanab (easily) is by automobile. The nearest car rental agencies are in St. George, UT, and Cedar City, UT. Ground zero in Kanab is where Center and Main streets intersect. U.S. 89 comes in from the north on 300 West Street, turns east onto Center Street, south again on 100 East Street, and finally east again on 300 South. U.S. 89A follows 100 East Street south to the airport and, after about 7 miles, the smaller town of Fredonia, AZ.

FAST FACTS   The **Kane County Hospital & Skilled Nursing Facility** is at 355 N. Main St. (✆ **435/644-5811**). In an **emergency,** dial ✆ **911.** The **post office** is at 39 S. Main St. (✆ **435/644-2760**). **Glazier's Food Town** is located at 264 S. 100 E. (✆ **435/644-5029**), open daily 7am to 10:30pm (10pm during low season). A slightly larger store, **Honey's Jubilee Foods,** is at 260 E. 300 S. (✆ **435/644-5877**). It's open daily 7am to 10:30pm (10pm during low season).

WHAT TO SEE & DO

The citizens of Kanab are starting to acknowledge the existence of the sprawling, but still undeveloped 1.9-million acre **Grand**

Staircase–Escalante National Monument 愛愛, whose southwest boundary stretches to within just a few miles of town. Many Kanab residents still believe that protecting this area will interfere with southern Utah's economic development. So far, there are few developed areas for visitors to this rugged desert landscape, where erosion has carved out narrow canyons, broad mesas, amphitheaters, spires, and arches. There are, however, a few bumpy, beautiful roads through the area and many tantalizing places to hike. Before venturing into this mazelike country, the best thing to do is gather maps and advice from locals. **The Bureau of Land Management Kanab Field Office** (℗ 435/644-4600), 318 N. 100 E. in Kanab, sells USGS maps of the area and can help you plan your excursion. If you're considering hiking, stop at **Willow Creek Books Coffee and Outdoor Gear** (℗ 435/644-8884), 263 S. 100 E. in Kanab. The shop's friendly staff dispenses advice, maps, outdoor gear, books (including guidebooks of the area), and—in case you lack incentive—espresso.

Frontier Movie Town (Kids) Come here to visit pieces of old movie sets from Westerns shot around Kanab; to dress up as a cowboy or cowgirl (cost: $5); and to admire the many autographed photos of actors who visited Kanab while filming Westerns. On nights when groups are visiting, Frontier Movie Town employees dress in period clothing and stage a Wild West drama that culminates in a deafening shootout. Because most of the participants in this drama are pulled from the audience, the acting is as wooden as on the USA network, but your kids probably won't care. Best of all, it's free. Frontier Movie Town also has an outdoor cook shack that serves buffalo wings, burgers, and steaks; an ice cream parlor; and a gift shop. Call ahead to find out when a shoot-out might take place.

297 W. Center St., Kanab. ℗ 800/551-1714. Free admission. Daily 8am–10pm in summer; 10am–6pm rest of year. No food Mon.

WHERE TO STAY
EXPENSIVE

Kanab has one expensive chain hotel: **Holiday Inn Express Kanab** (℗ 435/644-8888), 815 E. Hwy. 89.

Viola's Garden Bed and Breakfast 愛愛 In 1912, a sheep rancher named James Swapp built this home using a $640 kit from the Sears Roebuck catalog. All the components of the home, including pre-cut beams, siding, roofing, and paint, were delivered by train from Chicago to Marysvale, UT, then carried an additional 200-odd miles on a buckboard wagon to Kanab. Today, Swapp's granddaughter, Nileen Whitlock, and her husband, Von, welcome guests to a remarkably comfortable B&B in the home. Nileen's influence is evident in the many silk flowers, floral patterns, and lace curtains. Von serves up heavenly breakfast fare, including French toast stuffed with either baked apples or cherries and cream cheese. Two guest rooms—The English Garden Room and The Rose Garden Room—are in the original home, while three others are in an addition. My favorite, the English Garden Room, has a fully tiled shower, dormers, a Victorian-style bed, and, best of all, a private second-story balcony. The Rose Garden Room, meanwhile, boasts a claw-foot bathtub painted in a fairy motif, among other luxuries.

250 N. 100 W., Kanab, UT 84741. ©/fax **435/644-5683.** www.violas-garden.com. 5 units, each with private bathroom, shower only in 4 units. $89–$135 double. Rates include gourmet breakfast. DISC, MC, V. Older children acceptable. **Amenities:** Jacuzzi. *In room:* TV.

MODERATE

Kanab has three moderately priced chain hotels: **Best Western Red Hills** (© **435/644-2675**), 125 W. Center St; **Shilo Inn Kanab** (© **435/644-2562**), 296 W. 100 N.; and **Super 8 Motel** (© **435/ 644-5500**) 70 S. 200 W.

Parry Lodge ⊛ Many of the older rooms (known as "movie units") in this 1929 colonial-style lodge display plaques bearing the names of stars who stayed in them while filming Westerns (Dean Martin, Gregory Peck, and Sammy Davis, Jr., among others). One unit (no. 131) was built specially to house Frank Sinatra's mother-in-law while the famed crooner starred in *Sergeants Three*. (Sinatra stayed in an adjoining room.) The movie units are smaller and closer to Center Street than the motel's newer rooms, but they're far more charming. Most have tile bathroom floors and classic American furnishings inside, and they're shaded by hardwood trees. (If you want a bathtub, you'll have to take a newer unit.) At Parry Lodge, you do pay a little extra to stay where the stars once stayed—other, comparable motels in town cost less. Open from April 1 through October 30, the lodge's restaurant serves good breakfasts.

89 E. Center St., Kanab, UT 84741. © **435/748-4104** or 435/644-2601. Fax 435/644-2605. www.infowest.com/parry. 89 units. May 1–Oct 31 $45–$70 double; Nov 1–Apr 30 $30–$60 double. AE, DISC, MC, V. Pets accepted for $5 extra. **Amenities:** Restaurant (seasonal); outdoor pool (heated); Jacuzzi. *In room:* A/C, TV.

INEXPENSIVE

Clean, inexpensive rooms can also be found at **Grand Canyon Motel and Old Travelers Inn** (© **928/643-7646**), 175 S. Main St. (Hwy. 89A), Fredonia; **Crazy Jug Motel** (© **928/643-7752**), 465

S. Main St. (Hwy. 89A), Fredonia; **Blue Sage Motel and RV Park**
(© 928/643-7125), 330 S. Main St. (Hwy. 89A), Fredonia.

Treasure Trail Motel 𝒢   Built in the 1950s and '60s, this family-
run motel recalls the days when enormous gas guzzlers that were not
SUVs prowled the American West. Its showers, which pre-date today's
water-saving plumbing, slam you like fire-hose spray; surrounded by
lounge chairs and beached floatation toys, the tiny swimming pool
calls to mind a 5¢ post card; and the gaudy neon motel sign would
look right at home in a Rat Pack movie. Best of all, the motel remains
clean, comfortable, and relatively quiet. My favorite rooms—the corner units in the older, one-story building—have space to spare and
feel as solid as pyramids. Built in the 1960s, the adjacent two-story
building has central air-conditioning—as opposed to wall units in the
one-story building—but it feels less sturdy.

150 W. Center St., Kanab, UT 84741. © 800/603-2687 (reservations only) or
435/644-2687. Fax 435/644-2754. www.treasuretrailmotel.com. 29 units. May 15–
Oct 31 $40–$58 double; Nov 1–May 14 $32–$44 double. AE, DC, DISC, MC, V. 1
small pet per room for $5 extra. **Amenities:** Swimming pool (heated); coin-op
washer/dryer. *In room:* A/C, TV, fridges and microwaves (in some rooms).

WHERE TO EAT

Houston's Trails End Restaurant STEAKS/BURGERS/
SEAFOOD   Generations of ranchers have eaten in this restaurant,
as evidenced (sort of) by the many rifles, branding irons, and spurs
hanging on the walls. While country music plays over the stereo,
waitresses wearing their own toy side arms serve up meaty courses,
including the house special, a chicken-fried steak, and baby back
ribs, which are slathered in sauce and baked all day. The soup is
made fresh daily, as are the enormous yeast rolls that come with each
dinner. Breakfast includes a choice of omelettes, and lunch consists
primarily of burgers and sandwiches.

32 E. Center St. © 435/644-2488. Reservations accepted. Breakfast $4.20–$8.50;
lunch $4.95–$9.50; dinner $4.95–$18.75. AE, DISC, MC, V. Daily 6am–10pm. Closed
mid-Nov to Mar 15.

Nedra's Café 𝒢 MEXICAN   Because this restaurant in Fredonia,
AZ, serves hearty Mexican food at a moderate price, it's a great place
to fill up after completing a North Rim backpacking trip. In addition
to enchiladas, tostadas, burritos, and tacos, Nedra's serves less-com-
mon Mexican dishes such as *carnitas* (seasoned roast pork topped with
fresh cilantro and green onions) and *machaca* (shredded beef cooked
with tomatoes, onion, green chilies, cilantro, and egg). The only thing
missing is beer. In Kanab you'll find a similar restaurant, **Nedra's Too,**

but the tastiest Mexican fare in that community is at **Escobar's Mexican Restaurant** (© **928/644-3739**), 373 E. 300 S.

Hwy. 89A. © **928/643-7591**. Reservations not accepted. Breakfast items 3.25–$8.50; lunch and dinner $3.25–$16. AE, DISC, MC, V. Mon–Thurs 8am–10pm; Fri–Sun 7am–10pm (may vary in winter). Closed Thanksgiving and Christmas.

Rocking V Café ⓐⓐ *(Finds)* ECLECTIC   In 2000, Vicky Cooper left her stressful job as a TV news reporter to open this eclectic cafe, easily the best restaurant in Kanab. If you're here at dinnertime, start with the bruschetta—a house-baked focaccia topped with freshly sliced Roma tomatoes, slivered garlic, basil, and olive oil. Then, indulge in the chicken and mushroom Alfredo—a creamy Alfredo sauce atop spinach fettuccine, sautéed mushrooms, and grilled chicken. Or try the charbroiled filet mignon surrounded with a thyme port demi-glacé. Finish with the raspberry almond torte or the key lime pie. The restaurant, which also serves lunch, occupies a glass-fronted 1892 building that has seen duty as a general store, mortuary, grocery, and bank. The wine cellar occupies the old safe, and there's a gallery with local and regional art upstairs.

97 W. Center St. © **435/644-8001**. Reservations accepted. Lunch $6–$9.50; dinner $9–$21. MC, V. Daily 11:30am–9:30pm.

Vermilion Espresso Bar and Café *(Finds)* COFFEE   I've always had mixed feelings about trendy espresso bars cropping up in cow country: It depresses me to know that people who share my yuppified tastes (and who may, in fact, be like me) are becoming ubiquitous; yet I always appreciate java that doesn't resemble water from a rusty bucket. For better or worse, the Vermilion Espresso Bar and Cafe brings dark coffee, teeny ceramic cups, hip music, cushy sofas, Internet connections, and delectable pastries to Kanab—not to mention an "espresso-cam" that broadcasts, over the Internet (www.xpressweb.com/~espresso/cam.htm), live images of people standing in line at the counter. All these luxuries may help ease the pain for homesick city dwellers. Then again, they might make you wonder why you left home in the first place.

78 E. Center St. © **435-644-3886**. Coffee $1–$2.85; sandwiches $3.90–$5.25. MC, V. Open for breakfast and lunch year-round 7am–2:30pm.

Wok Inn HUNAN/SZECHUAN   For the past 11 years this Chinese restaurant has occupied a historic building that in the 1920s served as a rest station for bus passengers traveling between Grand, Zion, and Bryce canyons. If, as rumored, the building really is haunted, its ghosts are probably gorging on spicy dishes such as Mongolian beef and kung pao chicken; vegetarian fare (including

spicy tofu and snow peas with black mushrooms); and sizzling platters of meat and shrimp. In addition to serving good food, this
restaurant dispenses liquor—a rarity in Kanab. Be forewarned, however, that the wine list is ghastly. Your choices: Almaden, Almaden,
and Almaden.

86 S. 200 W. (next to Super 8 Motel). (✆ **435/644-5400** or 866/2-WOKINN. Reservations accepted. Lunch $4.50–$5.50; dinner $6.95–$16. AE, DISC, DC, MC, V.
Mon–Fri 11am–9pm; Sat 1–9pm; Sun 5–9pm. Closed in winter.

7 Havasu Canyon & Supai

70 miles N of Hwy. 66; 155 miles NW of Flagstaff; 115 miles NE of Kingman

In the heart of the 185,000-acre Havasupai Indian Reservation,
south of the Colorado River in the central Grand Canyon, you'll
find the town of Supai. It's nestled between the red walls of Havasu
Canyon, alongside the spring-fed Havasu Creek. Two miles downstream are some of the prettiest waterfalls on earth. In order to get
here, you must hike, ride a horse or mule, or take a helicopter.

ESSENTIALS

GETTING THERE   By Car   You can't drive all the way to Supai
Village or Havasu Canyon. The nearest road, Indian Road 18, ends
8 miles from Supai at Hualapai Hilltop, a barren parking area where
the trail into the canyon begins. The turnoff for Indian Road 18 is 6
miles east of Peach Springs and 21 miles west of Seligman on Route
66. Once you're on Indian Road 18, follow it for 60 paved miles to
Hualapai Hilltop. There's no gas or water available anywhere in this
area, so be sure to top off in either Seligman or Kingman.

By Helicopter   The easiest and fastest (and by far the most expen-
sive) way to reach Havasu Canyon is by helicopter from the Grand
Canyon National Park Airport. Daily flights linking Grand Canyon
National Park Airport and Supai are operated by **Papillon Grand
Canyon Helicopters** (✆ **800/528-2418** or 928/638-2419). A 30-
minute tour costs $109 for adults and $89 for children 12 and
under. The round-trip fare from Papillon's heliport in Tusayan to
Supai is $442, $126 of which goes to the Havasupai tribe. **Skydance
Helicopters** (✆ **800/882-1651**) shuttles passengers between Supai
and Hualapai Hilltop, the trailhead for Supai and Havasu Canyon,
from 10am to 3pm every Sunday, Monday, Thursday, and Friday.
One-way fare is $70 (cash only) per person. Seating is first-come,
first-served, with tribe members and goods taking priority. Each
passenger is allowed to bring one backpack weighing no more than
40 pounds.

By Horse or Mule   The next-easiest and most traditional way to get to Havasu Canyon is by horse or mule. Both you and your luggage can ride either to Havasupai Lodge or to the campground from Hualapai Hilltop. For the 10-mile trip from Hualapai Hilltop to the campground, pack and saddle horses can be rented through the **Havasupai Tourist Enterprise** (© **928/448-2121** or 928/448-2141), which is based in Supai. The cost is $150 round-trip, or $75 one-way. If you're only taking the 8-mile trip to the **Havasupai Lodge,** call the lodge (© **928-448-2111**) itself to rent your mule or pack horse. Round-trip fare between Hualapai Hilltop and the lodge is $120; a one-way ride costs $70.

Day tours from the lodge to Havasu Falls are available for $60. Riders must weigh under 250 pounds, be at least 4 feet, 7 inches tall, be comfortable around large animals, and have at least a little riding experience. Be sure to confirm your horse reservation a day before driving to Hualapai Hilltop. Sometimes no horses are available, and it's a long drive back to the nearest town. Entrance ($20 per person) and camping ($10 per person per night) fees are not included in the mule-trip price. Many people who hike into the canyon decide that it's worth the money to ride out, or at least have their backpacks packed out. Pack mules, which can carry up to four articles weighing up to 130 pounds (total), are available for the same price as a mule ride. The gatekeeper at the campground can usually help you arrange for a ride out.

On Foot   To reach Supai on foot, you'll follow a trail that begins at Hualapai Hilltop and descends 8 miles and about 2,000 vertical feet to the village. It covers a shorter vertical drop than the rim-to-river trails in the canyon, but has no drinking water or restrooms until you reach town. From Supai, it's another 2 miles, mostly downhill, to the campground. The steepest part of the trail is the first 1½ miles from Hualapai Hilltop. After this section it's relatively gradual. See below for more information on the hike to Supai.

FEES & RESERVATIONS   There's a $20 per-person entry fee to Havasu Canyon, effective year-round.

To make camping reservations, contact the **Havasupai Tourist Enterprise** at © **928/448-2141.** The tourist enterprise accepts Visa and MasterCard for both mule and camping reservations. After making reservations, you'll need to check in at the Tourist Enterprise office upon arriving in Supai, 8 miles into your hike.

To make lodging reservations, call **Havasupai Lodge** directly at © **928/448-2111** or 928/448-2201. Also, be sure to get a map and

---

Tips **Making Reservations**

The Havasupai ask that visitors secure reservations for camping or lodging before arriving at the parking area at Hualapai Hilltop. It's good to make reservations as far in advance as possible, especially for holiday weekends. If you show up in Supai without a reservation, you may be asked to hike all the way back to your car.

---

full trail description of this area before starting your hike. The best is the *Havasu Trail Guide* written by Scott Thybony and published by the Grand Canyon Natural History Association.

HIKING TO SUPAI & BEYOND TO THE WATERFALLS

Initially, the surroundings on the trail to Supai from Hualapai Hilltop aren't particularly pleasant. Helicopters buzz overhead, bits of paper rot alongside the trail or hang impaled on cacti, and phone lines parallel the path. Unannounced by the wranglers trailing them, horses canter past, startling hikers.

The trail drops in switchbacks down the Coconino Sandstone cliffs below Hualapai Hilltop, then descends a long slope to the floor of Hualapai canyon. Most of the hike consists of a descent down the gravelly, gradually sloping creek bed at the bottom of the canyon. Usually dry, this wash is prone to flash flooding, so exercise caution during stormy weather. At the confluence with Havasu Canyon, go left, following the blue-green waters of Havasu Creek downstream into the town of Supai.

When you see the two large hoodoos (rock spires) atop the red-rock walls, you'll know you're near town. The 450 Havasupai Indians living here believe that if either rock falls, disaster will befall their people. Unconcerned, children chase each other through town, ducking barbed wire strung between sticks, cottonwood trees, and metal poles. Prefabricated wood houses, some with windows boarded up, line the dirt paths that crisscross this sleepy community, which has a post office, a small grocery, a lodge (see information below), and a cafe.

Roughly 1½ miles past town you'll come to 75-foot-high **Navajo Falls,** then to 150-foot-high **Havasu Falls.** Just past the campground, more than 10 miles from the trailhead, is 300-foot-high **Mooney Falls,** named for a miner who fell to his death there in 1880. The milky water in the creek seems deceptively clear where shallow. It's turquoise at deeper points and emerald at its deepest, under falls so lovely as to make a swimmer laugh with delight. The creek's milky appearance comes from calcium carbonate, which precipitates around the falls in formations resembling enormous drooping mustaches. These formations are colored brownish red by the mud and iron oxide contained in runoff.

Three miles past the campground is the smaller Beaver Falls. Below them, travertine repeatedly dams the river, forming a series of seductive swimming holes. Getting there requires doing one long and relatively tricky descent down a rock face, using a fixed rope for assistance, and several shorter climbs without ropes. Four miles past these dams, Havasu Creek empties into the Colorado River. The hike downstream from the campground involves numerous river crossings, so bring your river sandals in addition to your hiking boots.

As you travel, remember that tourists often inundate this village, and that many of the Havasupai have grown weary of outsiders. Don't expect all of them to shout cheerful greetings on the trail.

OTHER AREA ACTIVITIES

Grand Canyon Caverns 🌟 *Kids*   In addition to visiting Havasu Canyon, you may want to tour the Grand Canyon Caverns. Discovered by a drunken cowboy in 1927, these caverns are notable not for pristine limestone formations but for sheer size. One cavern room is at least as large as a basketball court—or a football field, if the guides here can be believed.

The 45-minute tour recalls the days when entrepreneurs continually dreamed up new, more creative ways of luring tourists off Route 66. After descending 210 feet by elevator, you'll see an enormous fake ground sloth, a dead mountain lion that presumably fell into the hole and was preserved here, and an emaciated road-killed coyote, which the cavern's owners dragged into the cave in 1958 to test their theories on underground preservation. (They were wrong.) There are even some glowing rocks, which our tour guide told us had been "found elsewhere and brought down here strictly for your viewing."

The adjacent gift shop also has its share of novelties, including sharks' teeth and Hoover Dam placemats. The cafeteria serves burgers and sells cold cans of beer.

On Rte. 66 (12 miles east of Peach Springs). ✆ **928/422-3223.** Admission $12 adults, $7.95 kids 4–12, free for children under 4. AE, DISC, MC, V. 8am–6pm (last tour at 5:45pm) high-season; 10am–6pm low-season. Tours every 30 min.

WHERE TO STAY
IN HAVASU CANYON

Havasu Canyon Campground 🌟🌟   First, a few reasons for not coming: Dog-haters will want to avoid this campground, where dusty, scarred, but ultimately content canines nap under picnic tables by day and howl at their own echoes by night. The outhouses seldom if ever have paper in them. And, oh yes, the crowds can be thick on weekends. The Havasupai Tourist Enterprise allows 200 campers before cutting off reservations—this is 150 fewer than in the recent past, but still enough to crowd the place. There are no showers, public phones, fire pits, or grills. (Open fires are not allowed.)

When uncrowded, however, the campground is a delight. The milky creek flows past on one side, perfect for cooling off. Drinking water is available at the aptly named Fern Spring, where chlorinated water is now available. The ground, dusty from heavy use, nonetheless is soft enough to make for excellent tenting, and cottonwood trees provide ample shade. And then there are the falls.

During monsoon season, pitch your tent in an area high above the creek. During my last visit, a half-dozen mangled picnic tables in Havasu Creek served as evidence of recent flash floods through the area. If you're seeking solitude, travel farther downstream from the campground's entrance. The camping area is nearly a half-mile long, and few people lug their packs all the way to the end nearest Mooney Falls. However, bear in mind that you may have to walk all the way back to the entrance to find a useable toilet.

10 miles from Hualapai Hilltop on the Havasu Canyon Trail. ✆ **928/448-2141.** $20 per person entrance fee, plus $10 per person per night. MC, V. Open year-round.

Havasupai Lodge   For a place halfway to the bottom of the Grand Canyon and 8 miles from the nearest road, this motel is appealing enough. The rooms, which open onto a grassy courtyard, could use new fixtures and drapery. (Simply put, a lot of things are broken.) But they're clean and air-conditioned—a real blessing when the red rock walls around the town begin radiating the midsummer heat. And, after a long mule ride or hike, the mattresses will feel just right. Even if there were televisions, the coolest entertainment would be the waterfalls, which you can reach on horseback from the lodge for $60, or on foot for free.

The Havasupai Cafe, across from the general store, serves breakfast, lunch, and dinner. It's a casual place where people fritter time over french fries and fry bread. The food is relatively inexpensive despite the fact that most ingredients are packed in by horse.

General Delivery, Supai, AZ 86435. ✆ **928/448-2111.** . 24 units. $80 double, plus $20 per person entry fee. MC, V.

NEAR HUALAPAI HILLTOP

Grand Canyon Caverns Inn *Value*   The closest lodging to Hualapai Hilltop, this motel sits as far off the beaten path as you can get in the Grand Canyon area. The rooms probably look much the same as they did in the 1950s. In mine, polished rocks and crystals had been mounted, framed, and hung on a wall that had striped wallpaper. The main attractions are the outdoor swimming pool, the nearby caverns, and the space itself. Come sunset, that is more than enough to make the stay enjoyable.

P.O. Box 180 (on Hwy. 66, 12 miles east of Peach Springs, 25 miles west of Seligman), Peach Springs, AZ 86434. © **928/422-3223.** Fax 928/422-4470. www.gccaverns.com. 48 units. Mar 1–Oct 31 $62 double; Nov 1–Feb 29 $42 double. AE, DC, DISC, MC, V. Pets accepted ($50 deposit required). **Amenities:** Outdoor pool. *In room:* A/C, TV (barely).

8

A Nature Guide to Grand Canyon National Park

A photograph of the Grand Canyon may tell a thousand words, but a thousand words don't begin to tell the canyon's story, which spans more than 2 billion years. This chapter tells more of that story. The landscape section discusses the rock layers and how the canyon was carved. The flora section describes common plants, ranging from fir trees on the rims to barrel cacti on the canyon floor. The fauna section covers the creatures that flourish in the canyon's forbidding climes. And the ecology section explores a very recent development—the effects of humans.

1 The Ecosystem

Grand Canyon National Park is a continuation of the land around it—land that's far from pristine. Its air is clouded by distant industry and not-so-distant automobiles, its largest river constricted by dams, its silence shattered by high-flying jets and low-flying sightseeing planes. Theodore Roosevelt's dictum—to "leave it as it is"—now seems oversimplified. In the new millennium, the canyon's ecology depends nearly as much on far-reaching public policy as on nature.

EFFECTS OF THE GLEN CANYON RIVER DAM Some of the most significant changes in the ecology of the Grand Canyon result from the Glen Canyon Dam, which constricts the Colorado River just northeast of Grand Canyon. Finished in 1963, the dam provides large amounts of subsidized hydroelectric power for cities such as Phoenix and recreational opportunities for approximately four million visitors to Lake Powell every year.

In addition to inundating the once majestic Glen Canyon area, the dam has completely altered the biological communities in and around the Colorado River inside Grand Canyon. Water temperatures in the canyon used to fluctuate from near freezing in winter to 80°F (27°C) or warmer in summer. A mere trickle in winter, the river surged during the spring snowmelt to levels five times higher than the largest floods today. Now, penstocks 230 feet below the surface of Lake Powell take in water that varies only slightly from 48°F (9°C) year-round, at a rate that hardly changes. And the water itself has been sanitized. In pre-dam days, the Colorado carried tons of reddish silt that had washed into it from the canyons of the Four Corners area (thus the name "Rio Colorado," Spanish for "red river"). Today, that silt settles to the bottom of the torpid waters of Lake Powell, and the river emerges from the dam as clear as snowmelt.

These changes decimated the canyon's native fish, which had evolved to survive in the extreme temperatures, powerful flows, and heavy silt of the old river. Four of the eight native fish species died off, and one—the humpback chub—is breeding only where warmer tributaries enter the Colorado. In their places, rainbow trout, which were introduced below the dam for sport fishing, have flourished. Along the shores, tamarisk and coyote willow choke riverbanks that pre-dam floods once purged of vegetation. This vegetation now is home to a variety of small lizards, mammals, and waterfowl, which, in turn, attract birds of prey such as the peregrine falcon.

Another effect of the dam has been the loss of an estimated 45% of the beaches along the Colorado River. Before the dam was built, the canyon's huge floods lifted sand off the bottom of the river and deposited it in large beaches and sandbars. The post-dam flows are too weak to accomplish this. There's also a shortage of sand: the reservoir captures approximately 95% of the sand that would otherwise come into the canyon from upstream.

In March 1996, the Bureau of Reclamation, the National Park Service, and a group of concerned environmental groups sought to find out whether a man-made flood released from the dam would restore some of the beaches. For 7 days in March and April 1996, the dam unloosed a sustained flow of 45,000 cubic feet per second—the maximum it could safely release. Although the flood packed only a fraction of the force of pre-dam deluges, it temporarily restored parts of 80 canyon beaches, and most scientists initially deemed the experiment—known as the Beach Habitat Restoration Flood—to be a success.

Still, the long-term prognosis for the beaches isn't good. With the dam in place, years can pass before enough sand accumulates for a productive man-made flood. And the beaches created during the 1996 flood eroded faster than expected—85% of them had washed away within 6 months. Today, most scientists value the project for what it taught them about spiked flows, but as little more than a Band-Aid in restoring beaches and natural aquatic habitats.

The Hoover Dam, near Las Vegas, also affects the canyon. The last 35 miles of the Colorado River in the Grand Canyon are submerged in the still waters of Lake Mead, the reservoir above Hoover Dam.

EFFECTS OF AIR TRAFFIC   While the dams control the river, airplanes and helicopters break the natural silence. For years, planes and helicopters were free to fly anywhere over the canyon and below the rims. Then, after a collision between sightseeing aircraft killed 25 people in 1986, the FAA established strict flight corridors for the aircraft and forced helicopters and planes to fly at different altitudes.

Although sightseeing flights have long been forbidden over Grand Canyon Village, their droning is still audible at popular destinations, and public opinion supports reductions in noise. In 2000, the FAA implemented a new set of regulations for sightseeing flights over Grand Canyon. These rules froze the maximum number of air-tour flights per year at the number between May 1997 and April 1998, tightened requirements for the reporting of flights, and replaced one meandering flight route in the western canyon with two straighter ones.

Unfortunately, most visitors won't notice any changes. The busiest flight corridors still thrive, and only a small part of the canyon is out of earshot of aircraft noise, which travels an average of 16 miles laterally from aircraft in the eastern canyon and even farther in the west. However, the cap on flights does ensure that, at the very least, the problem shouldn't worsen much in the future.

By keeping the number of flights relatively constant, the FAA made it easier for researchers to monitor the acoustics in the park. The Park Service and Federal Aviation Administration may use this data in the years ahead, when they discuss ways to achieve Congress's goal of restoring "natural quiet" to at least 50% of the park at least 75% of the time by the year 2008.

The Park Service believes this goal can be safely achieved through a combination of smaller flight corridors, quieter aircraft, and fewer (or shorter) flights. But many obstacles loom. For starters, the Park Service and FAA must agree on exactly what Congress meant. The safety of air traffic over the canyon cannot be compromised. And, while environmental groups press for quiet, representatives from the area's air tour industry are likely to challenge any new limits on their operations.

Protecting the Environment

Here are a few things you can do during your stay to protect Grand Canyon National Park:

- **Respect the animals.** When accustomed to handouts, wild animals are nuisances at best, dangerous at worst. Deer will sometimes butt, kick, or gore people who have food; squirrels, which may carry rabies and even bubonic plague, won't hesitate to bite the hand that feeds them. And human food isn't good for wildlife. In recent years, the park has been forced to shoot deer that have become sickly from eating human food. So don't feed the critters. With your cooperation, they can live in the park in something akin to a natural state.

- **Report sightings of California condors and stay at least 300 feet away from them.** The endangered California condor, the largest land bird in North America, was reintroduced to the wild just north of Grand Canyon in 1996. Unafraid of people, many of the condors eventually began venturing to crowded areas on the South Rim. If the condors—identifiable by their grayish-black coloration, orangish heads, and triangular white patches under each wing—become accustomed to people, their survival will be jeopardized. Already, one has been killed by a poacher, another by flying into a power line. The park asks that visitors stay at least 300 feet from the birds and report any sightings to a ranger.

- **Stay on designated trails.** Short-cutting is riskier on the steep trails at Grand Canyon than at other parks. Besides falling, people who cut trails often kick off rockfall dangerous to those below. Short-cutting also digs paths that channel water during storms, causing unnecessary erosion of desert soils. Throughout the canyon, off-trail hikers frequently trample cryptogamic

AIR POLLUTION Another factor affecting the canyon's ecology is air pollution, which on some days decreases the visibility over the canyon from more than 200 miles to less than 50. In summer, much of the air pollution comes from urban areas in southern California,

soils—delicate plants that take as long as 100 years to form.

- **Pack it out.** Even when day-hiking, remember to carry out anything that you bring.

- **Pick up litter and recycle.** Even small bits of litter such as cigarette butts can add up to a big mess in the crowded areas on the rim. Pieces of paper that blow into the canyon can take decades to decay in the dry desert air. So can seemingly harmless organic material such as orange and banana peels and apple cores. Also note that plastic, glass, and aluminum are recycled in bins alongside trash receptacles throughout the park.

- **Leave plants, rocks, and artifacts in place.** Removing any of these things not only detracts from the beauty of the park but is against the law. While it may seem innocuous to pick a flower, imagine what would happen if each of the park's five million visitors did so.

- **Use the shuttles.** From March 1 to November 30, Grand Canyon Village, Hermits Rest Route, the Canyon View Information Plaza, and Yaki and Yavapai points are accessible via free shuttles, all of which pass through the Maswik Transportation Center. By using the shuttle, you can ease congestion, noise, and air pollution.

If you'd like to do something extra to help the park and make some new friends, sign up for the canyon's **Habitat Restoration Program,** which works to restore the park's natural environment. Activities include seed gathering, the removal of exotic species, and revegetating areas where the soils have been disturbed. During high season on the South Rim, a group usually meets in the morning and works for an hour or two. To find out more, ask at the Canyon View Center.

southern Arizona, Nevada, and northern Mexico. In winter, during periods of calm weather, nearby pollution sources play a more significant role. Overall, ozone levels in the park have been steadily rising, and visibility has declined.

The federal Clean Air Act mandates that natural visibility eventually be restored to all National Parks and Wilderness Areas by 2065. Seeking to accomplish this at Grand Canyon, the National Park Service regularly takes part in a commission that includes state and Environmental Protection Agency regulators, Native American tribal leaders, industry representatives, and other interested parties.

The commission achieved a major victory in 1999, when scrubbers were installed at the Navajo Generating Station in Page, Arizona. This coal-burning station may have been responsible for as much as half of the canyon's air pollution in winter, according to Park Service estimates.

Yet the problem extends far past obvious polluters in the immediate area. For natural visibility to be restored, pollution sources ranging from automobile emissions in Los Angeles to factories in Mexico must be addressed. WRAP (the Western Regional Air Partnership) targeted at least a few of these distant polluters in 2001, when it proposed a declining cap on sulfur dioxide emissions throughout the western states.

FOREST FIRES   Even as National Park Service scientists fret over air quality, they know that more forest fires are needed in the ponderosa pine forest on the canyon rims. Before humans began suppressing forest fires, these areas experienced low-intensity blazes every 7 to 10 years. These fires made the forest healthier by burning excess undergrowth and deadfall, thinning tree stands, and returning nutrients to the soil. After fire suppression began, however, deadfall and excess undergrowth accumulated on the forest floors, and trees grew too close together. With so much "fuel" available, the fires that did occur burned much hotter than before—hot enough, even, to kill old-growth ponderosas, which tend to be fire-resistant. Once dead, stands of these grand old trees were often supplanted by faster-growing aspen and fir trees.

In the late 1990s, Congress appropriated additional federal funding for land agencies to manage fire for ecological benefits, either through prescribed burns or what the government calls "fire-use fires"—unplanned blazes that are allowed to burn. The new funds will enable the National Park Service to burn more areas, more often, improving the health of its forests. Taking into account factors such as air quality, weather, location, fire-danger level, and available manpower, Grand Canyon National Park hopes to eventually do prescribed burns on 7,000 to 10,000 acres per year, far above levels in the early '90s.

Of course, fire use is not an exact science, and in May 2000, a prescribed burn on the North Rim spread faster and farther than expected, blackening over 14,000 acres near Point Imperial on the North Rim and closing parts of the park for weeks. Because the effects of the fire were obvious to visitors, the National Park Service in 2001 devoted much of the North Rim version of *The Guide* to a discussion of the ecological benefits of wild-land fires.

2 The Landscape

If you could observe 2 billion years pass in an hour, you'd see the land from which the Grand Canyon is carved wander across the globe, traveling as far south as the equator and perhaps even farther. You'd see it dip below sea level, rise as mountains, dry into dunes, and smother under swamps. You'd watch as different sediments such as silt, mud, and sand, were deposited (usually by water) atop it. Out of sight, compacted from above and cemented together by minerals, these sediments would eventually form *sedimentary* rocks such as sandstone, siltstone, limestone, and shale. Some of these rocks would resurface later, only to be eroded by wind and water. Others would remain safely buried. Because the canyon itself may be as little as 6 million years old, you probably wouldn't recognize it until the last 11 seconds of the hour, when two or more rivers began to cut down through the rocks of the Colorado Plateau. All of human history would require only a quarter second at the end of the hour.

Although you can't personally experience the canyon's two-billion-year history, the layers of rock in the Grand Canyon record much of what happened during that time. Because the rocks are both well-preserved and exposed down to very deep layers, the canyon is one of the best places in the world for geologists to learn about the Paleozoic era—and even earlier.

The record starts with the **Vishnu Formation,** consisting of schist, gneiss, and granite. The oldest and deepest layer in the canyon, it's the black rock draped like a wizard's robe directly above the Colorado River. Originally laid down as sedimentary rock, the layer was driven deep into the earth underneath a mountain range more than 1.7 billion years ago. There, it was heated to temperatures so extreme (1,100°F) and under pressure so great that its chemical composition changed, making it a *metamorphic* rock that's much harder and glossier than the others.

The Grand Canyon Supergroup, a group of sedimentary and *igneous* (volcanic) rocks laid down between 1.25 billion and 600 million years ago, appears directly above the schist in numerous locations in the canyon. These pastel-colored layers stand out because they're tilted at about 20 degrees. **Desert View** is one good place to see them. Once part of a series of small mountain ranges, the Supergroup was shaved off by erosion, disappearing from many parts of the canyon.

Where the Supergroup has disappeared, the **Tapeats Sandstone layer** sits right on top of the Vishnu Formation, even though a gap of over a billion years separates the two layers. Caused by erosion, this huge gap is commonly referred to as the **Great Unconformity.** Because of it, the layers have little in common. While the Vishnu Formation predates atmospheric oxygen, the Tapeats Sandstone contains fossils of sponges and trilobites that date to the Cambrian explosion of life. It also tells us about the beginnings of an incursion of the Tapeats Sea 545 million years ago. At that time, the water was so shallow and so turbulent that only the heaviest particles—sand—could sink. That sand eventually formed the sandstone.

The Bright Angel Shale forms the gently sloping blue-gray layer (known as the Tonto Platform) above the Tapeats Sandstone. It tells of a Tapeats Sea that had become deeper and considerably calmer in this area. Some 540 million years ago, the water was calm enough to let fine-grained sediment settle to the bottom. The sediment formed a muck that eventually became the shale.

Above it is the **Muav Limestone,** which dates back 530 million years. The Muav layer recalls a Tapeats Sea that was deeper still in this area—so deep that feathery bits of shell from tiny marine creatures sank. These bits of shell, together with other calcium carbonate that precipitated naturally out of the water, created limestone. Where not stained by the layers above, the Muav appears as a yellowish cliff underneath an obvious layer known as the Redwall Limestone.

About halfway between rim and river, the **Redwall Limestone** forms some of the canyon's steepest cliffs—800 feet in places. This imposing rock layer tells us about a Mississippian-age sea that deposited layers of calcium carbonate across all of what is now North America from 360 to 320 million years ago. Silvery gray under the surface, the Redwall is stained red by iron oxide from the red rocks above. To see the true color of the Redwall, look for places where pieces have recently broken off.

Just above the Redwall is the **Supai Group.** Formed about 300 million years ago, these layers of sandstone, shale, and siltstone were deposited in tidal flats along shorelines. They usually form a series of red ledges just above the Redwall cliffs. Right above them, and even deeper red, is the Hermit Shale, which was deposited in the flood plain of one or more great rivers around 285 million years ago. This soft shale usually forms a gentle slope or platform directly below the **Coconino Sandstone.**

The Coconino may be the easiest layer in the canyon to identify. The third layer from the top, it's the color of desert sand and forms cliffs that are nearly as sheer as those of the Redwall. The Coconino was laid down as dunes in a Sahara-like desert that covered this land about 280 million years ago. Everywhere in this layer, you'll see the slanted lines caused by cross-bedding—places where new dunes blew in atop old ones. While the other layers display fossils that become increasingly complex through time (the Supai contains fossils of insects and ferns, and marine invertebrates are common in the Redwall), the only imprints in the Coconino are lizard and arthropod tracks that always go uphill. This seems odd until you watch a lizard on sand. It digs in while going up, making firm imprints in the process, then smears its tracks coming down. Some of these fossils are visible along the South Kaibab Trail.

On the top sit the canyon's youngest rocks—the yellow-gray **Toroweap Formation** and the cream-colored **Kaibab Limestone,** which forms the rim rock. Both were deposited by the same warm, shallow sea from 260 to 250 million years ago, when this land was roughly 350 feet below sea level. Younger rock layers once laid atop the Kaibab Formation, but they have eroded off in most areas around the canyon. However, a few remnants of these layers remain. To see them, look east from Desert View to nearby Cedar Mountain or northeast to the Vermilion and Echo cliffs.

MOVING MOUNTAINS   Today, the ancient rocks are part of the **Colorado Plateau.** Between 65 and 38 million years ago, this land was lifted by a process known as subduction. When a continental plate butts up against an oceanic plate, the heavier, denser oceanic plate slips underneath it. Like an arm reaching under a mattress, this slipping—or subduction—can elevate land (on the upper plate) that's far inland from the continental margins. This happened in the Four Corners area during an event known as the **Laramide Orogeny.** At that time, the Pacific plate was subducted under the North American plate, pushing the 130,000 square miles of land in the present-day Four Corners area to elevations ranging from 5,000 to 13,000 feet. This area, which consists of many smaller individual plateaus and landforms, is today known as the Colorado Plateau. The Grand Canyon area has six plateaus—the Coconino and Hualapai on the

South Rim; and the Kaibab, Kanab, Uinkaret, and Shivwits on the North Rim—that are part of the larger Colorado Plateau.

Because the earth's crust is very thick under the Grand Canyon area, the layers of rock here rose without doing much collapsing or shearing. In those places where significant faulting did take place, the rocks sometimes folded instead of breaking. Places where rocks bend in a single fold are known as **monoclines.** As you drive your car up the 4,800-vertical-foot climb from Lee's Ferry to Jacob Lake on the North Rim, you'll ascend the East Kaibab monocline. As you drive east from Grandview Point, you'll descend the Grandview monocline. In both cases, you'll remain on the same rock layer, the Kaibab Formation, the whole time.

The Colorado Plateau is an excellent place for canyon formation for three reasons. First, it sits at a minimum of 5,000 feet above sea level, so water has a strong pull to saw through the land. This makes the rivers here more active than, say, the Mississippi, which descends just 1,670 feet over the course of 2,350 miles. With an average drop of 8 feet per mile, the Colorado River in Grand Canyon is 11 times steeper than the Mississippi. Second, its desert terrain has little vegetation to hold it in place, so it erodes quickly during rains. Third, those rains often come in monsoons that fall hard and fast, cutting deep grooves instead of eroding the land more evenly, as softer, more frequent rains would.

The different layers and types of rock make the resulting canyons more spectacular, perhaps, than any in the world. In addition to being different colors, the rocks vary in hardness and erode at different rates. Known as **differential erosion,** this phenomenon is responsible for the **stair-step effect** one finds at the Grand Canyon.

Here's how it works: The softer rocks—usually shales—erode fastest, undercutting cliffs of harder rock above them. During melt-freeze cycles in winter, water seeps into cracks in these now-vulnerable cliffs, freezes, and expands, chiseling off boulders that collapse onto the layers below. These collapsed rocks tumble down into boulder fields such as those at the bases of the canyon's temples. The biggest rock slides sometimes pile up in ramps that make foot descents possible through cliff areas. Where soft rock has eroded off of hard rock underneath it, platforms are formed. One such platform, known as the Esplanade, is obvious in the western canyon. The end result is a series of platforms and cliffs.

Runoff drives the process, and more of it comes from the North Rim. This happens for two reasons. First, the land through which the canyon is cut slopes gently from north to south. So runoff from the North Rim drains into the canyon while runoff from the South Rim drains away from it. And more precipitation falls at the higher elevations on the North Rim—25 inches, as opposed to 16 for the South Rim. As this water makes its way—often along fault lines—to the Colorado River, it cuts side canyons that drain into the main one.

These side canyons tend to become longer and more gradual through time. Since the runoff can't cut any lower than the Colorado River, it tends to eat away the land near the top of each side canyon. As this happens, the head of each canyon slowly moves closer to its water source—a process known as headward erosion. If you're standing at Grand Canyon Village looking down the Bright Angel fault, you may notice that the gorge formed along it is longer on the north side of the Colorado River. This is typical of the side canyons in the Grand Canyon. Because more water comes off the North Rim, more erosion has taken place on that side of the river, and longer canyons have been formed.

AND THEN CAME THE FLOODS   The eroded material has to go somewhere. The rocks that fall into the side canyons are swept into the Colorado River, usually by flash floods during the canyon's August monsoon season. While it may be hard to imagine a current this strong in what is usually a dry or nearly dry side canyon, look again at how thousands of tiny drainages converge like capillaries into a single significant creek bed. In most cases, several square miles of hard land drains into one relatively narrow rock chute. When a downpour falls at the canyon, it can generate floods that are immensely powerful and very dangerous.

Below each significant side canyon are boulders, swept into the Colorado River by these floods. These boulders form dams in the larger river, creating rapids where the water spills over them. The water above each set of rapids usually looks as smooth as a reservoir. Below the first rocks, however, it cascades downstream, crashing backward in standing waves against large boulders. Before Glen Canyon dam was built, the Colorado River broke up many of the biggest rocks during its enormous spring floods. These floods, which commonly reached levels five times higher than an average flow today, swept along small rocks, which would in turn chip away and break apart boulders, eventually moving *them* downstream. For the canyon to have reached its present size, the river had to sweep away more than 1,000 cubic miles of debris. Now, with the enormous spring floods a thing of the past, less debris is being moved, and the rapids have become steeper and rockier.

While it's fairly easy to explain how the side canyons cut down to the level of the Colorado River, it's much harder to say how the Colorado cut through the plateaus that form the sides of the Grand Canyon. Unless the river was already in place when these adjoining plateaus started rising roughly 60 million years ago, it would have had to first climb 3,000 feet uphill before it could begin cutting down. The explorer John Wesley Powell, who mapped the Colorado River in 1869, assumed that the river had cut down through the land as the land rose. The river in the eastern canyon may indeed be old enough to have accomplished this. The western canyon, however, is much younger. In fact, there's no evidence of a through-flowing Colorado River in the western Grand Canyon before about five million years ago.

Geologists have proposed a number of theories about how the river assumed its present course, none of which is supported by a strong body of evidence. Most center on the idea of an ancestral Colorado River that flowed through the eastern canyon, exiting the canyon via a channel different from its current one. The ancestral Colorado River would have been diverted onto its present course by another, smaller river that probably reached it via headward erosion. Depending on the theory you choose, this "pirate" river may have cut headward all the way from the Gulf of California, or it may have originated on the Kaibab Plateau during a period when the climate was wetter than it is today. No one is sure what happened, and the debate is still open.

3 The Flora

C. Hart Merriam, an American zoologist who studied the plant life around the canyon in 1889, grouped the species here in geographical ranges that he called "life zones." According to Merriam, different life zones resulted from "laws of temperature control" that corresponded to changes in elevations. Each life zone began and ended at a particular elevation, much like the rock layers that ring the canyon walls.

Merriam's theory was a good one at the time, but he didn't immediately recognize the significance of other variables. Today, naturalists understand that the Grand Canyon's flora are strongly affected by factors such as air currents, water flows, soil types, slope degree, and slope aspect. Most naturalists now prefer to talk about biological communities, avoiding the mistake of fixing species in any particular "zone."

However, if your goal is to identify a few major plant species and the general areas where you might find them, life zones still work fairly well. So we'll use them, with thanks to Dr. Merriam. The canyon's five life zones are: **Boreal,** from 8,000 to 9,100 feet; **Transition,** from 7,000 to 8,000 feet; **Upper Sonoran,** from 4,000 to 7,500 feet; **Lower Sonoran,** from the bottom of the canyon to 4,000 feet; and **Riparian,** along the banks of the Colorado River and its tributaries. Some of the more common or unusual plants in each zone are as follows:

BOREAL ZONE

Douglas fir   Found on the North Rim and on isolated north-facing slopes below the South Rim, the Douglas fir grows up to 130 feet high and 6 feet in diameter. You'll often find it in areas close to the North Rim itself. Its soft 1-inch-long needles generally grow in pairs. Its hanging cones, which grow to about 3 inches long, each have three-pronged bracts between their scales. The Douglas fir is built for cold weather; its branches, while cupped, are flexible enough to slough off snow.

Douglas fir

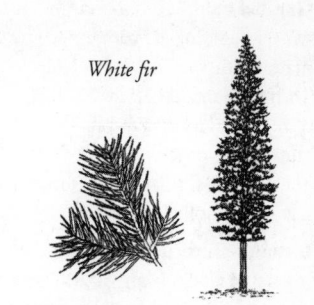

White fir

White fir   You'll know you've moved into spruce-fir forest when you start tripping over deadfall and running into low branches. One of the more common trees in this high-alpine forest, the white fir has smooth, gray bark; cones that grow upright to about 4 inches long; and 2-inch-long, two-sided curving needles. The white fir closely resembles the subalpine fir. But the branches of the subalpine fir, unlike those of the white fir, grow to ground level, and its needles are about an inch shorter. Another common tree in this forest is the blue spruce, recognizable by its blue color and sharp needles.

TRANSITION ZONE

Big sagebrush   More common on the rims than in the canyons, this fuzzy gray-green plant grows to 4 feet high on thick wood stalks. To make sure you haven't misidentified it as rabbit brush (another gray-green plant of comparable size), look at a leaf—it should have three tiny teeth at the end. Or simply break off a sprig (outside the park) and smell it. If it doesn't smell divine, it's not sagebrush. Some Indian tribes burned sage bundles during purification rituals.

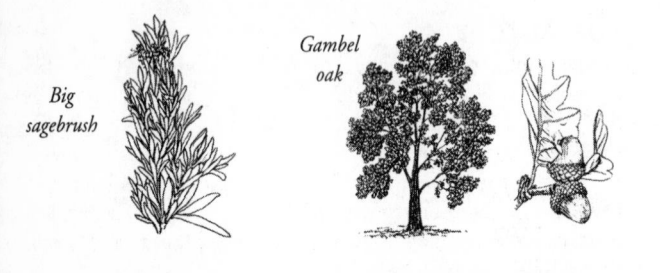

Gambel oak

Big sagebrush

Gambel oak   To find Gambel (or scrub) oak on the South Rim in winter, look for the bare trees. The only deciduous tree in the immediate vicinity of the South Rim, its leaves turn orange before falling. To find Gambel oak in summer, look for its acorns, its long (up to 6 in.) lobed leaves, and its gray trunk. It grows in thick clumps that clutter the otherwise open floor of the ponderosa pine forest. A plant with a similar name, shrub oak, grows lower in the canyon and has sharp, hollylike leaves.

Indian paintbrush   You should be able to identify this plant from the name alone. Many of its leaves are colored red or orange at their tips, making them look as if they've been dipped in paint.

Indian paintbrush

Lupine

Lupine   Common on both rims, this purple flower blooms from spring to late summer. You can spot lupine by its palmate leaves and tiny purple flowers growing in clusters at the top of its main stem.

Ponderosa pine   Found on both rims and in isolated places in the canyon, this tree can withstand forest fires, provided the fires come often enough to keep the fuel on the forest floor to a minimum. Its thick bark shields the inside of the tree from the heat. When the fires are over, the ponderosa thrives on the nutrients in the ash-covered soil. Once the tree's low branches have burned off, fires can no longer climb to the crown. So the trees that survive grow stronger. To spot a mature ponderosa pine, look for its thick red-orange bark (younger ones have blackish bark), its 6-inch-long needles in groups of three, and its absence of low branches. Once you've identified one, smell its bark—you'll be rewarded with a rich vanilla-like scent.

Quaking aspen   The ponderosa pine may smell the best, but tree-huggers should save the last dance for the quaking aspen, which grows alongside it in many North Rim forests. Its cool, dusty white bark feels great against your cheek on a hot day. Its leaves, on long, twisted stems, shudder at the very idea of a breeze. If you hug one aspen you're probably hugging many. Dozens and sometimes hundreds of these trees have been known to sprout from a common root system, meaning they're technically one plant. In fact, one of the world's largest organisms is a quaking aspen in Utah.

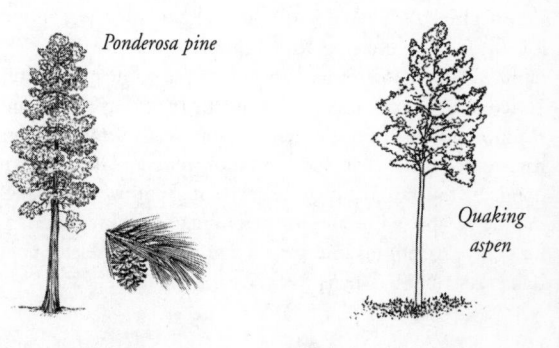

Ponderosa pine

Quaking aspen

UPPER SONORAN
Cliff rose & Apache plume   These flowering shrubs, which grow both on the rims and in the canyon, have much in common. Both are members of the rose family, grow tiny five-lobed leaves, and send up numerous delicate flowers from which feathery plumes sometimes

protrude. However, a few differences do exist: Cliff rose is the larger of the two, growing to a maximum of 25 feet, compared to 5 feet for the Apache plume. Its flowers are a creamy yellow, as opposed to white for the Apache plume. And its leaves, unlike those of the Apache plume, are hairless. The Apache plume blooms a few weeks longer—from early spring into October.

Cliff rose

Apache plume

Mormon tea   Common throughout the park, this virtually leafless plant has hundreds of jointed, needlelike stems that point skyward. Once the plants are full-grown, they remain largely unchanged for as long as 500 years. Photos of desert scenes taken more than 50 years apart show the same Mormon tea plants with every stem still in place. The only difference between young and old plants is color—the older plants are yellow-green or even yellow-gray; the younger ones are light green. Both the early Mormon pioneers and the Indians used the stems, which contain pseudoephedrine and tannin, for medicine.

Piñon pine   Wherever a new juniper tree sprouts, a piñon pine usually follows, growing to about the same size (30 ft.) as the juniper. Shorter and rounder than most pines, the piñon pine grows 1-inch-long needles, usually in pairs. It commonly takes root in the shadows of juniper trees, which are more heat-tolerant. Their system has worked well. Together, the piñon pine and the Utah juniper dominate much of the high desert in the Southwest. Packing 2,500 calories per pound, piñon (or pine) nuts have always been a staple for Native Americans in this area, and today they're also popular in Italian restaurants, where they're used to make pesto.

Piñon pine

Utah agave & banana yucca   The plants consisting of 3-foot-long spikes are most often agave or yucca. Agave leaves have serrated edges, while yucca leaves have rough, sandpaper-like sides. The Indians in the canyon used fibers and leaves from these plants to make sandals, baskets, and rope. If you were to break off a particularly sharp leaf and peel away the fibers from its edge, you would eventually end up with a thread with a needlelike tip. The agave blooms only once every 15 to 25 years. When it does, it's easy to spot—its spiky base sends up a wooden stalk, about 14 feet high, atop which yellow flowers grow. Because this flourish occurs so rarely, the agave is often referred to as the century plant. After flowering, it dies. Some naturalists theorize that the agave, whose leaves become rich in nutrients just before it flowers, evolved to bloom rarely so animals would not grow accustomed to eating it. This trick didn't fool the Ancestral Puebloans, who discovered that the roasted hearts of the plant were always nutritious. Unlike the agave, the banana yucca blooms every 2 to 3 years, sending up 4-foot-high stalks on which yellow flowers hang. Its fruit, which tastes a bit like banana, ripens later in summer.

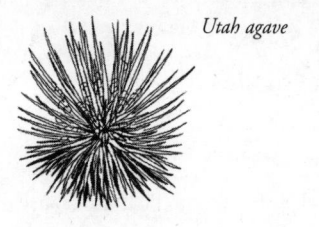

Utah agave

Banana yucca

Utah juniper   This tree, which seldom grows higher than 30 feet, *looks* like it belongs in the desert. Its scraggy bark is as dry as straw, its tiny leaves are tight and scalelike, and its gnarled branches appear to have endured, well, everything. Burned in campfires since the dawn of time, juniper wood releases a fragrant smoke that evokes the desert as much as the yipping of coyotes. Its dusty-looking blue berries are actually cones, each with one or two small seeds inside.

Utah juniper

LOWER SONORAN

Barrel cactus The barrel cactus does indeed resemble a small green barrel. One of the more efficient desert plants, it can survive for years without water. Contrary to the popular myth, however, there's no reservoir of drinking water inside.

Barrel cactus

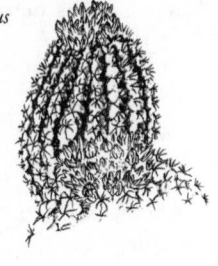

Blackbrush The blue-gray color of the Tonto Platform (above the Tapeats Sandstone) doesn't derive solely from the Bright Angel Shale. It also comes from blackbrush, a gray, spiny, 3-foot-high plant that dominates the flora atop the platform. Blackbrush grows leathery half-inch-long leaves on tangled branches that turn black when wet. Because the plant's root system is considerably larger than the plant itself, each blackbrush bush commands plenty of area. There are usually 10 to 15 feet between plants.

Hedgehog cactus The hedgehog cactus looks like a cluster of prickly cucumbers standing on end. Of the four species in the canyon, the most colorful is the claret cup, which sprouts crimson flowers every spring.

Honey mesquite & catclaw acacia   These two species of tree, which favor the walls above rivers or creek beds, show us the heights reached by the Colorado River's pre-dam floods. After a flood recedes, acacia and mesquite seedlings take root in the moist soil. Later, the maturing trees send pipelike roots down to the river or creek bed. Both species have dark branches and leaves with small paired leaflets, reach heights of about 20 feet, and grow seedpods several inches long. The mesquite's leaflets, however, are longer and narrower than the acacia's. And while the acacia has tiny barbs like cat claws for protection, the mesquite grows paired inch-long thorns where the leaves meet the stems. Mesquite beans were a staple for the Ancestral Puebloans.

Hedgehog cactus

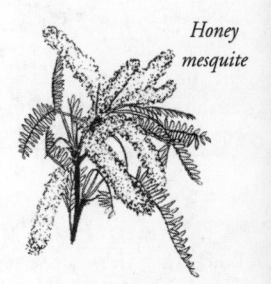
Honey mesquite

Opuntia cactus   Most members of this family are known as prickly pear. Although prickly pears do grow on the South Rim, the most impressive are lower in the canyon. There, the prickly pear's flat oval pads link up in formations that occasionally sprawl across 40 or more square feet of ground. Look closely at each pad and you'll notice that, even in the most contorted formations, the narrow side always points up, cutting down on the sunlight received. Because this cactus tends to hybridize, it produces a variety of yellow, pink, and magenta flowers from April to June. Put a finger inside one of these flowers, and the stamens will curl around it, a reflex designed to coat bees with pollen. Prickly pear pads can be roasted and eaten, and the fruit, which ripens in late summer, is often used to make jelly. There are several species of opuntia, ranging from very prickly (grizzly bear) to spineless (beavertail).

Opuntia cactus/
prickly pear

RIPARIAN

Fremont cottonwood To cool off, look for the bright green canopy of this tree, which grows near many of the tributaries to the Colorado River but seldom by the large river itself. The tree's spreading branches and wide, shimmering leaves shade many of the canyon's springs. Covered with grooved, ropelike bark, the cottonwood's trunk can grow as wide as a refrigerator. Its flowers, which bloom in spring, drop tiny seeds that look like cotton and can ride breezes to distant water sources. A nice grove of these trees shelters the picnic area at Indian Garden.

Tamarisk This exotic species was once used for flood-bank control by the CCC. Today, it is the plant that boaters and hikers love to hate. Before the Glen Canyon dam was built, the Colorado River's annual spring floods thinned or wiped out most of the tamarisk along its banks. Now tamarisk and coyote willow have taken over many beaches, creating thickets that can make hiking miserable. Other animals don't mind the thickets, as they're home to a diverse population of birds, lizards, and insects. Soft as ostrich feathers, the plant's stems grow tiny scalelike leaves and sprout small white flowers in spring. While young tamarisk consists of skinny, flexible stalks, the older plants have wood trunks.

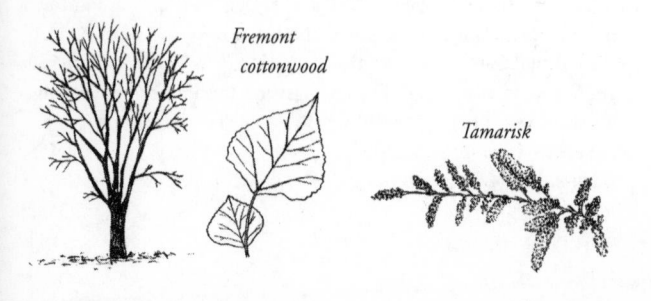

Fremont cottonwood

Tamarisk

4 The Fauna

To view wildlife during your stay at Grand Canyon, bring a flashlight. Most desert animals are either *nocturnal* (active at night) or *crepuscular* (active at dawn and dusk). By laying low during the day, they avoid the powerful sun, cutting their water needs and enabling them to forage or hunt without overheating. All have specialized mechanisms to survive this harsh environment, and many, if provoked, can be as prickly as the plants around them.

MAMMALS

Bats The **western pipestral** is the most common bat at Grand Canyon. At sunset you'll see them flutter above the rim, rising and falling as if on strings. Gray with black wings, they send out supersonic sounds that echo differently off of different objects. The bats then "read" the echoes to determine what they're approaching. If it's an insect, they know what to do. They'll sometimes eat 500 bugs in an hour.

Bighorn sheep If there's a hint of a foothold, a bighorn sheep will find it. Its hooves are hard and durable on the outside but soft and grippy underneath, a perfect design for steep, rocky terrain. You'll often hear them clattering before you spot their stocky, gray-brown bodies and white rumps. Six feet long, the males weigh up to 300 pounds. Their horns are coiled; the females' are straight. Look for bighorn sheep in side canyons that have water, and sometimes on the rims.

Bat

Bighorn sheep

Coyotes Coyotes will eat almost anything—bugs, carrion, plants, rodents, and bird eggs included. Their versatile diet has helped them flourish, and today you'll find them all around the canyon. They look like lanky mid-sized dogs. But their noses are more sharply pointed, and their tails hang between their legs when they run. During summer, their bodies are tan, their bellies white, and their legs rust-colored. In winter, the ones on the rims turn mostly gray. If you camp during your visit, you'll probably hear their squeaky yips and howls at sunset. Look for them at dusk in the meadows on the North Rim or at daybreak around the Tusayan garbage dumpsters.

Coyote

Desert cottontails   Common even in the canyon's most populated areas, these oval-eared rabbits feed on grasses, twigs, juniper berries, and leaves. Their bodies are mostly tan, but sometimes all you'll see is their white tails as they dash away from coyotes and bobcats.

Desert cottontail

Elk

Elk   Merriam's elk, which were native to this area, were hunted off in the 1920s. Transplanted from Yellowstone, Roosevelt elk have flourished on the South Rim. Their bodies are tan; their heads and necks dark brown and shaggy. These long-legged, thick-bodied animals grow to enormous sizes. The bulls weigh as much as 1,000 pounds and stand up to 5 feet high at the shoulders; the cows average 550 pounds. Unlike deer, which prefer bushes and shrubs, elk feed primarily on grasses on the forest floor. Rather than migrate far, they'll dig through snow for forage. Every year the bulls grow large racks, used to battle one another for the cows. In fall, during mating season the bulls can be dangerously aggressive. At this time, you may hear their high-pitched "bugling" inside the park. Herds of elk can often be seen roaming the National Forest on the South Rim near Grandview Point, and less commonly along the North Rim entrance road.

Mountain lions   These solitary cats, whose legs are as powerful as springs, will probably see you before you see them. Sightings around the canyon are rare, even among people who have spent their lives studying them. This isn't because the animals are small—they grow up to 6 feet long and weigh 200 pounds, with cylindrical tails as long as 3 feet. Their coat is tawny everywhere except the chest and muzzle, which are white. Their retractable claws let them alternately sprint across rocks and dig in on softer slopes—bad news for deer and elk, on which they prey. Hunted to near extirpation in this area in the early 1900s, the mountain lion has recovered of late, especially on the North Rim, where over 100 are believed to live.

Mountain lion

Mule deer

Mule deer   These tan or gray ungulates, which grow to as much as 200 pounds, are common everywhere in the park, including developed areas. They often summer on the rims, then move into the canyon or lower on the plateaus in winter, when their fur turns grayish-white. Every year the bucks grow antlers, then shed them in March after battling other males during mating season. Mule deer feed on a variety of bushes and shrubs, but their favorite food may be cliff rose. Active at night, they frequently dart in front of cars, making night driving risky.

Raccoons   Recognizable by their black "bandit" masks, their gray bodies, and tails with black stripes, raccoons are common around the rim campgrounds.

Ringtails   A relative of the raccoon, ringtails frequently raid campsites near the Colorado River. Their tails have luminous white bands. Their ears are pink and mouselike, their bodies gray-brown. They're smart enough and dexterous enough to untie knots. If cornered, they may spray a foul-smelling mist like skunks do. When not raiding campsites, they feed on mice and other small animals. Look for ringtails at night on the rafters inside the El Tovar Restaurant. (The hotel has tried unsuccessfully to move the population.)

Raccoon

Ringtail

Squirrels The Kaibab and Aberts squirrels were once the same species sharing the same ponderosa pine forest. After the canyon separated the squirrels, subtle genetic differences between the groups took hold in later generations. Although both still have tufts of fur above their ears, the Kaibab squirrel, which lives only on the North Rim, is gray with a white tail. The Aberts squirrel, on the South Rim, has a gray body, a reddish back, and a dark tail with white sides. Both still nest in, and feed on the bark of, ponderosa pines, and both are notoriously clueless (even by squirrel standards) around cars. Among the other species, the grayish-brown squirrels seen begging along the rim are rock squirrels. The ones that look like oversized chipmunks are golden-mantled ground squirrels.

Aberts squirrel

Kaibab squirrel

BIRDS

Bald eagles It's hard to mistake a mature bald eagle for any other bird. Dark plumage, a white head and tail, and yellow beak combine to give this bird, with its 6-foot wingspan, a look as distinctive as America itself. During winter, bald eagles frequently sit in trees along the river in the eastern canyon, where they like to fish for trout.

Common ravens These shiny blue-black birds soar like raptors above the rims when not walking like people around the campgrounds. They're big—up to 27 inches long—and smart. In addition to unzipping packs and opening food containers, they've been known to team up and take trout from bald eagles.

Common raven

Bald eagle

Golden eagles Golden-brown from head to talon, this bird is commonly spotted soaring above the rims, its wings spanning to 6 feet or more. Wings tucked, the golden eagle can dive at speeds approaching 100 mph. Although known to kill fawns, it usually prefers smaller mammals. It sometimes can be mistaken for an immature bald eagle.

Great horned owls This bird often perches in trees along the rims. Look for black circles around its eyes, puffy white feathers on its chest, and feathery tufts that resemble horns above its ears.

Golden eagle

Great horned owl

Peregrine falcons Identifiable by its gray back, black-and-white head, and pointed, sickle-shaped wings, this bird frequently preys on waterfowl, sometimes knocking them out of the air. Once endangered, the peregrine has benefited from the outlawing of the harmful pesticide DDT. The canyon is now home to the largest population of peregrines in the continental United States.

Peregrine falcon

Red-tailed hawk

Red-tailed hawks One of the more commonly sighted raptors, the red-tailed hawk flies with its wings on a plane the way an eagle does, but has a smaller (4-ft.) wingspan. Identifiable by its white underside, reddish tail, brown head, and brown back, the red-tailed hawk sometimes drops rattlesnakes from great heights to kill them.

Swifts and swallows Two small birds—**white-throated swifts** and **violet-green swallows**—commonly slice through the air above the rims, picking off bugs. The swift's black-and-white colored body is uniformly narrow from head to tail. Its wings, which curve back toward its tail, seem to alternate strokes as it flies. The swallow, which has a rounder body and green feathers on its back and head, flies more steadily than the swift.

Violet-green swallow

Turkey vultures If you see a group of birds circling, their wings held in "Vs," rocking in the wind like unskilled hang-glider pilots, you're watching a group of turkey vultures. Up close, look for the dark plumage and bald red head. California Condors sometimes follow turkey vultures because the vultures have a better sense of smell and can more easily locate carrion.

Turkey vulture

Wild turkey

Wild turkeys Growing to 4 feet long, the males of this species are easiest to spot. They have bare blue heads, red wattles, and 6-inch-long feathered "beards" on their chests. The females are smaller and less colorful. Common on both rims but seen most often in the meadows on the North Rim, wild turkeys were once raised in pens by the Ancestral Puebloans.

INVERTEBRATES

Black widows These black spiders often spin their irregularly shaped, sticky webs in crevices in the Redwall Limestone. Although they're most active at night, you can occasionally spy one in the shadows. Their large, round abdomens give them a unique appearance. Only the females, recognizable by the red hourglass shape under the abdomen, are poisonous, with bites lethal enough to endanger small children.

Scorpions Like a crayfish, each scorpion has two pincers and a long tail that curls toward its head like a whip. At the end of the tail is a stinger. Of the two species commonly found in the canyon, the most numerous by far is the giant hairy scorpion. Three to four inches long, this tan-colored scorpion inflicts a bite that's usually no worse than a bee sting. The bark (or sculptured) scorpion is more dangerous. Up to 2 inches long and straw-colored, it injects a neurotoxic venom much stronger than that of its larger counterpart.

These bites are very painful and can be deadly in rare cases. The best way to see scorpions is to shine an ultraviolet light on the canyon floor at night—in this light, they glow!

Scorpion

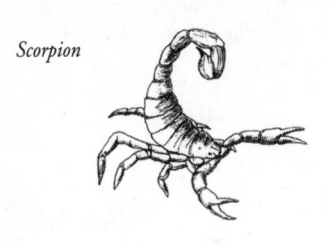

REPTILES

Chuckwallas   Common in the lower parts of the canyon, chuckwallas look as if they've just completed a crash diet, leaving them with skin that's three sizes too big. When threatened, they inflate that loose skin, wedging themselves into crevices in rock piles and cliffs. From 11 to 16 inches long, chuckwallas have blackish heads and forelegs.

Collared lizards   At the middle and lower elevations of the canyon, you'll see a variety of collared lizards, all of which grow to 14 inches long and have big heads, long tails, and two black bands across their shoulders. Usually tan, black-collared lizards change shades when the temperature shifts. Western collared lizards are among the more colorful in the park, with blue, green, and yellow markings supplementing the black bands. These lizards are not the least bit shy around people. Sometimes, they'll stare you down for hours.

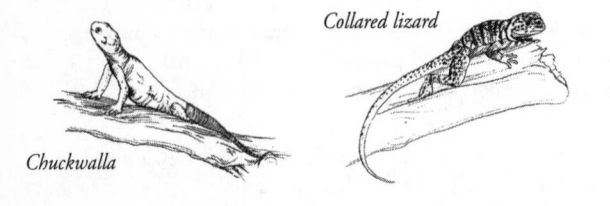

Collared lizard

Chuckwalla

Rattlesnakes   If something rattles at you below the rim, it's probably the Grand Canyon rattlesnake, the most common rattler inside the canyon. Its pinkish skin with dark blotches blends well with the canyon's soil. Like other rattlers, it has a triangular head, heat-sensing pits between its eyes, and a rattle used to warn larger animals. To maintain an acceptable body temperature, this snake becomes active only when the temperature along the ground approaches 78°F (26°C). At other times it's sluggish. It may sun itself on a ledge or curl up under a rock pile or log. Although venomous, the Grand Canyon rattlesnake is more reluctant to bite than other rattlesnakes. They're often seen near water, where they prey on small rodents. Other rattlesnake species are found closer to the rims. On the South Rim, the only common rattlesnake is the Hopi rattlesnake; on the North Rim, it's the Great Basin rattlesnake.

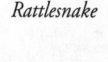
Rattlesnake

Short-horned lizards   These lizards can be found sunning themselves or scurrying across the forest floors on the canyon rims. With horizontal spines on their heads and rows of barbs on their backs, these short, stout lizards look like tiny dinosaurs or "horny toads," as they're commonly called. They'll sometimes ooze blood from their eyes at attackers.

Short-horned lizard

Index

See also Accommodations and Restaurant indexes, below.

ACCOMMODATIONS

Frommer's Portable Guides
Complete Guides for the Short-Term Traveler

FROMMER'S® COMPLETE TRAVEL GUIDES

Alaska
Alaska Cruises & Ports of Call
Amsterdam
Argentina & Chile
Arizona
Atlanta
Australia
Austria
Bahamas
Barcelona, Madrid & Seville
Beijing
Belgium, Holland & Luxembourg
Bermuda
Boston
Brazil
British Columbia & the Canadian
  Rockies
Brussels & Bruges
Budapest & the Best of Hungary
California
Canada
Cancún, Cozumel & the Yucatán
Cape Cod, Nantucket & Martha's
  Vineyard
Caribbean
Caribbean Cruises & Ports of Call
Caribbean Ports of Call
Carolinas & Georgia
Chicago
China
Colorado
Costa Rica
Cuba
Denmark
Denver, Boulder & Colorado Springs
England
Europe
European Cruises & Ports of Call

Florida
France
Germany
Great Britain
Greece
Greek Islands
Hawaii
Hong Kong
Honolulu, Waikiki & Oahu
Ireland
Israel
Italy
Jamaica
Japan
Las Vegas
London
Los Angeles
Maryland & Delaware
Maui
Mexico
Montana & Wyoming
Montréal & Québec City
Munich & the Bavarian Alps
Nashville & Memphis
New England
New Mexico
New Orleans
New York City
New Zealand
Northern Italy
Norway
Nova Scotia, New Brunswick &
  Prince Edward Island
Oregon
Paris
Peru
Philadelphia & the Amish Country
Portugal

Prague & the Best of the Czech
  Republic
Provence & the Riviera
Puerto Rico
Rome
San Antonio & Austin
San Diego
San Francisco
Santa Fe, Taos & Albuquerque
Scandinavia
Scotland
Seattle & Portland
Shanghai
Sicily
Singapore & Malaysia
South Africa
South America
South Florida
South Pacific
Southeast Asia
Spain
Sweden
Switzerland
Texas
Thailand
Tokyo
Toronto
Tuscany & Umbria
USA
Utah
Vancouver & Victoria
Vermont, New Hampshire & Maine
Vienna & the Danube Valley
Virgin Islands
Virginia
Walt Disney World® & Orlando
Washington, D.C.
Washington State

FROMMER'S® DOLLAR-A-DAY GUIDES

Australia from $50 a Day
California from $70 a Day
England from $75 a Day
Europe from $70 a Day
Florida from $70 a Day
Hawaii from $80 a Day

Ireland from $60 a Day
Italy from $70 a Day
London from $85 a Day
New York from $90 a Day
Paris from $80 a Day

San Francisco from $70 a Day
Washington, D.C. from $80 a Day
Portable London from $85 a Day
Portable New York City from $90
  a Day

FROMMER'S® PORTABLE GUIDES

Acapulco, Ixtapa & Zihuatanejo
Amsterdam
Aruba
Australia's Great Barrier Reef
Bahamas
Berlin
Big Island of Hawaii
Boston
California Wine Country
Cancún
Cayman Islands
Charleston
Chicago
Disneyland®
Dublin
Florence

Frankfurt
Hong Kong
Houston
Las Vegas
Las Vegas for Non-Gamblers
London
Los Angeles
Los Cabos & Baja
Maine Coast
Maui
Miami
Nantucket & Martha's Vineyard
New Orleans
New York City
Paris
Phoenix & Scottsdale

Portland
Puerto Rico
Puerto Vallarta, Manzanillo &
  Guadalajara
Rio de Janeiro
San Diego
San Francisco
Savannah
Seattle
Sydney
Tampa & St. Petersburg
Vancouver
Venice
Virgin Islands
Washington, D.C.

FROMMER'S® NATIONAL PARK GUIDES

Banff & Jasper
Family Vacations in the National
  Parks

Grand Canyon
National Parks of the American West
Rocky Mountain

Yellowstone & Grand Teton
Yosemite & Sequoia/Kings Canyon
Zion & Bryce Canyon

FROMMER'S® MEMORABLE WALKS

Chicago
London

New York
Paris

San Francisco

FROMMER'S® WITH KIDS GUIDES

Chicago
Las Vegas
New York City

Ottawa
San Francisco
Toronto

Vancouver
Washington, D.C.

SUZY GERSHMAN'S BORN TO SHOP GUIDES

Born to Shop: France
Born to Shop: Hong Kong,
  Shanghai & Beijing

Born to Shop: Italy
Born to Shop: London

Born to Shop: New York
Born to Shop: Paris

FROMMER'S® IRREVERENT GUIDES

Amsterdam
Boston
Chicago
Las Vegas
London

Los Angeles
Manhattan
New Orleans
Paris
Rome

San Francisco
Seattle & Portland
Vancouver
Walt Disney World®
Washington, D.C.

FROMMER'S® BEST-LOVED DRIVING TOURS

Britain
California
Florida
France

Germany
Ireland
Italy
New England

Northern Italy
Scotland
Spain
Tuscany & Umbria

HANGING OUT™ GUIDES

Hanging Out in England
Hanging Out in Europe

Hanging Out in France
Hanging Out in Ireland

Hanging Out in Italy
Hanging Out in Spain

THE UNOFFICIAL GUIDES®

Bed & Breakfasts and Country
  Inns in:
  California
  Great Lakes States
  Mid-Atlantic
  New England
  Northwest
  Rockies
  Southeast
  Southwest
Best RV & Tent Campgrounds in:
  California & the West
  Florida & the Southeast
  Great Lakes States
  Mid-Atlantic
  Northeast
  Northwest & Central Plains

Southwest & South Central
  Plains
  U.S.A.
Beyond Disney
Branson, Missouri
California with Kids
Central Italy
Chicago
Cruises
Disneyland®
Florida with Kids
Golf Vacations in the Eastern U.S.
Great Smoky & Blue Ridge Region
Inside Disney
Hawaii
Las Vegas
London
Maui

Mexio's Best Beach Resorts
Mid-Atlantic with Kids
Mini Las Vegas
Mini-Mickey
New England & New York with
  Kids
New Orleans
New York City
Paris
San Francisco
Skiing & Snowboarding in the West
Southeast with Kids
Walt Disney World®
Walt Disney World® for
  Grown-ups
Walt Disney World® with Kids
Washington, D.C.
World's Best Diving Vacations

SPECIAL-INTEREST TITLES

Frommer's Adventure Guide to Australia &
  New Zealand
Frommer's Adventure Guide to Central America
Frommer's Adventure Guide to India & Pakistan
Frommer's Adventure Guide to South America
Frommer's Adventure Guide to Southeast Asia
Frommer's Adventure Guide to Southern Africa
Frommer's Britain's Best Bed & Breakfasts and
  Country Inns
Frommer's Caribbean Hideaways
Frommer's Exploring America by RV
Frommer's Fly Safe, Fly Smart

Frommer's France's Best Bed & Breakfasts and
  Country Inns
Frommer's Gay & Lesbian Europe
Frommer's Italy's Best Bed & Breakfasts and
  Country Inns
Frommer's Road Atlas Britain
Frommer's Road Atlas Europe
Frommer's Road Atlas France
The New York Times' Guide to Unforgettable
  Weekends
Places Rated Almanac
Retirement Places Rated
Rome Past & Present

C I T Y P A C K
Prague

By Michael Ivory

Fodor's

Fodor's Travel Publications, Inc.
New York • Toronto • London • Sydney • Auckland

HTTP://WWW.FODORS.COM/

While every care has been taken to ensure the accuracy of the information in this guide, time brings change, and consequently the publisher cannot accept responsibility for errors that may occur. Prudent travelers will therefore want to call ahead to verify prices and other "perishable" information.

© 1997 by The Automobile Association
© Maps copyright 1997 by The Automobile Association
Fold-out map:
© RV Reise- und Verkehrsverlag Munich, Stuttgart
© Cartography: GeoData

Published in the United States by Fodor's Travel Publications, Inc.

Published in the United Kingdom by AA Publishing

Fodor's is a trademark of Fodor's Travel Publications, Inc.

ISBN 0-679-03168-5

First Edition

Fodor's Citypack Prague

Author: Michael Ivory
Cartography: The Automobile Association
RV Reise- und Verkehrsverlag
Cover Design: Fabrizio La Rocca, Allison Saltzman

Special Sales

Fodor's Travel Publications are available at special discounts for bulk purchases (100 copies or more) for sales promotions or premiums. Special editions, including personalized covers, excerpts of existing guides, and corporate imprints, can be created in large quantities for special needs. For more information write to Special Marketing, Fodor's Travel Publications, 201 East 50th St, New York NY 10022.

Origination by BTB Colour Reproduction Ltd, Whitchurch, Hampshire.
Printed by Dai Nippon Printing Co. (Hong Kong) Ltd.

10 9 8 7 6 5 4 3 2 1

Page 87b: Soldiers, Hrad

Page 87a: Civic forum umbrella

Page 61b: Detail over well, Malé Náměstí

Page 61a: Café sign

Page 49b: House of Artists, detail of lamp outside

Page 49a: Door, St. Peter & St. Paul, Vyšehradská

Page 23a: Decorative Arts Museum

23b: Astronomical clock, Old Town Square

Page 13b: Statue, Vyšehrad garden

Page 13a: Sentry, Hrad gates

Page 5b: Hat seller

Page 5a: Astronomical clock

Page 2: Badge, Hrad guard

Page 1: View from Charles Bridge Tower

Contents

About this book

Citypack *Prague* is divided into six sections to cover the six most important aspects of your visit to Prague.

1. PRAGUE LIFE *(pages 5–12)*
Your personal introduction to Prague by Michael Ivory
An overview of the city today and yesterday
Facts and figures
Leading characters
The big events in Prague's history

2. HOW TO ORGANIZE YOUR TIME *(pages 13–22)*
Make the most of your time in Prague
Four one-day itineraries
Two suggested walks
Two evening strolls
Four excursions beyond the city
Calendar of events

3. PRAGUE'S TOP 25 SIGHTS *(pages 23–48)*
Your concise guide to sightseeing
Michael Ivory's own choice, with his personal introduction to each sight
Description and history
Highlights of each attraction
Each sight located on the inside cover of the book

4. PRAGUE'S BEST *(pages 49–60)*
What Prague is renowned for
Panoramas
Galleries and museums
Palaces and churches
Twentieth-century buildings
For music lovers
Green spaces
Attractions for children
Communist mementoes

5. PRAGUE: WHERE TO... *(pages 61–93)*
The best places to eat, shop, be entertained, and stay
Seven categories of restaurant
Eight categories of store
Eight categories of entertainment spot
Hotels in four districts

6. PRAGUE TRAVEL FACTS *(pages 87–93)*
Essential information for your stay
Arriving and departing
Using public transportation
What to do in an emergency
Money, telephones, and tipping
Short language guide
and much more

SYMBOLS

Throughout the guide symbols are used to denote the following categories:

+ map reference to the fold-out map accompanying this book (see below)
⊠ address
☎ telephone number
⏰ opening times
🍴 restaurant or café on premises or nearby
Ⓜ nearest metro station
🚌 nearest bus/trolleybus/tram route
🚉 nearest overground train station
♿ facilities for visitors with disabilities
💲 admission charge
↔ other places of interest nearby
? tours, lectures, or special events
▶ indicates the page where you will find a fuller description

MAPS

All map references are to the separate fold-out map accompanying this book. For example, the National Theater on Národní 2, New Town, has the following information: + D/E5 indicating the grid squares of the map in which the National Theater will be found. All entries within the Top 25 Sights section are also plotted by number (not page number) on the downtown plan located on the inside front and back covers of this book.

PRICES

Where appropriate, an indication of the cost of an establishment is given by $ signs: $$$ denotes higher prices, while $ denotes lower charges.

PRAGUE
life

A Personal View

St. Nicholas's Church
from Hradčany

Urban decay

Visitors are sometimes shocked at Prague's shabbiness. Under Communism, showpieces were restored at great public expense, but less-favored buildings moldered away, encased in straitjackets of scaffolding to stop them falling into the street. Privatization and restitution (the return of property to its former owners) are expected to remedy the situation.

"Golden Prague," "Prague the hundred-towered," "the most beautiful city in Europe": such clichés are certainly true, though they tell only part of the story. Ocher in color, many of the city's buildings can gleam like gold, especially in the glow of the late afternoon sun; the skyline is punctuated by the uncountable towers, turrets, and steeples; and Prague's beauty is incontestable.

The site is superb, with rock bluffs above a broad and curving river and steep slopes rising through orchards and woodland. Human activities have enhanced what Nature provided so generously, crowning the heights with great churches and palaces, emphasizing the slopes with terraced gardens, precipitous streets, and flights of stairs, and marking the course of the river with a sequence of foaming weirs and bold bridges.

Over a thousand years of history is expressed in stone; the foundations of the first Christian churches can still be seen, while below the sidewalks of the Old Town are vaulted cellars that formed the ground floor of medieval merchants' houses. In the 17th and 18th centuries the baroque style transformed the city's appearance, as did great landmarks like the National Museum and National Theater—all testimony to the Czech nation's self-confidence—in the 19th century, followed by the extravagances of art nouveau. Even the radical architects of the first half of the 20th century managed to insert their innovative buildings into the urban scene with a minimum of disturbance.

In spite of (or perhaps as a result of) military defeats, occupation, and denial of citizens' rights, the four distinct quarters that form Prague's historic core are in a near-perfect state of preservation. They are the Castle district (Hradčany), the Lesser Town (Malá Strana) at its foot, the Old Town (Staré město) across the river, and the New Town (Nové město) laid out in the 14th century.

Beyond is a ring of rundown suburbs, largely 19th-century, then an outer circle of high-rise housing projects and satellite towns built during the last 40 years. These suburbs are where the vast majority of Praguers live. Most people are relieved at being freed from Communism but apprehensive about a future full of uncertainty. For many, life remains gray, the struggle to make ends meet greater than ever. Others have embraced the new freedom with alacrity; there's an obvious enjoyment in the previously forbidden pleasures of making and spending money. The continuing stream of visitors from abroad (90 million people come to the Czech Republic every year) adds an extra element of vibrancy and has vastly improved the places to eat and to stay. Entrepreneurs are everywhere, opening shops, cafés, and bars. There's excitement in the air, particularly among the young, as Prague claims its rightful place in a Europe from which it has been long excluded.

Get lost

Prague is a labyrinth, a warren of winding roads and alleyways, courtyards and passageways leading deep into buildings. Don't mind getting lost—treat disorientation as a pleasure and enjoy the unexpected treats along the way. The historic center is small, and sooner or later you will recognize a landmark or emerge by the riverside.

Míšeňská Street, Malá Strana

Prague in Figures

GEOGRAPHY
- In Central Europe, on the River Vltava, Prague is the capital of the Czech Republic (and was until 1993 the capital of Czechoslovakia).
- Prague lies 50 degrees 5 minutes north and 14 degrees 25 minutes east.
- Area: 191 square miles.
- Lowest point (River Vltava): 577 feet above sea-level.
- Highest point (Kopanina): 1,299 feet above sea-level.
- Distance from Berlin: 217 miles.
- Distance from Vienna: 181 miles.
- Distance from Paris: 643 miles.
- Distance from London: 853 miles.

PEOPLE
- Population: 1,225,000; 95.5 percent of Czech nationality.
- Living conditions: about half the population live in "panelaks," the high-rise apartments built under Communism. The largest housing project is "Southwest Town" with a planned population that should reach a total of 140,000 inhabitants.
- Nearly half Prague's population leaves the city on summer weekends, many to spend time in their *"chata"* or country cottage.
- 43,000 students attend universities in the city.

ENVIRONMENT
- Conservation: the city's historic core, designated by UNESCO as being of world importance, covers an area of 2,224 acres and includes some 10,000 protected artifacts and works of art.
- The city has nearly 25,000 acres of green spaces (parks, cemeteries, etc).
- Nearly half a million vehicles fill the 1,593 miles of city streets. Prague's Metro, 27 miles long and with 43 stations, carries more than a third of all the city's passengers. There are 80 miles of tram lines within the city.
- Prague is a heavily polluted city. Its industries, heating plants and motor vehicles emit more than 50,000 tons of sulfur dioxide per annum.

PRAGUE PEOPLE

VÁCLAV HAVEL

Playwright and one-time prominent dissident President Havel has, by attempting to combine political activity and ethical principles, not always endeared himself to market-obsessed politicians keen to rush the new republic into the embrace of modern capitalism. Gruff of voice and short of stature, Havel presents a conventional image when reviewing the troops or receiving ambassadors, but seems happiest dressed in an old sweater, chain-smoking with old cronies, or propelling himself along the Castle's long corridors aboard a child's scooter.

IVAN PLICKA

Engineer Plicka has spent most of his working life in the section of the City Architect's Department responsible for the planning of Greater Prague. Now near retirement, he's proud of the city's beauty and of his office's role in preserving it. He hopes

Engineer Ivan Plicka

his department's forthcoming masterplan to take Prague into the next millennium will protect the downtown from the commercial pressures that have destroyed the traditional character of many western cities.

ZUZANA ŽEŽULKOVÁ

Lawyer Zuzana comes from the small town of Litorměřice in Bohemia. Like many Czechs she was surprised by the rapidity and completeness of the collapse of Communism in 1989, but she has been quick to adapt. Her experience in commercial law and command of German are proving valuable as foreign firms move into Czech markets. Because of the partial collapse in law and order, she feels less safe than she used to, but she is happy to realize her full working potential—and she loves living in Prague.

Jo Williams

One of a number of young Americans attracted to post-Communist Prague, art historian Jo hails from New York City. An enthusiast for Czech culture, she has not only mastered the language but works in a Czech environment at a local salary. Her job: to promote abroad the hidden treasures of the National Gallery's modern collection in the Veletržní palác.

Lenka Drstičkova

Lively Lenka has been studying math and physics at Prague's venerable Charles University since moving here from a country town (a change she found more dramatic than the events of 1989). She expects to find a rewarding job in banking or finance, though she would rather teach. But with the starting salary for a teacher now a quarter of those in commerce, bright young things like Lenka have little choice.

A Chronology

7th or 8th century AD	Prague's legendary foundation by Princess Libuše and her plowman husband, Přemysl
Late 9th century	Slav stronghold established on Hradčany Hill, where Prince Bořivoj builds the first timber church
10th century	Trading settlements established in Malá Strana and Staré město
1231	King Wenceslas I fortifies the Old Town with 13 towers, walls 39 feet high, and a moat (today's Na Příkopě Street)
1253–1278	Reign of King Otakar II, who extends and fortifies Malá Strana, inviting German merchants and traders to settle there
1346–1378	Under King/Emperor Charles IV, St. Vitus's Cathedral is begun, the New Town (Nové město) laid out, and Charles Bridge built
1415	Religious reformer Jan Hus burned at the stake for heresy
1576–1611	Reign of eccentric Habsburg Emperor Rudolph II, whose interests include alchemy, astrology, and astronomy
1620	Battle of the White Mountain just outside Prague, in which the Protestant army is routed. In the following years, Protestant leaders are executed in Old Town Square. Czechs who refuse to reconvert to Catholicism emigrate en masse. A largely foreign nobility is installed, loyal to the Habsburgs, and Prague is beautified with baroque churches and palaces. Eventually the court is removed to Vienna, and Prague becomes a sleepy provincial town
1848	A revolt led by students is put down by Austrian General Windischgrätz, but Czech nationalism continues to grow
1914–1918	Czechs are dragged into World War I on the Austrian side. Many soldiers desert or join the

Czech Legion fighting for the Allies in Russia, Italy and France

1918 Establishment of the democratic First Republic of Czechoslovakia under liberal President Tomáš Masaryk

1938 At Munich, Britain and France agree to cede the Sudetenland to Hitler's Germany, depriving Czechoslovakia of most of its industry and all its defenses

1939 Hitler dismembers what is left of Czechoslovakia. The Czech Lands become the "Protectorate of Bohemia-Moravia," and Prague is declared the "Fourth City of the Third Reich" (after Berlin, Vienna and Hamburg)

1942 Assassination of Reichsprotektor Heydrich by Czechoslovak parachutists flown in from Britain leads to brutal repression by the Nazis

1945 The people of Prague liberate their city and welcome the subsequent arrival of the Red Army. More than 2.5 million Germans expelled from the Sudetenland

1948 Communists, the most powerful party in the democratically elected government, stage a coup d'état. Stalinist repression follows

1968 The Prague Spring crushed by Soviet tanks

1977 Dissident intellectuals sign Charter 77, a call for the government to apply the Helsinki Agreements of 1975. Many, including Václav Havel, are harrassed and imprisoned on trumped-up charges

1989 Velvet Revolution. The Communist government resigns and is replaced by the dissident-led Civic Forum. Václav Havel elected president

1993 Czechoslovakia splits into the independent states of Slovakia and the Czech Republic (with Prague as the latter's capital). The Czech Republic presses ahead with privatization of nationalized industries and looks forward to early entry into the European Union

PEOPLE & EVENTS FROM HISTORY

Fall from power

Yet another Prague defenestration (not officially referred to as such) was the fall of much-loved foreign minister Jan Masaryk from his office window in the Černín Palace when the Communists seized power in 1948. His opposition to Communism led many to think that he was pushed, but it is more likely that he jumped, in despair at the prospect facing his country and at his powerlessness to prevent it.

DEFENESTRATIONS

The first defenestration in Prague, in 1419, seems to have happened spontaneously. A crowd of Hussites demonstrating in Charles Square were pelted with stones from the New Town Hall by their Catholic adversaries who— to make matters worse—were German. The infuriated mob stormed the building and threw the culprits from the upstairs windows onto the cobbles of the square, where they were brutally killed. A window of the Old Town Hall provided the means for expressing discontent in 1483, when the mayor of Prague was the victim of the second defenestration.

The third defenestration, in 1618, marked the start of the Thirty Years War. Accompanied by an enthusiastic mob, a group of Protestant noblemen forced their way into the castle and hurled a pair of Catholic councellors and their secretary into the dung-heaps that had accumulated in the moat. The victims' survival—the manure broke their fall—was widely attributed to divine intervention.

FALSE SPRING

By the mid-1960s, the inefficiencies and the oppressiveness of the Communist system in Czechoslovakia were becoming all too apparent. In what came to be known as the "Prague Spring" of 1968, the party under the leadership of Alexander Dubček promised to create "Socialism with a human face." Terrified at this prospect, the Soviet Union in August sent in tanks and took the government off to Moscow in chains. A humiliated Dubček was told to reverse his reforms, then dismissed. Two decades of social and political winter followed, until 1989, when the whole Communist house of cards came tumbling down.

Alexander Dubček

PRAGUE
how to organize your time

ITINERARIES

These four one-day itineraries, all beginning from the "Golden Cross"—
the pedestrianized area where Wenceslas Square meets the boulevards of
Národní třída and Na příkopě (Metro Můstek)—are based on Prague's
four historic districts: Old Town (Staré město), Hradčany (the Castle area),
Lesser Town (Malá Strana), and New Town (Nové město).

ITINERARY ONE	OLD TOWN & JOSEFOV
Morning	Walk east along Na příkopě (Moat Street) Obecní dům (► 46) Walk along Celetná Street to the Old Town Square (Staroměstské náměstí ► 42) Coffee at one of the cafés in Old Town Square Climb the tower of the Old Town Hall Astronomical Clock (► 59) Take in Týn Church and Týn Court Walk along Paris Boulevard (Pařížská) to the Old/New Synagogue (► 39)
Lunch	Restaurant of the Jewish Town Hall or restaurants on Pařížská
Afternoon	Old Jewish Cemetery (► 40) Decorative Arts Museum (► 37)
ITINERARY TWO	HRADČANY, THE CASTLE HILL
Morning	Go west along 28 října and Národní streets Catch Tram No 22 at the Národní třída stop (Bila Hora direction) to Pohořelec stop Strahov Monastery (► 24) Coffee in Pohořelec Square Continue to the Loretto Shrine (► 26) Walk down Černínska Street and turn right into Nový Svět (► 25) Hrad (Prague Castle ► 29)
Lunch	One of the castle restaurants
Afternoon	St. Vitus's Cathedral (► 30) St. George's Basilica and Convent (► 31) Leave Castle via eastern gateway, double back through Castle Gardens (► 58) and go via Nerudova (► 32) to Malá Strana Square Return to the Golden Cross by Tram No. 22 or on foot across Charles Bridge

ITINERARY THREE	**BOTH ENDS OF THE BRIDGE**
Morning	Enter the Old Town via Na můstku and Havelská ulička, turn left into the market held on Havelská and V kotcích streets, and continue west via Uhelný trh and Skořepka Street into Bethlehem Square Bethlehem Chapel (► 55) Náprstek Museum (► 53) Coffee in café and restaurant on Bethlehem Square Follow Husova Street and turn left onto the Royal Way on Karlova Street Cross Charles Bridge Turn right into Josefská Street and again into Letenská Street Wallenstein Palace (► 34)
Lunch	Cafés and restaurants in Malá Strana Square
Afternoon	St. Nicholas's Church (► 33) Schönborn and Lobkovic Palaces (► 54) Church of Our Lady Victorious (► 55) Walk via Mostecká and Lázeňská to Maltese Square and Grand Priors' Square with the John Lennon Wall Cross the Čertovka brook to Na kampě on Kampa Island Return via Legions' Bridge (Most legií) and the National Theater (► 36)
ITINERARY FOUR	**NEW TOWN & VYŠEHRAD**
Morning	Walk west into Jungmann Square (Jungmannovo náměstí) Stroll in the Franciscans' Garden (Františkánská zahrada) behind the Church of Our Lady of the Snows Wenceslas Square (► 43), stop for coffee National Museum (► 44)
Lunch	Restaurants and cafés in Wenceslas Square
Afternoon	Metro to Vyšehrad Palace of Culture Go west along Na Bučance and V pevnosti Vyšehrad (► 38) Tram No. 3 and return to Wenceslas Square via Vodičkova Street and Novák building (U Novaku ► 56)

15

WALKS

IN THE FOOTSTEPS OF KINGS—THE OLD TOWN TO THE CASTLE

The walk follows the Royal Way, the ancient coronation route taken by Czech kings from their downtown residence to the cathedral high up in Hradčany. It starts in Old Town Square and is deservedly popular, so you are likely to have plenty of company.

Go west into Little Square (Malé náměstí) with its delightful fountain, and turn into twisting Karlova Street with its tempting gift shops. The street's final curve brings you into Knights of the Cross Square (Křížovnicke náměstí). Look out for the traffic as you rush to enjoy the incomparable view of the castle across the river.

Pass through the Old Town Bridge Tower on to Charles Bridge; admire the stunning procession of saintly statues that adorn the bridge. As it approaches Malá Strana the bridge becomes a flyover, and then, after the Malá Strana Bridge Tower, it leads you to Bridge (Mostecká) Street. Cross Malá Strana Square (Malostranské náměstí), dominated by the great bulk of St. Nicholas's Church, with care. Grit your teeth in preparation for the long climb up Nerudova Street and don't forget to turn sharp right on to the final leg of the Castle approach named Ke hradu. Regain your breath while leaning on the wall of Hradčany Square and soaking up the panorama of the city far below, which rewards the climb.

THE SIGHTS

- Old Town Hall (►42)
- Clam-Gallas Palace
- Old Town Bridge Tower (►35)
- Charles Bridge (►35)
- St. Nicholas's Church (►33)
- Neruda Street (►32)

INFORMATION

Distance 1.2 miles
Time 1 hour
Startpoint Old Town Square
🚇 E4
Ⓜ Staroměstská
End point Hradčany Square
🚇 C4
🚋 Tram 22

Surface restoration

With their often ambivalent attitude to tradition, the Communists decided to promote the Royal Way as a tourist route, and poured considerable resources into restoring the buildings along it. But the treatment was sometimes more of a face-lift than a complete rejuvenation.

Café in Old Town Square

WALKS

Schwarzenberg Palace, ceiling

THE SIGHTS

- Schwarzenberg Palace (Military Museum ►53)
- Strahov Monastery (►24)
- Černín Palace (►54)
- Loretto Shrine (►26)
- Nový Svět (►25)
- Šternberg Palace (►27)
- Archbishop's Palace (►54)
- Royal Gardens (►58)
- Letná Plain (►50)
- Josefov, the Ghetto (►39, 40)

INFORMATION

Distance 2.5 miles
Time 2 hours
Start point
   Hradčany Square
🔲 C4
🚊 Tram 22
End point
   Old Town Square
🔲 E4
Ⓜ Staroměstská

BACK TO THE OLD TOWN VIA SOME OF PRAGUE'S GARDENS

From Hradčany Square walk up Loretánská Street, turning 180 degrees left as you enter Pohořelec Square. A short way down Úvoz, make a sharp right and stop to enjoy the view from the vineyard lying just below Strahov Monastery. Go through the monastery courtyard, turning right into Pohořelec, then left into Loretto Square (Loretánské náměstí). Narrow Černinska Street leads downhill into Nový Svět.

Return to Hradčany Square via Nový Svět and Kanovnická. Go through the Matthias Gate of the Castle, then out of the north gate from the Castle's Second Courtyard. Turn into the Royal Gardens; leave them near the Belvedere summer palace and enter the Chotek Gardens (Chotkovy sady). Cross the footbridge into Letná Plain (Letenské sady) and view the city first from the Hanava Pavilion (Hanavský pavilon) and then from the plinth where Stalin's statue stood. Descend the steps and ramps to the Cech Bridge (Čechův most) and return to Old Town Square via Josefov—the former Jewish ghetto.

Rustic retreat

The tiny vineyard below Strahov Monastery is a reminder of the days when vines clad most of the slopes hereabouts. Young apple, pear, cherry, and almond trees have been planted, giving a landscape unique in the heart of a metropolitan city.

17

EVENING STROLLS

THE OLD TOWN

Survey the busy downtown scene from the terrace in front of the National Museum at the top of Wenceslas Square before leaving through the underpass (don't try to cross the road) and walk down either side of the square, having first ensured that your wallet or handbag is safe. Keep going in the same direction at the foot of the square, along Na můstku and Melantrichova into Old Town Square. Follow the Royal Way (► 16), turning left into Husova Street, then right into Bethlehem Square (Betlemské náměstí), a quieter focus of night life. Go down Náprstkova Street and join the Vltava embankment, crossing the road carefully. The best point to absorb the view of the river, Malá Strana, and Castle, is from the tip of Novotného lávka, by the statue of Smetana.

View over Malá Strana

NEW TOWN

Finish your beer or coffee in one of the cafés by the Smetana statue and go through the arcade leading to Knights of the Cross Square at the Old Town end of Charles Bridge. Continue in the same direction, then cross the Vltava by the restored Mánes Bridge (Mánesův most). Head for Malostranská Metro station and walk through what is probably the only subway garden in the world to palace-lined Valdštejnská Street with its unusual close-up view of the Castle high above. Tomášská Street leads into Malá Strana Square. Return to the Smetana statue down Mostecká Street and across Charles Bridge, particularly enchanting at night.

ORGANIZED TOURS

There are plenty of organized tours available to take visitors on general tours of the city, more detailed explorations of particular districts, or out into the surroundings. The difficulty is in choosing between the various excursions on offer. It's also worth considering whether to do it yourself, using your own two feet and public transportation; this will certainly be cheaper and —as far as the historic downtown is concerned— probably more enjoyable than a bus tour (though a walking tour with a local guide to tell you what lies behind the façades has its own allure). Local trains or buses to attractions outside Prague will cost a fraction of an organized tour. It's advisable to spend some time shopping around and considering the alternatives.

A good starting point for finding out about organized tours are the various bureaus of the official Prague Information Service (Pražská informační služba – PIS) at:

⊠ Na příkope 20, New Town ☎ 54 44 44-7
🕚 Mon–Fri 9–6, Sat 9–3 🚇 Náměstí Republiky
or ⊠ Můstek or Staroměstské náměstí 1
(Old Town Hall) ☎ 54 44 44-7
🕚 Mon–Fri 9–6, Sat, Sun 9–5
🚇 Staroměstská or Můstek

PIS runs its own tours in a reliable way, as do a number of other operators, including:

CEDOK (the longest established travel company of all) at:
⊠ Na příkope 18, New Town
☎ 24 19 76 43, fax 232 16 56 🚇 Náměstí Republiky or Můstek
⊠ Pařížská 6, Old Town ☎ 231 25 81, fax 232 17 28 🚇 Staroměstská
⊠ Rytířská 16, Old Town
☎ 26 27 90, fax 26 27 96 🚇 Mustek or Staroměstská

PREMIANT CITY TOUR at:
⊠ Na příkopě 16, New Town
☎ 53 36 84.

Castle tour
A stroll around the Castle in the company of a well-informed guide can be instructive. Tours start from the Information Center of Prague Castle in the Chapel of the Holy Rood in the Second Courtyard.
✠ C4
⊠ Hradčany
☎ 33 37 33 68

View across Vltava to Castle

EXCURSIONS

Karlštejn Castle

INFORMATION

Karlštejn Castle

- Hrad Karlštejn
- 031 19 42 11
- Mar–Apr, Oct–Dec Tue–Sun 9–12, 1–4; May–Sep 8–12, 1–6
- Suburban trains from Prague-Smíchov to Karlštejn: travel time 40 min

Mělník Castle

- Svatoslavska 19, Mělník
- 02 06 62 68 53
- Mar–Dec daily 10–4 (to 6 in summer)
- Bus from Florenc bus station: travel time 50 min

KARLŠTEJN CASTLE
(Hrad Karlštejn)

This mighty fortress, one of the great sights of Bohemia, towers above the glorious woodlands of the gorge of the River Berounka. There's no motor transportation up from the riverside village, but nevertheless the long climb up should be braved—the superb panorama from the castle walls will fully compensate you. The name of the castle, which was started in 1348, celebrates the Emperor Charles IV. He conceived it as a sort of sacred bunker, a repository for the Crown Jewels and his collection of holy relics. Not merely a fortress, the castle was also planned as a personal, processional way that the Emperor would follow to its climax—the Great Tower containing the Chapel of the Holy Rood—reached only after much prayer and contemplation. This gorgeous chamber has had to be sealed off from the public, whose breath was destroying its exquisite artifacts.

MĚLNÍK

Built on a bluff near the confluence of the Vltava with the Elbe, this ancient town is famous for the vineyards that rise up in terraces beneath its imposing castle. Following the demise of Communism, Mělník's castle and estates have been returned to the original aristocratic Lobkovic owners. Long before the Lobkovic family, however, it was a royal seat, the abode of the Czech queens, one of whom raised her grandson Wenceslas (later the "Good King") here. The castle courtyard, with both Gothic and Renaissance wings and ancient wine cellars, is approached via the charmingly arcaded town square.

LIDICE

Nowhere could seem more ordinary than this modern little mining village in the dull countryside just beyond Prague airport. But on June 10,

1942, on the flimsiest of pretexts, its male population was shot and its women and children sent off to a concentration camp—and Lidice's name resounded round the world as a synonym for Czech suffering and German ruthlessness. Days before, Reichsprotektor Heydrich had been assassinated, and the Nazis needed revenge. Lidice was razed to the ground and its name removed from the records "forever." After the war the village was rebuilt a short distance away, while the site of the atrocity became a memorial museum and park.

KONOPIŠTĚ CASTLE
(Zámek Konopiště)

Konopiště Castle's round towers rise in romantic fashion from the surrounding woodlands. The place's origins go back to the 14th century, but it owes its present appearance largely to Archduke Franz Ferdinand, heir to the Habsburg throne, who acquired it in 1887. The corridors are filled with trophies of the countless wild creatures he slaughtered while waiting for the demise of his long-lived uncle Franz Josef. The arch-duke met his own violent end when he was cut down by an assassin's bullet in Sarajevo, thereby triggering the start of World War I. The castle is full of Franz Ferdinand's fine furniture and his extraordinary collection of weapons. His other obsession was landscape gardening, and the splendid parklands and rose garden are a delight.

St. Peter and St. Paul Church, Mělník Castle

INFORMATION

Lidice
- ✉ Monument
  10 cervna 1942, Lidice
- 🕐 Daily 8–4 (to 5 in summer)
- 🚌 Bus from Dejvice

KonopištěCastle
- ✉ Zámek Konopiště, Benesov u Prahy
- 🕐 Tue–Sun 9–3; May–Aug to 4
- 🚆 Train to Benesov (1 hr) then bus or taxi

Konopiště: armor detail

21

WHAT'S ON

MAY 12 TO EARLY JUNE	*Prague Spring Music Festival* This internationally important event consists of an array of concerts of classical music in churches, palaces, and halls. It starts off with a procession from Smetana's grave in the National Cemetery in Vyšehrad to the great Hall named after him in the Obecni dům (Municipal House) where a rousing performance of his orchestral tone poem *Ma Vlast* ("My Country") is given. (But note that the Obecni dům is closed until 1997.)
JUNE	*Dance Prague* An international dance festival with events at various venues, including some public outdoor spaces
OCTOBER	*Mozart Festival* The cultural program for the month includes even more than the usual Prague allowance of the maestro's masterworks
DECEMBER 5	*St. Nicholas* The streets are roamed by a multitude of St. Nicks, each accompanied by an angel (who rewards good children with candy) and a devil (who chastises appropriately)
CHRISTMAS	Live carp are sold on the street for Christmas Eve dinner
NEW YEAR'S EVE	The more respectable attend a "Sylvester" ball, while others celebrate the arrival of the New Year on the streets

TICKETS

Tickets for events can be obtained at individual box offices (which may be cheaper) or through one of a number of agencies. These include:
Bohemia Ticket International ✉ Václavské náměstí 25, New Town
☎ 24 22 72 53.
Prague Information Service ✉ Na příkope 20, New Town ☎ 26 40 22
Ticketpro ✉ Rytířská 31, Old Town ☎ 24 91 22 43.

ENTERTAINMENT INFORMATION

The best source of information for English readers about what's on is probably the tabloid section *"Night and Day"* of the weekly newspaper *Prague Post*. This gives listings of stage, screen and cultural events likely to be of interest to visitors from abroad, as well as interesting comment and analysis. A comprehensive review of the month's events is contained in *Culture in Prague*, published monthly by the Prague Information Service.

PRAGUE's
top 25 sights

The sights are numbered from west to east across the city

23

1

STRAHOV MONASTERY

INFORMATION

- C4
- Strahovská,
  Hradčany
- 24 51 03 55
- Daily 9–12, 12:30–5
- Peklo (Hell)
  restaurant in
  monastery cellars
- Tram 22 to Pohořelec
- Fair
- Moderate
- Loretto Shrine (➤ 26),
  Petřín Hill (➤ 28)

Baroque spires rising toward Heaven, a gilded image of an enemy of the Faith, monks profiting from an enterprise in Hell ... this hilltop monastery (Strahovský klášter) seems to encapsulate something of this most paradoxical of cities.

Persuasive priests A major landmark in the cityscape, the Strahov monastery crowns the steep slope leading up from Malá Strana (its name derives from *strahovní*, meaning "to watch over"). It is a treasure house of literature and its ornate library halls with their splendid frescoes are among the most magnificent in Europe. As befits a monastery devoted to books, Strahov owed much to its abbots' way with words. Its 12th-century founder, Abbot Zdik, persuaded Prince Vladislav II to back his project by making flattering comparisons of Prague with the holy city of Jerusalem. Much later, in 1783, Abbot Meyer exercised equal powers of persuasion on Emperor Joseph II to exempt Strahov from the reforming ruler's edict that closed down many of the Habsburg Empire's monasteries. The canny cleric was so eloquent that Strahov actually benefited from the misfortune of other institutions; books from the suppressed monastery at Louka were brought here by the wagonload. A gilded medallion of the emperor over the library entrance may also have helped to persuade Joseph that the Strahov monks deserved special treatment.

Returnees' revenge Chased out of Strahov by the Communists in 1952, the monks, who belong to the Premonstratensian Order, have now come back. They have made the upper floor of the cloisters into a gallery for the works of art now returned to them and converted the cellars into a restaurant called Hell (Peklo).

NOVÝ SVĚT

Chambermaids and scullions, footmen and flunkies, these were the folk for whom the humble homes of Nový Svět ("New World") were originally erected back in the 14th century. The area has moved upscale since.

Wizards and weird doings A mysterious place of crooked alleyways and secret gardens hidden behind high walls, Nový Svět has never been in the mainstream. As well as the castle servants, others able to cater for the more esoteric interests of their masters came here. They included the Danish astronomer Tycho Brahe and his German colleague Johannes Kepler, both employed by Rudolph II to investigate the more arcane secrets of the universe.

La Bohème Their successors are artists and writers, who have colonized the pretty 18th-century houses along this charming cobbled street that wobbles its way westward just uphill from the Castle. The painter's studio at No. 19 is crammed with pictures of curvaceous girls and grimacing gnomes, and the Czech master of animated film, Jan Švankmajer, a long-time resident, has recently set up a gallery devoted to Surrealist art.

Connecting the worlds "New World" is linked to the outside world by short streets (Loretanská, Capucinská, U Kasaren, and Kanovnická) running down the hill from the main tourist trail between the Strahov Monastery and the Castle, or by flights of steps from the old ramparts whose course is followed by today's tram No. 22.

HIGHLIGHTS

- Nepomuk statue in Černínská Street
- Birthplace of violinist F. Ondříček at No 25
- Tycho Brahe's house at No. 1
- Church of St. John Nepomuk
- No. 3, the president's favorite restaurant

INFORMATION

- ✚ C4
- ✉ Nový Svět, Hradčany
- 🍴 Restaurant
- 🚋 Tram 22 to Brusnice
- ♿ Few
- ↔ Loretto Shrine (➤ 26)

St. John Nepomuk

3

LORETTO SHRINE

HIGHLIGHTS

- The main façade, with statuary and carillon
- The Santa Casa
- Interior of the Church of the Nativity
- Diamond monstrance in the Loretto Treasure
- Cloister painting of St. Starosta

Loretto Shrine, Hradčany

INFORMATION

✚ C4

✉ Loretánské náměstí, Hradčany

☎ 24 51 07 89

🕐 Tue–Sun 9–12:15, 1–4:30

🚌 Tram 22 to Pohořelec

♿ Moderate

↔ Strahov Monastery (► 24), Nový Svět (► 25)

A bearded lady, skeletons rattling their bones to the sound of chiming bells, severed breasts on display, a flying house ... no freak show, but all features of the sumptuously decorated Loretto Shrine (Loreta) high up on Hradčany Hill.

Counter-Reformation fireworks No showman's trick was spared to bring the wayward Czechs back into the Catholic fold after their long flirtation with Protestantism was brought to an end by the Battle of the White Mountain in 1620. Protestant austerity, with its dislike of images, was replaced by the idolatry of the cult of the Virgin Mary, dripping with sensuality and symbolism. Of all the flights of architectural fantasy that the Roman Catholic Counter-Reformation perpetrated on Prague, the Loretto is the most bizarre as well as the most beautiful, its church and courtyard a theater of cults, miracles, and mysteries designed to dazzle doubters and skeptics.

Weird wonders The kernel of the complex is a Casa Santa, a facsimile of the Virgin Mary's holy home in Nazareth, supposedly flown by angels from the Holy Land and deposited at Loreto in Italy. Fifty such shrines were once scattered around the Czech countryside, but this is far and away the most important, an ornate little Renaissance pavilion built in 1631 and later encased in an equally ornate baroque setting of courtyard, carillon tower, and richly decorated church. Pilgrims once flocked here in huge numbers to marvel at the macabre: St. Agatha offering up her bloody bosom to the angels; the skeletons in their death masks made of wax; unhappy Saint Starosta, whose father killed her in a fury on finding she'd grown a beard to discourage a favored suitor ...

4

ŠTERNBERG PALACE

Who would guess that the unpretentious little alley beside the Prague archbishop's pompous palace on Hradčany Square would lead to one of the continent's great art collections, housed in the Šternberg Palace (the Šternberský palác), dazzling visitors with a multitude of Old Masters, plus many modern works.

Ambitious aristocrats Having built Château Troja (► 48), the Bohemian Versailles, on the edge of Prague, Count Šternberg, one of the city's richest men, needed a town house closer to the Castle. The Italian architect Giovanni Alliprandi was commissioned to design the palace, and work began on the count's Hradčany home in 1698. However, the money ran out before a main façade was built on the square to outface his neighbor the archbishop. The interior was decorated with fine ceiling and wall paintings. It was a later Šternberg who donated much of the family's great picture collection to the fledgling National Gallery in the early 19th century, and the nation's finest foreign paintings were housed here from 1814 to 1871. They are once more in this grand setting.

Picture palace Despite being tucked away behind the square, the Šternberg Palace is an edifice of some substance, arranged around an imposing courtyard, with grand stairways and an oval pavilion facing the garden. The National Gallery of European Art attracts a stream of tourists—as well as art thieves, tempted (until recently) by laughably lax security. The pictures could keep an art lover busy for a whole day or more, though some star exhibits are no longer on view: "restitution" has returned them to the owners from whom they were confiscated by the Communists.

HIGHLIGHTS

- Triptych of the *Adoration of the Magi*, Giertgen tot Sint Jans
- *Adam and Eve*, Cranach
- *Feast of the Rosary*, Dürer
- *Scholar in his Study*, Rembrandt
- *Head of Christ*, El Greco
- Icons from 2nd-century Egypt
- *Beheading of St. Dorothy*, Hans Baldung Grien
- *Martyrdom of St. Florian*, Altdorfer
- *St. Jerome*, Ribera
- *The Thames*, Canaletto

INFORMATION

- ✚ C4
- ✉ Hradčanské náměstí 15, Hradčany
- ☎ 24 51 05 94–5
- 🕐 Tue–Sun 10–6
- 🚊 Tram 22 to Pražský hrad
- ♿ Few
- 🈺 Moderate
- ↔ Schwarzenberg Palace (► 53), Castle (► 29)

5

PETŘÍN HILL

HIGHLIGHTS

- Rozhledna—viewing tower
- 14th-century Hunger Wall
- Mirror Maze (Bludiště)
- Charles Bridge Battle diorama
- Observatory and Planetarium
- Rose Garden
- Alpine Garden
- Baroque Church of St. Lawrence
- Calvary Chapel and Stations of the Cross
- Ukrainian timber Church of St Michael

INFORMATION

- ✛ C/D 4/5
- ◉ Rozhledna: Tue-Sun 9:30–5; Mirror Maze: Apr–Oct, Tue–Sun 9:30–5; Observatory: Mon–Fri 6PM–8PM, Sat–Sun 10–noon and 2–8
- 🍴 Café and restaurant
- 🚋 Tram 22 to Strahov and walk
- 🚠 Funicular railway, Újezd in Malá Strana
- ♿ Few
- 🎟 Rozhledna, Mirror Maze, Observatory: moderate
- ↔ Strahov Monastery (► 24)

When the press of the crowd on Charles Bridge becomes too much and the sidewalks become too hard, there's always the glorious green of the Petřín to retire to, its orchards and woodlands a cool retreat from the pressures of the city center.

Funiculi-funicula to the view In 1891, the thoughtful city fathers provided a jolly little funicular railway (the "Lanovka") to the top of Petřín Hill, and it's recently been restored to carry passengers effortlessly up (or down) the steep slope. At the top there's a whole array of attractions, including the Rozhledna ("Lookout"), the little brother of the Eiffel Tower. This, too, was built in 1891, for the city's great Jubilee Expo that celebrated the achievements of the Czech Lands when they still formed part of the Austrian Empire. The Rozhledna has 299 steps to a viewing platform; some claim to have seen, on a clear day, not only the Czech Republic's Giant Mountains (90 miles to the northeast) but also the Alps (even farther away to the southwest). And there's all of Prague at your feet.

Country matters With its woods and orchards (splendid with blossom in the springtime) the Petřín brings a real breath of the countryside into the metropolis. Once there were vineyards

on the hill, but these didn't survive the Thirty Years War, and they were replaced by the superb gardens that link the palaces of Malá Strana into the surrounding hillside parklands.

Rozhledna tower, Petřín

PRAGUE CASTLE

Nothing in Prague escapes the blank gaze of the castle's thousand windows. Pražský hrad is the citadel of the Czech nation, the holder of its collective memory. It is a place of palaces, churches, streets, squares, and alleyways, a city within a city, sheltering the homes of some of the country's greatest treasures.

Age-old stronghold The princes of Prague first built a fortress on the limestone spur high above the Vltava in the 9th century, and the Czech Lands have been ruled from here ever since (except when rulers preferred to live in a long-vanished palace downtown or on the summit of the upstream rock at Vyšehrad). Every age has left its imprint on the castle; it is a storehouse of architectural styles, ranging from the foundations of Romanesque churches a thousand years old to Professor Plečnik's premature Postmodernism of the interwar years. Even now, a committee is hard at work adapting the ancient complex in an attempt to make it more inviting and accessible to the citizens of a new and democratic order.

Castle denizens Teeming with tourists, the castle's courtyards also echo with the tread of countless ghosts: Emperor Charles IV with his dreams of Prague as a great Imperial capital; the cranky Habsburg ruler Rudolph II attended by his retinue of alchemists and necromancers, soothsayers and erotic painters; the Protestant mob who flung the hated Catholic councellors down from the palace windows; philosopher-president Tomáš Masaryk, creator of Czechoslavakia; Adolf Hitler Heil-ing his hysterical helots; and, most recently, the Communists enjoying their privileges while they lasted.

HIGHLIGHTS

- Giants guarding western gateway
- Mihulka (Powder Tower)
- Vladislav Hall in Old Royal Palace
- Tiny houses in Golden Lane
- Lobkovic Palace (History Museum)
- Outline of Matthias Gate in First Courtyard
- Second Courtyard with Holy Rood Chapel
- Third Courtyard with statue of St. George
- Plečnik's canopy and stairway to gardens
- Riders' Staircase in Old Royal Palace

INFORMATION

- ✚ C/D4
- ✉ Pražský hrad, Hradčany
- ☎ 33 37 11 11
- ◉ Courtyards and streets daily until late; buildings Tue–Sun 9–5
- 🍴 Cafés and restaurants
- 🚌 Tram 22 to Pražský hrad
- ♿ Few
- ⊞ Moderate
- ↔ Šternberg Palace (➤ 27)

St. Vitus's Cathedral

HIGHLIGHTS

- South Portal with 14th-century mosaic
- St. Wenceslas's Chapel
- Crypt with royal tombs
- Silver tomb of St. John Nepomuk
- Sculptures on west front

INFORMATION

- ✚ C/D4
- ✉ Pražský hrad, Hradčany
- 🕐 Daily 9–5 (tower to 4)
- 🍴 Cafés and restaurants in castle
- 🚃 Tram 22 to Pražský hrad
- ↔ Castle (▶ 29)

Tomb of St. John Nepomuk, St. Vitus

To emerge into Prague Castle's Third Courtyard and see the twin towers of the cathedral (katedrála svatého Víta) lancing skyward is a truly breathtaking experience, all the more compelling when you realize that the great Gothic edifice was completed within living memory.

Spanning the centuries The cathedral was begun by Emperor Charles IV in the middle of the 14th century. It is built over the foundations of much earlier predecessors, a round church erected by "Good King" Wenceslas in the early 10th century and a big Romanesque building resembling the present-day St. George's Basilica (▶ 31). The glory of the architecture is largely due to the great Swabian builder Petr Parléř and his sons, who worked on the building for some 60 years. Work was abruptly halted by the troubles of the 15th century, and the cathedral consisted of an east end only until the formation of an "Association for the Completion of the Cathedral," in 1843. Decades of effort saw the nave, western towers and much else brought to a triumphant conclusion; in 1929, a thousand years after King Wenceslas was assassinated, the cathedral, dedicated to the country's patron saint St. Vitus, was consecrated.

Cathedral treasures The cathedral is a treasure house of Bohemian history, though the Crown Jewels, its greatest prize, are seldom on display. The spacious interior absorbs the crowds with ease and provides a fitting context for an array of precious artifacts that range from medieval paintings to modern glass.

St. George's Basilica & Convent

A bull's-blood-colored baroque façade conceals a severe ancient interior, the Romanesque Basilica of St. George (Bazilika a Klášter sv Jiří). To the north, the nuns have long since left their convent, which is now a worthy setting for fine collections of Gothic, Renaissance, and Baroque painting and sculpture.

Bare basilica The basilica is the biggest church of its date in the Czech Lands, its twin towers and pale and sober stonework a reminder of the great antiquity of the castle complex. Very well preserved after restoration, it is no longer a church but is now a concert hall, and the austere interior, a great hall with wooden ceiling, houses a small number of impressive artworks.

Paintings and princesses Founded in 973, St. George's Convent was a prestigious institution, a place to which princesses and other young ladies of noble birth were sent to receive the best possible education. Shut down like many other religious houses by Emperor Joseph in 1782 (he turned it into a barracks), it had to await the coming of the Communists for its rehabilitation; they planned to turn it into a "Museum of the Czechoslovak People." A painfully long period of restoration has provided a more than adequate home for one of the country's greatest and most distinctive galleries, the National Gallery of Old Bohemian Art. In the Middle Ages, artists from Bohemia led Europe in their ability to convey the serene beauty of undisturbed faith; their sculpture and painting, displayed in the atmospheric setting of the convent's cellars, is unsurpassed. The upper floors contain the work of Prague's equally creative Renaissance and Baroque periods.

HIGHLIGHTS

- Sculpture of *St. George and the Dragon*
- Sculpture of Krumlov *Madonna and Child*
- Painted panels by the Master of Vyšší Brod
- Portraits of saints by Master Theodorik
- *Christ on the Mount of Olives,* The Třeboň Master
- Tympanum from Tyn Church in Old Town
- Statue of Hercules
- *Tobias Restoring his Father's Sight,* Petr Brandl
- Landscapes by Roland Savary
- Genre scenes by Norbert Grund

INFORMATION

- ✚ D4
- ✉ Jiřské náměstí, Hradčany
- ☎ 24 51 03 68
- 🕐 Tue–Sun 10–6
- 🍽 Restaurants and cafés in castle
- Ⓜ Malostranská, then an uphill walk
- 🚊 Tram 22 to Pražský hrad
- ♿ Few
- 🔡 Moderate
- ↔ Castle (▶ 29)

9

NERUDA STREET

INFORMATION

- C/D4
- Nerudova, Malá Strana
- Restaurants and cafés
- Tram 22 to Malá Strana Square
- Few
- St. Nicholas's Church and Malá Strana (► 33), Castle (► 29)

Toil up to the castle from Malá Strana Square via steep, cobbled Neruda Street (Nerudova), and you will be rewarded by a sequence of exquisite town houses. Baroque and rococo, on medieval foundations, most have elaborate house signs.

Eagles and other emblems It is the elegant façades and their emblems that catch the eye. There's an Eagle, Three Little Fiddles, a Goblet, a Golden Key and a Horseshoe. The Two Suns indicate the house (No. 47) of author Jan Neruda (1843–1891), who gave his name to the street; he was the Dickens of Malá Strana, a shrewd observer of the everyday life of the area. Most of the people who lived here were prosperous burghers, but there were some aristocrats like the Morzins who built their palace at No. 5; the muscular Moors holding up the balcony are a pun on the family name. Their home is now an embassy, as is the Thun-Hohensteins' palace at No. 20; here the Moors' job is being carried out by a pair of odd-looking eagles.

Spur Street The secret of savoring Neruda Street to the full is to coast gently downward, like the coachmen from whom the road derived its earlier name of Spur Street (Spornergasse in German), the spur in this case being the skid-like brake that slowed their otherwise precipitous progress down the steep slope.

Violins depicted on Neruda Street façade

10

St. Nicholas's Church, Malá Strana

Crawling insect-like around the base of this cliff of a church you feel the full power of the Catholic Counter-Reformation expressing itself in what is surely one of the boldest and most beautiful Baroque buildings of Central Europe.

Counter-Reformation citadel When the Jesuits came to Prague following the rout of the Protestants at the Battle of the White Mountain, the existing little 13th-century church at the center of Malá Strana Square was far too modest for their aspirations. The new St. Nicholas (Chrám svatého Mikuláše) was eventually completed in the 18th century and became one of the dominant features of the city with its lofty walls and high dome and bell tower. The Jesuits intended their church to impress, but not through size alone. They employed the finest architects of the day (the Dientzenhofers, father and son, plus Anselmo Lurago) along with the most talented interior designers. The exterior has a subtly undulating west front adorned with statues proclaiming the triumph of the Jesuit Order under the patronage of the Imperial House of Habsburg. Inside, no effort was spared to enthrall the eye—with the dynamic play of space, statuary, and painting—and the ear—with words (declaimed from the fantastically decorated pulpit) and music (through the 2,500 pipes of the great organ).

Princely palaces and humbler households In front of the church swirls the life of Malá Strana, locals waiting for the trams mixing with tourists following the Royal Way. Malá Strana Square is lined with a fascinating mixture of ancient town houses and grand palaces, while attached to St. Nicholas's is the Jesuits' college, now part of the university.

HIGHLIGHTS

St. Nicholas's Church
● West front
● St. Barbara's Chapel
● Organ with fresco of St. Cecilia
● Dome with Holy Trinity fresco
● Huge sculptures of four Church Fathers
● Trompe l'oeil ceiling fresco, Kracker

Malá Strana Square
● Arcaded houses
● No. 10, Renaissance House
● No. 13, Liechtenstein Palace of 1791
● Nos. 18 and 19, Smiřicky Palace and Šternberg House

INFORMATION

✚ D4
✉ Malostranské náměstí
🕐 Sun, Tue–Fri 10–12, plus Wed 2–5
🍴 Cafés and restaurants in square
🚇 Malostranská
🚌 Tram 12, 22 to Malostranské náměstí
♿ Few
🔲 Inexpensive
↔ Neruda Street (▶ 32), Charles Bridge (▶ 35), Wallenstein Palace (▶ 34)

11

WALLENSTEIN PALACE

Think of this palace—Prague's biggest—as an awful warning, an admonition to eschew excessive ambition and arrogance of the kind shown by its builder, Albrecht von Wallenstein, whose aspirations to power and fame led to his ignominious assassination.

Greedy generalissimo Wallenstein's huge late Renaissance/early Baroque palace (Valdštejnský palác) crouches at the foot of the castle as if waiting to gobble it up. A whole city block, previously occupied by a couple of dozen houses and a brickworks, was demolished to make way for the complex of five courtyards, a barracks, a riding school, and a superb garden that were intended to display Wallenstein's overweening ambitions. Wallenstein (Valdštejn in Czech) turned the troubled times to his advantage. Having wormed his way into the emperor's favor, he became governor of Prague, then duke of Friedland. He married for money (twice), and great tracts of land (even whole towns) fell into his hands following the Battle of the White Mountain in 1620. His fortunes grew further as he quartermastered the imperial armies as well as leading them. Rightly suspicious of his subject's intentions—Wallenstein was negotiating with the enemy—the emperor had him killed (the assassins were an Englishman, an Irishman, and a Scotsman).

The general's garden The great hall of the palace, with its ceiling painting of Wallenstein as Mars the god of War, makes a magnificent setting for the occasional concert. The formal garden is more freely accessible. It's dominated by the superb Sala Terrena, modeled on the loggias of Italy, and has convincing copies of the statues stolen by Swedish soldiers during the Thirty Years War.

CHARLES BRIDGE

I like to linger here all day, watching the sun come up over the Old Town, enjoying the day-long antics of the buskers and hucksters, then remaining to savor the almost sinister atmosphere of dusk, when the bridge's sculpted saints gesticulate against the darkening sky.

Gothic overpass For centuries Karlův most was Prague's only bridge, built on the orders of Emperor Charles IV in the 14th century. It's a triumph of Gothic engineering, 16 massive sandstone arches carrying it more than 1,600 feet from the Old Town to soar across Kampa Island and touch down almost in the heart of Malá Strana. It is protected by sturdy timber cutwaters and guarded at both ends by towers; the Old Town Bridge Tower is richly ornamented on its eastern face; its opposite number is accompanied by a smaller tower, once part of this bridge's predecessor, the Judith Bridge.

Starry saint Charles Bridge has always been much more than a mere river crossing. Today's traders succeed earlier merchants and stallholders. Tournaments, battles, and executions have been held on the bridge. The heads of the Protestants executed in 1620 in Old Town Square were displayed here. Later that century the bridge was beautified with baroque sculptures, including the statue of St. John Nepomuk. Falling foul of the king, this unfortunate cleric was pushed off the bridge in a sack. As his body bobbed in the water, five stars danced on the surface. Nepomuk became the patron saint of bridges and is always depicted with his starry halo.

HIGHLIGHTS

- Old Town Bridge Tower
- Malá Strana Bridge Tower (viewpoint)
- Nepomuk statue with bronze relief panels
- Bruncvik (Roland column) to southwest
- Statue of St. John of Matha
- Bronze crucifix with Hebrew inscription
- Statue of St. Luitgard (by Braun)

INFORMATION

- 🟦 D4
- 🔲 Staroměstská
- 🚊 Tram 12, 22 to Malá Strana Square
- ♿ Good
- ↔ St. Nicholas's Church, Malá Strana (▶ 33)

St. Anthony of Padua

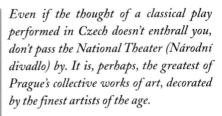

National Theater

Even if the thought of a classical play performed in Czech doesn't enthrall you, don't pass the National Theater (Národní divadlo) by. It is, perhaps, the greatest of Prague's collective works of art, decorated by the finest artists of the age.

National drama In the mid-19th century, theater in Prague still spoke with a German voice. Money to build a specifically Czech theater was collected from 1849 onward, without support from German-dominated officialdom. The foundation stone was laid in 1868 with much festivity, then in 1881, just before the first performance, the whole place burned down. Undiscouraged, the populace rallied, and by 1893 the theater had been completely rebuilt. The opening was celebrated with a grand gala performance of the opera *Libuše* by Smetana, a passionate supporter of the theater project.

Expanded ambition The National Theater stands at the New Town end of the Legions Bridge (most Legii), its bulk carefully angled to fit into the streetscape and not diminish the view to Petřín Hill on the far bank. It was given a long-deserved restoration in time for its centenary, and when the theater reopened in 1983 it had gained a piazza and three annexes, whose architecture has been much maligned, the least unkind comment being that the buildings seem to be clad in bubble-wrap. Prague's well-known Laterna Magika performs in one of these additional buildings, the Nová scéna.

HIGHLIGHTS

- Bronze troikas above the entrance loggia
- Star-patterned roof of the dome
- Frescos in the foyer by Mikuláš Aleš
- Painted ceiling of the auditorium by Frantisek Ženíšek
- Painted stage curtain by Vojtěch Hynais
- View of the theater from Střelecký Island
- Any performance of an opera from the Czech repertoire

INFORMATION

- D/E5
- Národní 2, New Town
- 24 91 34 37
- Bar
- Národní třída
- Few
- Bethlehem Chapel (► 55)

Reflection of the National Theater

Decorative Arts Museum

Don't be put off by the uninviting build-ing. The forlornly flapping banner that proclaims the museum's name (Uměleck-oprůmyslové muzeum) is a harbinger of better things. At the top of a steep flight of stairs are little visited treasure chambers full of fine furniture, glass, porcelain, clocks, metalwork ...

Riverside reclaimed Looking something like a miniature Louvre, the museum was built in 1901 in an area that, by the end of the 19th century, had turned its back on the river and had become a jumble of storage depots and timber yards. The city fathers determined to beautify it with fine public buildings and riverside promenades on the Parisian model. The School of Arts and Crafts (1884) and the House of Artists (1890) preceded the Decorative Arts Museum; the University's Philosophy Building (1929), which completed the enclosure of what is now Jan Palach Square, followed it.

Decorative delights The museum's collections are incredibly rich and diverse, numbering nearly 200,000 items. Unfortunately only a fraction has ever been on display at any one time. In particular, the extraordinary Czech contribution to the development of 20th-century art and design has never been dealt with adequately, a situation that will be partly remedied by the opening of the Museum of Modern Art (▶ 47). In the meantime, the Decorative Arts Museum offers antiques enthusiasts a treat. Although the museum's scope is international, the focus is on the beautiful objects originating in the Czech Lands from Renaissance times to the 19th century. They are displayed in an endearingly old-fashioned way, in sumptuous settings.

HIGHLIGHTS

- *Pietra dura* scene of a town by Castnicci
- Beer glasses with card players
- Boulle commode and cabinet
- Monumental baroque furniture by Dientzenhofer and Santini
- Meissen Turk on a rhino
- Holic porcelain figures
- Harrachov glass
- Klášterec figurines of Prague characters
- Biedermeier cradle
- Surprise view down into the Old Jewish Cemetery

INFORMATION

- ➕ E4
- ✉ 17 listopadu 2, Old Town
- ☎ 24 81 12 41
- 🕐 Tue–Sun 10–6
- 🍽 Café Mon–Fri 10:30–10:30, Sat, Sun 10:30–6
- Ⓜ Staroměstská
- ♿ Few
- 🔲 Moderate
- ↔ Old/New Synagogue (▶ 39), Old Jewish Cemetery (▶ 40)

VYŠEHRAD

HIGHLIGHTS

- National Cemetery (Slavín) graves and memorials
- St. Martin's Rotunda (Romanesque church)
- Brick Gate (Cihelná brana) with Prague Fortifications Museum
- Vyšehrad Museum with historical exhibits
- Baroque Leopold Gate
- Ramparts walk
- Neo-Gothic Church of St. Peter and St. Paul
- Freestanding sculptures of Libuše and other legendary figures (by Josef Myslbeck)

INFORMATION

✚ E7

Museum

✉ Soběslavova 1, Vyšehrad

☎ 29 66 51

◉ Museum and National Cemetery daily 9:30–4:30

🍴 Cafés

Ⓜ Vyšehrad

♿ Few

🎫 Park free, museum and cemetery inexpensive

↔ Palace of Culture (► 51)

Rising high above the river, Vyšehrad—High Castle—was where the soothsaying Princess Libuše foresaw the founding of Prague, "a city whose splendor shall reach unto the stars", and where she married her plowman swain, Přemysl.

Romantic rock Beneath Vyšehrad's 19th-century neo-Gothic Church of St. Peter and St. Paul are the remains of a far earlier, Romanesque church that once served the royal court. But it was in the 19th century, with the rise of Romantic ideas about history and nationhood, that poets, painters and playwrights celebrated the great fortress-rock, elaborating the story of Libuše. Most of their efforts have been forgotten, though Smetana's "Vyšehrad," part of his glorious tone-poem *Má vlast*, is still popular. The nation's great and good have been buried in the Slavín, the National Cemetery (or Pantheon) at Vyšehrad, since the later 19th century. Smetana himself is here, along with fellow-composer Dvořák.

Devil's Pillars, Karlach's Park

Vltava views Everyone driving along the main riverside highway has to pay homage to Vyšehrad, as the road and tram tracks twist and turn and then tunnel through the high rock protruding into the Vltava. In the 1920s the whole hilltop was turned into a public park, with wonderful views up and down the river (► 51).

JOSEFOV – OLD/NEW SYNAGOGUE

To step down from the street through the low portal of the Old/New Synagogue (Staronová synagóga) is to enter another world, one that endured a thousand years until brought to a tragic end by Nazi occupation.

Ghetto memories The Old/New Synagogue stands at the heart of the former Jewish Ghetto. Prague's Jews moved here in the 13th century; by that time they had already lived at various locations in the city for hundreds of years. High walls kept the Jews in and their Christian neighbors out, though not in 1389, when 3,000 died in a vicious pogrom and the synagogue's floor ran with blood. The ghetto community produced some extraordinary characters, such as Rabbi Loew, Renaissance scholar, confidant of emperors, and creator of that archetypal man-made monster, the Golem. Molded from river mud, the mournful Golem first served his master dutifully, but eventually ran amok until the rabbi managed to calm him down. Legend has it that the monster's remains are hidden in the synagogue's loft. Far worse monsters marched in as the Germans annexed Czecho-slovakia in 1939; by the end of World War II most of the country's Jews had perished, some in the prison town of Terezín/Theresienstadt, the majority in Auschwitz.

Ghetto Gothic With its pointed brick gable and atmospheric interior, the Gothic Old/New Synagogue of 1275 is the oldest building of its kind north of the Alps, a compelling reminder of the age-old intertwining of Jewish and Christian culture in Europe. It is at its most evocative when least crowded with visitors. Remember that it is still a place of worship for Prague's few remaining Jews and not a mere museum.

HIGHLIGHTS

- Vine carving in entrance portal
- Unconventional five-ribbed vaults
- Gothic grille of the bimah (pulpit)
- Rabbi Loew's seat
- Imperial banner in recognition of Jewish bravery in Thirty Years War
- Ark with foliage carving

INFORMATION

- E4
- Pařížská and Červená
- Sun–Thu 9–5, Fri 9–1
- Restaurant in Jewish Town Hall
- Staroměstská
- Few
- Moderate
- Old Jewish Cemetery (► 40), Old Town Square (► 42), Decorative Arts Museum (► 37)

17

OLD JEWISH CEMETERY

INFORMATION

🞖 E4
✉ U starého hřbitova, Old Town
☎ State Jewish Museum: 24 81 00 99
🕑 Sun–Fri 9–4:30
🍴 Restaurant in Jewish Town Hall
Ⓜ Staroměstská
♿ None
🔅 Moderate
↔ Old/New Synagogue (► 39), Old Town Square (► 42), Decorative Arts Museum (► 37)

Just as the sunlight filtering through the tall trees is reduced to a dappled shade, so visitors' voices diminish to a hush as they contemplate the 12,000 toppling tombstones of this ancient burial place (Starý židovský hřbitov).

Improving the Ghetto Over the centuries, hemmed in by its walls, the Jewish Ghetto became intolerably crowded. By the time Emperor Joseph II gave the Jews partial emancipation, toward the end of the 18th century, the Ghetto had 12,000 inhabitants, crammed together within it in increasingly sordid conditions. During the course of the 19th century many moved out to more salubrious quarters in the suburbs. Around 1900, the city fathers decided to "improve" the Ghetto, now named Josefov (Joseph's Town) in honor of the emperor. Most of it was flattened to make way for broad streets and boulevards, though the rococo Jewish Town Hall and a clutch of synagogues around the cemetery were spared. They survived under the German occupation, because Hitler hoped to preserve what was left of the Ghetto as a "Museum of a Vanished Race." The stolen valuables of the Jewish communities of Bohemia and Moravia were brought to Prague, where some are now on display in the synagogues administered by the State Jewish Museum.

Solemn cemetery The cemetery is evocative of the long centuries of Jewish life in Prague. Unable to extend it, the custodians were forced to bury the dead one on top of the other, up to 12 deep in places. The total number laid to rest here may amount to 80,000. Visitors leave wishful notes under pebbles on the more prominent tombstones (like that of Rabbi Loew).

St. Agnes's Convent

I gave up believing a long time ago that the restoration of St. Agnes's Convent (Anežský klášter) would ever be finished. I was wrong! The city's most venerable Gothic complex is open to the public at last, a fit setting for a fascinating and unfamiliar art collection.

Canonized Czech Agnes was a 13th-century princess, sister of Wenceslas I and founder of a convent of Poor Clares here. In its glory days a mausoleum for the royal family, the convent was sacked by the Hussites in the 15th century. In 1782, it was closed down by Joseph II, and for more than a century it was a slum, its noble interior partitioned and crammed with tenants. At the turn of the century, the convent was saved from demolition by public protest. It was another hundred years before it was restored—by the Communists. On November 12, 1989, just days before the Communist regime ended, Agnes was made a saint. An auspicious augury?

Czech collection The convent now houses the National Gallery's extensive collections of 19th-century Czech art. Watch for works by Josef Mánes (painter and revolutionary), Mikuláš Aleš (painter and graphic artist), Josef Myslbek (sculptor and graphic artist) and a painter of very atmospheric urban scenes—Jakub Schikaneder.

Below the Cottage, *Josef Mánes*

HIGHLIGHTS

- Rustic idyll *Below the Cottage*, Josef Mánes
- History painting *Oldřich and Bozena*, F. Ženíšek
- *Winter Evening in Town*, Jakub Schikaneder
- Study for the Wenceslas statue, Josef Myslbek
- *Primeval Forest*, Julius Marak
- Vaulted medieval cloister
- Church of St. Francis (concert hall)
- Church of the Holy Savior

INFORMATION

- ✚ E3
- ✉ U milosrdných 17, Old Town
- ☎ 24 81 06 28
- 🕐 Tue–Sun 10–6
- 🍴 Café
- Ⓜ Staroměstská
- 🚎 Tram 17 (Pravnická fakulta stop) or Tram 14, 26, 5 (Dlouhá třída stop)
- ♿ Few
- 🔳 Moderate
- ↔ Postal Museum (➤ 53)

OLD TOWN SQUARE

Visitors throng this spacious square (Staroměstské náměstí) at all times of year, enchanted by the Astronomical Clock and the cheerful façades of the old buildings, entertained by buskers, and refreshed at outdoor cafés.

Martyrs and mournful memories The Old Town Square has not always been so jolly. A medieval market-place, it soon became a place of execution, where Hussites lost their heads in the 15th century and the 27 prominent Protestants were put to death in

Square and Tyn Church

1621 (they are commemorated by white crosses in the paving). In 1945, in a final act of spite, diehard Nazis demolished a whole wing of the Old Town Hall; the site has still, thankfully, not been built on. On February 21, 1948, Premier Gottwald proclaimed the triumph of Communism from the rococo Goltz-Kinský Palace.

Round the square The hub of the square is the Jan Hus Memorial, an extraordinary art nouveau sculpture whose base is one of the few places in the square you can sit without paying! From here, to your left rise the blackened towers of the Tyn Church, while to your right is the Old Town Hall, an attractively varied assembly of buildings and, further round, the city's second St. Nicholas's Church. The fine town houses surrounding the square are a study in different architectural styles from the genuine Gothic of the House at the Stone Bell to the 19th-century mock-Gothic of No. 16.

WENCESLAS SQUARE

Despite its sometimes rather seedy air, Wenceslas Square (Václavské náměstí) is still for me the place where the city's heart beats most strongly, and to meet someone "beneath the horse" (the Wenceslas statue) remains a special thrill.

When is a square not a square? When it's a boulevard. "Václavak," 2,300 feet long, slopes gently up to the imposing façade of the National Museum (▶ 44), which is fronted by the statue of Wenceslas on his sprightly steed. This is a good place to arrange a rendezvous—whatever the time of day there's always some action, with daytime shoppers and sightseers replaced by every species of night owl as darkness falls.

Many of the dramas of modern times have been played out here. In 1918, the new state of Czechoslovakia was proclaimed here, and in 1939 German tanks underlined the Republic's demise. In 1968, more tanks arrived—this time to crush the Prague Spring of Alexander Dubček. To protest the Soviet occupation, Jan Palach burned himself to death here the following year, and in 1989, Dubček and Václav Havel waved from the balcony of No. 36 as half a million Czechs crowded the square to celebrate the collapse of Communism.

Museum of modern architecture The procession of buildings lining both sides of the square, from the resplendent art nouveau of the Hotel Evropa to the bare and elegant Functionalism of the Bata Store, tell the story of the distinctively Czech contribution to 20th-century design. Even more intriguing are the arcades ("pasáž") that burrow deep into the buildings' interiors, creating a labyrinthine world of boutiques, theaters, cafés, and cinemas.

HIGHLIGHTS

- *St. Wenceslas* statue, J. V. Myslbek (1912)
- Arcades of the Lucerna Palace
- Grand Hotel Evropa, completed 1905 (Nos. 25/27)
- 1920s Functionalist Bata and Lindt buildings (Nos. 6, 12)
- Ambassador, late art nouveau hotel of 1912 (No. 5)
- Memorial to the victims of Communism
- 1950s Soviet-style Jalta Hotel (No. 45)
- Former Bank of Moravia of 1916 (Nos. 38/40)
- Art nouveau Peterka building of 1901 (No. 12)
- Koruna Palace of 1914 (No. 1)

INFORMATION

- ✚ E4/5, F5
- ✉ Václavské náměstí, New Town
- 🍴 Many cafés and restaurants
- Ⓜ Můstek or Muzeum
- ♿ Fair
- ↔ National Museum (▶ 44)

21

NATIONAL MUSEUM

HIGHLIGHTS

- Allegorical sculptures on the terrace
- The Pantheon and dome
- Coin collection
- Collection of precious stones
- Skeleton of a whale

INFORMATION

- ✚ F5
- ✉ Václavské náměstí 68, New Town
- ☎ 24 23 04 85
- 🕐 Wed–Mon 9–5
- 🍴 Café
- Ⓜ Muzeum
- ♿ Few
- 💰 Moderate
- ↔ Wenceslas Square (► 43)

Some people find Prague's prestigious National Museum terribly disappointing, crammed as it is with cabinets full of beetles and mineral specimens. My advice is to enjoy it as a period piece in its own right, its dusty showcases as venerable as the building itself.

Top building Its gilded dome crowning the rise at the top of Wenceslas Square, the National Museum (Národní muzeum) provides a grand finale to the capital's most important street. The neo-Renaissance building was completed in 1891, and at the time was as much an object of pride to the Czech populace as the National Theater (► 36). Such is its presence that some visitors have mistaken it for the Parliament building, as did the Soviet gunner who raked its façade with machine-gun fire in August 1968.

An array of -ologies Even if you are not an enthusiastic entomologist, paleontologist, zoologist, mineralogist, or numismatist, you can't fail to be impressed by all the evidence assembled here of the 19th century's great passion for collecting and classifying. Perhaps more immediately attractive for the casual visitor will be the temporary exhibitions that draw on the museum's vast collections. A recent dinosaur display proved at least as compelling to young visitors as the famous film that may have inspired it. Above all, the building itself is a most impressive exhibit, with grand stairways, statuary, mosaics, and patterned floors. And, unlike virtually all other attractions in Prague, it's open on Mondays!

Recumbent figure, on stairway to the National Museum

NATIONAL TECHNICAL MUSEUM

Did you know... That Czechoslovakia had one of the world's biggest auto industries and that Škoda cars were a byword for toughness and reliability?... That a horse-drawn railroad once linked Bohemia with Austria?... That a Czechoslovak fleet once sailed the oceans?

Past glories The answer to all these questions is "yes," based on the evidence piled high in this wonderful museum (Národní technické muzeum), located off the beaten track on the edge of Letná Plain. The facelessness of the building belies the richness and fascination of its contents, a celebration of the longstanding technological prowess of inventive and hard-working Czechs. The Czech Lands were the industrial powerhouse of the Austro-Hungarian Empire, steel works and coal mines providing the foundation for excellence in engineering of all kinds, from the production of weapons to locomotive manufacture. Later, between the two world wars, independent Czechoslovakia's light industries led the world in innovativeness and quality.

Trains and boats and planes The museum displays its collection of technological artifacts to spectacular effect in the vast top-glazed and galleried main hall, where balloons and biplanes hang in space above the ranks of sinister-looking streamlined limousines and powerful steam engines. The side galleries tell the story of "The Wheel" and of navigation, from rafting timber on the Vltava to transporting ore across the oceans in the Czechoslovak carrier *Košice*. Deep underground there's a exhibit of a coal mine, and other sections tell you all you ever wanted to know about time, sound, geodesy, photography, and astronomy.

HIGHLIGHTS

- 1928 Škoda fire engine
- Laurent and Klement soft-top roadster
- President Masaryk's V-12 Tatra
- Soviet ZIS 110B limousine
- Express locomotive 375-007 of 1911
- Imperial family's railway dining car of 1891
- Bleriot XI Kaspar monoplane
- Sokol monoplane

INFORMATION

- E3
- Kostelní 42/44, Holešovice
- 37 36 51
- Tue–Sun 9–5
- Tram 26 to Letenské náměstí, or Metro Vltavská then Tram 1 to Letenské náměstí
- Few
- Moderate
- Letná Park (► 50), Veletržní palác/Museum of Modern Art (► 47)

45

OBECNÍ DŮM

HIGHLIGHTS

- Entrance canopy and mosaic *Homage to Prague*
- Smetana Hall, with frescoes symbolizing the dramatic arts
- Mayor's Suite with paintings by Mucha
- Rieger Hall, with Myslbek sculptures
- Palacký Room with paintings by Preisler

INFORMATION

- E/F4
- Náměstí Republiky 5, Old Town
- Closed until 1997
- Náměstí Republiky
- St. James's Church (► 57), Black Madonna (► 58)

The prosaic name Municipal House fails utterly to convey anything of the character of this extraordinary art nouveau building, a gloriously extravagant turn-of-the-century confection on which every artist of the day seems to have left his stamp.

City council citadel Glittering like some gigantic, flamboyant jewel, the Obecní dům is linked to the blackened Powder Tower, last relic of the Old Town's fortifications and for long one of the city's main symbols. The intention of the city fathers in the first years of the 20th century was to add an even more powerful element to the cityscape that would celebrate the glory of the Czech nation and Prague's place within it. The site of the old Royal Palace was selected, and no expense was spared to erect a megastructure in which the city's burgeoning life could expand.

Ornamental orgy The building program included meeting and assembly rooms, cafés, restaurants, bars, even a patisserie, and the mayor was provided with particularly luxurious quarters. The 1,300-seat Smetana Hall, later the home of the Czech Philharmonic, is a temple to the muse of Bohemian music. Everything, even the elevators, is encrusted with lavish decoration in stucco, metalwork, glass, mosaic, murals, textiles. The Obecní dům is likely to reopen in 1997 after a complete restoration.

The glorious Municipal House

MUSEUM OF MODERN ART

"What I found to be a truly great experience was a tour of the Prague Trades Fair Building. The first impression created by the enormous palace is breathtaking." So enthused the great architect Le Corbusier, when he visited Prague in 1928 shortly after this monumental structure, the Veletržní Palác, was completed.

Trailblazer Never lacking in ego, Le Corbusier was nevertheless vexed to find that his Czech colleagues had got in first in completing what is one of the key buildings in the evolution of 20th-century design, a secular, modern-day cathedral constructed in concrete, steel, and glass. Set in the suburb of Holešovice, the palace was intended to be a showpiece for the products of Czechoslovakia. However, trade fairs moved away from Prague to Brno, and for many years the great building languished in neglect and obscurity, its originality forgotten as its architectural innovations became the norm throughout the world.

Disguised blessing After fire gutted the palace in 1974, it was decided to use its elegant, spacious interiors to display the city's rich hoard of modern art treasures, which had never found a proper home. In all, it took nearly 20 years to complete restoration work, but the wait was well worthwhile. As well as showing the French Impressionists and other modern foreign paintings from the National Gallery, the palace promotes contemporary arts of all kinds and stages the kind of major international art shows of which the Czechs were so long deprived. But the core of the collection is the amazing achievements of Czech painters and sculptors in the early part of the 20th century.

HIGHLIGHTS

- *Reader of Dostoyevsky,* Emil Filla
- *Serie C VI,* František Kupka
- *Melancholy,* Jan Zrzavy
- *Sailor,* Karel Dvožák
- *Self-portrait,* Picasso
- *Self-portrait,* Douanier Rousseau
- *Green Rye,* Van Gogh (pictured above)
- *Virgin,* Gustav Klimt
- *Pregnant Woman and Death,* Egon Schiele

INFORMATION

- F2
- Dukelských hrdinů 7, Holešovice
- 24 30 11 11
- Tue–Sun 10–6
- Restaurants and cafés
- Tram 5 from Náměstí Republiky
- Few
- Moderate
- National Technical Museum (▶ 45)

25

TROJA CHÂTEAU

INFORMATION

Out here you can catch a glimpse of how delightful Prague's countryside must have been three centuries ago... vine-clad slopes, trees in abundance and, in the midst, a resplendent Baroque palace (the Trojský zámek) set among its allées and parterres.

Prague's Versailles This extravagant palace was built not by the monarch, but by the second richest man in Prague, Count Wenceslas Adelbert Šternberg. The Šternbergs profited from the Thirty Years War, and at the end of the 17th century were in a position to commission Jean-Baptiste Mathey to design a country house along the lines of the contemporary châteaux of the architect's native France. The south-facing site by the river, oriented directly on the cathedral and castle on the far side of the Royal Hunting Grounds (now Stromovka Park), was ideal for Šternberg to be able to offer the monarch the right kind of hospitality following a day's hunting.

Ornamental extravagance The palace boasts grand proportions, and its painted interiors go over the top in paying homage to the country's Habsburg rulers. And over the top, too, goes a turbaned Turk as he topples, in stunning trompe l'oeil, from the mock battlements in the grand hall. Troja was acquired by the state in the 1920s, but only restored (some think excessively) in the late 1980s. It contains part of Prague's collection of 19th-century paintings, few of which can compete with the flamboyance of their setting.

Ornamentation at Troja

PRAGUE's *best*

PANORAMAS

Unpopular neighbor

Building the unlovely TV tower in Zizkov necessitated the destruction of part of an old Jewish cemetery and was resisted (insofar as any resistance was possible in Communist days) by locals and other protesters. Some people are still uneasy with their giant neighbor, claiming to be able to pick up transmissions on virtually any metal object, or that their bodies are being slowly microwaved.

Malá Strana from Petřín

CATHEDRAL TOWER

Climb the 287 steps of St. Vitus's Cathedral tower for one of the best all-round panoramas of the city and its surroundings as well as close-ups of the intricate exterior of the cathedral itself, with its bristling buttresses, diamond-tiled roofs, and copper cockerels atop their spiky perches.

🕂 C/D4 ⊠ Pražský hrad ⏰ Daily 10–4, closed in bad weather 🍴 Cafés and restaurants 🚋 Tram 22 to Pražský hrad 💰 Inexpensive

KAMPA ISLAND EMBANKMENT

From the shady parkland of Kampa Island there is an unusual view across the Vltava to the Old Town over Charles Bridge and the foaming weir.

🕂 D4 ⊠ U Sovových mlýnů ⏰ Permanently open 🚋 Trams 12, 22 to Hellichová 💰 Free

LETNÁ PLAIN

The parks and gardens of Letná Plain stretch from the eastern end of the castle high above the north bank of the Vltava. Between 1955 and 1962 a monster statue of Stalin stood here. The plinth, now infested with skateboarders, is occupied by a giant metronome and makes an excellent vantage point for views of the river, its bridges and the Old Town.

🕂 D/E3 ⊠ Letenské sady ⏰ Permanently accessible 🚇 Malostranská and uphill walk 🚋 Tram 18 to Chotkovy sady or 22 to Kralovský letohrádek 💰 Free

OLD ROYAL PALACE (STARÝ KRÁLOVSKÝ PALÁC)

After admiring the interiors of the Old Royal Palace and the Vladislav Hall, take a stroll on the south-facing terrace or peep out of the windows from which the Catholic councellors were defenestrated in 1618. All Prague lies at your feet.

🕂 D4 ⊠ Pražský hrad ☎ 33 37 33 68 ⏰ Tue–Sun 9–5 (Nov–Mar to 4) 🍴 Cafés and restaurants 🚋 Tram 22 to Pražský hrad 💰 Moderate

OLD TOWN HALL TOWER

Whether or not the creaking elevator is working, the climb up is well worthwhile for the dizzying view it gives of the swarming activity in Old Town Square, as well as of the higgledy-piggledy red-tiled roofs of the medieval Old Town.

🕂 E4 ⊠ Staroměstské náměstí ☎ 24 81 16 83 ⏰ Tue–Sun 9–6 🍴 Restaurants in Square 🚇 Staroměstská 💰 Moderate

PETŘÍN HILL LOOKOUT TOWER (ROZHLEDNA)

This little brother of the Eiffel Tower was erected for Prague's great Jubilee Expo of 1891. Prepare to climb 299 steps!

🚩 C4 ⊠ Petřín ⏰ Tue–Sun 9:30–5 (summer only) 🚋 Tram 12 or 22 to Hellichova, then Lanovka funicular (from Újezd) 🔧 Moderate

POWDER TOWER

The sumptuous roofscape of the adjoining Obecní dům (Municipal House) makes an immediate impact, but this panorama is particularly appealing because of the vista along Celetná Street into the heart of the Old Town.

🚩 E/F4 ⊠ Náměstí Republiky ⏰ Daily 10–5 (to 6 in summer) 🚇 Náměstí Republiky 🚋 Trams 5, 14, 26 to Náměstí Republiky 🔧 Moderate

SMETANA STATUE

The walkway leading to the museum devoted to the composer Bedřich Smetana is in fact a pier (known as Novotného lávka), built out into the river, and the museum itself is in a building that once housed the offices of the city's waterworks. At the very tip of the pier are café tables and a statue of the composer; the view across the river, whose roaring weir drowns all intrusive noises, is the classic one of Charles Bridge, Malá Strana, and the castle above.

🚩 D4 ⊠ Novotného lávka ⏰ Permanently open 🍴 Café and restaurant 🚇 Staroměstská 🚋 Trams 17, 18 to Karlový lázně 🔧 Free

Old Town Square from Town Hall Tower

TELEVISION TOWER (TELEVIZNÍ VYSÍLAČ)

This immensely tall (853 feet) television transmitter tower in the inner suburb of Žižkov may be a blot on Prague's townscape, but its viewing gallery does give visitors stupendous views over the city and its surroundings. The best time to take the elevator to the top is fairly early in the day before the sun has moved too far round to the west.

🚩 G5 ⊠ Mahlerovy sady ☎ 27 61 63, 27 63 07 🍴 Restaurant 🚇 Jiřího z Poděbrad 🚋 Trams 5, 9, 26 to Lipanská 🔧 Moderate

VYŠEHRAD

A walk around the ramparts of the old fortifications of Vyšehrad gives contrasting views along the Vltava flowing far below. Upstream, Prague is surprisingly countrified, with rugged limestone crags and rough woodland, while downstream the panorama reveals the city, especially Hradčany, from an entirely new angle. Nearby, the terraces of the Communists' huge Palace of Culture offer a view across the deep Nusle ravine toward the New Town, guarded by the walls and cupolas of the Karlov Monastery.

🚩 E6/7 ⊠ Vyšehrad ⏰ Permanently accessible 🍴 Café and restaurant 🚇 Vyšehrad 🚋 Trams 3, 7, 17 to Vytoň

Across the river

Some of the finest views of Prague are those in which the city is seen across the broad waters of the Vltava, as from the Smetana statue or Kampa Island. A stroll along the embankments and footpaths on both sides of the river is equally rewarding, nor should you neglect the islands—Slavonic Island (Slovansky ostrov) and Shooters' Island

GALLERIES

Unseen art

Housing Prague's vast and varied art collections has always posed problems. Under Communism, the temptation to keep pictures and other art objects more or less permanently in store was not always resisted, and the unique Czech contribution to 20th-century art has never been properly celebrated. The big issue is now a financial one. If there are particular works you want to see, it's worth checking whether they are actually on display.

House at the Stone Bell

GOLTZ-KINSKÝ PALACE

Changing exhibitions, based on the National Gallery's vast collections of prints and drawings. It was from a balcony here that Klement Gottwald proclaimed the victory of the working classes in 1948.
🔲 E4 ⊠ Staroměstské náměstí 12 ☎ 24 81 07 58
🕐 Tue–Sun 10–6 🍽 Cafés and restaurants in Old Town Square 🚇 Starom/stská 🔲 Moderate

HOUSE AT THE STONE BELL

For many years this fine town house was thought to be a rococo palace. When the restorers began work on it, that rarity, a Gothic mansion, was discovered behind the 18th-century work. After much debate, the building was restored to its medieval state. Exhibitions of art by young Czech contemporaries.
🔲 E4 ⊠ Staroměstské náměstí 13 ☎ 24 81 00 36
🕐 Tue–Sun 10–6 🍽 Cafés and restaurants in Old Town Square 🚇 Staroměstská 🔲 Moderate

LAPIDARIUM

Classical and modern sculpture, including some of the original statues from Charles Bridge brought here to protect them from Prague's polluted atmosphere.
🔲 F2 ⊠ Výstaviště, Holešovice
🕐 Tue–Fri 12–6, Sat, Sun, & hols 10–12, 1–6 🍽 Cafés and restaurants in grounds 🚇 Nádraží Holešovice
🚊 Trams 5, 12, 17 to Výstaviště
🔲 Inexpensive

RIDING SCHOOL OF PRAGUE CASTLE

This big Baroque building is used by the National Gallery for temporary exhibitions.
🔲 C3 ⊠ U Prašného mostu 55, Hradčany ☎ 33 37 32 32
🕐 Tue–Sun 10–6 🍽 Cafés and restaurants in Castle 🚊 Tram 22 to Pražský hrad 🔲 Moderate

MUSEUMS

CITY MUSEUM
(MUZEUM HLAVNÍHO MĚSTA PRAHY)
This pompous late 19th-century building contains exhibits telling the story of Prague's evolution from the earliest times. The star is an extraordinary scale model of the city as it was in the 1820s and 1830s, meticulously put together by a person of infinite patience named Antonín Langweil. Most of the extensive collections are in store, but selections (posters, postcards, etc.) are shown in rotation.
➕ F4 ✉ Na poříčí 52, north New Town ☎ 24 22 31 79 🕓 Tue–Sun 10–6 🚇 Florenc ▦ Inexpensive

MILITARY MUSEUM, SCHWARZENBERG PALACE
(VOJENSKÉ MUZEUM)
Behind the stunning sgraffito façades of this Renaissance palace is an array of militaria of all kinds —guns, uniforms, models, paintings, maps—proving what a bloody battleground Bohemia always was.
➕ C4 ✉ Hradčanské náměstí 2, Hradčany ☎ 53 64 88 🕓 Tue–Sun 10–6 🚇 Malostranská 🚊 Tram 22 to Pražský hrad ▦ Inexpensive

NÁPRSTEK MUSEUM (NÁPRSTKOVO MUZEUM)
Surprisingly few visitors climb the stairs to the intriguing ethnographical exhibits assembled here by a 19th-century collector in love with the indigenous cultures of the Americas and Pacific.
➕ E4 ✉ Betlémské náměstí 1, Old Town ☎ 24 21 45 37 🕓 Tue–Sun 9–12, 1–5:30 🚇 Staroměstská or Narodni třída ▦ Inexpensive

POLICE MUSEUM (MUZEUM POLICIE CR)
This museum recovered quickly from the collapse of the old order in 1989 and gives an upbeat account of Czech policing, with plenty of gore and weaponry on show in, incongruously, the former Karlov monastery.
➕ E6 ✉ Ke Karlovu 1, New Town ☎ 29 52 09 🕓 Tue–Sun 10–5 🚇 I P Pavlova then Bus 272 ▦ Inexpensive

POSTAL MUSEUM (POŠTOVNÍ MUZEUM)
A delightful little museum of great appeal and not just to philatelists. It's housed in an attractive building with some charming 19th-century frescos.
➕ F3 ✉ Nové mlýny 2, northern New Town ☎ 23 12 060 🕓 Tue–Sun 9–5 🚇 Náměstí Republiky, then Tram 5, 14, 26 to Dlouhá třída ▦ Inexpensive

More militaria

Almost unknown abroad, the tale of Czech and Slovak involvement in the conflicts of the 20th century is told in the Museum of the Resistance and History of the Army (Muzeum odboje a dějin armady) at the foot of the National Memorial in the inner suburb of Žižkov.

The big guns

Czech and Slovak involvement in the big conflict that never happened, the face-off of the Cold War, is chillingly displayed in the huge collection of military hardware on display at the Aircraft Museum (Letecké muzeum) at Kbely airfield on the eastern outskirts. Some of the aircraft go back to World War I, but above all it's the MiGs that remain in the memory.

PALACES

High diplomacy

The Anglophile and athletic first president of Czechoslovakia, Tomás Masaryk, is reputed to have maintained good relations with the British ambassador in the Thun Palace by lowering a ladder down the castle walls and dropping in for tea.

Coat of Arms, Archbishop's Palace

Auto sculpture

In the summer of 1989, the streets around the West German Embassy were clogged with Wartburgs and Trabants abandoned by their East German owners. The memorial to these stirring days lurks in the shrubbery in the embassy garden—a fiberglass Trabant on mighty, seven-league legs.

See Top 25 Sights for
ROYAL PALACE ►29
ŠTERNBERG PALACE ►27
WALLENSTEIN PALACE ►34

ARCHBISHOP'S PALACE (ARCIBISKUPSKÝ PALÁC)

The lusciously restored rococo façade hides a sumptuous residence, unfortunately accessible only on special occasions.

✚ C4 ⊠ Hradčanske náměstí 16 ⓘ Not normally open to the public 🚊 Tram 22 to Pražský hrad

ČERNÍN PALACE (ČERNÍNSKÝ PALÁC)

It was from this huge baroque structure (completed 1720), now the Foreign Ministry, that Jan Masaryk fell to his death in 1948.

✚ C4 ⊠ Loretánské náměstí, Hradčany ⓘ Not open to the public 🚊 Tram 22 to Pohořelec

HOUSE OF THE LORDS OF KUNŠTAT AND PODĚBRADY (DŮM PANU Z KUNŠTATU A PODĚBRAD)

Possibly the most ancient interior accessible to the public, this is the 13th-century mansion of King George of Podebrady.

✚ E4 ⊠ Řetezová 3, Old Town ⓘ Tue–Sun 10-6 (summer only) Ⓜ Staroměstská 🔳 Inexpensive

LOBKOVIC PALACE (LOBKOVICKÝ PALÁC)

The residence of the German ambassador, this superb Baroque structure (not to be confused with the Lobkovic Palace within the castle precinct) saw strange scenes in the summer of 1989, when it became temporary home to thousands of East Germans seeking refuge.

✚ C4 ⊠ Vlašská 19 ⓘ Not open to the public 🚊 Tram 12, 22 to Malostranské náměstí

SCHÖNBORN-COLLOREDO PALACE (SCHÖNBORNSKÝ PALÁC)

The U.S. Embassy occupies a Baroque palace whose grandeur equals that of the nearby German Embassy.

✚ D4 ⊠ Tržiště 15, Malá Strana ⓘ Not open to the public 🚊 Tram 12, 22 to Malostranské náměstí

SCHWARZENBERG PALACE ►53

THUN PALACE (THUNOVSKÝ PALÁC)

The British Embassy since 1918. Presented by the Emperor in 1630 to Walter Leslie, a Scotsman, who had helped to remove his great rival Wallenstein.

✚ D4 ⊠ Thunovská 25, Malá Strana ⓘ Not open to the public Ⓜ Malostranská

CHURCHES

See Top 25 Sights for
LORETTO SHRINE ➤26
ST. GEORGE'S BASILICA ➤31
ST. NICHOLAS'S CHURCH, MALÁ STRANA ➤33
ST. VITUS'S CATHEDRAL ➤30

BETHLEHEM CHAPEL (BETLEMSKÉ KAPLE)
This barn-like structure, where Jan Hus preached, has to be visited in order to appreciate the deeply nonconformist traditions so thoroughly obscured by centuries of imposed Catholicism and its extravagant baroque architecture.
➕ E4 ✉ Betlemské náměstí, Old Town 🕐 Daily 9–6
🍴 Restaurants and cafés near by 🚇 Národní třída
🎫 Inexpensive

CHURCH OF OUR LADY VICTORIOUS (KOSTEL PANNY MARIE VÍTĚZNÉ)
After Czech Protestantism was crushed in 1621, this church became a center of the Counter-Reformation, not least thanks to miracles wrought by the little waxwork known as the Bambino di Praga.
➕ D4 ✉ Karmelitská 9, Malá Strana 🕐 Daily 7–9
🚊 Tram 12, 22 to Malostranské náměstí

ST. JAMES'S CHURCH (KOSTEL SVATÉHO JAKUBA)
Beneath the Baroque froth is an ancient Gothic church, though you'd hardly guess it. The acoustics of the long nave are particularly impressive, and concerts held here are generally well attended.
➕ E4 ✉ Malá Štupartská, Old Town 🕐 Daily 9:30–4
🚇 Náměstí Republiky

ST. NICHOLAS'S CHURCH, OLD TOWN (KOSTEL SVATEHO MIKULÁŠE, STARÉ MĚSTO)
St. Nicholas's twin towers and grand dome are the work of the great Baroque architect, Kilian Ignaz Dientzenhofer. His church is now one of the more prominent features of Old Town Square, but Dientzenhofer designed it to fit into the narrow street that once ran here.
➕ E4 ✉ Staroměstské náměstí, Old Town 🕐 Tue–Fri, Sun 10–12, Wed also 2–5 🚇 Staroměstská

TYN CHURCH (KOSTEL PANNY MÁRIE PŘED TÝNEM)
Among the city's best-known landmarks, the Gothic Tyn Church's twin towers stick up spikily behind the houses east of Old Town Square. Inside are some fascinating tombs, including that of Tycho Brahe.
➕ E4 ✉ Tynská and Celetná, Old Town 🕐 Daily 3–5
(possibly longer in summer) 🍴 Cafés and restaurants near by 🚇 Staroměstská or Náměstí Republiky

Tyn Church

Rough justice
A withered hand hangs from the altar in St. James's Church, severed by a butcher when the thief to whom it belonged was apprehended by the Virgin Mary, who refused to let go.

Bambino di Praga
The Bambino di Praga was given to the Church of Our Lady Victorious in 1628 as part of the compulsory re-Catholicization of the wayward Czechs. The miracles performed by the diminutive effigy of the infant Jesus are even more numerous than its 60 sumptuous changes of outfit.

Twentieth-Century Buildings

See Top 25 sights for
OBECNÍ DŮM (MUNICIPAL HOUSE) ➤46
VELETRŽNÍ PALÁC, MUSEUM OF
  MODERN ART ➤47

Art nouveau

The glorious effusions of art nouveau (known here as Secession) mark the townscape all over Prague. Along with Vienna, Prague is probably the richest source of this style, with its use of sinuous lines and motifs from the natural world.

Black Madonna, Cubist House

Czech innovations

Art nouveau/Secession was an international style, but later Czech architects created unique movements of their own—Rondo-Cubism, and the more sober, functionalist style that then followed.

BANK OF THE LEGIONS (BANKA LEGIÍ)

Czechoslovak legionaries fought on many fronts in World War I, and the sculptures decorating the façade of this handsome Rondo-Cubist (see panel) building of 1923 commemorate their exploits.
⊞ F4 ⊠ Na poříčí 24, northern New Town
🕐 Accessible during banking hours to customers of Komercní Bank 🚇 Náměstí Republiky

CUBIST STREET LAMP

An echo of Czech Cubism, this extraordinary little object still seems to vibrate with the artistic excitements of early 20th-century metropolitan life.
⊞ E5 ⊠ Jungmannovo náměstí, New Town 🚇 Metro Můstek

HOUSE AT THE BLACK MADONNA (DŮM U ČERNÉ MATKY BOŽÍ)

This striking example of Czech Cubist architecture (1912) stands challengingly at the corner of Celetná Street in the heart of the Old Town, yet somehow manages to harmonize with its venerable surroundings. Look for the Black Madonna in her cage.
⊞ E4 ⊠ Ovocný trh 19, Old Town 🕐 Art gallery open Tue–Sun 10–12, 1–6 🍴 Restaurant 🚇 Náměstí Republiky 🎟 Inexpensive

MAIN STATION (HLAVNÍ NÁDRAŽÍ)

Above the modern concourses rise the richly ornamented art nouveau buildings of the station of 1909, originally named after Emperor Franz Josef, then after President Wilson.
⊞ F4 ⊠ Wilsonova 8, New Town 🕐 24 hours
🍴 Buffet 🚇 Hlavní nádraží 🎟 Free

NÁRODNÍ TŘÍDA PAIR

Fascinating variations on the theme of art nouveau can be traced in the façades of these adjoining office buildings. No. 9 was built for the publisher Topic, No. 7 for an insurance company.
⊞ E5 ⊠ Národní třída 7, 9, New Town 🚇 Národní třída

U NOVAKU

This lavishly decorated art nouveau structure, now a casino, was built as a department store in 1903. The colorful mosaic represents Trade and Industry.
⊞ E5 ⊠ Vodičkova 30, New Town 🕐 Open to customers of Varieté Praga 🍴 Restaurant 🚇 Můstek

FOR MUSIC LOVERS

See Top 25 sights for
NATIONAL THEATER
(NÁRODNÍ DIVADLO) ►36
ST. NICHOLAS'S CHURCH, MALÁ STRANA ►33

BERTRAMKA, MOZART MUSEUM
Mozart's closest friends in Prague were the Dušeks, and the Bertramka was their rural retreat. This is the place where the great composer dashed off the last lines of *Don Giovanni* before conducting its premiere in the Estates Theater (► 75).
➕ C6 ✉ Mozartova 169, Smíchov ☎ 54 00 12
🕐 Tue–Sun 9:30–6 🚇 Anděl, then Tram 4, 7, 9 to Bertramka (one stop) ⚑ Inexpensive

DVOŘÁK'S BIRTHPLACE
Dvořák was born the son of an innkeeper in the unassuming little village of Nelahozeves on the Elbe River. His birthplace, at the foot of the Lobkovic family's huge Renaissance castle, is now a museum.
➕ Off map, about 20 miles northwest of Prague
✉ Nelahozeves 12 🕐 Tue–Thu, Sat, Sun 9–12, 2–5
🚉 Nelahozeves ⚑ Inexpensive

ESTATES THEATER (STAVOVSKÉ DIVADLO) ►75

SMETANA HALL (SMETANOVA SÍŇ)
The highly decorated Smetana Hall is the grandest space in the Obecní dům (► 46), with seating for 1,300. The Prague Spring is heralded here every year with a rousing rendition of *Ma vlast*.
➕ E/F4 ✉ Obecní dům, Náměstí Republiky 🕐 Closed for restoration 🍴 Café and restaurant 🚇 Náměstí Republiky

SMETANA MUSEUM (MUSEUM BEDŘICHA SMETANY)
The museum dedicated to the composer of "Vltava" is appropriately sited in a building that rises directly out of the river.
➕ D4 ✉ Novotného lávka 1, Old Town ☎ 72 65 371
🕐 Temporarily closed 🚇 Staroměstská

STATE OPERA (STATNI OPERA PRAHA – SMETANA DIVADLO) ►75

VILA AMERIKA, DVOŘÁK MUSEUM
This exquisite little villa was built for Count Michna in 1720 as a summer retreat, when this part of the New Town was still countryside. It now serves as a fascinating repository for Dvořák memorabilia (► 76).
➕ E6 ✉ Ke Karlovu 20, New Town ☎ 29 82 14
🕐 Tue–Fri 10–12, 1–5; Sat , Sun 1–5 🚇 I P Pavlova
⚑ Inexpensive

A musical nation
Co Cech—to musikant!— "All Czechs are musicians!"—goes the saying, and this is certainly one of the most musical of nations. Eighteenth-century Bohemia supplied musicians and composers to the whole of Europe.

Music for free
By all means go to concerts at the places listed on this page. But bear in mind that "all Czechs are musicians," and enjoy the often very high-quality music made by street performers. If you keep your ears cocked, you may even catch one of tomorrow's virtuosi practicing at an open window.

Dvořák's piano, Vila Amerika

GREEN SPACES

See Top 25 Sights for
PETŘÍN HILL ►28
WALLENSTEIN GARDENS ►34

BAROQUE GARDENS BELOW THE CASTLE

The aristocrats in their palaces at the foot of the castle in Malá Strana turned their interconnecting gardens into a paradise of arbors, gazebos, fountains, and stairways. Closed for restoration, they can be enjoyed from the castle's Ramparts Garden above.

KAMPA ISLAND

Separated from the mainland of Malá Strana by the old millrace known as the Devil's Brook (Čertovka), Kampa Island was flooded regularly until the Vltava was tamed in the 1950s, which explains why most of it has happily remained undeveloped.
🚊 D4/5 🕐 At all times 🚋 Tram 12, 22 to Hellichova or Malostranské náměstí 💲 Free

LETNÁ PARK ►50

RAMPARTS GARDEN (ZAHRADA NA VALECH)

The gardens just to the south of the castle were redesigned in the 1920s and provided with carefully placed sculptural objects, including a miniature pyramid.
🚊 C/D4 ⊠ Praťsky hrad, Hradčany 🕐 10–6 summer only 🚇 Metro Malostranská and uphill walk 🚋 Tram 22 to Pražsky hrad 💲 Free

ROYAL GARDENS (KRÁLOVSKÁ ZAHRADA)

Fine old trees and formal gardens make a superb setting for several pleasure pavilions to the north of the castle: the baroque Riding School, the sgraffitoed Ball-Game Hall, and the beautiful little Belvedere.
🚊 C/D3 ⊠ Královsky letohradek, Hradčany 🕐 10–6 summer only 🚋 Tram 22 to Králskový letohradek 💲 Free

VOJAN GARDENS (VOJANOVÝ SADY)

A quiet retreat hidden away behind Malá Strana.
🚊 D4 ⊠ U lužického semináře 🕐 Daily 8–7 🚇 Malostranská 💲 Free

VRTBA GARDEN (VRTBOVSKÁ ZAHRADA)

This is Prague's finest individual baroque garden, with a splendid staircase, superb sculptures, and a view over Malá Strana.
🚊 D4 ⊠ Karmelítská 25, Malá Strana 🕐 Closed for restoration 🚋 Tram 12, 22 to Malostranské náměstí

Monkish retreat

The old garden of the Franciscan monks between Wenceslas Square and Jungmann Square (Jungmannovo náměstí) has recently been freshened up by Prague Parks Department and makes a welcome oasis in the heart of the city.

Stromouka Park, Holešovice

Charles Square

Charles Square (Karlovo náměstí) is more of a park than a square, a useful resting place when pounding the sidewalks becomes too tiring in this spread-out part of town.

ATTRACTIONS FOR CHILDREN

See Top 25 Sights for
NATIONAL TECHNICAL MUSEUM ►45
PETŘÍN HILL, WITH FUNICULAR,
VIEWING TOWER, HALL OF MIRRORS,
OBSERVATORY ►28

ASTRONOMICAL CLOCK (ORLOJ)
Crowds gather every hour on the hour in front of the
Old Town Hall to enjoy the performance put on by
this fascinating clock, which not only tells the time
but gives the position of the sun, moon, and much
more, while the splendid painted calendar shows
saints' days, the signs of the zodiac, and the labors of
the months. Legend has it that Hanus, the master
technician who perfected the mechanism, was blind-
ed by the city fathers to stop him passing his secrets
on. But Hanus persuaded an apprentice to lead him
up inside the clock. He then plunged his hands into
the mechanism, putting it out of action for 80 years.
➕ E4 ⊠ Staroměstské náměstí ⏺ Performances daily
on the hour 🚇 Staroměstská 🎟 Free

CHANGING OF THE GUARD.
The blue-uniformed Castle Guard are ceremonially
relieved every day at noon, with extra helpings of
pomp on Sundays (buglers, etc.).
➕ C4 ⊠ Pražský hrad, Hradčany ⏺ Daily at noon
🚋 Tram 22 to Pražský hrad 🎟 Free

HISTORIC TRAM RIDE.
A vintage tram trundles round a circuit linking the
city center, Malá Strana, and the Exhibition Grounds.

MILTARY MUSEUM ►53

PUPPET THEATERS ►80

VÝSTAVIŠTĚ (EXHIBITION GROUNDS)
The extensive Exhibition Grounds in the inner sub-
urb of Holešovice have a fine old-fashioned funfair
and a number of other attractions that should appeal
to children.
➕ E/F2 ⊠ U Výstaviště, Holešovice ☎ 872 92 04
⏺ Tue–Sun 10–6 (evening opening for performances)
🍴 Cafés and restaurants 🚋 Tram 5, 12, 17 to
Výstaviště 🎟 Inexpensive

ZOO (ZOOLOGICKÁ ZAHRADA)
Not the world's outstanding zoological garden, but
useful to know about and conveniently placed oppo-
site Troja Château.
➕ D1 ⊠ U Trojského zámku 3, Troja ☎ 66 41 04 80
⏺ Daily 9–7 🍴 Buffet 🚇 Nádraží Holešovice, then
Bus 112 to Zoologická zahrada 🎟 Inexpensive

Keeping 'em happy
At least for a short visit,
Prague is a child-friendly
city. There are enough
sword-swallowers, jazz
bands, and other enter-
tainers on the streets to
keep kids happily staring
for hours and any number
of tall towers to climb.
Incorrigible junior con-
sumers will find their
favorite soft drinks on
sale, the local ice cream
is excellent, and Prague
is no longer a "One-Mac-
city"; the famous ham-
burgers are on sale at
several locations, and
there are plenty of pizzas
and similar snacks
available as well.

Getting around
Tram rides will be a
novelty to many children
—and are an excellent
way of getting to know
the city. Other entertain-
ing ways of moving
around include the "train"
that chugs up to the
castle from Old Town
Square and the horse-
drawn carriages also
based in Old Town
Square.

COMMUNIST MEMENTOES

Communist corruption

Despite being lowered every evening into a refrigerated chamber and receiving the attentions of the best embalmers available, the corpse of Klement Gottwald ("First Working Class President"), in the National Memorial, continued to putrefy. When platoons of Young Pioneers were brought to admire their leader most of what they saw was not Klement, but skilfully crafted replacement parts.

Home sweet home

Paneláks are regarded with a mixture of affection and exasperation. Any accommodations are desirable in a city with an acute housing shortage, especially if they are supplied with hot and cold running water and central heating like most paneláks. The downside is the dreariness of the surroundings.

BAROLOMĚJSKÁ POLICE STATION

The police station where Václav Havel was regularly brought in for interrogation in his dissident days has now been returned to its former owners, an order of nuns, who have leased part of it as a pension. If you book far enough ahead, you can sleep in Havel's cell.
E4/5 ✉ Unitas Pension, Bartolomějská 9, Old Town ☎ 232 77 09 🚇 Národní třída ♿ Accessible only to pension guests

HOTEL INTERNATIONAL

A totally authentic example of the monumental wedding-cake architecture of the Stalinist era.
C2 ✉ Koulova 15, Dejvice ☎ 24 39 31 11 🍽 Café and restaurant 🚇 Dejvická 🚊 Tram 20, 25 to Podbaba ♿ Expensive to stay

JAN PALACH'S GRAVE

The grave of the self-immolating student Jan Palach (► 43) is in the vast cemetery at Olšany (🚇 Flóra), a square in the Old Town is named after him, and flowers are regularly placed on the spot in Wenceslas Square where he died.
H/J5 ✉ Olšanske hřbitov (Olšany cemetery), Vinohradská 🕐 daily 8–7 🚇 Flóra or Želivského ♿ Free

MEMORIAL TO NOVEMBER 17, 1989

In an arcade on Národní třída, a little memorial panel of hands raised in supplication marks where 50,000 student demonstrators were attacked by riot police—an event seen as the genesis of the Velvet Revolution.
E5 ✉ Národní třída 16, New Town 🚇 Národní třída ♿ Free

THE METRO

Prague's immaculate Metro once sported a number of fine examples of Socialist Realist art. The only one remaining is the mosaic of a chisel-chinned worker and his mate at Anděl station.
D6 ✉ 5AM–midnight 🚇 Anděl

NATIONAL MEMORIAL (NÁRODNÍ PAMÁTNÍK)

Built in the interwar period, this great slab of a building atop the steep rise to the east of the downtown area served as a shrine to prominent Party men. The Memorial's future is uncertain.
G4 ✉ U památníku, Žižkov, Prague 3 🚇 Florenc and uphill walk

PANELÁKS

All around the outskirts of Prague are the monolithic housing estates composed of high-rise blocks nicknamed "paneláks," system-built on the Soviet model from concrete panels manufactured on site.

PRAGUE
where to...

CZECH & SLOVAK CUISINE

Prices
Expect to pay for dinner
per person without drinks
$$$ over Kč600
$$ Kč200–600
$ Kč100–200

Dumplings

Love them or leave them,
knedliky (dumplings) are
the inevitable
accompaniment to much
Czech cooking, adding
further solidity to an
already substantial
cuisine. Every housewife
has her prized recipe,
using bread, flour,
potatoes, or semolina,
and the homemade
knedlik may have a
lightness often absent
from a restaurant's
offering.

DERBY ($)
Excellent value includes
basic soup and sandwich
lunch for just a few
crowns.
🟦 F2 ✉ Dukelských
hrdinů 20 🚊 Tram 5,12,17
to Veletržní

FREGATA ($$)
An alternative to the
Vltava for traditional fish
dishes.
🟦 E6 ✉ Ladová 3 ☎ 29
31 21 🚇 Karlovo náměstí

MALOSTRANSKÁ
BESEDA ($)
Czech food served in
Malá Strana Square.
🟦 D4 ✉ Malostranské
náměstí ☎ 53 25 73
🚇 Malostranská

MYSLIVNA ($$)
Improbably located in a
back street in suburban
Vinohrady, this restaurant
("The Hunter's Lodge")
is worth seeking out for its
delicious game
specialities.
🟦 G5 ✉ Jagellonská 21,
Vinohrady ☎ 627 02 09
🚇 Jiřího z Poděbrad

NA OŘECHOVCE ($$)
Pub-restaurant with some
of the best Czech food,
deep in the garden suburb
of Ořechovka ("Walnut
Grove").
🟦 B3 ✉ Východní 7,
Dejvice ☎ 312 48 42
🚊 Tram 1, 2, or 18 to
Sibeliova

NA RYBÁRNĚ ($$)
Fishy delights in a
restaurant supposedly
once frequented by
President Havel and
cronies.
🟦 E5/6 ✉ Gorazdova 17,
New Town ☎ 29 97 95
🚇 Karlovo náměstí

PEZINOK ($–$$)
Genuine Slovak cuisine in
the pleasant surroundings
of what was formerly the
the cultural center of
eastern Czechoslovakia.
🟦 E5 ✉ Purkyňova 4,
New Town ☎ 24 91 56 30
🚇 Národní třída

POD KŘÍDLEM ($$$)
Stylish surroundings and
impeccable food,
conveniently close to the
National Theater.
🟦 E5 ✉ Narodni třída
10, New Town ☎ 24 91
23 77 🚇 Národní třída

STARÁ RADNICE ($$)
A useful lunch-stop along
the Hradčany tourist trail.
🟦 C4 ✉ Loretánská 1,
Hradčany ☎ 53 27 32.
🚊 Tram 22 to Pražský
hrad or Pohořelec

U BENEDIKTA ($$)
Conventional Czech
cooking done with more
than the usual degree of
sophistication and served
in a patio tucked away
behind the big Kotva
department store.
🟦 E4 ✉ Benediktská 11,
Old Town. ☎ 23 11 527
🚇 Náměstí Republiky

U ČIŽKŮ ($$)
Attractive Old Bohemian
farmhouse atmosphere
with meaty specialties to
match, such as a platter of
duck, pork, and sausage
with dumplings and
sauerkraut for light relief.
🟦 E5 ✉ Karlovo náměstí
(Charles Square) 34, New
Town ☎ 29 88 91
🚇 Karlovo náměstí

VEGETARIAN, SCENIC & KOSHER RESTAURANTS

VEGETARIAN

COUNTRY LIFE ($)
Healthy eating at a couple of central venues (stand-up buffet only at the Old Town branch).
✚ E5 ⊠ Jungmannova 1, New Town (also at Melantrichova 15, Old Town) ☎ 24 19 17 39 Ⓠ Národní třída or Můstek

RADOST CAFÉ FX ($)
Trendy café for the chic and cool.
✚ F6 ⊠ Bělehradská 120, Vinohrady ☎ 25 12 10 Ⓠ I P Pavlova

U GOVINDY
A Hare Krishna eating-place, in the unlikely surroundings of the city's eastern suburbs. As much wholefood as you can digest. Pay by donation.
✚ J2 ⊠ Na hrázi, Palmovka ☎ 82 14 38 Ⓠ Palmovka

RESTAURANTS WITH A VIEW OR TERRACE

BOTEL ADMIRAL ($)
Why not dine romantically on the deck of one of Prague's floating hotels, which also incorporates a dance floor?
✚ D6 ⊠ Hořejší nábřeží, Smíchov ☎ 24 51 16 97 Ⓠ Anděl

NA ZVONARCE ($)
Billiards and bulky Czech food with a fine view of the slopes that were once covered with the vineyards that gave Vinohrady its name.
✚ F6 ⊠ Šafaříkova 1, Vinohrady ☎ 691 13 11/691 01 94 ◻ Tram 8, 11 to Pod Karlovem or Nuselské schody

NEBOZÍZEK ($$)
The "Little Auger" looks the other way from the Parnas (see below), from the slopes of Petřín Hill toward the center. Reached by funicular.
✚ C5 ⊠ Petřínské sady 411, Malá Strana ☎ 53 79 05 ◻ Funicular

PARNAS ($$$)
For that special night out. Sumptuous turn-of-the-century setting and sophisticated cuisine combined with an unbeatable view of the Vltava and the castle (as long as you resereve a window table).
✚ D5 ⊠ Smetanovo nábřeží 2, Old Town ☎ 24 22 76 14 Ⓠ Národní třída

RESTAURACE NA VYŠEHRADĚ ($)
With its terrace and straightforward Czech cooking, this is a good place to cool off after visiting Prague's second citadel.
✚ E7 ⊠ K rotunde 2, Vyšehrad ☎ 24 23 92 97 Ⓠ Vyšehrad

KOSHER FOOD

KOSHER RESTAURANT SHALOM ($–$$)
Reliable kosher food served in the former meeting room of the Jewish Town Hall.
✚ E4 ⊠ Maislova 18, Old Town ☎ 24 81 09 29 Ⓠ Staroměstská

PUBS, BARS & CAFÉS

Czech beer

Lager beer was virtually invented in Bohemia, when the citizens of Pilsen/Plzen got together to form the "Burghers' Brewery" in 1842 and began producing the light and tasty liquid that has spawned endless imitation "pils" ever since but which has never been surpassed. But other Czech beers are just as good, better from the barrel than the bottle. Try Prague's own Staropramen or Braník, or the milder Budvar from Ceské Budejovice/ Budweis in southern Bohemia.

PUBS

BRANÍCKÁ FORMANKA

The suburban Braník brewery is one of four major breweries in Prague. This pub is its downtown outlet.

🔢 E5 ✉ Vodičkova 26, New Town ☎ 24 21 30 36 Ⓜ Můstek

ČERNÝ PIVOVAR

The "Black Brewery" pumps are constantly at work pulling up the dark beer for the crowds in this no-frills Charles Square establishment.

🔢 E5 ✉ Karlovo náměstí 15, New Town Ⓜ Karlovo náměstí

JAMES JOYCE

Should you ever tire of the wonders of Czech beer, here's one of the few places that offer the alternative of Guinness and other Irish beers (to a largely expatriate crowd).

🔢 E4 ✉ Liliová 10, Old Town Ⓜ Staroměstská

NOVOMĚSTSKÝ PIVOVAR

The "New Town Brewery" is Prague's other boutique brewery (after U Fleku), housed in a medieval building.

🔢 E5 ✉ Vodičkova 20, New Town Ⓜ Můstek

U FLEKU

Every visitor should sip the dark and tasty beer that has been brewed on the premises for 200 years and which is served in the raucous interior or—more congenial—in the big beer garden.

🔢 E5 ✉ Kremencova 11, New Town ☎ 24 91 51 18 Ⓜ Karlovo náměstí or Národní třída

U KOCOURA

The famous old "Tomcat" welcomes the thirsty tourist on the hard trek up from Malá Strana to the castle.

🔢 D4 ✉ Nerudova 2, Malá Strana 🚊 Tram 22 to Malostranské náměstí

U MEDVIKU

Budvar, from České Budějovice in southern Bohemia, is probably the best-known Bohemian beer apart from Pilsener. Try it here on tap—out in the garden in summer.

🔢 E4 ✉ Na Perštýně 7, Old Town Ⓜ Národní třída

U SVATÉHO TOMÁŠE

The monks no longer brew their own here, but the medieval ambience of St. Thomas' makes it a popular stop with tour groups who also enjoy the folk music performances.

🔢 D4 ✉ Letenská 12, Malá Strana Ⓜ Malostranská

U VEJVODU

Don't be put off by the scruffy appearance; this is one of the most ancient and authentic of Prague's downtown pubs, with local Staropramen on tap.

🔢 E4 ✉ Jilská 4, Old Town ☎ 24 21 05 91 Ⓜ Národní třída

U ZLATÉHO TYGRA

The perfect Pilsener drawn straight from the

13th-century cellars of the "Golden Tiger" has long made it a favorite with serious local drinkers who remain unimpressed by visitors, even when they turn out to be the president of the United States.

🗺 E4 ✉ Husova 17, Old Town ☎ 24 22 90 20 🚇 Staroměstská

CAFÉS & BARS

ARCHE

Next to one of the country's biggest publishing houses, this café attracts a youthful, even intellectual set.

🗺 F4 ✉ Na poříčí 26, northern New Town ☎ 232 41 49 🚇 Náměstí Republiky

CAFÉ MILENA

Another elegant café in Old Town Square.

🗺 E4 ✉ Staroměstské náměstí 22, Old Town. ☎ 26 08 43 🚇 Staroměstská

CAFÉ SAVOY

Turn-of-the-century elegance in a refined café at the Malá Strana end of the Legions' Bridge (Most legií).

🗺 D5 ✉ Vítězná 5, Malá Strana ☎ 53 97 96 🚋 Tram 6, 9, or 22 to Újezd

CAFFÉ DANTE

Clean-cut Italian café opposite the modern art collections of the Trades Fair Palace.

🗺 F3 ✉ Dukelských hrdinů 16, Holešovice ☎ 87 01 93 🚋 Tram 5, 12, 17 to Veletržní

DOLCE VITA

Authentic espresso close to Old Town Square.

🗺 E4 ✉ Široka 15 🚇 Staroměstská

EVROPA

In spite of the arrogance that charges an entrance fee, the art nouveau café of the Evropa Hotel on Wenceslas Square is an experience not to be missed.

🗺 E5 ✉ Václavské náměstí 29, New Town ☎ 24 22 81 17 🚇 Můstek

GULU GULU

You'll be lucky to get a table at this trendy locale in Bethlehem Square, which buzzes like a beehive until midnight.

🗺 E4 ✉ Betlémské náměstí 8, Old Town ☎ 24 22 25 25 🚇 Národní třída

H&S CAFÉ

Attractive open-air café enabling you to watch the busy boating activity that takes place on the Vltava.

🗺 D5 ✉ Slovanský ostrov (Slavonic Island) 🚇 Národní třída

INSTITUT FRANÇAIS

Pleasant French-style café in the New Town just off Wenceslas Square.

🗺 E5 ✉ Štěpánská 35, New Town ☎ 24 21 40 32 🚇 Můstek or Muzeum

VELRYBA

The "Whale" opens wide its jaws to accommodate its clientele of trendies.

🗺 E5 ✉ Opatická 24, New Town ☎ 24 91 23 91 🚇 Národní třída

Turkish coffee

Most kinds of coffee can now be found in Prague (espresso, cappuccino...), but don't be surprised if you get served a traditional *"turecka."* This is Turkish coffee, fine when you're accustomed to it and know when to stop swallowing—before you disturb the deposit of coffee grounds at the bottom of the cup.

BOOKS & ANTIQUES

Bargains ... perhaps

Czechs are great readers, and until recently new and secondhand books were very inexpensive, many of them in foreign (i.e. non-Czech) languages. Prices have risen considerably since 1989, but there are still many bargains. Prices for antique books are now well in line with the international market.

NEW BOOKS

ALBATROS

Children's books, an area of publishing in which Czech authors and illustrators have long excelled.

✚ E4 ✉ Na perštýně 1, Old Town ☎ 24 22 32 27–46 Ⓜ Národní třída

CIZOJAZYČNÁ LITERATURA

Fair-sized stocks of what its name ("Foreign-language Literature") implies and much else besides.

✚ E4 ✉ Na příkopě 27, Old Town ☎ 26 28 37 Ⓜ Můstek

FRANZ KAFKA

Stocks an excellent range of both new and secondhand books, mostly in German.

✚ D4 ✉ U lužického semináře 19, Malá Strana ☎ 87 76 85 Ⓜ Malostranská

THE GLOBE BOOKSTORE AND COFFEEHOUSE

A congenial home-from-home for Americans and anyone hungry for all kinds of literature in English as well as bagels and American-style coffee. The Globe is located in the inner-city suburb of Holešovice, on the north bank of the Vltava, but it is easy to reach by public transportation.

✚ F2 ✉ Janvoského 14, near Štrossmayerovo náměstí, Holešovice. ☎ 66 71 26 10 ⬚ Tram 5, 12, 17 to Štrossmayerovo náměstí

INTERNATIONAL BOOKSTORE

Large selection of English-language publications.

✚ E4 ✉ Corner Pařížska and 17 listopadu (first floor), Old Town Ⓜ Staroměstská ⬚ Tram 17 to Pravnická fakulta

KIWI

Don't be put off by the travel agency on the ground floor; the shop in the basement has one of the best selections of maps and guides in town. Small secondhand section.

✚ E5 ✉ Jungmannova 23, New Town ☎ 26 12 82 Ⓜ Národní třída

KNIKUPECTVÍ VYSOKÝ DŮM

A large range of both Czech and foreign books.

✚ D4 ✉ U lužického semináře 15, Malá Strana ☎ 49 70 16 81 Ⓜ Malostranská

MELANTRICH

A famous-name bookstore with an excellent selection of maps.

✚ E4 ✉ Na příkope 3, Old Town ☎ 24 22 72 58 Ⓜ Můstek

ORBIS

Good selection of new titles, including children's stories and books on Prague and the Czech Republic, some in non-Czech languages.

✚ E5 ✉ Václavské náměstí (Wenceslas Square) 42, New Town. ☎ 24 21 73 35 Ⓜ Můstek

U KNIHOMOLA

An enticing new basement

bookshop, "The Bookworm" attempts to supply the fullest possible range of foreign-language volumes. Bonus of an even deeper basement café with periodicals to read.

➕ G5 ✉ Mánesova 79, Vinohrady Ⓜ Jiřího z Poděbrad

ANTIQUES & ANTIQUARIAN BOOKSTORES

ANTIKVARIÁT EVA KOZAKOVA

Old photographs, prints and postcards plus innumerable old (mostly Czech) books.

➕ E5 ✉ Myslíkova 10, New Town ☎ 29 44 02 ⊙ Closed Saturday Ⓜ Karlovo náměstí

ANTIKVARIÁT GALERIE MŮSTEK

Printed treasures of all kinds in spacious Old Town basement, including many engravings, maps, and even paintings.

➕ E4 ✉ 28 října 13, Old Town ☎ 26 80 58 Ⓜ Můstek

ANTIKVARIÁT KAREL KŘENEK

Refined establishment near the start of the Royal Way, with an excellent range of prints and watercolors as well as fine old books.

➕ E4 ✉ Celetná 31, Old Town ☎ 231 47 34 Ⓜ Náměstí Republiky

ANTIKVARIÁT NA VALDŠTEJNSKEM NÁMĚSTÍ

The Malá Strana mecca for lovers of old books.

➕ D4 ✉ Valdštejnske náměstí 7, Malá Strana Ⓜ Malostranská

ANTIKVARIÁT U KARLOVA MOSTŮ

Fine old books and printed memorabilia of all kinds, not particularly cheap.

➕ E4 ✉ Karlova 2, Old Town ☎ 24 22 92 05 Ⓜ Staroměstská

GALERIE LUKAŠ

Exquisite objects of international as well as Czech origin.

➕ E5 ✉ Národní třída 21, New Town ☎ 24 21 33 38 Ⓜ Národní třída

PRAZSKÉ STAROZITNOSTI

"Prague Antiques" sells jewelry, porcelain, and paintings galore.

➕ E5 ✉ Mikulandská 8, New Town ☎ 29 41 70 Ⓜ Národní třída

VADAMO

Well-stocked antiques shop with wares at international prices.

➕ E4 ✉ Na příkopě 23, Old Town ☎ 26 02 59/26 56 10/26 50 73 Ⓜ Můstek or Náměstí Republiky

VLADIMIR ANDRLE

In Wenceslas Square, this antiques shop is a handy starting point for your hunt for collectables.

➕ E5 ✉ Václavské náměstí 17, New Town ☎ 231 16 25 Ⓜ Můstek

ZLATÁ KORUNA

Antique coins, medals, and paper money.

➕ E4 ✉ Parížská 8, Old Town Ⓜ Staroměstská

Wenceslas Hollar

One of the first artists to make accurate drawings of the English landscape was Wenceslas Hollar. Born in 1607 in Bohemia, Václav (to give him his Czech name) sought refuge abroad following the Protestant defeat at the Battle of the White Mountain and was employed as a draftsman by the Earl of Arundel. A trawl through Prague's antiquaries might turn up a Hollar original, such as his wonderfully detailed 1636 panorama of the city, but there are plenty of alternatives—drawings, engravings, maps—at affordable prices.

GIFTS, SOUVENIRS & MUSIC

Kafka at home

One of the many places
lived in by Jewish
novelist Franz Kafka was
the house on Celetná
Street adjoining Tyn
Church. In the bedroom
in which Kafka slept and
dreamed as a child, a
blank window faces
down the south aisle of
the church's nave.

Sgraffito

The Schwarzenberg
Palace on Hradčany
Square is probably
Prague's most splendidly
sgraffito-ed building.
Sgraffito work involves
picking out patterns in
two shades of
plasterwork either to
accentuate the
architectural character
of the building, or to
cover the façade with
lively pictures (as in the
Martinic Palace also in
Hradčany Square).

TOYS, PUPPETS & SOUVENIRS

ALBATROS
The place to look for soft
toys as well as children's
books.
➕ E4 ✉ Na Perštýně 11,
Old Town ☎ 24 22 32
27–46 🚇 Národní třída

ČESKÝ NÁRODNÍ PODNIK
Folksy artifacts include
Christmas cribs as well as
willow whips with which
to harass village maidens
at Eastertime.
➕ E4 ✉ Husova 12, Old
Town ☎ 24 21 08 86
🚇 Staroměstská

DIVADELNÍ KNIHKUPECTVÍ A LOUTKY
Looking for a puppet as a
souvenir? "Theater
Bookstore and
Marionettes" sells hand-
made marionettes of
superior quality to those
sold on the street and
correspondingly more
money. Worth visiting if
only to study the several
kinds of Devil ("Lucifer,"
"Old Nick," etc.) that play
such a prominent part in
Czech puppetry.
➕ E4 ✉ Celetná 17, Old
Town 🚇 Náměstí
Republiky

DŘEVENÉ HRAČKY
Sensible and imaginative
wooden toys.
➕ E4 ✉ Karlova 26, Old
Town 🚇 Staroměstská

ELEKTRICKÉ ŽELEZNICE
Immaculate old-time tin
trains especially for
nostalgic train buffs.

➕ D6 ✉ Na Bělidle 34,
Smíchov (also at Trigor,
Senovážné náměstí 28,
New Town) 🚇 Anděl

EXPOSICE FRANZE KAFKY
Prague's most famous
writer must have spun
round in his grave many
times at the souvenir
industry that has
impressed his haggard
features on countless
T-shirts. This is the least
tacky selection of
Kafkeriana that is sold
in the city.
➕ E4 ✉ Corner of
Maislova and Kaprova,
Old Town
🚇 Staroměstská

LIŠKA
Central Europeans still
wear their furs without
shame, purchased from
elegant outlets such as
"The Fox" near Old
Town Square. If you're on
a budget, fox-fur hats at
bargain prices can also be
found on a stall in the
Havelská market.
➕ E4 ✉ Železná 1, Old
Town 🚇 Staroměstská

MUSEUM SHOP
Unusually tasteful and
original souvenirs based
on the treasures of the
many Prague museums,
plus foreign art books not
available elsewhere in
Prague. An example to
other souvenir shops
worldwide; where else, for
example, could you buy a
china mug with elegant
sgraffito patterning?
➕ D4 ✉ Jiřská 6,
Hradčany ☎ 33 37 32 55
🚌 Tram 22 to Pražský
hrad

OPERA & CLASSICAL MUSIC

OPERA

ESTATES THEATER (STAVOVSKÉ DIVADLO)

The venue that saw the premiere of Mozart's *Don Giovanni* in 1787 has been restored to its pristine neoclassical glory. Regular performances of Wolfgang Amadeus' greatest hits.

✚ E4 ☒ Ovocný trh, Old Town ☎ 24 21 50 01, 26 77 97 Ⓜ Můstek

NATIONAL THEATER (NÁRODNÍ DIVADLO)

Operas from both the Czech and international repertoire in a sumptuous setting.

✚ D/E5 ☒ Národní třída, New Town ☎ 24 91 34 To Ⓜ Národní třída Ⓒ

STATE OPERA— SMETANA THEATER

Opened in 1887 as the Deutsches Theater (German Theater), this neo-Renaissance building changed its name to the Smetana Theater (Smetanovo divadlo) after World War II. It's now the home of the State Opera, with performances from the international repertoire. Classical ballet, too.

✚ F5 ☒ Wilsonova 4 ☎ 24 22 76 93, box office 26 53 53 Ⓜ Muzeum

CLASSICAL MUSIC

BERTRAMKA

The villa of Mozart's Prague patrons is now a museum and chamber concert hall (➤ 57).

✚ C6 ☒ Mozartova 169, Smíchov ☎ 54 00 12 Ⓜ Anděl 🚋 Tram 4, 7, 9 to Bertramka

HOUSE AT THE STONE BELL

Contemporary classical compositions augment the traditional repertoire in this Gothic mansion (Dům U kammeného zvonu) on Old Town Square.

✚ E4 ☒ Staroměstské náměstí 13, Old Town ☎ 23 27 677, 24 81 00 36 Ⓜ Staroměstská

KLEMENTINUM

Chamber concerts in the Hall of Mirrors (Zrcadlová síň) of this vast complex.

✚ E4 ☒ Křížovnické náměstí, Old Town ☎ 24 48 11 11 Ⓜ Staroměstská

LIECHTENSTEIN PALACE

Palatial setting (Lichtenstejnský palác) for symphonic and other perfomances.

✚ D4 ☒ Malostranské náměstí 13, Malá Strana Ⓜ Staroměstská 🚋 Tram 22 to Malostranské náměstí

LOBKOVIC PALACE

Chamber concerts in the banqueting hall of this palace (Lobkovický palác) in the castle precinct.

✚ D4 ☒ Jiřská 3, Hradčany ☎ 53 73 06 Ⓜ Malostranská and uphill walk 🚋 Tram 22 to Pražský hrad

NOSTIC PALACE

Count Nostic was the founder of the Estates Theater. His own palace (Nostický palác) makes a fine setting for chamber concerts.

✚ D4 ☒ Maltézské náměstí 1, Malá Strana 🚋 Tram 22 to Hellichova

---

Mozart in Prague

"My Praguers understand me," declared Mozart, who was far better received here than in Vienna. Both *Figaro* and *Don Giovanni* were hits in Prague, and after his pauper's death in Vienna, it was Prague that honored him with a great funeral mass in Malá Strana's St. Nicholas' Church, attended by a crowd of 4,000 mourners.

Josef Tyl

The Estates Theater (Stavovské divadlo) reverted to its original name in 1991. For many years it was called the Tyl Theater; almost unknown abroad, the 19th-century playwright Josef Kajetan Tyl is dear to Czech hearts for his comedy *Fidlovacka* which contains the song "Kde domov muj?" ('Where is my home?'), a plaintive call that later formed the first line of the Czechoslovak national anthem.

RUDOLFINUM

This splendid neo-Renaissance hall on the banks of the Vltava is the home of the Czech Philharmonic Orchestra who perform in the big Dvořák Hall. The Little (or Sük) Hall is used for chamber concerts.

🔲 E4 ⊠ Alšovo nábřeží 12, Old Town ☎ 24 89 33 52 🚇 Staroměstská

ST. AGNES'S CONVENT

One of the convent's two churches is used for chamber concerts.

🔲 E3 ⊠ U milosrdných 17, Old Town ☎ 24 81 08 35 🚃 Tram 17 to Pravnická fakulta or Tram 5, 14, 26 to Dlouhá

ST. GEORGE'S BASILICA (►31)

The castle's austere Romanesque church is now used as a chamber concert hall.

ST. JAMES'S CHURCH

The admirable acoustics in this superb Old Town church augment the concerts of sacred music held here.

🔲 E4 ⊠ Malá Štupartská, Old Town 🚇 Náměstí Republiky

ST. NICHOLAS'S CHURCH

The organ that Mozart played in Prague's greatest Baroque church still accompanies choral concerts.

🔲 D4 ⊠ Malostranské náměstí, Malá Strana 🚇 Malostranská 🚃 Tram 22 to Malostranské náměstí

ST. NICHOLAS'S CHURCH

The other Church of St. Nicholas, less sumptuous than the one in Malá Strana but an equally fine choice for organ and vocal recitals.

🔲 E4 ⊠ Staroměstské náměstí, Old Town 🚇 Staroměstská

SMETANA HALL

The home of the Czech Philharmonic, part of the sumptuously decorated Municipal House, is due to reopen in 1997 after restoration.

🔲 E4 ⊠ Obecní dům, Náměstí Republiky 5, Old Town 🚇 Náměstí Republiky

TROJA CHÂTEAU

The magnificence of Count Šternberg's out-of-town palace (Trojský zámek, ► 48) almost overwhelms the music.

🔲 D1 ⊠ Troja ☎ 84 07 61 🚇 Nádraží Holešovice, then bus 112 to Zoologická zahrada

VILA AMERIKA

Count Michna's jolly little 18th-century summer palace, home of the Dvořák Museum, puts on evening evocations of the composer's life and work.

🔲 E6 ⊠ Ke Karlovu 20, New Town ☎ 29 82 14 🚇 I P Pavlova

WALLENSTEIN PALACE (►34)

Summer evening concerts in the baroque gardens of the palace are a dream, and there are occasional performances in the superb interior as well.

JAZZ, POP & NIGHTLIFE

POP & ROCK

BELMONDO REVIVAL CLUB

On the far (northern) side of the Vltava from the Bunkr, a less tourist-prone alternative to its famous rival.

+ F3 ⊠ Bubenská 1, Holešovice ☎ 79 14 854 Ⓜ Vltavská

BORAT

Grimy, noisy haunt of a type that appeals to certain kinds of local and visitor alike.

+ D4 ⊠ Újezd 18 ☎ 53 83 62 🚊 Tram 22 to Hellichova

BUNKR

The archetypal post-1989 club, secure in its fame, frequented by visitors as much as locals. It actually was a nuclear bunker for the Communist bigwigs of Cold War days.

+ F4 ⊠ Lodecká 2, New Town ☎ 24 81 06 65 Ⓜ Náměstí Republiky 🚊 Tram 3, 8 to Těšnov

KAMYK

A different scene for the jaded: disco-dancing on the deck, of this boat moored to the quayside. Summer season only.

+ E3 ⊠ Alongside Sverm Bridge (Švermuv most), northern New Town 🚊 Tram 5, 14, 26 to Dlouhá

KLUB U ZOUFALCU

Downtown disco that also features some live bands.

+ E4 ⊠ Celetná 12, Old Town Ⓜ Náměstí Republiky

LÁVKA

Disco dancing in an unrivaled riverside setting close to Prague's most celebrated bridge, Karlův most (Charles Bridge).

+ D4 ⊠ Novotného lávka 1, Old Town ☎ 24 21 47 97 Ⓜ Staroměstská

LUCERNA

This is part of the vast complex of the Lucerna Palace, a labyrinth of arcades and passageways that were the work of President Havel's builder grandfather. It has a good-sized ballroom, able to accommodate visiting groups as well as locals.

+ E5 ⊠ Vodičková 36, New Town ☎ 24 21 70 98 Ⓜ Můstek

MALOSTRANSKÁ BESEDA

Something for everyone— ska, folk, reggae, and blues, as well as rock.

+ D4 ⊠ Malostranské náměstí 21, Malá Strana ☎ 53 90 24 Ⓜ Malostranská 🚊 Tram 22 to Malostranské náměstí

MUSIC PARK

Not the place for claustrophobes. You'll never be alone, least of all on a Saturday night, as the crowds cram into this biggest and most popular of all the city's discos a mere two Metro stops east of Wenceslas Square.

+ F6 ⊠ Francouská 4, Vinohrady ☎ 69 11 768 Ⓜ Náměstí Míru

RADOST FX

Disco plus occasional live

Rock Czech-style

Before 1989, groups like the Plastic People of the Universe were seen as genuinely subversive of the existing order and were relentlessly hounded by State Security. Nowadays the rock scene is a confused one, with a lot of fairly mindless imitation of Western trends but some innovation too, by groups like Sum svitsu (Latin influenced) and Shalom (obsessed by Judaism).

Prague jazz

Jazz has deep roots among the Czech people, as evidenced in the novels and short stories of the long-exiled writer Josef Skvorecky (for example *The Bass Saxophone*). Prague jazz is highly concentrated, with the majority of venues closely clustered in the area between the National Theater and Wenceslas Square.

music to the east of the downtown area.
➕ F6 ✉ Bělehradská 120, Vinohrady 🚇 I P Pavlova

ROCK CAFÉ

Downtown café and concert spot—the place to go if you like your rock hard and very loud.
➕ E5 ✉ Národní 20, New Town ☎ 91 44 14–5 🚇 Národní třída

ROXY

Unusual underground establishment that makes its point with visuals as well as music.
➕ E4 ✉ Dlouhá 33, Old Town 🚇 Staroměstská

JAZZ

AGHARTA JAZZ CENTRUM

Cramped but enjoyable setting for local and international jazz. There's a CD shop, too, and you can get cocktails and snacks.
➕ F5 ✉ Krakovská 5, New Town ☎ 24 21 29 14 🚇 Muzeum

HIGHLANDER

Daily jazz.
➕ E5 ✉ Národní třída 28, New Town ☎ 24 21 35 55 🚇 Národní třída

METROPOLITAN

Easy listening (swing, ragtime, blues...) to resident and visiting Dixielanders.
➕ E5 ✉ Jungmannova 14, New Town ☎ 24 21 60 25 🚇 Národní třída

REDUTA

Bill Clinton blew his sax

here during the presidential visit to Prague, as befitted the best-known of Prague jazz locales. You can hear Dixieland, swing, and modern jazz.
➕ E5 ✉ Národní 20, New Town ☎ 24 91 22 46 🚇 Národní třída

VIOLA

Saturday night specials only.
➕ E5 ✉ Národní třída 7, New Town ☎ 24 22 08 44 🚇 Národní třída

CASINOS & CABARETS

If you want to see a good old-fashioned floorshow, with music, dancing, and spectacle, the larger hotels are the best bet. Advance booking is essential.

CASINO DE FRANCE

Roulette, etc., played in the spacious modern surroundings of Prague's biggest hotel.
➕ F3 ✉ Hotel Atrium, Pobřežní 1, Karlín ☎ 24 84 20 05 🚇 Florenc

CASINO PALAIS SAVARIN

Roulette and other games of chance.
➕ E4 ✉ Na příkopě 10, New Town ☎ 24 22 16 36 🚇 Můstek or Náměstí Republiky

VARIETÉ PRAGA

Variety, brass bands, and gaming in a wonderful building in art nouveau style.
➕ E5 ✉ Vodičková 30, New Town ☎ 24 22 20 99 🚇 Můstek

MOVIES & THEATER

MOVIES

Prague has dozens of movie theaters, with a particular concentration around Wenceslas Square. Many show recent releases, often in the original version with Czech subtitles.

THEATER

The language barrier can limit enjoyment of theater for visitors. However, mime and multimedia are big on the Prague stage and can be enjoyed without knowledge of Czech. Most such shows are devised with the foreign visitor in mind.

ARCHA THEATER

This is a new establishment with a varied program, much of it designed to appeal to the visitor from abroad.
⊞ F4 ✉ Na poříčí 26, northern New Town ☎ 232 75 70/232 62 32 Ⓜ Náměstí Republiky

CELETNÁ THEATER

One of the establishments that orients itself to the needs of summer visitors eager to hear more about the life and times of Prague's literary giant, Franz Kafka.
⊞ E4 ✉ Celetná 17, Old Town ☎ 24 81 27 62 Ⓜ Náměstí Republiky

IMAGE THEATER (DIVADLO IMAGE)

Another visitor-oriented theater where the "Black Light" shows feature dance, mime, music—you name it!.

⊞ E4 ✉ Pařížská 4, Old Town ☎ 232 91 91 Ⓜ Staroměstská

JIŘÍ SRNEC BLACK THEATER

Legends of magic Prague presented in multimedia format as at the Image Theater.
⊞ E5 ✉ Národní třída 40, New Town ☎ 24 23 04 21 Ⓜ Národní třída

KARLÍN MUSICAL THEATER (HUDEBNÍ DIVADLO V KARLÍNĚ)

Operettas and musicals are the undemanding fare in this theater in an inner suburb.
⊞ F4 ✉ Křižíkova 10, Karlín ☎ 24 21 07 10 Ⓜ Florenc

LATERNA MAGIKA

The Magic Lantern's synthesis of film, music, theater, and mime was first developed in the 1950s by Alfréd Redok, and continues to intrigue and delight audiences. Some of the most successful shows are reworkings of ancient myths, such as Theseus and the Minotaur or the Odyssey.
⊞ E5 ✉ Nova scéna of the National Theater, Národní třída 2, New Town ☎ 24 91 41 29 Ⓜ Národní třída

NATIONAL THEATRE (NÁRODNÍ DIVADLO)

You can see classics of Czech theater here, as well as performances of opera and ballet
⊞ D/E5 ✉ Národní třída 2, New Town ☎ 24 91 34 37 Ⓜ Národní třída

Keeping you posted

Since 1989 there has been a boom in performances of all kinds intended to appeal to the visitor from abroad. Few hide their light under a bushel, and the ubiquitous posters and the leaflets proffered will keep you up to date with what's on.

Czech puppetry

In a country where the art of manipulating marionettes can be studied at university, no one whose imagination has been stimulated by the array of delightful little figures on sale on stalls and in shops should miss one of Prague's puppet performances. The colorful characters are mostly drawn from the fairy tales that are such a feature of Czech popular literature. They include water sprites and witches, devils, soldiers and highwaymen, villains and virgins.

ROKOKO
Some non-Czech performances are put on in this establishment, in Wenceslas Square
➕ E5 ⊠ Václavské náměstí 38, New Town
☎ 24 21 71 13 Ⓜ Můstek

TA FANTASTIKA
Another spectacle based on the Black Light fusion of dance, mime, and music—a spinoff from the hugely successful Laterna Magika.
➕ E4 ⊠ Karlova 8, Old Town ☎ 24 22 90 78
Ⓜ Staroměstská

THEATER ON THE BALUSTRADE (DIVADLO NA ZÁBRADLÍ)
Václav Havel shifted scenery here, and his later plays helped build the place's reputation. Performances sometimes include mime shows in addition to straight theater.
➕ E4 ⊠ Anenské náměstí 5, Old Town
☎ 24 22 95 17, box office 24 22 19 33/24 22 95 17
Ⓜ Staroměstská

PUPPETRY & FOLKLORE

CZECH FOLKLORE ENSEMBLE (ČESKÝ SOUBOR PÍSNI A TANCU)
Well-rehearsed rustic song and dance coming from Bohemia's Fields and Woods plus some operettas.
➕ D4 ⊠ Divadlo na Klarove (Klarov Theater), nábřeží E Benese 3, Malá Strana
☎ 24 51 10 22
Ⓜ Malostranská

LETNÍ SCÉNA AUS PRAHA
Shows based on Moravian and Slovak folklore. Location varies—look in the listings under *lidova skupina.*

MINOR THEATER (DIVADLO MINOR)
Live theater for children, as well as puppetry, performed in continuous programes.
➕ F4 ⊠ Senovážné náměstí 28, New Town
☎ 24 21 32 41
Ⓜ Náměstí Republiky

NATIONAL MARIONETTE THEATER (NÁRODNÍ DIVADLO MARIONET)
Adaptations of operas feature among other attractions. Matinee performances.
➕ E4 ⊠ Žatecká 1, Old Town ☎ 232 34 29
Ⓜ Staroměstská

PANTOMIME OF LADISLAV FIALKA BOMIEL
Cabaret-style opera presentations put on here provide a different experience.
➕ D4 ⊠ Novotného lávka 1, Old Town
☎ 24 21 47 97
Ⓜ Staroměstská

SPEJBL AND HURVINEK THEATER (DIVADLO SPEJBLA A HURVINKA)
Unmissable antics of Prague's famous comic duo. Location varies.

SPORTS & OUTDOOR ACTIVITIES

SOCCER

SPARTA STADIUM
First-class soccer at the home of the country's leading team, Sparta.
🔝 E3 ⊠ U Sparty, Letná
☎ 38 24 41 🚋 Tram 26 to Sparta

ICE HOCKEY

SPARTA PRAHA
Based in this big indoor hall behind the Sparta Stadium, Sparta tend to top the national league.
🔝 E2 ⊠ Korunovacní, Bubenec ☎ 872 74 43
🚋 Tram 26 to Sparta

SKATING

SPORTS HALL
This indoor ice rink is one of several in Prague. In winter there's skating on ponds, lakes, and reservoirs.
🔝 F2 ⊠ Exhibition Grounds (Výstaviště), Holešovice ☎ 37 11 42
🚇 Nádraží Holešovice
🚋 Tram 5, 12, 17 to Výstavistě

SWIMMING

HOSTIVAŘ RESERVOIR
Prague's biggest reservoir; windsurfing and boating as well as swimming.
🔝 Off map 🚇 Haje, then walk or Bus 165, 170, 212, 213

SLAPY DAM & LAKE
The Vltava upstream from Prague has been dammed to form a chain of lakes. Facilities include beaches of imported sand.
🔝 Off map, 20miles south of Prague 🚌 Bus from Anděl bus station

PODOLÍ POOLS (PLAVECKÝ STADION PODOLÍ)
Large complex of pools, sauna, etc.
🔝 E8 ⊠ Podolská 34, Podolí ☎ 61 21 43 43
🚋 Tram 3, 17 to Kublov

BIKING

LANDA
One of the few places to rent bikes. Biking is not a recommended activity in the city, but it is possible to find attractive and fairly traffic-free routes out into the countryside.
🔝 G5 ⊠ Šumavská 33, Vinohrady ☎ 253 99 82
🚇 Náměstí Míru
🚋 Tram 16 to Šumavská

HORSE RACING

CHUCHLE RACECOURSE (ZÁVODIŠTĚ CHUCHLE)
Flat races and trotting.
🔝 Off map ☎ 54 30 91/54 04 06/54 66 10
🚆 Suburban train from Smíchov to Velká Chuchle or 🚌 Bus 172, 453

GOLF

KARLŠTEJN
One of a number of recently built courses; this one has the benefit of Karlštejn Castle (▶ 20) as part of the scenery.
🔝 Off map, 20miles southwest ☎ 795 39 44

STIŘÍN CHÂTEAU (ZÁMEK STIŘÍN)
This impeccably restored country house hotel has a golf course in its park.
🔝 Off map, 20miles southeast ☎ 99 21 60

In-town biking
Urban bicyclists congregate on weekends in the city's extensive Stromovka Park, where there is a network of marked bike paths and some signposting indicating how bikers might reach other parts of Prague in relative safety.

HOTELS BY DISTRICT

Prices
Expect to pay per night
for a double room
$$$ Kč3,000 +
$$ Kč1,000–3,000
$ Kč500–1,000

Book ahead

Until recently, Prague suffered from an acute shortage of hotel accommodations, particularly in the middle price range, and was not an inexpensive place to stay. The situation has improved, but it is always wise to book well in advance, especially in summer and if you want to stay in the center.

82

HRADČANY & LESSER TOWN (MALÁ STRANA)

The castle quarter and the "Lesser Town" between the castle and the River Vltava.

DIPLOMAT ($$–$$$)

Modern, immaculate large hotel, not quite in Hradčany but only 10 minutes (uphill) on foot from the castle. A business person's favorite, with conference facilities, conveniently located on the run-in from the airport and next door to a Metro station a mere three stops from the downtown area.
✚ C3 ✉ Evropská 15, Dejvice ☎ 24 39 41 11 Ⓜ Dejvická

HOFFMEISTER ($$$)

In a historic building that has been carefully refurbished, "Prague's personal luxury hotel" enjoys an enviable position below the bend in the road up to the castle.
✚ D3 ✉ Pod bruskou ☎ 56 18 15 5–7 Ⓜ Malostranská

KAMPA ($)

In a delightful corner of the Lesser Town close to the Devil's Brook, this old building has been refurbished and is popular with tour groups.
✚ D4/5 ✉ Všehrdová 16 ☎ 24 51 04 09/24 51 06 00 🚊 Tram 12, 22 to Hellichova

PENSION DIENTZENHOFER ($$)

In a secluded side street, the home of the Dientzenhofers, the greatest of Prague's baroque architects, is now a small hotel.
✚ D4 ✉ Nosticova 2 ☎ 53 16 72 🚊 Tram 12, 22 to Malostranské náměstí

SAVOY ($$$)

Top-of-the-market luxury within easy (downhill) reach of the castle in a completely modernized hotel.
✚ C4 ✉ Keplerova 6 ☎ 24 30 21 11 🚊 Tram 22 to Pohořelec

SAX ($$)

There's no closer place to the castle than this little hotel just off Nerudova Street.
✚ C4 ✉ Janský vršek 3 ☎ 53 84 22/53 84 98 🚊 Tram 12, 22 to Malostranské náměstí

U PAVA ($$)

"The Peacock" preens itself on its perfect location by the Vojan Gardens in lower Malá Strana, a few short steps from Charles Bridge.
✚ D4 ✉ U lužického semináře 32 ☎ 24 51 09 22 Ⓜ Malostranská

U RAKA PENSION ($$)

Idyllically located among the stuccoed houses of Nový Svět is this extremely comfortable, rather exclusive small pension.
✚ C3 ✉ Černínská 10 ☎ 35 14 53 🚊 Tram 22 to Brusnice

U TŘÍ PŠTROSŮ ($$$)

"The Three Ostriches" was once the center of a

flourishing trade in feathers, then a coffeehouse. The exquisite gabled Renaissance building is now a rather expensive private hotel, from some of whose rooms you can almost exchange a handshake with people passing by on Charles Bridge.

🚩 D4 ✉ Dražického náměstí 12 ☎ 24 51 07 79 🚊 Tram 12, 22 to Malostranské náměstí

OLD TOWN (STARÉ MĚSTO)

The Old Town is linked to the Lesser Town by the superb Gothic Charles Bridge. From the eastern end of the bridge, a warren of streets gives a good idea of what medieval Prague was like, and the Royal Way leads through the center to the Old Town Square.

BETLEM CLUB ($–$$)
Small hotel offering central accommodations in the same square as Jan Hus's historic Bethlehem Chapel.

🚩 E4 ✉ Betlemské náměstí 9 ☎ 24 21 68 72 🚇 Národní třída

CENTRAL ($–$$)
Somewhat run-down but quite adequate accommodations in a convenient position behind the Obecní dům (Municipal House).

🚩 E4 ✉ Rybná 8 ☎ 24 81 20 41/24 81 27 34 🚇 Náměstí Republiky

INTERCONTINENTAL ($$$)
The epitome of pretension in Communist days and hypermodern when it opened back in the 1970s, the Intercontinental offers every comfort as well as spacious public rooms furnished with fine antiques.

🚩 E4 ✉ Náměstí Curieových 5 ☎ 24 88 11 11 🚇 Staroměstská

PAŘÍŽ ($$$)
The rampant early-1900s splendor of the "Paris" has recently been restored to perfection.

🚩 E4 ✉ U Obecního domu 1 ☎ 24 22 21 51 🚇 Náměstí Republiky

U KRÁLE JIŘÍHO ($)
A small hotel just off the Royal Way with comfortable rooms and the bonus (?) of a pub on the ground floor.

🚩 E4 ✉ Liliová 10 ☎ 24 22 20 13 🚇 Staroměstská

UNGELT ($$$)
Apartment hotel in ancient premises that once formed part of the city's customs house.

🚩 E4 ✉ Štupartská 1 ☎ 24 81 13 30 🚇 Náměstí Republiky

UNITAS PENSION ($)
Basic accommodations in what was part of State Security's malevolent empire.

🚩 E4/5 ✉ Bartolomejská 9 ☎ 232 77 00 🚇 Národní třída

Special offers

The number of moderately priced hotels has increased rapidly, but these properties are probably still outnumbered by expensive hotels. However, it's always worth checking to see if the latter are offering any special deals, particularly for weekend stays.

Breathe freely

Choosing a place to stay requires care. A central location may turn out to be noisy with traffic as the rush hour gets under way shortly after 5 AM. Somewhere in the suburbs may seem a long way from the action, but if it's near a Metro station, this is unlikely to be a problem, and your night's rest may be more relaxed because you are breathing marginally fresher air.

NEW TOWN (NOVÉ MĚSTO) AND NEARBY

"New" in the 14th century, but developed in the late 19th and early 20th centuries, this part of Prague centers on Wenceslas Square and the broad streets of Narodni and Na Příkopě.

ADRIA ($$$)

A stunningly restored old establishment amid the glitter of Wenceslas Square.

➕ E5 ⊠ Václavské náměstí 26 ☎ 24 21 65 43/24 23 13 80 ⓜ Můstek

AMETYST ($$–$$$)

A fresh and inviting medium-sized, family-owned hotel, the equal in luxury to most of the big names and only 10 minutes' walk from Wenceslas Square.

➕ F6 ⊠ Jana Masaryka 11, Vinohrady ☎ 691 17 58. ⓜ Náměstí Míru

ANNA ($–$$)

A reliable small hotel in the pleasant inner suburb of Vinohrady, which is less than a quarter of an hour's stroll from Wenceslas Square.

➕ G5 ⊠ Budečská 17, Vinohrady ☎ 25 75 39 ⓜ Náměstí Míru

ATLANTIK ($$)

A pleasant alternative to the Harmony (see below) if you want to stay on this busy central shopping street.

➕ F4 ⊠ Na poříčí 9 ☎ 24 81 10 84 ⓜ Náměstí Republiky

ATRIUM ($$$)

Around the vast interior space that gives this hotel its name are nearly 800 beds, just enough to house President Clinton's entourage when he came to Prague.

➕ F3 ⊠ Pobřežní 1 ☎ 24 84 11 11 ⓜ Florenc

CITY HOTEL MORAN ($$$)

Austrian-style elegance and comfort in a historic building close to Charles Square.

➕ E6 ⊠ Na Moráni 15 ☎ 24 91 52 08 ⓜ Karlovo náměstí

CITY PENSION ($)

Exceptionally pleasant pension, one Metro stop from Wenceslas Square.

➕ F6 ⊠ Belgická 10 ☎ 691 13 34 ⓜ Náměstí Míru

EVROPA ($–$$)

Nothing could be closer to Prague's heart than this art nouveau jewel on Wenceslas Square. Unfortunately, most of the rooms fail to live up to the promise of the exterior.

➕ E5 ⊠ Václavské náměstí 25 ☎ 24 22 81 17 ⓜ Můstek

HARMONY ($$)

A 1930s building that has been attractively refurbished to provide pleasant accommodations just east of Obecní dům.

➕ F4 ⊠ Na poříčí 31 ☎ 23 20 016 ⓜ Náměstí Republiky

HOTEL 16 U SV KATEŘINY ($–$$)

Excellent-value family

hotel just around the corner from the Dvořák Museum and a ten-minute walk from Wenceslas Square.

🚇 E5 ☎ 29 53 29/29 13 13 🚇 I P Pavlova

JULIS ($$)

A pioneering glass and concrete Functionalist building of 1933 makes an interesting contrast to the resplendent Evropa Hotel on Wenceslas Square, and is probably a more sensible choice.

🚇 E5 ⊠ Václavské náměstí 22 ☎ 24 21 70 92 🚇 Můstek

PALACE ($$$)

A sumptous art nouveau exterior conceals the completely refurbished ultramodern interior of the Palace, proud to be Prague's priciest hotel.

🚇 E4 ⊠ Panská 12 ☎ 24 09 31 11 🚇 Můstek

PAV ($$)

Family-run pension in a side street that also happens to be the location of Prague's most popular beer hall.

🚇 E5 ⊠ Křemencova 13 ☎ 24 91 32 86 🚇 Národní třída

THE SUBURBS

Beyond the four historic districts is a ring of suburbs, some dull, but most with their own attractions.

BILÝ LEV ($)

An economical place to rest your bones in the eastern suburb of Žižkov.

🚇 G4 ⊠ Cimburkova 20 ☎ 27 11 26 🚊 Trams 5, 9, 26 to Husinecká

COUBERTIN ($)

Small modern hotel named after the founder of the modern Olympics and located among the stadia and sports facilities of Strahov.

🚇 B5 ⊠ Atletická 4, Strahov ☎ 35 28 51 🚇 Dejvická, then Bus 149, 217

FORUM ($$$)

International luxury and all that that implies in a steel and glass tower overlooking the Nusle expressway bridge in Vyšehrad. Wenceslas Square is just five minutes away by Metro.

🚇 F7 ⊠ Kongresová 1, Vyšehrad ☎ 61 19 11 11 🚇 Vyšehrad

GOLF ($)

Large motel handily located on the main road from the west.

🚇 Off map to west of Prague ⊠ Plzenská 215 ☎ 52 10 98

INTERNATIONAL ($$)

Under new management, the unique and long-established International Hotel in a Socialist-Realist skyscraper retains all the atmosphere of the Stalinist '50s.

🚇 C2 ⊠ Koulova 15 ☎ 24 39 31 11 🚇 Dejvická 🚊 Tram 20, 25 to Podbaba

KAFKA ($)

Good-value accommodations on the wrong side of the tracks in

Botels

An alternative to conventional hotels are the "botels" moored at various points along the banks of the Vltava. However, being rather cramped, they are less romantic than they might sound. One such, close to the Palacky Bridge (Palackého most) on the Smíchov quayside, is the *Admiral* 🚇 D6 ⊠ Hořejší nábřeží ☎ 24 51 16 97 /54 86 85 🚇 Metro Anděl.

Home from home

An economical solution to the problem of accommodations is to stay in a private house or, more likely, an apartment. Most agencies have such places on their books, which is a better approach than allowing yourself to be solicited after your arrival at the main train station. Private rooms can also be booked from abroad. Check that it doesn't take three changes of bus and tram to get into town from your accommodation.

the seedy inner suburb of Žižkov but only ten minutes' walk from the main train station and a short tram ride to Wenceslas Square.
✚ G4 ✉ Cimburkova 24 ☎ 27 31 01 🚊 Tram 5, 9, 26 to Husinecká

LAUDA ($)
Pleasant pension usefully located on a residential road running off the main highway to northern Bohemia and eastern Germany.
✚ H1 ✉ Kubišova 10 ☎ 66 41 14 91

MOTEL STOP ($)
Another motel on the western outskirts for the price-conscious.
✚ Off map to west of Prague ✉ Jeremiášova 974 ☎ 52 56 48

OBORA ($$)
Well-appointed small hotel in the leafy surroundings of the royal hunting park and Hvezda Castle, in the western outskirts close to the airport.
✚ Off map to the west of Prague ✉ Libocká 271/1 ☎ 36 77 79

PRAHA ($$$)
The Praha perfectly expresses how Communist taste moved from the Stalinist certainties of the International Hotel in the '50s to the anonymous luxury of the '70s. Until 1989, the Praha, in its hilltop location in the western suburb of Dejvice, was reserved for privileged

and powerful Party people and their guests.
✚ B2 ✉ Sušická 20, Dejvice ☎ 24 34 26 50 🚇 Dejvická 🚊 Tram 2, 20, 26, to Hadovka

VILA VOYTA ($$$)
A splendid Secession villa in the southern suburbs caters for its mostly business clientele with great care and attention.
✚ Off map to south of Prague ✉ K novému dvoru 124/54, Lhotka ☎ 472 55 11

Accommodations advice

Any number of agencies stand ready to help you with advice on accommodations. AVE is one of the best established, with offices at the main train station (✉ Hlavní nádřaží, Wilsonova 8. ☎ 24 22 35 21), Holešovice train station, and the airport. Prague Information Service (Pražská informační služba – PIS. ☎ 24 21 28 44/45), the official city information agency, will also find lodgings. It has offices at the main train station, ✉ Staroměstské náměstí/Old Town Square 22, and ✉ Na příkopě 20.

PRAGUE
travel facts

ARRIVING & DEPARTING

Before you go
• Visas are not required for citizens of the United States.

When to go
• The best time to visit is in spring, when the fruit trees of Petřín Hill are in blossom, or in early summer.
• Winter weather can be depressingly gray and cold, with high levels of air pollution.
• High summer can become oppressively hot and humid with considerable rainfall.

Arriving by air
• There are direct flights to Ruzyně Airport from New York and Montréal.
• Prague is served by ČSA (the national airline) and by other major carriers.
• The best downtown link is by airport bus, either to Dejvická Metro station or to Revolucní Street on the eastern edge of the Old Town. An ordinary service bus is marginally less expensive but meanders all over the suburbs. For taxis, ➤ 91.
• The ČSA main office is at ✉ Revolucní 1, Old Town. ☎ 23 12 595. Departure tax is normally included in the price of your air ticket.

Arriving by train
• Express trains link Prague to all neighboring countries as well as to Paris and to Ostend in Belgium (ferry connection with Dover in England).
• Most trains terminate at the main station (Hlavní nádraží ✚ F4), though some stop (or terminate) at Holešovice in the northern suburbs and at Smíchov in the

southern suburbs, both of which have good onward connections by Metro.
• Czech Railways (ČD) has an information office at the north end of level 3 in the main railway station.

Arriving by bus
• Express buses link Prague with a growing number of international destinations, including London.
• The coach terminal is at Florenc, on the eastern edge of the downtown area, where there is a Metro station.
• Departure tickets can be obtained at Florenc, but it is easier to buy them through an agency.

Arriving by water
• Occasional passenger boats ply the Vltava and Elbe to Dresden and on to Hamburg.

Customs Regulations
• The duty-free allowance comprises 250 cigarettes or 100 cigars or 250g tobacco; 2 liters of wine; 1 liter of liquor; 50ml perfume, and 250ml eau de toilette.
• At the time of writing, the Czech crown is not convertible, and only small amounts may be imported or exported. There is no limit on the import or export of foreign currencies.
• In principle there are strict limits on the export of goods purchased in the Czech Republic, but the normal tourist souvenirs are unlikely to pose any problem. However, antiques and "rare cultural objects" require an official certificate from a recognized museum or art gallery (which the dealer may have already obtained).

ESSENTIAL FACTS

Travel insurance
- All visitors should have full travel insurance.

Opening hours
- Banks: Mon–Fri 9–3:30. Komerční banka ✉ Na příkopě 28 is open Mon–Fri 8–6, and Česká spořitelna ✉ Václavské náměstí 42 is also open Sat 9–1.
- Stores: Mon–Fri 9–6, Sat until 1 PM. Food stores may open as early as 6 AM; some late-night shopping (to 8 PM) Thu. Some shops in tourist areas also open on Sun.
- Museums and galleries: 9/10–5, closed Mon, except the National Museum (open Mon and closed Tues) and the Strahov Library (open every day). Some also close for lunch.

National holidays
- January 1, Easter Monday, May 8 (Liberation Day), July 5 (SS Cyril and Methodius), July 6 (Jan Hus' Day), October 28 (Independence Day), December 24–26.

Money matters
- The Czech crown (*koruna česká* or Kč) is divided into 100 virtually worthless hellers (*haléř*).
- There are coins for 10, 20, and 50 hellers and for 1, 2, 5, 10, 20, and 50 crowns, and notes in denominations of 20, 50, 100, 200, 500, 1,000, and 5,000 crowns.
- At the time of writing the Czech crown is not a convertible currency and its import and export is controlled.
- There are plenty of bureaux de change, but banks usually give better rates of exchange.
- Credit cards are in increasing use, particularly in places frequented by tourists.

Etiquette
- Czech manners tend to be formal. Titles such as Doctor and Professor must not be ignored, and hands should be shaken when offered.
- Dress has become less formal; neat casual wear is usually acceptable, though attendance at the opera requires a modicum of formality.
- Diners share tables in crowded restaurants, and exchange greetings like "*dobrý den*" ("Good day"), "*dobrou chuť*" ("Enjoy your meal"), "*na zdraví!*" ("Cheers!") and "*na shledanou*" ("Goodbye") at the appropriate moments.
- If you are invited into a Czech home, bring flowers or a small gift, and offer to take your shoes off before entering.

Women travelers
- Women travelers need take no more than the usual precautions.
- Unaccompanied females lingering at night in certain areas of the city—such as parts of Wenceslas Square—may be taken for prostitutes.

Places of worship
- Roman Catholic: St. Joseph's Church (sv Josefa), ✉ Josefská 4, Malá Strana, Ⓜ Malostranská. English mass Sun 11 AM.
- Anglican: St. Clement's Church (sv Klimenta), ✉ Klimentská, northern New Town, Ⓜ Něměstí Republiky. English-language service Sun 9:30 AM.

Student travelers
- Few discounts are available for students, but by keeping out of the most popular tourist spots, young people will find it an affordable city to get by in.
- All aspects of youth travel and

accommodations are dealt with by the ČKM agency ✉ Žitná 12, New Town, ☎ 24 91 57 67, Ⓜ Karlovo náměstí.

Time differences

• Central European Time applies, changed for daylight saving between March and September.

Toilets

• "WC," "OO," "muži/pani" (Men), and "ženy/damy" (Women) are useful signs to remember.
• Public facilities are rare; look for those in restaurants, cafés, etc.
• Tip the attendant (usally an old woman) with some smaller coins— these are her wages.

Electricty

• 220 volts, 50 cycles AC, fed through standard continental two-pin plugs.

PUBLIC TRANSPORTATION

• Prague's comprehensive transportation system is based on the immaculate underground Metro and the slightly less pristine but equally reliable trams and buses.
• One inexpensive ticket obtained at stations, kiosks, and some hotel receptions serves all three modes and must be validated by inserting it into the clipping machine as you enter a station or board a vehicle. A fresh ticket must be used for each change of mode.
• The best public transportation map is in the free city guide available from Prague Information Service. This shows all Metro and tram lines and, very usefully, names the tram stops as well as Metro stations.
• Expect crowding at the rush hours

(although they start and finish earlier than in many Western countries). The young and fit should give up their seats to the elderly, pregnant, and disabled.

Metro

• This showpiece system, with its fast and frequent trains and clean stations, consists of three lines: A (color-coded green), B (yellow), and C (red). They converge from the suburbs onto downtown where there are several interchange stations.
• To ensure you get on the right train, check the line (A, B, or C) and note the name of the terminus station at the end of the line in the direction you wish to travel; this station appears on the overhead direction signs.
• Outlying stations are relatively far apart and are intended more to feed commuters to connecting trams and buses than to take tourists to their favorite spots.
• Particularly useful stations are Můstek (for Wenceslas Square and Old Town Square), Staroměstská (for Old Town Square), and Malostranská (for Malá Strana and for Tram No 22). Hradčanská station is quite a long walk from the Castle.

Tram

• The tramway system operates in close conjunction with its underground equivalent. It is worthwhile studying the route map, because travel by tram can spare your legs on many of your likely itineraries.
• The name of every tram stop appears on the stop sign and on the route map.
• Tram routes are numbered, and the tram has a destination board. Timetables are usually pasted on

the stop and are almost always adhered to.

- There is a skeleton service of night trams with a different system of numbers and schedules from the daytime service.
- A particularly useful and scenic line is the No. 22, which runs from downtown (at Národní třída) right through Malá Strana, past Malostranská Metro station, then climbs to the back entrance to the castle (Pražský hrad stop) or farther on to Strahov Monastery.

Bus

- Kept out of the downtown to minimize pollution, buses serve all the suburban areas that the trams do not reach.

Discounts

- Special passes are valid for periods of one day upwards. They are only useful if you intend to make lots of trips—more than about eight a day.

Taxi

- Prague taxi drivers have an appalling reputation for over-charging and their disagreeable nature.
- If you have to use a taxi, agree the fare beforehand. Asking for a receipt can be helpful in reducing excessive demands.
- It may be better to flag down a moving taxi rather than go to a taxi stand.
- For taxis, telephone AAA Radiotaxi (☎ 33 99) or Profitaxi (☎ 61 04 55 55).
- The more upscale hotels have their own taxi service, reliable but expensive.

MEDIA & COMMUNICATIONS

Telephones

- The Czech Republic's phone system is being modernized, and making calls can be very frustrating. All Prague subscribers have been, or are being, allotted new numbers.
- Most public phones now take phone cards, on sale in kiosks and post offices in denominations of Kč50 upwards.
- Telephoning from your hotel may cost up to four times the standard rate.

Mail

- Postage stamps are on sale not only at post offices but also at kiosks and hotel receptions.
- The main post office, with fax and poste restante services, is at ✚ F4 ✉ Jindřišská 14, New Town ☎ 24 22 88 56 Ⓜ Můstek.

Newspapers and magazines

- Foreign-language newspapers are on sale at downtown newsstands and at some hotel reception desks.
- Local English-language publications include the weekly *Prague Post* and its rival *Prognosis*; both contain useful listings of events.
- The English-language *Central European Business Weekly* is much as its title suggests.
- The German-language weekly *Prager Zeitung* is oriented toward the minuscule German population still living in the Czech Republic.

Radio and television

- Local TV consists of four channels, ČT1 and ČT2

(state-owned), Nova and Premiera (private), none of which are likely to be of much interest to the non-Czech speaker, though Premiera puts out NBC's Superchannel news. Major hotels have multiple satellite channels.

- Local Radio 1 puts out news of tourist interest in English at 3:30 PM on weekdays.
- Voice of America and the BBC World Service can be picked up on 106.2 FM and 101.0 FM respectively.
- Most local stations play "golden oldies" from the rock era. Country Radio (89.5 FM) plays country music; Radio One (91.9 FM) plays avant-garde rock; and Radio Kobra (98.7 FM) plays classical music.

EMERGENCIES

Sensible precautions

- Despite some horror stories, Prague is still safer than most comparable Western cities. But after dark it's not a bad idea to avoid the main train station.
- The main hazard is the pickpockets who operate in tourist areas—on Wenceslas Square, on Charles Bridge, and in Old Town Square. Keep a good hold on your handbag and don't carry your wallet protruding from a back pocket.
- Bear in mind that your casually acquired consumer accessories (like a camcorder) are likely to be worth several months' wages here.

Lost property

- The lost property office is at ⊠ Karoliny Světlé 5, Old Town, ☎ 24 23 50 85.

Medical treatment

- Emergency medical treatment is free for visitors from abroad, but it is still advisable to arrange medical insurance in advance of your trip.
- Foreigners' Polyclinic ⊠ Roentgenová 2, Motol (off map), ☎ 52 92 21 46. Tram 4, 7, 9, 58, or Bus 167 from Anděl Metro. Bring your passport to this former Communist Party clinic, which is part of the Nemocnice, Na Homolce, the huge hospital complex just off the main highway to Pilsen in the western suburb of Motol. It is the best place to go for serious treatment.
- Fakultní poliklinika 🏥 E5. ⊠ Karlovo náměstí 32, New Town, ☎ 24 91 48 24. 🚇 Karlovo náměstí. A downtown alternative to the above for less serious ailments.
- Drugs and medications must be paid for. Remember to bring supplies of any regular medication with you.
- 24-hour pharmacies are at ⊠ Opletalová 30 and ⊠ Na příkopě 1.

Emergency phone numbers

- Ambulance 155
- Police 158
- Fire brigade 150

Embassy

- USA 🏥 D4 ⊠ Tržiště 15, Malá Strana ☎ 24 51 08 47 🚇 Malostranská, then Tram 12, 22

LANGUAGE

- Czech is a Slavic language, and anyone who knows other Slavic languages, such as Russian or Polish, should have little

LANGUAGE

- Czech is a Slavic language, and anyone who knows other Slavic languages, such as Russian or Polish, should have little difficulty in muddling through in Czech.
- It will be rewarding to master a few words and phrases, if only to be able to ask if anyone speaks your language and to recognize some signs.
- Czech is pronounced as it is written (unlike English).

Vowels

a	as in mammoth	á	as in father
é	as in air	e	as in yes
i,y	as in city	í,ý	as in meet
o	as in top	ó	as in more
u	as in book	ů	as in boom

Consonants

c	as in its	č	as in china
ch	as in Scottish loch		
j	as in yes	n	as in onion
r	rolled or trilled r	ř	combination of r and z (as in Dvorak)
š	as in shine		
z	as in zero	ž	as in pleasure

Basic words and phrases

yes ano
no ne
please prosím
thank you děkuji
do you speak English/German?
   mluvíte anglicky /německy?
I don't understand nerozumím
I don't speak Czech nemluvím česky
hello ahoj
good morning/good day dobrý den
good evening dobrý večer
goodnight dobrou noc
goodbye na shledanou
sorry promintě
where? kde?
how much? kolik?
when? kdy?
what? co?

Numbers

1	jeden/jedna /jedno	15	patnáct
2	dva/dvě	16	sestnáct
3	tri	17	sedmnáct
4	čtyři	18	osmnáct
5	pět	19	devatenáct
6	šest	20	dvacet
7	sedm	30	třicet
8	osm	40	čtyřicet
9	devět	50	padesát
10	deset	60	šedesát
11	jedenáct	70	sedmdesát
12	dvanáct	80	osmdesát
13	trináct	90	devadesát
14	čtrnáct	100	sto
		1,000	tisíc

Days of the week

Monday pondělí	Friday pátek
Tuesday úterý	Saturday sobota
Wednesday středa	Sunday neděla
Thursday čvrtek	

Months of the year

January leden	July červenec
February únor	August srpen
March březen	September září
April duben	October říjen
May květen	November listopad
June červen	December prosinec

Useful words

beer pivo
big velký/á/é
bus or tram stop zastávka
café kavárna
castle hradhrad
closed zavřeno
Danger! pozor!
entrance vchod/vstup
exit vychod/vystup
forbidden zakáz
market trh
open otevřeno
pharmacy lekarna
pull (sign on door) sem
push (sign on door) tam
small maly/á/é
station nádraží
water voda

INDEX

Acknowledgments

The Automobile Association wishes to thank the following photographers, libraries and associations for their assistance in the preparation of this book.

M IVORY 25a, 25b
NATIONAL GALLERY IN PRAGUE 41b, 47
REX FEATURES LTD 12

All remaining pictures are held in the Association's own library (AA PHOTO LIBRARY) with contributions from **C. SAWYER** 1, 2, 5b, 13a, 13b, 18, 19, 20, 26b, 28a, 29, 30a, 32b, 36b, 37, 38b, 41a, 48a, 49b, 50, 52, 54, 55, 56, 58, 61b, 87b; **A. SOUTER** 5a, 7, 23b, 24, 33, 34, 36a, 42a, 46a, 46b, 87a; **J. WYAND** 6, 16, 17, 21a, 21b, 23a, 26a, 27, 28b, 30b, 31, 32a, 35a, 35b, 38a, 39, 40, 42b, 43, 44a, 44b, 45, 48b, 49a, 51, 57, 61a

Copy editor **Audrey Horne**
Verifier **Nick Parsons**
Indexer **Marie Lorimer**
Original design **Design FX**